Rural Labour Relations in India

Editors

T.J. BYRES
KARIN KAPADIA
JENS LERCHE

FRANK CASS
LONDON • PORTLAND, OR

First published in 1999 in Great Britain by
FRANK CASS PUBLISHERS
Newbury House, 900 Eastern Avenue,
London IG2 7HH, England

Transferred to Digital Printing 2004

and in the United States of America by
FRANK CASS PUBLISHERS
c/o ISBS
5804 N.E. Hassalo Street
Portland, Oregon 97213-3644

Website: www.frankcass.com

Copyright © 1999 Frank Cass & Co. Ltd.

British Library Cataloguing in Publication Data
Rural labour relations in India. – (The library of peasant
studies; no. 18)
1. Agricultural laborers – India 2. Industrial relations –
India 3. India – Economic conditions – 1947– – Regional
disparities
I. Byres, T.J. (Terence James), 1936– II. Kapadia, Karin
III. Lerche, Jens
331′.0954′091734

ISBN 0 7146 4983 X (cloth)
ISBN 0 7146 8046 X (paper)
ISSN 1462-219X

Library of Congress Cataloging in Publication Data
Rural labour relations in India / edited by T.J. Byres, Karin Kapadia,
and Jens Lerche.
      p.   cm. – (The Library of peasant studies; no. 18)
Papers presented at the Workshop on Rural Labour Relations in
India Today, held at the London School of Economics on 19 and 20
June 1997.
Includes bibliographical references and index.
ISBN 0-7146-4983-X (cloth). – ISBN 0-7146-8046-X (pbk.)
1. Agricultural laborers – India – Congresses. 2. Women
agricultural laborers – India – Congresses. 3. Industrial relations –
India – Congresses. 4. Labor policy – India – Congresses. I. Byres,
T.J. II. Kapadia, Karin. III. Lerche, Jens. IV. Worshop on
Rural Labour Relations in India Today (London: 1997). V. Series.
HD1537.I4R874   1999
331′.043′0954–dc21   99-19731
                                                                                    CIP
This group of studies first appeared in a Special Issue on
'Rural Labour Relations in India' of *The Journal of Peasant Studies*
(ISSN 0306 6150) Vol.26/2 & 3 (January/April 1999) published by Frank Cass.

Contents

Introduction

KARIN KAPADIA and JENS LERCHE

This collection is the outcome of the Workshop on 'Rural Labour Relations in India Today' held at the London School of Economics (LSE) on 19 and 20 June 1997. We are grateful to Professor Jan Breman, Centre for Asian Studies Amsterdam (CASA), Professor Terry Byres, School of Oriental and African Studies (SOAS), Professor Ashwani Saith, LSE, and Professor Henry Bernstein, SOAS, for the strong moral support they gave us, from the very start, when we first thought of organising a workshop on rural labour in India. We are also grateful for financial support to Professor Breman and the International Institute of Asian Studies (IIAS), Leiden, to the British Academy and to Professor Saith and the Development Studies Institute at the London School of Economics.

The Workshop aimed to analyse emerging development trajectories of rural labour relations and rural labour struggles in India, based on studies from its regions and states. It brought together a group of scholars most of whom had conducted recent fieldwork on rural labour relations. It took place against the background of certain developments taking place in the Indian countryside. Macro-economic data pointed to sustained agricultural growth in several regions outside the classical Green Revolution belts, indicating that capitalism was penetrating the agrarian sector more deeply than previously expected. Moreover, the interrelationship between the wider Indian social formation and agrarian labour relations was underlined by a pronounced, if regionally differentiated, increase in non-agrarian employment and a decrease in rural poverty during the 1970s and 1980s. Importantly, this process was gendered: as men entered occupations outside agriculture, women took over a higher proportion of work within agriculture. The set-backs in some of these developments (poverty increased as non-agricultural employment fell) in the early 1990s following new structural adjustment policies, and the fact that it still is too early to

Karin Kapadia, Christian Michelsen Institute, PO Box 6033, 5020 Bergen, Norway - email kapadia@amadeus.cmi.no; and Jens Lerche, Department of Development Studies, School of Oriental and African Studies, University of London, Thornhaugh Street, Russell Square, London, WC1H OXG - email jl2@soas.ac.uk chart the overall developments of the 1990s, highlight the consistency of the trends of the previous decades.

Importantly, state intervention, always crucial to Indian agrarian development, played a part in the trajectories of both the 1980s and the 1990s. Politically, it appeared that both politicisation and polarisation had taken place in the countryside, though to a very varying extent, and primarily along caste and religious fault lines. Most notable was the strong support that the low caste BSP party garnered among rural workers in many parts of North India.

However, the case studies focusing on rural labour relations and labour struggles of the 1980s and early 1990s rarely engaged with general developments such as these. Moreover, the picture they painted of labour relations pointed in several different directions. For example, a casualisation of the labour force was emphasised by some studies, but an increase in unfree labour relations was indicated by others. The studies saw changes in labour relations as made up of different core elements, some of the central ones being: (a) continuous capitalist development in agriculture, (b) the tightening of the labour market resulting from the increase in non-agricultural employment opportunities, (c) emancipatory processes from below, or (d) collective oppression from above. These differences represent differences in analytical angle, between enquiry concentrated on economic issues and a perspective focusing on class struggles, and also differences in the actual analysis of economic processes and of the balance of power between the agrarian classes.

From the late 1960s to the early 1980s the debate on modes of production in Indian agriculture, that was sparked off by the Green Revolution, occurred. Since then, there has been a theoretical shift towards more disaggregated analyses of rural capitalism, and the Workshop reflected this development. The task we intended the Workshop to fulfil was to analyse local developments as part of wider class structures and capitalist development trajectories, contextualised within a broad political economy framework. Our aim was to pinpoint all-Indian developments as well as regional differentiation within India (in practice, often state-wise differentiation) regarding labour regimes and labour relations.

Regional differences in the Indian countryside regarding agrarian development are well acknowledged. This is hardly surprising, given significant regional variations in class constellations, colonial agrarian history, and political and economic development trajectories since Independence. However, while the 1990s have seen an increase in detailed labour relations and labour regime studies, there are still very few attempts to extend such regional analyses to labour relations and labour struggles. It is therefore still difficult to identify general all Indian trends as well as specific regional developments. Hence the Workshop aimed at combining local and regional labour relations studies based on long-term fieldwork and detailed insight into local social relations with papers analysing the macro-level.

The organisers were, among other issues, interested in examining how accumulation patterns and the balance of power between the classes facilitated and shaped labour relations, and set the conditions for labour struggles. An important point was the extent to which agricultural employment was being substituted by non-agricultural employment, and especially whether, due to this, rural labourers were being de-linked from their old masters in ways which broke previous exploitative relations, or whether such relations were being maintained or even extended to new groups. Moreover, the question of specific caste and gender trajectories was posed.

We also called for discussion of the role of the state in rural labour relations. Here, both the implications of government policies such as the liberalisation/structural adjustment policies of the 1990s, or the presumably more labour friendly policies of the few left-wing Indian State governments, as well as the direct involvement of local state institutions in power relations between labour and landowner were our concern.

When investigating the relationship between labour relations and class struggles, an assessment of the forms and outcomes of class struggle from below and class struggle from above in different Indian regions and states becomes essential. Disagreements exist within the academic community. Is the contemporary development of rural labour relations part of a process of politicisation of rural labourers, as the new vigour of the caste-based subaltern movements and parties of north India seemed to suggest? Or is such emancipatory development being stalled by class struggle from above, not least through the increased imposition of debt bondage and, if necessary, violent oppression? And, returning to the wider canvas, which accumulation patterns and what balance of class power facilitate and shape such class struggle from above and from below?

Two aspects of these closely linked themes were of special interest to the organisers, namely that of the politicisation / emancipation of rural labourers, and that of gendered changes in labour relations.

PROCESSES OF POLITICISATION AND EMANCIPATION AMONG RURAL LABOURERS

Regarding the first theme, several authors have argued that agricultural labourers in India have become politicised, emancipated or empowered. However, the positive value of such processes has been questioned on at least two counts: first, because substantial class actions from above render the emancipatory processes from below ineffectual; and secondly, because to the extent that emancipatory processes do influence labour relations, they often take a non-class perspective, therefore harming the development of class consciousness and a genuinely socialist movement. These different assessments of the importance of emancipatory processes in the Indian countryside are forcefully represented by Jan Breman and Tom Brass.

Jan Breman's influential study of the Halpatis, a Scheduled Caste labour community in Gujarat, spans over 30 years (Scheduled Caste is a euphemistic term meaning 'untouchable' castes – politicised SCs use the term 'Dalit', meaning 'the oppressed', to refer to themselves). He argues that following the rise of free labour relations, 'a groundswell of social emancipation' has taken place. He submits that this is more important than the limited material improvements that the Halpatis have experienced, even though this emancipation has not yet been 'converted and consolidated into organized action' [Breman, 1993: 354–5, 364]. Tom Brass, on the other hand, argues against the celebration of empowerment as it is often a substitute for analysing the class perspective of the concerned processes. This may legitimise 'communal discourses and practice' instead of creating, at least, 'prefigurative socialist forms' [Brass, 1994: 263].

For both authors, the emancipatory processes are analysed against the backdrop of overall class struggle. An important aspect of Breman's cautious optimism is that, in Gujarat, emancipatory processes are part of structural changes in labour relations and society in general, breaking down the classical dependency of labourers on their old masters [Breman, 1993: 297–316]. Brass, on the other hand, does not see such a link. Basing himself on fieldwork he conducted in the 1980s in Haryana, he argues that the landed classes are succeeding in increasingly imposing unfree labour relations on rural labourers, in order to counter any class struggle from below [Brass, 1990].

The Workshop, with its regionally diverse papers, was in a good position to analyse specific politicisation processes among rural labourers in relation to the development of labour relations and class struggle in general. An important issue was the understanding of these processes and the division of rural labourers along caste lines. This importance of caste-based divisions had been well acknowledged in the past but, in spite of this, recent emancipatory processes linked to caste categories, such as those occurring in north India, were yet to be analysed from a class perspective and, more specifically, from a labour relations perspective.

The other central theme pertaining to the debate on emancipatory processes was that of free/unfree labour relations and their link to emancipatory processes. This was discussed by most papers. The case-study based papers showed important regional variations and different interpretations of the phenomena, while one paper centred on the debate on unfree labour relations and class power more generally. To pinpoint just a few of the conclusions, the general, theoretical paper by J. Mohan Rao argues that there is no archetype for bonded labour in India. His argument for diversity is strikingly illustrated by the fact that while da Corta and Venkateshwarlu find that bondage is becoming more prevalent in rural Andhra Pradesh, Lerche argues that the opposite development is occurring in Uttar Pradesh. In both contexts local socio-political changes have powerfully influenced developments in labour relations. In the Andra Pradesh case study, gender-based divisions within the workforce are central to this development. While similar gendered processes are discernible in the Uttar Pradesh case study, unfree labour relations are generally losing some of their importance there, a development that is being aided by emancipatory processes organised along caste lines.

THE 'FEMINISATION' OF AGRICULTURAL WAGE LABOUR AND ITS IMPACT ON EMANCIPATORY PROCESSES

From the outset, the organisers were concerned to bring gender analysis into the discussion of changing labour relations. From the mid seventies and early eighties important studies by anthropologists and economists had analysed the impacts of gender-differentiation on the situation of agrarian labour. These studies focused, *inter alia*, on women labourers' increasing responsibility for household income, the increase in female-headed households, the ways in which caste norms prohibited some women's entry into better-paid 'outside' work, the growing work participation rate of labouring women, women's greater contribution to the household, and gender differentiated participation in strikes and resistance. Despite this impressive body of work, much writing on labour relations remains gender-blind: the subjects, in much discussion of agrarian labour – 'the labourers' and 'the Scheduled Castes' – are implicitly male. The organisers challenged this, by calling for a gendering of all the papers, on the premise that research that is not gender-sensitive, and data that are not disaggregated by sex, cannot comprehend the implications of the major structural changes in employment that are under way.

Recent research has noted that over the past two decades, there have been striking differences between trends in female and male employment. First, from 1975 to 1991 there was a general trend for male labour, throughout rural India, to move from agricultural labour to rural non-agricultural employment [*Sen*, 1997; *Bhalla*, 1997; *Sen and Ghosh*, 1993]. However, female labour remained very largely in agriculture, and as men vacated agriculture for better-paid non-agricultural jobs, wage labour in agriculture became increasingly 'feminised' throughout rural India [*Bennett*, 1992; *Duvvury*, 1989; *Chadha*, 1997]. Rural women have had very little access to non-agricultural jobs, which are not only better paid but also of significantly higher status than agricultural labour.

Secondly, while it has been argued that there is a growing assertiveness on the part of rural labour it is not clear whether this is largely limited to male labour or equally shared by female labour. Discourses of workers' rights and human dignity are strongly voiced by men, in the contributions to this volume, rather than by women. Wilson's contribution is the exception: she argues that in central Bihar women wage labourers are active in resistance too. Her findings connect with the limited gendered research that has been done so far on rural emancipatory struggles, that indicates that women's agency is important in many rural struggles [*Agarwal*, 1994; *Basu*, 1992; *Kelkar*, 1992; *Omvedt*, 1980]. More research is needed on this subject, as also on contemporary contexts where bonded labourers are seeking emancipation [*Kapadia*, 1995].

Thirdly, recent field studies, including some of the papers in this volume, suggest that in the process of male wage labour moving into better-paid non-agricultural occupations, attached male workers are becoming 'free'. However, female wage labour remains largely in agriculture (Lerche, this volume; Srivastava, this volume). The research of da Corta and Venkateshwarlu from Andhra Pradesh (this volume) and Kapadia from Tamilnadu [1995, forthcoming a and b] suggests that, in contexts of existing tied labour, female labour may be becoming even more attached. Female labourers who work as the wives of male bonded workers are regarded as mere helpers, not as main tied labourers. Employers allow male tied labourers to leave more easily if they substitute their female kin, usually their wives, in their place. This insertion of women into main bonded worker positions effectively allows men to walk free. This process, noted in these two case studies from south India, may be more widespread. Further investigation is necessary to find out whether these studies are representative of a new trend. If so, this would imply that in rural India unfree labour is increasingly female labour.

These two case studies also note that male labourers are contributing less to their households than they used to – partly because women's earning opportunities are increasing and men use this as their excuse to retain more of their own earnings for personal spending. Consequently, the burden of feeding their children is falling increasingly on women, who often become *de facto* family breadwinners. Because they have to rely more on their employers, than on their husbands, to feed their households, women wage labourers become particularly vulnerable to offers of credit based on tied labour. Involvement in direct patron--client relations and in attached labour constrains their ability to challenge employers.

Several of the contributions to this volume illustrate how the increasing politicisation of landless workers has transformed their self-perceptions and thus their strategies in relation to employers. However, when considering these emancipatory processes of politicisation and solidary action, it is important to recognise that men's bargaining power increases – among other reasons – because they are able to draw on the support of women to aid their emancipatory strategies. They draw on women's support in a variety of forms – including women's unpaid domestic labour, women's paid labour and women's tied labour.

The critical point is that the ability to count on assistance from female kin (especially wives) strengthens male labourers in their struggles for their rights. The contribution to this volume which illustrates this most clearly is that of da Corta and Venkateshwarlu. In their study, poor Scheduled Caste men in rural Andhra Pradesh are found to assert their new claims to social dignity and status by refraining from doing agricultural labour even when they have no other employment. It is because their wives agree to enter into short-term tied labour relations – with all the lack of freedom and social humiliation that tied status entails – that their households are able to survive. The cost of this avoidance of low-paid agricultural work by Scheduled Caste men is borne by Scheduled Caste women who end up having to do a very great deal of work, as they have to perform all the domestic work too.

In short, the relations of women wage labourers to production, to tied labour and to credit are significantly different from those of men. The contributions of Srivastava, Lerche and Wilson throw further light on these issues. Srivastava's account, from Uttar Pradesh, indicates that poor women enter tied labour arrangements with wealthy farmers in order to access fodder for the household's cattle. Lerche's analysis, also from Uttar Pradesh, notes that men's presence in the agricultural labour force has fallen and that, due to the massive movement of male labour from agriculture to non-agricultural employment, employers have been forced to rely more on two new categories of main labourers, namely local female workers and migrant male workers. Significantly, both categories of labour are frequently attached in a variety of ways.

Wilson's contribution indicates the growing importance of women in Bihar's agrarian workforce. An index of this trend is that a central reason for the tying of male labour is to enable employers to access the labour of men's female kin. This indirect tying of female labour through tied male labour is connected with employers' growing need for female labour. Wilson notes that it is women, not men, who take the lead in strikes. It is partly because these women have access to non-agricultural employment (brick kiln and construction work) that they do not have to become attached labourers – and their free status encourages them to strike for higher wages. These women labourers use much the same discourse of rights as men, declaring that they are fighting employers in order to protect their own dignity. This suggests that where women wage workers have the same access to new employment opportunities as men, they are just as ready to stand up for their rights.

Sen has noted that the 'freeing' of labour from long-term ties has continued for the last two decades [1997]. This observation is not contradicted by the tying – or, more precisely, re-tying – of female labour discussed here. The field studies of da Corta and Venkateshwarlu (this volume), Kapadia [forthcoming a and b] and Lerche [this volume], indicate that it is specifically with new, non-permanent forms of attached labour that women are involved. This trend towards 'neo- bondage' [*Breman*, 1996] or 'deproletarianisation' [*Brass*, 1990], which involves the re-tying of female labour as main attached labour, does not contradict the larger trend, noted by many writers, that permanent forms of attached labour are becoming increasingly rare. However, while da Corta and Venkateshwarlu's study appears to find an overall increase in unfree labour relations, both Kapadia's and Lerche's case studies show that unfree labour relations are, on the whole, becoming less common.

The central question that is raised by an analysis of changing labour relations is how to conceptualise a sociologically nuanced and disaggregated analysis of capitalism in rural India today. The analyses provide an insight into the main issues of labour relations within different regions, and through this, contribute to our understanding of contemporary rural labour relations in India. They throw light on accumulation patterns, the balance of power between rural classes, and the actual development of labour relations and labour struggles. No exhaustive answers were expected from the Workshop. It is clear that politicisation among rural labourers is developing in complex ways. Evaluated from a class perspective, some trends may seem negative, because this politicisation may strengthen, or may depend on, intra-class divisions such as gender and caste. However, recent political history shows that caste-based solidarities can be the precursors of wider class mobilisations. Thus present trends do hold out some promise for the future.

REFERENCES

Agarwal, Bina, 1994, *A Field of One's Own: Gender and Land Rights in South Asia*, Cambridge: Cambridge University Press.

Basu, Amrita, 1992, *Two Faces of Protest: Contrasting Modes of Women's Activism in India*, Berkeley, CA: University of California Press.

Bennett, Lynn, 1992, *Women, Poverty and Productivity in India*, Economic Development Institute Seminar Paper No.43, Washington, DC: The World Bank.

Bhalla, Sheila, 1997, 'The Rise and Fall of Workforce Diversification Processes in Rural India', in Chadha and Sharma (eds.) [1997: 145–83].

Brass, Tom, 1990, 'Class Struggle and the Deproletarianisation of Agricultural Labour in Haryana (India)', *The Journal of Peasant Studies*, Vol.18, No.1, pp.36–67.

Brass, Tom, 1994, 'Post-Script: Populism, Peasants and Intellectuals, or What's left of the Future? 'New Farmers' Movements in India', Special Issue, *The Journal of Peasant Studies*, Vol.21, Nos.3/4, pp.246–86.

Breman, Jan, 1993, *Beyond Patronage and Exploitation. Changing Agrarian Relations in South Gujarat*, Delhi: Oxford University Press.

Breman, Jan, 1996, *Footloose Labour: Working in India's Informal Economy*, Cambridge: Cambridge University Press.

Chadha, G.K., 1997, 'Access of Rural Households to Non-Farm Employment: Trends, Constraints and Possibilities', in Chadha and Sharma (eds.) [1997: 184–215].

Chadha, G.K. and Alakh N. Sharma (eds.), 1997, *Growth, Employment and Poverty: Change and Continuity in Rural India*, New Delhi: Vikas Publishing House.

Duvvury, Nata, 1989, 'Work Participation of Women in India: A Study with Special Reference to Female Agricultural Labourers, 1961 to 1981', in A.V. Jose (ed.), *Limited Options: Women Workers in Rural India*, New Delhi: ILO- ARTEP.

Kapadia, Karin, 1995, 'Women Workers in Bonded Labour in Rural Industry (South India)', in the Agrarian Questions Organising Committee (eds.), *Agrarian Questions: The Politics of Farming Anno 1995*, Vol.2, Wageningen: Wageningen Agricultural University.

Kapadia, Karin, forthcoming a, 'Responsibility Without Rights: Women Workers in Bonded Labour in Rural Industry', in Deborah Bryceson, Cristobal Kay and Jos Mooij (eds.), *Disappearing Peasantries? Rural Land and Labour in Latin America, Asia and Africa*, London: IT Publications.

Kapadia, Karin, forthcoming b, 'The Politics of Difference and the Formation of Rural Industrial Labour in South India Today', in Jonathan Parry, Jan Breman and Karin Kapadia (eds.), *The Worlds of Indian Industrial Labour*, New Delhi: Sage.

Kelkar, Govind, 1992, *Women, Peasant Organisations and Land Rights: A Study from Bihar, India*, Gender Studies Series, Bangkok: Asian Institute of Technology.

Omvedt, Gail, 1980, *We Will Smash This Prison*, London: Zed Press.

Sen, Abhijit, 1997, 'Structural Adjustment and Rural Poverty: Variables that Really Matter', in Chadha and Sharma (eds.) [1997: 110–22].

Sen, Abhijit and Jayati Ghosh, 1993, *Trends in Rural Employment and the Poverty-Employment Linkage*, New Delhi: ILO-ARTEP.

Rural Labour Relations in India: Persistent Themes, Common Processes and Differential Outcomes

T.J. BYRES

I. THE AGENDA AND SOME CAUTIONARY OBSERVATIONS

In the Introduction by Karin Kapadia and Jens Lerche, the considerations which gave rise to the conference on Rural Labour Relations in India from which this special issue derived are noted. Here I concentrate on the papers from the conference published in this special issue. One important theme given particular attention in the Introduction, that of gender, I will pay less attention to than would be necessary in the absence of the Introduction.

We have a collection in which there is one general account, by Mohan Rao, which considers unfree and free employment relations and six studies on individual states (two of them on one state, Uttar Pradesh, which is by far the most populous state of India). The contributions, then, with the exception of Mohan Rao's, relate to the individual states of India, or some of them.

Our concern is to suggest what conclusions we may derive from these papers, and what hypotheses for future research. We may start with two notes of caution. The first is that we do not, unfortunately, in this collection, manage individual treatment of all of the states of India. That would be impossible, even on the scale attempted here. Rather, we cover the states of Andhra Pradesh, Bihar, Haryana, Kerala and Uttar Pradesh: five out of those 17 states with a population of five million or more. We do not cover the states of Assam, Gujarat, Himachal Pradesh, Jammu and Kashmir, Karnataka, Madhya Pradesh, Maharashtra, Orissa, Punjab, Rajasthan, Tamil Nadu and West Bengal. That these 'missing states' have distinctive histories of rural labour relations and characteristic outcomes is likely. In what follows I will not mention them, although their individual experiences are extremely important and have much of substance to add to any serious treatment of Rural Labour Relations in India. A full treatment would require

T.J. Byres, Department of Economics, School of Oriental and African Studies, University of London, Thornhaugh Street, Russell Square, London WC1H 0XG. email tb1@soas.ac.uk consideration of them all. Our coverage, then, is no more than partial.

Secondly, we need to exercise some caution over the nature of the conclusions we may draw from the different kinds of evidence deployed in the regional studies. Thus, two analyses proceed in terms of the state as a whole: Bhalla on Haryana and Kannan on Kerala. They also seek to relate their treatment, indeed, to the all-India level and sometimes to other individual states. Another two, those on Uttar Pradesh (UP) by Lerche and Srivastava, while focussing on particular fieldwork areas, have chosen those areas as representative of the diversity of Uttar Pradesh itself (a very large state, with a population of 139 million in 1991): a diversity often seen in terms of the contrast between a backward eastern UP and a progressive western UP. The final two contributions, by da Corta and Venkateshwarlu on Andhra Pradesh and Wilson on Bihar, relate to particular fieldwork areas – the former to Chittoor District in the Rayalaseema region of Andhra Pradesh and the latter to Nalanda District in Central Bihar – although seeking to relate their treatment to the all-Andhra level and the all-Bihar level.

With these cautions in mind, we may, nevertheless, attempt an analytical distillation from a set of carefully worked and richly informative analyses. In these accounts, certain persistent themes emerge. Here my aim is threefold: first, to identify and consider those major persistent themes; secondly, to distinguish, within those themes, whatever common processes, with respect to labour relations in the Indian countryside, can be observed in the contributions published; and, thirdly, to suggest what the accounts reveal about differential outcomes within the Indian social formation. Clearly, what can be only a partial statement would have been added to considerably by full coverage of the states of India. Yet, while partial, it has much to offer.

II. THE PERSISTENT THEMES: CLASS CONFLICT AND THE NATURE AND IMPACT OF STATE INTERVENTION

A difficult analytical task set by these accounts is that of capturing, with respect to rural labour relations in India and within a political economy framework, both the general and the particular. We may conceptualise India as a whole: in the vocabulary of political economy, as a social formation. It is important that we do so. In so doing, we may seek the general: which we may identify as powerful convergent processes, or dominant tendencies. However, within such a large social formation there are likely to be substantive, divergent tendencies, which manifest themselves regionally. We need to capture both if we are to portray the full nature of the social formation, in all its complexity.

In so proceeding, it is illuminating to focus upon Marx's distinction between class-in-itself and class-for-itself. I have used this distinction in a previous contribution [*Byres*, 1981: 407–8 and *passim*]. That it is appropriate here seems obvious.

The subject of this collection is rural labour relations in India. These relations, for the political economist, are about class formation and class action in the Indian countryside, with respect to both subordinate and dominant classes: about the processes and outcomes associated with class-in-itself and class-for-itself in contemporary rural India. In one paper, that by Kannan, the class-in-itself/class-for-itself distinction is used explicitly, and to excellent effect, to analyse rural labour relations in Kerala. It is implicit, and, indeed, strongly present , in all of the other papers.

The idea that rural labour relations are about class conflict and the results of class conflict is common to all of the contributions. That is the major overarching theme. In those papers, such class conflict focuses upon rural labourers and their struggles with employers. They also include, as they must, treatment of poor and middle peasants and processes of differentiation of the peasantry: although this is less prominently pursued. Certainly, consideration of rural labour relations in India cannot be complete without treatment of poor and middle peasants and their struggles.

If such rural class conflict is the overarching theme, it is one that is intimately linked with the nature and impact of state intervention: both the central state and the state at the level of the individual regional polities. That theme is clear and persistent for each of the states covered. What, then, emerges from these studies? What do they suggest about both convergent and divergent processes with respect to these two major themes?

III. CONVERGENT AND DIVERGENT ELEMENTS: STYLISED
SHIFTS AND EMANCIPATORY PROCESSES

We may start with the general, with whatever common or convergent elements and processes may be identified. Mohan Rao argues the following: that 'while neither the robust elements of continuity nor the substantial variations over space should be underplayed' certain 'stylised shifts seem fairly widespread'. In other words, he seeks to identify clear general tendencies for the Indian social formation.

He does so cogently and with unerring accuracy with respect to the papers on the individual states, although he does not mention those papers. The general tendencies, or 'stylised shifts', which he identifies are as follows:

from caste-based or personally bonded labour sometimes secured by debt frequently extending across generations to long- and short-duration credit contracts apparently with no such tying; from informally defined and open-ended obligations to formal contractual arrangements; from relations based on 'extra-economic' sanctions to ones based on voluntary agreements; from a reliance on intra-village labour exchanges to the conjoint employment of local and migrant workers; and, from permanent farm labour to casual labour. These shifts seem broadly to be correlated also with the growth of non-agricultural employment.

Such are some of the major 'stylised shifts'. All of these emerge very clearly from the studies on the individual states: significantly more markedly in some states than in others but more or less without exception. What may we make of them?

We must not understate the continuing power of dominant rural classes, and the concerted class-for-itself action taken by such classes. In particular, we must not minimise the powerful agency of a self-confident capital, red in tooth and claw, that has emerged in the countryside of post-colonial India, in the half century of its existence, albeit in uneven fashion. This has ensured that, even as these changes have taken place,

> poor peasants' and labourers' livelihoods remain precarious as they continue to carry land leases at very low returns to their labour, often pay high interest rates especially for consumption loans and face insufficient and uncertain employment in the labour market.

The balance of power and control remains firmly with dominant classes. Yet, as Mohan Rao insists, plausibly, 'even without radical changes in the distribution of control over land and other means of production … employment relations seem to have evolved qualitatively during this half century'. The value of the present collection of papers is that it demonstrates the nature of that qualitative evolution, in all of its complexity; it suggests the major contributory influences; and it indicates its limitations and the contradictions it has entailed. We may point to some of this.

Without, then, romanticising these 'stylised shifts' and their outcome, we may say that it seems clear that in post-colonial India there have been vigorous emancipatory processes at work. In the five states covered, they have been at their most marked in Kerala, where, as Kannan points out:

> the highly contested nature of distributive issues … [and] the highly politicised and militant nature of labour struggles until the recent past … [have meant that] Kerala is unique among Indian states in that labour, including rural labour, has acquired a dominant position in the development discourse and in the development process.

The achievements for rural labourers have been significant:

> From the perspective of labour in general and rural labour in particular, Kerala's record in achieving a measure of human dignity and social progress is remarkable, viewed especially from an all-India perspective. The oppressive and degrading conditions, still prevalent in many parts of rural India, involving organised violence by landowning classes, indignities to women workers, and degrading conditions of work are no longer prevalent in Kerala. The emergence of trade unions as a strong labour institution and the overall social progress have led to a remarkable decline in the incidence of child labour (around one per cent as against eight per cent in all-India), social acceptance of such work norms as an eight-hour day, intervals and formal labour relations as against patron–client relations. It has also witnessed a sustained increase in wages and the securing of non-wage benefits in several occupations which are not officially categorised as 'formal' or 'organised'.

These are undeniable achievements. They have been secured, to an important degree, by sustained class struggle.

That progress in India has been uneven is suggested by the statement by Kannan just quoted. Yet the outcome of class struggle is by no means negligible elsewhere in India. Thus da Corta and Venkateshwarlu show, for Andhra Pradesh, an important improvement in the economic position of labourers in several respects: including a decline for men in traditional, permanent bonded relations and significant increases in real agricultural wages for both men and women. That this has been, to a significant extent, the outcome of class conflict, waged by landless labourers, is clear:

> Male labourers' movement out of joint daily wage labour also has its basis in their fierce struggle conducted against higher caste employers for freedom from tied labour work obligations, for improved wages and for improved status. Among the obligations contested by men are low/unpaid ploughing/irrigation tasks, beck-and-call arrangements, and the denial of their right to seek better paid work elsewhere, in the process either shirking or refusing work.

Again, the achievement is undeniable.

For Uttar Pradesh, Srivastava documents an active struggle between landless labourers and Jat landholders, which has had a notable outcome. He demonstrates a clear increase in class consciousness and in class-for-itself action, including strikes, by landless labourers, and action, moreover, which has had considerable success:

While conflict and struggle between the poor and dominant classes has never been absent from the rural scene in Uttar Pradesh, evidence examined in this study suggests that recent changes may have added new dimensions and assertiveness to the poor. The changes in the nature of dependence, contradictions and ensuing resistance analysed in this paper have significant implications for the restructuring of labour relations within villages, and still wider ramifications for the political articulation of the labouring classes.

There have been significant increases in real wages; and in some parts of Uttar Pradesh, at least, a notable change in employer–labourer relations:

> Employers report that earlier labourers started work at dawn, now they rarely report for work before 8 am and their working hours have shrunk to merely 6 hours. They complain that labourers have become more assertive, vocal and demanding. They will not take up work under pressure and have to be requested to come to the fields to take up work. Whether they accept or not is entirely up to their discretion.

Lerche has similar findings to report for Uttar Pradesh: 'rural labourers have experienced a number of important positive changes since Independence, and are increasingly able to assert what they now perceive to be their rights. Rural labour struggles have intensified and, in spite of counter actions by middle and big peasants, the position of labourers has improved.' Class struggle has secured clear gains for rural labourers. That appears to be undeniable.

Even in Bihar – or in Central Bihar, at least – class struggle has brought positive, if more limited, change for agricultural labourers and poor peasants. Wilson considers the struggle of landless labourers and small cultivators and concludes:

> An initial spurt of capital accumulation among a section of larger landowners employing wage labour provided the catalyst for the emergence in the late 1970s of an organised movement of mainly dalit agricultural labourers. This movement has continued to develop despite a subsequent slowing down of the process of accumulation in agriculture in the face of constraints rooted in the agrarian structure itself and the nature of State power in Bihar.

Wilson illustrates the changing relationship between agricultural labourers and their employers – complex and partial, yet substantive – thus:

> Naresh Ram, a dalit agricultural labourer who lives in a village dominated by large landowners of the Kurmi caste in Hilsa, a block of Bihar's Nalanda District, uses the following example to explain how

things have and haven't changed in his village during the last fifteen years:

> 'Before if I remained sitting on the khatia outside my house when a landowner walked through this tola, he would abuse me or even beat me up. Now after we have got organised, I can carry on sitting here and invite him to sit down. But if I were to go to his house and sit down next to him on the khatia outside, it would be a different matter …'.

She looks at

> the specific impact upon production relations of sustained struggles waged by agricultural labourers … [and she considers] a number of changes in production relations during the last fifteen years, relating in particular to wages, the nature and extent of attached and casual labour, and changes in patterns of tenancy and of credit.

The struggle has been complex in its outcome, as it has been throughout India. In part the outcome has been a defensive attempt by landowners to maintain the *status quo*, as elsewhere in India: in this instance, for example, the withdrawal of credit and of sharecropped land. But in part it has, too, represented 'acceptance by employers of demands put forward by agricultural labourers'. That constitutes a clear major gain in the least propitious of circumstances.

Of the five states covered, agricultural labourers would appear to have been least assertive in Haryana, one of the most agriculturally prosperous and dynamic of all Indian states. Here we may identify a divergent element. In that state, of course, the 'stylised shifts' we have noted had taken place before they had done so in most other states, as capitalist relations penetrated the countryside. In that transformation, however, class struggle would seem not to have been a major influence. Here we have a state that seems to be unique in several respects. These are considered with some cogency by Bhalla. The ones I would here stress are the following. It is unique in the timing of militant farmers' agitations, which took place in Haryana during the 1990s, whereas elsewhere in north and north-west India these peaked a decade earlier; and unique in the surprising acquiescence of rural labour as a class. Those militant farmers' agitations were pursued in the name of all peasants and agricultural labourers, yet to the extent that they were successful they were very predominantly so for rich peasants and capitalist farmers. Indeed, in rural Haryana dominant classes have gained remarkable control over labour processes: remarkably because it has been so weakly contested.

Bhalla identifies two elements of control. The first was permanent labour contracts, with a series of effects very powerfully in line with the interests of dominant classes. This was calculated to prevent, or dampen, class-for-itself action by subordinate classes. The second was the classic ploy of reaching for technical change: mechanisation, in order to hold down the wage bill. Such devices, or variants of them, were reached for in other states: for example, in Andhra Pradesh (various tied labour arrangements) and in Uttar Pradesh (the priority labour relationships described by Lerche). A central question must be: how is it that these weapons in the armoury of dominant classes are reached for with such comprehensive success in some instances – for example, in Haryana – while they are less successful in others, and so resolutely opposed in still others? In Kerala, for example, Kannan points to Luddite breaking up of tractors by agricultural labourers and a remarkable compromise over the introduction of tractors, whereby organised labour allowed such introduction but secured the payment of labourers who would have been employed in the absence of tractors. There appears to be no example of anything remotely like this in Haryana – or, indeed, elsewhere in India.

Addressing this question, surely, is critical in our efforts to capture the political economy of the Indian social formation's regional diversity. Only detailed historical treatment can unlock the secret of why class struggle takes a particular form and has a particular outcome in one instance and totally different ones in another, within the same social formation. Let us see what explanations, or hypotheses emerge from the contributions. I will turn to that presently. First we may stress some of the limitations and contradictions of the processes described.

IV. LIMITATIONS AND CONTRADICTIONS INHERENT IN EMANCIPATORY PROCESSES

We do well to remind ourselves of the broad limitations of these emancipatory processes, and the high costs borne by subordinate classes engaged in struggle. These are stated in each of the regional studies.

Thus, da Corta and Venkateshwarlu identify what they term a 'Standard of Living Paradox' in Andhra Pradesh, which translates into the proposition 'that despite a near doubling of real wages since 1970, food consumption levels and general standard of living were lower than expected and this is reflected in a heavy dependence on employers and merchants for exploitative loans'. In Uttar Pradesh, Srivastava notes the powerful nature of employer resistance to action by labourers:

By and large employers in all the study areas have resisted collective demands for wage increases by organising counter-boycotts. The important aspects of employer strategy in all three study areas have been sanctions against workers on the use of fields for grass and fodder, for movement and for easing themselves, and the use or threat of violence (their own violence or that of the state machinery) against workers. Some of these arenas constitute areas of 'one-sided dependence' in which labourers have no direct bargaining power. The sanctions succeed or fail depending on the extent that they affect the workers, which in turn depends on such factors as the location of their habitations and their dependence on fodder and grass, and the extent to which the employers can collectively implement them.

That this has powerful effect is undeniable. Srivastava further cautions, lest we be carried away by romantic notions, that 'the evidence that we have presented ... demonstrates the limited nature of the organisation and absence of sustained mobilisation among the poorer classes in the study areas' . Lerche also expresses some caution: pointing out that landowners in Uttar Pradesh in the 1990s continue to use 'harsh and direct means of oppression to maintain a cheap, reliable and docile labour force'. Wilson reminds us of ' the continuing stranglehold of the dominant classes over rural society' in Bihar, now deploying criminal gangs against landless labourers. She begins her study by noting 'the unprecedented scale of the massacre of 61 women, children and men belonging to low caste labouring families at Lakshmanpur Bathe in Jehanabad district on the night of 1 December 1997, the latest in a concerted campaign of terror by the landlord-sponsored Ranvir Sena'. The costs of struggle for subordinate classes in Bihar are high.

These limitations may be further expressed in two crucial contradictions inherent in the emancipatory processes analysed in these accounts. The first contradiction, which emerges most clearly in the study by da Corta and Venkateshwarlu on Andhra Pradesh, which is noted for Uttar Pradesh by Lerche, and which is likely to have wider significance, is what Lerche refers to as the 'progressive feminisation of unfree labour relations'. Da Corta and Venkateshwarlu point out that part of the counter-offensive, mounted by agrarian capitalists, to the struggle waged by male agricultural labourers, to compensate for the consequent rise in wage costs, was to intensify non-permanent forms of attached labour:

The latter were designed to secure male labour for exclusively male work and in order to replace male workers seeking emancipation and higher wages with cheaper, unfree female labour for the remaining agricultural tasks. Female labour was cheaper and less free than male labour because men shifted more of the responsibility for family provisioning on to women by spending more outside the home and by refusing wage work as a protest against low, tied wages. As a consequence, the cost of men's struggle for emancipation was women's unfreedom. Under these circumstances, feminisation of labour was largely disempowering for women.

They argue, indeed, that this is by no means confined to South India, and cite evidence for Haryana. Kannan notes the far higher proportion of women who are agricultural labourers than men in Kerala , although he does not pursue this. Lerche finds that in Uttar Pradesh:

> in the fieldwork villages the main breadwinners had de-linked themselves from all but the most profitable peak season processes in agriculture, and it might be that they were not particularly concerned about the unfree character of many of the slack season labour relations as these relations did not concern them personally. If this is the case, then any further struggle against unfree labour relations awaits initiatives by or on the part of female labourers.

We certainly need to establish quite how widespread such 'progressive feminisation of unfree labour relations' is; and whether, indeed, there have been active struggles against it. The papers here published are richly suggestive but by no means conclusive.

A second contradiction is given cogent expression by Kannan for Kerala, where emancipatory processes have gone furthest in India. He describes 'a process of social development without a commensurate transformation of the productive forces', giving rise to a central dilemma faced by Kerala: that of technological progress being blocked, and accumulation being slowed down significantly, by militant agricultural labour.

> While the organised power of labour enabled real increases in wage rates as well as securing better conditions of work, the employers resorted to a strategy of technological change to increase productivity and to prevent increases in the share of wages. Faced with a situation of displacement of labour in a context of labour surplus in the economy, trade unions opposed such technological change. This resulted in the employers seeking strategies to reduce the quantum of employment in an effort to reduce, or prevent further increase, in wage cost. In agriculture, this led to crop substitution in favour of low labour-absorbing crops. In a number of rural industries, this meant the migration of capital to low-wage areas in neighbouring states where the organised power of labour is quite weak. The decade of the seventies witnessed this phenomenon.

This, in turn, led to a worsening employment situation. Yet immiserisation of rural labour was, to use Kannan's expression, 'partly thwarted' . Two crucial elements intervened to secure such an outcome. One was large-scale migration of labour to Middle East countries. The second was of more general significance, and is an element which recurs in all of the accounts, and which proves to be central in any discussion of emancipatory processes: the role of the state.

V. THE SEVERAL INFLUENCES WHICH CONDITION CLASS STRUGGLE AND THE CRUCIAL ROLE OF THE STATE

Clearly, class struggle has been central to the emancipatory processes discussed in the contributions to this volume. But class struggle, and its relative success or failure, is itself the product of several influences, which may be difficult to disentangle.

The nature, and the degree of success, of such struggle will in part depend on the particular manifestations of 'the hard core of class', class-in-itself, in any particular context. The Kerala example is a clear-cut case in point. Kannan points to 'the early proletarianisation of a large segment of the traditional workforce' and the predominance of agricultural labourers in the workforce. This surely does, as I have said in a previous account, 'involve men and women with a common relationship to the means of production, a common relationship to the appropriation of surplus product, and a common relationship, therefore, to one another: these relationships giving rise to an objectively given, common set of economic interests *vis-à-vis* other classes' [*Byres*, 1981: 407]. But class-for-itself action requires a perception of class interests (class consciousness) and a willingness, and a capacity, to pursue these interests. This, in its turn, requires collective organisation, perhaps in unions. It may, further, entail wide-ranging social and political action, perhaps via political parties. All of this may be seen, in fascinating detail, in the contributions here published. There is one aspect of this to which I would draw attention: the crucial role of the state.

The state here exists at two broad levels: that of the national state and that of the regional state. Both are important in the interaction between state and class. Initiatives may be taken at both levels with important implications for rural labour relations/class struggle. Here, however, the state at the regional level takes on a particular significance. Even where a critical initiative is taken at the central level – say, liberalisation policies or poverty alleviation programmes – how it works out in the regional polities may differ strikingly from regional polity to regional polity, with differing implications for rural labour relations. And, certainly, there are dramatic differences among regional polities in autonomous, endogenous initiatives.

Among our authors there is agreement on the role of the state, but that role pursued in different ways and with differing outcomes.

Kannan argues that the state in Kerala is a 'soft institution': soft inasmuch as, on the one hand, it has limited freedom with respect to the central government (being dependent on it for finance and having no decisive say in public sector decisions); and on the other because it has not been able to operate independently of organised labour – 'coalition politics and governments', he tells us, 'have had to reckon with the power and demands of labour'. Yet, when he stresses that 'much of the energy of the state has been directed at mediating disputes between labour and capital and/or labour and the state' he is, in effect, underlining the powerful influence of the state upon the possibilities of class struggle and the outcomes. If, as he says, the state in Kerala has 'limited autonomy' it is a 'limited autonomy' that has been exercised powerfully on behalf of labour. One cannot possibly grasp the nature of rural labour relations in Kerala without reference to the important role of the state.

In the contribution by da Corta and Venkateshwarlu state interventions are given some prominence. They tell us, for example, that 'some policies had a direct and fairly strong impact on male labourers' economic position, such as the 1969 policy of opening up formally restricted government wasteland for use by landless labourers' . In Uttar Pradesh, Lerche lays considerable stress on the ' extraordinary development in UP [in the 1990s], whereby low caste BSP governments have actually been voted in' and argues that this has been a catalyst for many of the positive changes that have taken place for rural labourers: bringing about, he argues, the politicisation of labourers/untouchables and, without doubt, their far greater assertiveness and a net improvement in their economic position. He contrasts the BSP's success with the failure of the communist parties to gain a position of strength in agricultural labour struggles in UP. Indeed, agricultural labourers remain unorganised. In Haryana, Bhalla stresses that 'it is noteworthy that whatever victories were won [by agricultural workers], were won largely through the intermediation of governments – central, state or local. No major agricultural workers' union victories were recorded in Haryana which emerged from direct confrontations of agricultural labourers with their employers'. The state – as the Kerala, Andhra Pradesh, Uttar Pradesh and Haryana studies suggest – is crucial to whatever gains, be they substantial or meagre, accrue to agricultural labourers.

So far, then, we see a positive role exercised by the state. The contributions suggest, further, that poverty alleviation programmes in these states – in Kerala, in Andhra Pradesh, and in Uttar Pradesh, at least – have played a more significant role in emancipatory processes, and in maintaining gains made by rural labour, than the general literature on such programmes would suggest. This further underlines the positive role of the state.

Kannan holds that in Kerala poverty alleviation programmes played a prominent part in the 1980s in maintaining the gains made previously by agricultural labourers: stemming the immiserisation that had taken place in the 1970s. He argues that 'the combined impact of all "poor-relief" programmes, equivalent to the consumption of one out of five members in the family, played a significant role in the ability of the younger generation to remain unemployed until employment could be secured in the non-agricultural sector'. In Andhra Pradesh, it is argued by da Corta and Venkateshwarlu,

> there is a tendency to confuse the effects of 'growth' with the cumulative impact of government anti-poverty policies on tightening the labour market ... Strategic attempts of both Congress and the Telugu Desham Party in Andhra Pradesh to win the allegiance of rural male labourers [in the 1980s and early 1990s] have led to a series of ad hoc populist state welfare interventions ... [which] ... despite many problems supported male agricultural labourers' movement out of traditional permanent bonded labour relations and into employment on encroached government land and in government related non-agricultural work.

The benefits of these went chiefly to male agricultural labourers, and they had a strong impact 'on the political consciousness of men by encouraging them to emancipate themselves from the economic and symbolic humiliation of bondage and casteism as well as to vote independently from their employers'. In Uttar Pradesh, too, considerable significance is attached to such programmes by Srivastava: which are held to 'have reduced landlessness and assetlessness and put upward pressure on the supply price of labour'. He suggests:

> even though government programmes such as JRY have themselves created a minuscule amount of jobs in the rural areas, the wage offered under the schemes was higher than the prevailing wage rate, which, both employers and labourers concede, fuelled labourer expectations regarding wages. Moreover, employment generating public works programmes such as the JRY implemented though the village councils (panchayats) have given a small boost to rural infrastructure such as village approach roads which has tended to make labour more mobile. The increased mobility of labourers to nearby as well as distant destinations has created more alternative opportunities for employment.

It is difficult to resist these conclusions of careful scholars, made on the basis of scrupulously pursued fieldwork.

We see a far less positive role of the state in Bihar, however. There, no positive role of poverty alleviation programmes is mentioned by Wilson. There, rather, the appropriation of surpluses by unproductive upper caste landlords through manipulation of state apparatuses is noted as a common phenomenon, a path now being followed by rich peasants. State power is wielded consistently on behalf of dominant rural classes, and against subordinate classes in the countryside. In Bihar the major force in the pursuit of the interests of agricultural labourers seems to have been a movement led by the CPI(ML).

VI. ON NOT COLLAPSING THE REGIONAL INTO THE GENERAL AND A FUTURE ANALYTICAL AGENDA

We may return to Mohan Rao, with whom we started. Mohan Rao, in fact, before identifying the general tendencies we noted at the outset, distinguishes the general and the particular and raises the issue of 'regional variations in [agricultural] performance'. Although, having raised it, he does not, in fact, address seriously the matter of such variations , he stresses the danger of seeking simplistic explanations for them: such as the appearance of the high-yielding varieties, that is, 'agro-climatic differences and the relative availability of suitable new varieties' . No such simplistic explanations, we may note, are to be found in the accounts here published.

Mohan Rao alerts us to the significance, for a massive social formation such as India, of not collapsing the regional into the general. This is important if we are to capture a true concrete analysis of the concrete Indian situation, in all its complexity. The contributions that follow his are cogent testimony to that.

We note, in so proceeding, that we must seek to avoid both the aforementioned resort to simplistic explanation and the sterility of empiricism. The former abdicates adequate historical analysis and serious political economy treatment, in terms of processes of class formation and class action; while empiricism takes one no further than the proposition that there is regional diversity.

Mohan Rao observes that 'historical changes and regional variations in production relations and political processes which structure investments and incentives, in both public and private domains, have deservedly commanded wide attention'. That is so. But we are far from a satisfactory treatment of such variety. Indeed, one might say that it has barely begun. What the contributions here published demonstrate is that we need to capture, with great care and rigorously, how, precisely, developments vary substantively between regions. I would regard that as extremely important. There is a need to consider, within an appropriate analytical grid, the nature of the substantive regional diversity that constitutes rural India. For that we require full coverage of the states of India.The studies published help us take a few steps on that analytical path. The strong conclusion which I draw from them is that this is a primary analytical task facing scholars of rural India. A full set of accounts on the states of India, of the quality of those published here, would allow such a task to begin to proceed seriously.

In the chapter which gave rise to the celebrated Brenner debate, Robert Brenner argues: 'it is in the outcome of ... class conflicts – the reaffirmation of the old property relations or their destruction and the consequent establishment of a new structure – that is to be found perhaps the key to the problem of long-term economic development in late medieval and early modern Europe, and more generally of the transition from feudalism to capitalism' [*Brenner*, 1985: 12]. Brenner seeks to demonstrate, in a rich comparative political economy, that class relationships and class struggle are central to differential historical outcomes. We might seek to apply Brenner's fundamental insight more widely than Europe, and suggest a Brennerian analytical agenda for India. We need just such a powerful comparative political economy, with a sensitive treatment of class struggle at its centre, to be deployed in relation to the large social formation that is India. That might be the basis for a far more systematic interpretation of regional variations than we have currently. The analytical rewards are likely to be many.

REFERENCES

Brenner, Robert, 1985, 'Agrarian Class Structure and Economic Development in Pre-Industrial Europe', in T.H. Aston and C.H.E. Philpin (eds.), *The Brenner Debate: Agrarian Class Structure and Economic Development in Pre-Industrial Europe*, Cambridge: Cambridge University Press. The Brenner contribution was first published in *Past and Present* in 1976 (No.70, Feb.).
Byres, T.J., 1981, 'The New Technology, Class Formation and Class Action in the Indian Countryside', *The Journal of Peasant Studies*, Vol.8, No.4.

Liberalisation, Rural Labour Markets and the Mobilisation of Farm Workers: The Haryana Story in an All-India Context

SHEILA BHALLA

I. THE CONTEXT: RURAL MARKET TRENDS IN THE 1980s AND 1990s AND THE SPECIAL CASE OF HARYANA

This study traces the development of the Haryana unit of the All India Agricultural Workers Union (AIAWU), in close association with the peasants' movement, under conditions in which employment was contracting or stagnant in both agriculture and manufacturing, but working age population was growing. The Haryana case is a special one. This is the only state in India which has combined high farm output growth rates with an absolute decline in the number of workers engaged in agriculture during the liberalisation era. It is also unique in the timing of its militant farmers' agitations during the 1990s. In other northern and north-western states, such movements peaked a decade earlier, and then in the 1990s caste-based, ethnic or communal groupings flourished instead. This did not happen in Haryana.

The first half of the analysis concentrates on rural labour market trends in the 1980s and 1990s at the all-India level and in Haryana. An analysis of changes in workforce structure, labour productivity, real wages and poverty constitutes the core, and provides the context for the subsequent account of the rural response to these changes, and to others arising in the sphere of public policy, especially after 1991.

The Haryana case is important, because this state along with Punjab and western Uttar Pradesh, constitutes the heartland of India's Green Revolution. Not only was Haryana among the pioneers in the adoption of high-yielding varieties of wheat in the mid-1960s, it also maintained the pace of innovation throughout the 1970s and beyond when high yielding varieties of rice, then longer staple cotton and later crops new to the region, such as sunflower, were introduced. Of the two prime Green Revolution

Sheila Bhalla, Centre for Economic Studies and Planning, Jawaharlal Nehru University, New Delhi 110 067, India.

regions, Punjab and Haryana, Punjab still records the higher yield values: well over Rs.13,000 per hectare at 1990–93 constant prices, as compared to a little more than Rs.10,000 per hectare in Haryana.[1] However, Haryana agriculture has been able to sustain, and even to improve upon, its previous growth rates during the 1990s, while in Punjab the initially spectacular growth figures have gone down from decade to decade over the last 30 years. In the 1990s, Haryana's agricultural growth performance was significantly better than Punjab's.[2]

This may be one reason why, in Haryana during the past 20 years, real wages for farm workers generally have remained higher than those in Punjab,[3] despite the lower levels of farm output per worker in Haryana. Adam Smith's dictum that in the determination of real wages, it is not the level of a nation's wealth that matters, but rather the rate at which that wealth is growing, seems to hold at the state level in this case.[4] It may be added here also that in the Adam Smith universe, as in the Indian rural ground reality, improvements in wages do not depend directly on changes in labour productivity.[5]

In India, in recent decades, the factor which has mattered most in the determination of farm wages is the availability of alternative, non-farm jobs as reflected in shifts in the structure of a growing workforce in favour of industrial, trade, transport, communications and service sector employment.[6] The Haryana experience in the 1990s, with respect to such changes in the employment structure, is unique.

In Haryana, during the five years from 1987–88 to 1993–94, the share of the workforce accounted for by non-agricultural activities went up by almost ten percentage points; the absolute number of workers in the farm sector went down; and employment in the tertiary sector (covering transport, communications, trade and services) expanded until, by the middle of the 1990s, it absorbed 35 per cent of all ' usual principal status' workers.[7] No other state records figures like these.

These Haryana workforce developments were, of course, largely a response to very rapid output growth rates in the non-farm sectors of the economy. In Haryana, industrial and service sector growth rates have run consistently at roughly double the rates achieved by the farm sector. Thus Haryana should not be thought of as a predominantly agricultural state, at least not any more. In employment terms, Haryana today is one among a small handful of states – only four – where non-farm employment accounts for more than half of all 'principal status' jobs when rural and urban areas are taken together.[8]

Given the relentless build-up of demographic pressure on land in all other states, except Kerala, it is something of a tragedy that in eight out of 17 Indian states, during the 1990s, events were moving in a different direction. The farm workforce share in a growing worker population expanded instead of contracting. This constituted a reversal in the direction of longstanding trends in workforce structure. That this happened in about half of all major states in the country is just one aspect of an important new development in the regional workforce configuration within the Indian economy. At the state level, the regional economies have taken increasingly divergent paths during the liberalisation era.[9]

One measure of this divergence is the coefficient of variation for four points of time – the National Sample Survey employment survey years: 1977–78, 1983, 1987–88 and 1993–94. This measure of inter state variations reveals that up to the mid or late 1980s, the structurally backward states tended to record more rapid industrialisation of their workforces, together with relatively more rapid expansion of tertiary sector employment, generating a constructive kind of catching up process. This trend is reflected in falling coefficients of variation from year to year, indicating an unambiguous convergence in workforce structures, in directions commonly associated with 'modern economic growth'.[10]

The coefficient of variation figures which measure inter state contrasts in the share of manufacturing employment tell the main story. Between 1977–78 and 1983, the coefficients fell from 0.436 to 0.372, indicating a very substantial narrowing of the gaps between industrially backward and advanced states. Between 1983 and 1987–88, there was convergence also, but much less of it; the process of catching up by less industrialised states had evidently slowed down a great deal. (The 1987–88 coefficient of variation, at 0.368, was not much below the corresponding 1983 figure.) Then came the turning of the tide. By 1993–94, the coefficient of variation for manufacturing workforce shares had shot up to 0.476. In terms of timing, it is obvious that the process of reducing inter-state contrasts in workforce structure slowed down during the decade of the 1980s, characterised in India by indigenous efforts towards liberalisation, while divergence in the 1990s coincided with the period of externally sponsored stabilisation and structural adjustment programmes.[11]

While it may not be possible yet even to identify the complex set of factors which could explain the recent rise in regional diversity, one thing is certain. The implications of this new trend are likely to be far reaching. There are reasons to think that it could herald an era of widening inter regional inequalities, in labour productivity, in per capita incomes, as well as in access to jobs in the relatively high wage non-farm sectors. However, on this we have mainly the logic of past convergent development experience to go by. In independent India, divergent regional development at the state level is something new.

II. THE LOGIC OF NATIONAL LONG TERM RURAL LABOUR MARKET TRENDS AND RECENT REVERSALS IN THEM

(a) *Some General Trends and Reversals: and Haryana against the Stream in the 1990s*

In Haryana, as in India as a whole, during the 30 years up to 1991, poverty, wages and employment structure moved together, or failed to move. And this was as much the case in the decade preceding the 1970s, when levels of poverty and real wages, and the share of agriculture in the workforce resisted all efforts to change them, as it was later on, when poverty declined, real wages went up, and the share of the workforce engaged in agriculture, at last started creeping down.

But in one other crucial development indicator, the economy failed to achieve a much needed turnaround. At the all-India level, the gap between labour productivity in agriculture, on the one hand, and labour productivity in all other sectors of the economy, on the other, grew wider and wider, from the fifties to the 1960s, throughout the 1970s and 1980s, and right into the 1990s. However, in this matter, as in several others during the 1990s, Haryana managed to move against the stream.

At the national level, in 1951, non-farm labour productivity was less than twice the corresponding figure for the farm sector. By 1983, this ratio had gone up to more than three is to one. By 1993–94, despite the fact that labour productivity had risen in both sectors, the figure for the non farm sector had gone up to more than four times that for agriculture. The reason was simple. In India as a whole, the decline of the share of the workforce in agriculture, which began in the 1970s, and was aborted in the 1990s, never picked up enough strength to reduce this cruel contrast between what a typical worker can produce and earn in the farm sector, and what he (or she), can get if he (or she), is able to secure a job in a secondary or tertiary sector activity. In general, India is still an economy where labour markets conspicuously do not clear; that is, they do not operate so as to equate the available supplies, of casual work days in particular, to the demand for them. It is also one where the vast army of the rural self-employed, along with their hired labourers, continue to suffer the impact of policy changes inimical to their absorption in activities where labour productivity is higher.

In all the other key indicators – poverty, wages, and the farm sector's weight in the total workforce structure – there was a common turning point somewhere in the middle of the 1970s. We may consider these indicators: examining a) workforce, b) poverty and c) real wage levels.

(b) Changes in the Workforce Structure: From Before the 1970s to the
    Early 1980s

Workforce structure exhibited no clear trend up until 1970. Then, during the period commonly known as the decade in which India suffered a deceleration in industrial output growth rates, the Indian economy also experienced a retrogression of the employment structure. The 1971 Census showed that the share of the workforce engaged in agriculture had risen, and that the agricultural labour subset had grown at the expense of the share of self-employed cultivators. In the absence of significant expansion of employment opportunities outside of agriculture, workers had moved into the farm labour force, rapidly in those states enjoying the employment boom of the early Green Revolution, such as Haryana, and more slowly in states where no substantial change in the labour absorptive capacity of agriculture had taken place.[12] It is now generally known that, by 1981, in India taken as a whole, the share of non agriculture in the total workforce had recovered to better than 1961 levels. What is not commonly realised is that in rural areas it did not. This implies that a substantial part of the initial workforce shift out of agriculture involved a shift to urban areas.

The Haryana workforce urbanised at an exceptionally rapid rate. Moreover, Haryana also was one of the very few states where, even in rural areas, non-farm employment grew fast enough during the 1970s to regain all the ground lost during the industrial recession years, and more.

The deceleration of industrial output growth rates during the period from the mid-1960s to the early 1970s spawned a rich theoretical and empirical literature, which identified, as explanatory factors, combinations of the following: changes in the terms of trade in favour of agriculture, the decline in public and private investment during the 'Plan Holiday' period (1966 to 1969), the exhaustion of the easier opportunities for import substitution, and the emergence of domestic demand constraints.[13] But it does not seem to have been recognised in the wide-ranging literature on this recessionary period that rural areas generally bore the brunt of the workforce restructuring that took place, especially in the manufacturing segment. But not only there. In the tertiary sector also, the workforce grew rapidly in the cities during the 1970s, while the negative employment effects of tertiary sector workforce adjustments were evident in rural areas.[14] During the early 1990s, in a number of important respects, this bit of history was repeated. I will come back to the workforce developments of the 1990s, in greater detail, later. But before that a similar review of first the background to recent changes in poverty[15] and then in real wage levels is illuminating.

(c) Poverty Trends and a New Disturbing Shift Specific to Haryana

In India, the prevalence of poverty remained unchanged from 1950–51 to the mid-1970s. There were year-to-year fluctuations, but no long-term trend, either upwards or downwards. In years of good harvests poverty went down; in years of rising foodgrains prices, poverty went up – and simultaneously real wages went down. It was established that the level of agricultural output and foodgrains prices were the main determinants of year-to-year variations in poverty, and in real wage rates.

Then, from the mid-1970s onwards, poverty in India declined continuously up to the end of the 1980s, reaching its lowest point ever, at about 34 per cent of the population in 1989–90. It then crept up slightly in 1990–91, recorded a substantial jump in 1992, and subsequently moved down again somewhat in 1993–94, which is the latest year for which data are available. The outcome of these variations is that, by 1993–94, there was more poverty in percentage terms than in 1989–90, and about the same as in 1987–88.

The Haryana poverty profile matches the all-India one up to 1989–90 in directional terms, but there the resemblance ends. To begin with, Haryana's rural poverty ratios started out much lower than those for India as a whole. Then they not only fell far faster than all-India's during the 1980s, to an all-time low of about 13 per cent in 1989–90, they also rose much more steeply in 1990–91, and, after falling somewhat in 1992, finally peaked at close to 29 per cent in 1993–94 – a figure more than double the ratio in 1989–90, and higher than any Haryana poverty ratio since 1973–74!

In short, we have just seen, in the first half of the 1990s, a period during which the prevalence of poverty in terms of shares, has varied around an almost constant trend line from 1987–88 to 1993–94 in India as a whole, while the absolute number of people in poverty rose despite the facts that: (i) the performance of agriculture has been consistently good, except in 1992, and that (ii), per capita incomes generally have increased, albeit at a modest rate. In rural Haryana, the disappearance of the old relationships between poverty on the one hand, and agricultural output as well as per capita income growth, on the other, is even more striking.

This delinking from agricultural performance, of poverty, especially rural poverty trends, is something new for India, and for Haryana. Per capita income growth, without any poverty reduction, is also a new story, at least as far as the past twenty years is concerned. But it is a story which has been repeated in a number of countries in recent years. One common factor – common to countries from the UK to certain countries of south-east Asia – is worsening income distributions.[16] If income distribution worsens enough, even respectable per capita income growth rates may not lead to a decline in poverty.

(d) Real Wage Rates and Poverty: And Haryana Stands out Again

We may now consider the behaviour over time of real wage rates – particularly the wages paid to the poorest category of labour – rural casual agricultural labourers. Their real wages also remained constant until after the mid 1970s. There were fluctuations, related mainly to changes in foodgrains prices, but the long term trend was flat. Real wages started to move up exactly when rural poverty started to move down. Year-by-year wages followed the same pattern as poverty, only inversely. In years when poverty fell fast, real wages moved up substantially; when poverty declined more slowly, or increased, real wages rose more slowly, or, as in the first two years of stabilisation and structural adjustment, actually fell.

In Haryana, however, real agricultural wage rates[17] rose to record levels during the first four years following 1991, but the poverty figures failed to reflect the apparent improvement in rural labour market conditions. This new disjunction turned out to be just one facet of Haryana's unique response to rural labour market compression. Before considering that, we may identify the forces behind the ubiquitous wage gains of the 1970s and 1980s.

Studies of the period after the mid 1960s showed that the rise of real wages had very little to do with labour productivity in agriculture.[18] Initially, in the late 1960s and early 1970s, when agricultural labour productivity went up, real wages had stagnated. After the mid-1970s, real wages went up everywhere, even in states where agricultural labour productivity was in long-term decline, like Bihar. What real wages did have to do with was increases in the share of the workforce in non-agricultural employment, in each state. It was also established that the rise of non-agricultural employment reduced the incidence of bonded labour in rural areas.[19] And since wages in non-agricultural employment have been consistently above wages in agriculture, it was realised that a part of the significant decline in rural poverty was also related to the opening up of opportunities for non-farm work.

In the 1990s, in India taken as a whole, such opportunities collapsed, and in terms of time periods, the timing of the decline in the share of workforce engaged in rural non-farm activities exactly matches the timing of the rise in rural poverty. Real wage rates in agriculture, even in the most recent period, are still inversely related to poverty in most states, and directly related to the availability of non farm employment.

In Haryana, however, the inverse relation with poverty has, for the time being, vanished, but the direct connection between wages and the share of labour absorbed in the non-farm sector seems more robust than ever. The causes of the rise in rural poverty lie elsewhere, notably in the long term –

1983 to 1993–94 – stagnation in the absolute number of persons who could find steady work in any sector. (See the 'usual principal status' figures in Table 5.)

In India, academic attention was initially distracted from this wider set of factors influencing poverty by a narrow focus on one single feature of post-1991 experience, namely, increases in food prices. As a matter of policy in the 1990s, foodgrains price increases were deliberately pitched above the rate of inflation of non farm commodity prices.

The rationale for doing this was clearly set out in the 1996 Interim Budget Speech, as well as in the 1996 Economic Survey.[20] To judge by Manmohan Singh's reported statements at the February 1996 Davos meetings of the annual World Economic Forum, he visualised increases in foodgrain prices, phased over a long period, as one element of a reform programme which would also see concurrent reductions in farm subsidies. Such statements, it may be noted, are not consistent with an alternative account of the reasons for the sharp increases in foodgrain prices during the early 1990s, put forward by Tendulkar and Jain [1995]. They argue that the price increases are the result of domestic political forces 'totally unrelated to the basic rationale underlying the economic reforms' [1995: 1377].

(e) The New Economic Policy in the 1980s and After

At this stage, a few words about the new economic policy in the 1980s and after are in order, to place the more recent developments on the employment front in their proper context.

In its first phase, running from the start of the 1980s or a bit earlier, India's new economic policy was marked by the gradual relaxation of industrial licensing policy, moves to encourage the modernisation and upgradation of industrial technology, and measures to liberalise the import of industrial inputs. Papola [1989, 1991] has argued that these measures accelerated the normal process of development and structural change within manufacturing in favour of industries using processed intermediates and inputs, (including imported inputs), and labour saving technologies. In addition, the notion of a 'small scale' unit was repeatedly redefined by raising the ceiling investment limit from Rs 7.5 lakhs in the late 1970s to Rs 35 lakhs in 1985. Since a broad spectrum of protective and promotional legislation applies to small scale units, one of the consequences was that many of the really small units suddenly found themselves competing on the same terms with the relatively bigger ones recently brought under the protective umbrella. These changes contributed both to the subsequent decline in employment elasticities[21] in industry, and to the collapse of rural household industry in the 1980's, recorded by the 1991 Population Census.

The second phase was, of course, precipitated by the political, fiscal and balance of payments crises of 1990–91. The IMF-World Bank sponsored policy package for dealing with it included both stabilisation and structural adjustment programmes. The former aimed to reduce budgetary deficits, the inflationary gap and the balance of payments deficit. The latter sought to make the economy more efficient and competitive by replacing an inward looking growth strategy by a more outward oriented one, and by reducing the role of the state in the economy. Specific measures included: a sharp devaluation of the rupee, a squeeze on public investment and social expenditure, and wide ranging measures to liberalise the import of capital and intermediate goods. Simultaneously, the industrial licensing system was virtually wound up. There was a partial withdrawal of fertiliser subsidies, and foodgrain procurement prices were increased.

In the immediate aftermath, growth rates collapsed and poverty soared. It was officially conceded that: 'Stabilisation policies for containing fiscal and current account deficits are inherently contractionary ... and tend to depress output growth as well as employment growth', and that, in India in 1991–92, there had been a sharp fall in growth rates and very little employment generation.[22] However, India's growth rates bounced back to modestly respectable, if not spectacular, figures within two or three years. For a restructuring economy, this has been described as typical 'J-curve' behaviour,[23] but in the Indian case, the turn around time has been exceptionally short. The question now is: what are the longer term employment and earnings prospects, particularly for the rural poor? The answers lie as much in what happened during the 1980s, as in the subsequent events of the 1990s.

III. THE DECLINE IN THE EMPLOYMENT GENERATING CAPACITY OF ECONOMIC GROWTH IN THE 1980s

(a) Trends and Outcomes in Employment

One of the most serious developments in India during the years of indigenously sponsored liberalisation in the 1980s, was the decline of employment growth rates to levels below population and workforce growth rates. This happened during a decade in which India achieved record rates of growth in all major sectors. By 1987–88, employment growth had fallen to just over one-and-a-half per cent per year. The problem was mainly in rural areas, as can be seen in Table 1. The 'recovery' of overall employment growth rates in the 1990s is, again, largely the product of what happened in rural areas. It will be noted that, in Haryana, where output growth stood far above the all India averages between 1987–88 to 1993–94, rural workforce growth rates did not recover to the levels achieved during the previous

TABLE 1
EMPLOYMENT GROWTH BY RESIDENCE AND EMPLOYMENT STATUS:
HARYANA AND INDIA: 1972–73 TO 1993–94

Residence	Status	1972-73 to 1977–78	1977-78 to 1983	1983 to 1987–88	1987-88 to 1993–94
HARYANA					
Rural	UPSS	1.43	1.88	2.21	1.30
	UPS		2.98	–0.45	0.51
Urban	UPSS	6.44	5.06	5.27	3.48
	UPS		5.52	4.06	2.93
Total	UPSS	2.20	2.46	2.84	1.78
	UPS		3.50	0.60	1.15
INDIA					
Rural	UPSS	2.52	1.83	1.17	2.27
	UPS		1.56	1.45	2.11
Urban	UPSS	4.31	3.56	2.97	3.51
	UPS		3.51	2.92	3.63
Total	UPSS	2.82	2.15	1.53	2.53
	UPS		1.94	1.76	2.45

Notes:

1. Compound growth rates based on absolute figures, derived from National Sample Survey (NSS) data and mid-NSS Round population estimates computed from the 1971, 1981 and 1991 Population Censuses.
2. The NSS defines a person's 'Usual Principal Status' (UPS) as working, or employed, if he/she pursued any combination of gainful activities on most days in a 365 day reference period. Everyone else is a non-worker by the UPS criterion, but such UPS 'non-workers' who pursued a gainful activity in a subsidiary capacity are referred to as 'Subsidiary Status' workers. Together, the 'Usual Principal and Subsidiary Status'(UPSS) set covers all employed persons. The sole NSS 27th Round (1972-73) category, 'workers' is comparable to the UPSS category.
3. In the most recent period, the Haryana UPS worker growth rates stand far below UPSS growth rates, especially in rural areas. This implies a burgeoning 'Subsidiary Status' subset, described in the *NSS Revised Report No. 406* (1996) as a 'transient' employment component. (See page 20).

decade. Further, as we shall see shortly, there is a dark side to the apparently rosy picture of improved rural labour absorption in India as a whole.

Simultaneously, there was a tremendous increase in the share of casual workers, mainly at the expense of the self employed in rural areas, and mainly at the expense of regular hired workers in urban areas. Both these trends were accentuated in the 1990s.

The immediate cause of the shortfall in job creation in India during the

TABLE 2
EMPLOYMENT ELASTICITIES WITH RESPECT TO GDP BY SECTOR AND
EMPLOYMENT STATUS: HARYANA AND ALL-INDIA

Residence/Status Sector		All India				Haryana	
		1972–73 to 1977–78	1977–78 to 1983	1983 to 1987–88	1987–88 to 1993–94	1983 to 1987–88	1987 to 1993–94
1.Agriculture and allied	UPS			0.35	0.52	–0.95	–0.28
activities	UPSS	0.54	0.49	0.26	0.54	1.48	0.01
PRIMARY							
2. Mining	UPS			0.79	0.37	7.47	–0.87
& Quarrying	UPSS	0.95	0.67	0.81	0.36	8.81	–1.14
3. Manufacturing	UPS			0.41	0.32	0.77	–0.38
	UPSS	1.05	0.68	0.35	0.39	0.70	–0.32
4. Electricity, gas	UPS			0.77	0.38	2.14	0.26
& water supply	UPSS	1.67	0.74	0.74	0.53	2.28	0.03
5. Construction	UPS			3.20	0.12	1.23	3.97
	UPSS	0.35	1.00	3.43	0.01	1.29	3.63
SECONDARY	UPS			0.76	0.26	0.86	0.22
	UPSS			0.72	0.28	0.84	0.15
6 Transport, Storage	UPS			0.44	0.58	0.04	1.56
and Communication	UPSS	0.76	0.92	0.39	0.62	–0.18	1.57
7. Trade, hotels	UPS			0.83	0.56	1.02	0.39
hotels & restaurant	UPSS			0.76	0.59	1.07	0.45
8. Services	UPS			0.44	0.70	–1.81	7.29
	UPSS			0.39	0.76	–3.77	8.34
(7+8) Services including	UPS	—	—	—	—	—	—
trade	UPSS	0.80	0.90	0.52	0.68	—	—
TERTIARY	UPS			0.57	0.61	0.04	1.04
	UPSS			0.53	0.65	0.12	1.14
9. All Sectors	UPS			0.36	0.46	0.11	0.18
	UPSS	0.61	0.55	0.32	0.47	0.54	0.28

Source: Based on NSS Usual Principal, and Usual Principal and Subsidiary Status data and CSO National Accounts Statestics GDP and SGDP data. The all India figures for the first twoyears are taken from Planning Commission documents.

Note: GDP/SGDP data on a financial year basis has been converted to the NSS Round basis, by taking a weighted average of the relevent financial year figures.

1980s was a decline in the impact of economic growth on employment, in all major sectors: agriculture, manufacturing and services. The employment elasticity figures of Table 2 (measured as the rate of growth of employment divided by the rate of growth of gross domestic product) reveal the weakening of the employment response, in terms of new jobs, to any given rate of economic growth. What the bottom line of the table tells us is that in the 1970s, a one per cent increase in gross domestic product led to an increase in employment of the order of 0.61 per cent in the economy as a whole. Ten years later, in the 1980s, the same one per cent increase in India's gross domestic product resulted in an employment increase of only 0.32 per cent. The recovery of most elasticities in the 1990s was led by agriculture and services. The all-India employment elasticity for manufacturing, it may be noted, persisted in the 1990s at about the same low level that was established in the 1980s.

(b) Interpreting the Trends

To interpret the more recent all India elasticities, and the starkly contrasting Haryana ones, examination of the underlying gross domestic product and employment growth rates is revealing (see Table 3). The fact is that in the major commodity producing sectors, in trade, and overall, the Haryana economy did much better than the national economy during the mid-1980s, despite the drought which produced negative farm output growth in 1987–88 as compared with the preceding crop year. The negative Haryana elasticities which appear in Table 2 for this period are therefore all due to an absolute fall in hard core 'usual principal status' (UPS) employment, most importantly in agriculture and services, under circumstances in which business is booming in manufacturing, basic infrastructure, transport and trade. Evidently a major bout of privately initiated workforce restructuring was underway in Haryana during the 1980s. What these tables do not show, however, is that in rural areas, the absolute number of UPS workers actually declined in all sectors combined. A substantial shift into transient subsidiary status work brings up the rural 'usual principal and subsidiary status' (UPSS), workers growth to a respectable-looking positive 2.2 per cent.

In the 1990s, workforce restructuring in Haryana proceeded apace, in apparently even more favourable circumstances, to judge by the State GDP figures for 'all sectors'. Indeed, what 'saved' Haryana workers, by producing a small positive UPS worker growth rate for all sectors combined in the 1990s, was the relatively high rates of GDP growth in trade, transport and services. None the less, with negative or negligible rates of growth of UPS farm employment, and the crash of elasticities in the secondary sector, many workers really had no option but to find a niche in the tertiary sector. They joined it in such large numbers, however, that despite high rates of

TABLE 3
GROWTH OF GDP AND GROWTH OF EMPLOYMENT (UPS) IN THE 1980s AND
1990s BY SECTOR: ALL-INDIA AND HARYANA

Residence/ Sector	All India				Haryana			
	1983 to 1987–88		1987-88 to 1993–94		1983 to 1987–88		1987 to 1993–94	
	GDP	Workers	GDP	Workers	GDP	Workers	GDP	Workers
Agriculture and allied activities	1.29	0.45	4.26	2.22	1.51	−1.43	6.76	−1.90
PRIMARY								
Mining and Quarrying	0.62	5.07	6.30	2.54	3.23	24.12	12.83	−11.15
Manufac-turing	7.05	2.93	4.73	1.50	11.57	8.86	5.98	−2.30
Electricity gas and water supply	9.72	7.47	8.48	3.20	7.35	15.74	9.42	2.43
Constru-ction	4.06	13.00	5.71	0.68	2.66	3.26	3.29	13.07
SECONDARY	6.71	5.11	5.29	1.39	10.00	5.97	8.63	1.31
Transport, Storage and Communication	8.15	3.56	6.15	3.58	7.40	0.31	8.41	13.13
Trade,hotels & resturant	5.65	4.67	6.23	3.46	8.68	8.88	5.82	2.29
Services	7.08	3.08	6.37	4.43	6.82	−1.81	5.67	7.29
TERTIARY	6.75	3.84	6.29	3.85	7.73	0.33	6.09	6.61
All Sectors	4.84	1.76	5.38	2.45	5.28	0.60	6.35	1.15

Source: as Table 2.

tertiary sector product growth, tertiary sector elasticities rose to greater than one, implying, of course, a decline in labour productivity in this expanding sector.

The evidence presented so far leads to a number of questions. First, why did employment elasticities go down generally during the 1980s? Second, what lies behind the national level 'improvements' recorded during the 1990s, which stand in such contrast to the discouraging Haryana employment elasticity figures? At the present time, only superficial answers can be given to the second question. The data are not yet available which would enable researchers to probe more deeply. But a great deal of evidence has been sifted to produce answers to the first one. Let me begin with the record in agriculture during the 1980s.

In India, as long as the expansion of net sown area provided most of the observed increases in output, employment went up, almost automatically, whenever output increased. The typical farmer, in effect, simply replicated the existing input combinations on an additional field. But now that increases in yield account for 90 per cent, or more, of all output growth, increases in production may, or may not, be associated with increased demand for labour. It all depends on what the least cost combination of labour with other inputs actually is.

Initially, in the first phase of the Green Revolution, when real wages stagnated, despite substantial increases in demand for labour, the least cost combination was highly labour absorbing. On the material inputs side, the key inputs were HYV seeds, a controlled water supply, in particular tubewell irrigation, and chemical fertilisers. In the second phase of the Green Revolution, however, mechanisation was increasingly adopted, partly, but not entirely, in response to rising real product wage rates from the mid 1970s onwards. The other important factor was that for annual crop cycles involving wheat with some other high value crops, such as rice, cotton or sugarcane, timeliness in sowing the wheat crop became crucial to obtaining optimum yields. Thus the cost of production per unit of output was reduced by mechanisation which speeded up land preparation before sowing, and harvesting operations, even in the absence of any rise in wage rates.

In the case of manufacturing, much of the spectacular collapse of employment elasticities during the 1980s can be traced to the substantial restructuring of the industrial sector which took place then. Segments like capital goods and consumer durables, where production processes are characterised by low labour intensity, grew the fastest, while more highly labour intensive lines of production, such as cotton textiles, grew slowly or actually contracted. In addition, both domestic and foreign demand shifted in favour of more sophisticated, higher quality goods. This tended to reduce labour absorption even within particular elements of the industrial structure.[24] The effects of these changes, almost all adverse to employment prospects, will persist, although some industries, such as textiles, now that their restructuring process is, for the time being, complete, are likely to record more favourable elasticities in future than they did in the recent past. Much of this restructuring, it may be noted, took place in the organised manufacturing sub-sector, located largely in urban centres.

Not only this. In rural areas specifically, the 1991 Census tells us that an absolute decline in the household industry workforce took place during the 1980s for the first time since India gained independence. (In earlier decades, although the share of household industry had declined, the absolute numbers had always risen.) This contraction of the household manufacturing workforce was not fully compensated for by the increased employment in the non-household manufacturing sector. The prospects are that this decline of employment in rural household industry will continue. Household manufacturing will tend to be driven out of business by more efficient units, typically using power driven machinery and relying mainly on hired labour instead of on self employed family workers.

IV. THE EVENTS OF THE 1990s: VARIETIES OF EXPERIENCE IN RURAL AREAS SPECIFICALLY

What happened during the 1990s to rural workforce structure at the national level, was even more serious than what had gone before. Agriculture reverted to its historic role as the residual sector for workers who could not find more productive jobs elsewhere. At the same time, Haryana recorded an unprecedented shift out of agriculture, much of it into the tertiary sector, providing striking evidence that workforce restructuring can proceed along more or less approved lines, and yet reflect distressed conditions in the rural labour market.

In Indian conditions, how does one judge when labour markets are under pressure? One does so, first and foremost, by the behaviour of poverty ratios, and by changes in the absolute number of people who are poor. Secondly, one does so by the appearance of a major sector or combination of sub sectors, into which a comparatively large number of workers shift despite low, and/or declining average labour productivity there. Finally, one does so by the mere fact that labour absorption in usual principal status work stagnates or declines in absolute terms over a protracted period, despite substantial positive rates of population growth during those years.

The Haryana developments differ so markedly from those reflected in the all India aggregates, that the two experiences will be considered sequentially below.

V. THE ALL-INDIA RURAL EXPERIENCE IN THE 1990s

At the end of the 1980s, the share of the rural non-agricultural workforce reached its highest level ever, just before the era of structural adjustment began. This time profile is the same for wage rates, and a sort of inverse of the time profile for poverty ratios.

TABLE 4A
THE DECADE TO 1993-94: SECTORAL DISTRIBUTION OF THE RURAL
WORKFORCE BY EMPLOYMENT STATUS: INDIA

Sector	Status	1983	1987–88	1989–90	1990–91	1992	1993–94
Agriculture	UPS	80.0	76.6	74.2	74.5	78.5	76.9
	UPSS	81.2	78.2	75.1	75.5	79.4	78.4
Non-Agriculture	UPS	20.0	23.4	25.8	25.5	21.5	23.1
	UPSS	18.8	21.8	24.9	24.5	20.6	21.6
Secondary	UPS	9.4	12.0	12.3	11.1	9.7	10.6
	UPSS	9.0	11.3	12.2	10.9	9.5	9.6
Tertiary	UPS	10.3	11.4	13.5	14.4	11.6	11.9
	UPSS	9.5	10.4	12.7	13.6	11.1	11.4

Source: As in Table 1.

Notes:
1. 1983, 1987–88 and 1993–94 are NSS 'full sample' Rounds. 1989–90, 1990–91 and 1992 are NSS 'thin sample' years. Figures for thin sample years should be interpreted as indicating qualitative changes only, even at the all India level.
2. Non-agriculture is taken as a residual. The sum of secondary plus tertiary sector workers does not always add up to the non-agriculture share. Some, but not all, of this is due to rounding. Another part is due to the existence of a small number identified variously by the NSS as 'others' and 'unrecorded'. When there is a difference in the NSS data, between the sum of the parts and the whole, the 'difference..is adjusted with the row/column having the maximum entry': page 45/1 NSS revised Report No. 406. *Key Results on Employment and Unemployment* NSS 50th Round (July 1993–June 1994).

TABLE 4B
THE DECADE TO 1993-94: SECTORAL DISTRIBUTION OF THE RURAL
WORKFORCE BY EMPLOYMENT STATUS: HARYANA

Sector	Usual Principal and Subsidiary Status			Usual Principal Status		
	1983	1987–88	1993–94	1983	1987–88	1993–94
Agriculture	77.4	78.5	71.9	74.5	73.1	62.4
Non-agriculture	22.71	21.5	28.1	25.5	26.9	37.6
Secondary	9.4	9.8	9.2	9.9	11.9	12.7
Tertiary	13.4	11.7	18.9	15.6	15.0	24.9

Source: As in Table 1.
Note: All the data used here are from NSS 'full sample' Rounds.

TABLE 5
THE DECADE TO 1993–94: RURAL WORKFORCE AND ITS GROWTH
BY SEX AND EMPLOYMENT STATUS: INDIA AND HARYANA

Residence/Status/Sex		Number (000s)			Growth Rate (Compound)	
		1983 to 1987–88	1987–88 to 1993–94	1993–94	1983	1987–88
INDIA						
Male	UPS	148,158	157,940	184,077	1.43	2.59
	UPSS	153,489	164,050	189,209	1.49	2.41
Female	UPS	65,978	70,538	74,855	1.50	0.99
	UPSS	90,454	92,995	104,925	0.62	2.03
Persons	UPS	214,136	228,478	258,932	1.45	2.11
	UPSS	243,943	257,045	294,134	1.17	2.27
HARYANA						
Male	UPS	2,698	2,788	3,140	0.73	2.00
	UPSS	2,836	2,956	3,260	0.93	1.64
Female	UPS	759	600	353	–5.09	–8.46
	UPSS	1,296	1,604	1,667	4.85	0.64
Persons	UPS	3,458	3,387	3,492	–0.45	0.51
	UPSS	4,132	4,560	4,927	2.21	1.30

Source: As in Table 1.
Note: All years are 'full sample' NSS Rounds.

In Table 4, we note also the tendency for the share of the secondary sector in the rural workforce to stagnate or decline, in the years before the watershed of 1991. This reflects the collapse of employment in household industry. After 1991, not only the rural secondary sector, but all of non-agriculture, suffered a rout. By 1993–94, although the shares of the secondary and tertiary sectors had both recovered somewhat from the trough of 1992, the non-agricultural sector as a whole continued to provide jobs to a relatively smaller proportion of the workforce than in either 1987–88 or 1990–91. To sum up: structural retrogression correctly describes the character of changes in the sectoral distribution of the rural workforce in India in the post 1991 era.

The outcome, in terms of the numbers of people who found work or lost jobs in each sector is set out in Table 6.

The influx of 24 million usual principal status workers into agriculture – roughly 19 million men and 5 million women between 1987–88 and 1993–94 – is recorded in the second column, top line, of each section. (The

TABLE 6
THE RECORD IN TERMS OF CHANGES IN WORKFORCE NUMBERS IN RURAL
AREAS: BY SECTOR AND EMPLOYMENT STATUS: ALL INDIA

Sex/Sectors Status		Change in Absolute Numbers (000s) by year			
		1983 to 1987–88	1987–88 to 1993–94	1990–91 to 1992	1990–91 to 1993–94
MALES					
Agriculture	UPS	+2,369	+18,946	+11,732	+12,128
	UPSS	+3,217	+17,987	+14,153	+13,266
Non-agriculture	UPS	+7,413	+7,190	−7,322	−3,280
	UPSS	+7,344	+7,172	-6,557	−2,843
Secondary	UPS	+4,315	+1,374	-2,511	−753
	UPSS	+4,501	+1,341	-2,249	−441
Tertiary	UPS	+3,414	+5,606	−4,810	−2,896
	UPSS	+3,093	+5,995	−4,307	−2,401
FEMALES					
Agriculture	UPS	+1,308	+5,208	+4,895	+1,564
	UPSS	−389	+11,679	+9,448	+15,210
Non-agriculture	UPS	+3,252	−891	−559	−151
	UPSS	+2,931	+251	+176	+1,099
Secondary	UPS	+2,754	−1,088	−29	+716
	UPSS	+2,606	-590	+484	+1,530
Tertiary	UPS	+613	+268	−530	−867
	UPSS	+596	+842	−309	−432
PERSONS					
Agriculture	UPS	+3,677	+24,155	+16,626	+13,691
	UPSS	+2,828	+29,665	+23,60	+28,476
Non-agriculture	UPS	+10,665	+6,298	−7,881	−3,341
	UPSS	+10,274	+7,423	-6,380	−1,744
Secondary	UPS	+7,068	+268	−2,541	−36
	UPSS	+7,107	+751	−1,765	+1,089
Tertiary	UPS	+4,027	+5,873	−5,341	−3,763
	UPSS	+3,697	+6,837	−4,616	−2,833

Notes:
1. Absolute figures have been derived from NSS ratios, using mid-Round population estimates derived by interpolation for the years before 1991, and by projection for subsequent years.
2. Absolute figures for the 'thin sample' years (1990-91 and 1992), should be interpreted as indicative of qualitative trends only.

figures are even higher if subsidiary status workers are included.) Most of this tremendous buildup of relatively low productivity workers took place after 1991, as is evident from the last two columns of the table. The number of persons who settled for work in agriculture, it is worth noting, is roughly four times the number who obtained work in the non farm sectors from 1987–88 to 1993–94. This compares decidedly unfavourably with the numbers for the preceding quinquennium. From 1983 to 1987–88, roughly three times as many fresh jobs had been generated in non-agriculture as were generated within the farm sector.

Again, the damage was done mainly in the years following 1991. Over the most recent period covered by the data at present available (i.e. 1987–88 to 1993–94), the worst hit have been women workers in the rural secondary sector, where more than one million usual principal status jobs were lost. (Compare this with the more than two-and-a-half million fresh jobs generated in the preceding quinquennium.) The net result for men and women workers taken together is that while seven million new secondary sector jobs were created between 1983 and 1987–88, this stream of fresh secondary sector workers dwindled to a mere trickle, amounting to an addition of just 286,000 persons to the rural secondary sector workforce in the most recent five years. To top it all off, the casual labour subset grew the fastest.

Under these circumstances, we should expect an increase in the prevalence of rural poverty, both because it is among the poorest groups that the workforce has expanded, while the relatively better off workforce categories have contracted, and also because the key factor which had made for rising real wage rates in agriculture has ceased to operate. If workforce diversification (in rural and urban areas combined and separately) was the main force behind rising real agricultural wage rates during the preceding 15 years, the reverse process in the 1990s is bound to exert downward pressure on rural real wage rates generally. And all this is quite aside from the damaging effects of rising foodgrains prices on the poorer sections of the rural population. Evidently the rural poor had not one, but several factors working against their interests during the first years of the present decade.

Behind the depressing figures in Tables 4A and 6 lie some readily identifiable causal factors. One of them is certainly the large negative rates of growth of both public and private investment in 1991–92, and the subsequent decline of public gross fixed capital formation in 1992–93. Another is the substantial absolute fall in public spending, particularly in the social sector, and most notably in education. At the level of the central government, this rot had set in from 1989–90 onwards, that is, a full year before the rigours of budgetary compression fell on social sector spending.

TABLE 7
THE RECORD IN TERMS OF CHANGES IN WORKFORCE NUMBERS IN RURAL
AREAS 1983 TO 1993-94 BY SEX, SECTOR AND EMPLOYMENT STATUS:
HARYANA

| | | Change in Absolute Numbers by year | |
| | | 1983 to 1987–88 | 1987-88 to 1993–94 |
Secto	Status		
MALES			
Agriculture	UPS	+37,928	65,382
	UPSS	+69,512	−109,271
Non-agriculture	UPS	+51,590	+417,002
	UPSS	+50,132	+413,077
Secondary	UPS	+59,486	+48,172
	UPSS	+58,173	+31,931
Tertiary	UPS	−7,326	+368,830
	UPSS	−8,608	+378,538
FEMALES			
Agriculture	UPS	135,965	−232,235
	UPSS	+317,454	+70,124
Non-agriculture	UPS	23,750	−14,346
	UPSS	8,496	6,972
Secondary	UPS	− 192	6,972
	UPSS	+1,159	−24,528
Tertiary	UPS	159,715	7,374
	UPSS	10,286	+19,264
PERSONS			
Agriculture	UPS	98,037	−297,617
	UPSS	+386,966	39,147
Non-agriculture	UPS	+27,840	+402,456
	UPSS	+41,134	+406,146
Secondary	UPS	+59,294	+41,200
	UPSS	+59,332	+7,403
Tertiary	UPS	30,838	+361,456
	UPSS	18,894	+396,498

Notes: As in Table 6.

Figures giving the value of output per worker (at constant 1980–81 prices) for agriculture and non-agriculture, bring home the seriousness of a related problem – the widening gap between agricultural and non-agricultural labour productivity. Although labour productivity in agriculture and related activities has crept up, the gains per worker in the non-farm sectors are far greater. The worsening income distribution implications of the figures in Table 8 are obvious. The gap between the wage rates of rural agricultural and rural non-agricultural labourers has also increased.

TABLE 8
LABOUR PRODUCTIVITY IN AGRICULTURE AND NON-AGRICULTURE, BY SECTOR 1983 TO 1993–94: INDIA AND HARYANA

Residence/Sector	Basis	1983	1987–88	1993–94
A. ALL INDIA				
Agriculture,	UPSS	2526.73	2636.04	2952.62
Forestry, Fishing	UPS	2932.60	3045.70	3429.89
Non-Agriculture	UPSS	9309.60	10497.59	12425.57
	UPS	9797.59	10931.43	13028.58
Ratio: Non-Agriculture	UPSS	3.68	3.98	4.21
to agricultural labour	UPS	3.34	3.59	3.80
productivity				
B. HARYANA				
Agriculture,	UPSS	5712.27	5529.34	8157.79
Forestry, Fishing	UPS	7070.12	8068.15	13403.39
Non-Agriculture	UPSS	10515.60	12857.31	14080.11
	UPS	10990.80	13676.34	14974.85
Ratio: Non-Agricultural	UPSS	1.84	2.33	1.73
to agricultural labour	UPS	1.55	1.70	1.12
productivity				

Notes:
1. Labour productivity is calculated as GDP by sector at constant 1980–81 prices/NSS employment figures. The latter is shown on both the NSS 'usual principal and subsidiary' status and the 'usual principal' status basis.
2. Haryana suffered a major drought in 1987–88.

In addition, there is a widening rural–urban divide in terms of the direction of changes in workforce structure. While in rural areas women have lost jobs in the non-farm sector, even in absolute terms, in urban areas they have gained. In the urban female usual principal status workforce, the share of non-agriculture rose continuously from one 'full sample' NSS

Round[25] to the next, from 1983 to 1993–94. The major gains were recorded in the tertiary sector. Shares of the secondary sector in the urban female workforce went down by a smaller amount. The changes in the structure of the urban male workforce were negligible, with the result that, for persons, the urban tertiary sector shares rose at the expense of the secondary sector, while the share of non-agriculture as a whole recorded an inconsequential gain.

In short, as in the late 1960s and early 1970s, in India generally, rural areas have borne the brunt of the workforce restructuring process, with agriculture in particular reverting to its traditional role as the residual sector for rural born workers who have not been able to find more productive non-farm jobs, either in rural areas, or in the cities. Given declining real wage rates and increasing poverty in rural areas during the early 1990s, combined with a persistent widening of the productivity gap between an expanding workforce in agriculture, and those employed in non-farm activities, at the very least, a fresh look at the impact of recent policies is called for.

The Haryana story, which follows, brings home much more pointedly the inherent defect of India's new economic policy. It ignores distribution. Even in economic circumstances such as Haryana's, which by the usual neo-classical criteria produce outcomes close to the best of all possible worlds, poverty rises because of the propensity of the system to generate large increases in inequality, whenever labour markets come under pressure.

VI. THE HARYANA STORY: RISING REAL WAGES, RISING SHARE OF RURAL WORKFORCE IN NON-AGRICULTURE, RISING OUTPUT PER WORKER ... AND RISING POVERTY

The bare bones of the Haryana story in the 1990s can be set out as follows. Real wages went up; the share of the rural workforce in non-agricultural pursuits went up; output per agricultural worker in the aggregate and per capita incomes went up (at constant 1980–81 prices) ... and poverty also went up, a lot. For that to happen, there has got to have been a substantial increase in inequalities somewhere. The recent evidence suggests that in Haryana, this may have happened at more than one level. Consider, first, the following configuration of facts in relation to real wages. Real wages in agriculture are higher in Haryana than in any other state, including Punjab. In rural Haryana both agricultural and non-agricultural wages rose during the early 1990s; personday unemployment did not. So it is not as though Haryana workers, on the average, were getting fewer days work. The fact is that, although 1993–94 rural personday unemployment rates are slightly above the average for 14 major plains states (and far above those in Punjab) they are much below the corresponding Haryana figures for 1987–88.[26]

Thus the rural wage earnings of the typical Haryana worker must also have risen during the 1990s. If a substantial subset of them got poorer, again, inequalities must have increased.

By way of contrast, in India as a whole, the real wage rates for agricultural workers rose up to 1990, declined in 1991 and 1992, and then rose again in 1993. Subsequently they stagnated. In non-agriculture, the decline in the real wage rate set in before 1991, with the result that in recent years the gap between farm and non-farm wages has been closing. In Haryana, on the contrary, the gap between agricultural and non-agricultural real wages seems to have widened continuously ever since 1974–75. Haryana is, in fact, the only state where this wage gap has increased.

On the face of it, the Haryana wage data suggest growing earnings disparities between those mainly dependent on casual agricultural work, on the one hand, and those similarly occupied in the rural non-farm sector, on the other. Discussions with people engaged in organising rural labourers during early 1997 tend to confirm this assessment. People classified as agricultural workers, on the majority of time criterion, it seems, are now generally getting the major part of their income from non-farm work, be it wage labour, or part-time self-employment.

While these adjustments to widening disparities in wage rates reflect the stress under which participants in rural labour markets now operate, they do not produce the rising poverty ratios. They reflect rather the efforts made by agricultural workers to stay above the poverty line. If the past is any guide, both resort to such activity diversification strategies and the prevalence of poverty are likely to be greatest among the landless agricultural labour households.

In this context, an astonishing increase in the proportion of agricultural labour households recorded as possessing land is worth noting. The latest Rural Labour Enquiry suggests that in 1987–88, 67 per cent of rural labour households in Haryana cultivated land. The figures ranged between seven and eight per cent in the preceding decade. There was, of course, no land redistribution programme which could have accounted for this extraordinary rise. What had happened was that members of households which had formerly stuck mainly to cultivation accepted jobs as hired agricultural labourers in large numbers. Members of other households possessing land probably also joined the casual farm labour force.[27]

The explanation offered by Unni [1997: 20] is that a 'a large proportion of households with small and marginal land holdings were forced to enter the wage labour market due to failure of the monsoons'. This is, perhaps, a somewhat partial picture of the ground realties. The wider evidence, on the long-term downward drift of cultivating households in the acreage class structure, for example, suggests that the drought merely exacerbated the effects of what was going on already. Subsequent events lend support to this amended interpretation.

Already, in the decade ending in 1991, demographic pressure on land had reduced the number of males who reported their main work as cultivation by close to six per cent, according to the Census. Simultaneously, the agricultural labour group grew by more than four percent. In the course of the overlapping, but slightly later time span, from 1987–88 to 1993–94, the absolute number of NSS principal status agricultural workers of all descriptions (males, females, cultivators and agricultural labourers combined) had declined by 0.26 per cent, and the number of principal plus subsidiary status farm workers by 3.05 per cent. Clearly the subsidiary status workers, at least the males, were leaving agriculture on a large scale. (The number of female subsidiary status farm workers, however, went up. See Table 7.)

What links these recorded events together is the following. Field surveys have demonstrated that in Haryana, when members of landed households move into the hired labour market in substantial numbers, workers from landless agricultural labour households are offered fewer days work. This is not a new phenomenon.

In Haryana, it was first observed during an extensive field survey conducted in 1972–73.[28] The rapid expansion of demand for hired workers, which characterised the early years of Haryana's Green Revolution, attracted a surge of workers from small farm households into the hired labour force. By 1972–73, this had become a source of grievance for the landless, who complained that landed households were taking away 'their' jobs. In the two most technologically advanced regions of the state, the entry of landed household members into the new market for farm labour hired under long term 'permanent' labour contracts so depressed the number of casual days work available that landless households got fewer days casual work than their counterparts in less developed districts. This was identified as one of the factors which contributed to the persistence of high poverty ratios among landless farm labour households well into the 1970s.

A second, large scale study by Sidhu [1991], based on data collected a few years later, confirmed that the practice of hiring labourers on long term contract 'reduced the work availability for casual workers in terms of number of days' [1991: 261].[29] He also found 'a definite negative relationship between the proportion of attached labourers and the level of unemployment' [1991: 260].

It therefore seems reasonable to suppose that the fresh influx of landed household members into the hired labour market in the late 1980s is likely to have reduced the number of days work available to landless workers once again, and that some of them have been pushed down below the poverty line as a result, notwithstanding the fact that the NSS reports a considerable improvement in the persondays unemployment rate. In short, a redistribution of the available work among competitors for hired labour jobs may be a source of growing inequality in farm labour earnings. Another major field survey would be required to confirm, or refute, this conjecture. In the meantime, it can at least be argued that something of this sort is needed to account for the Haryana 'paradox' of higher wages, lower unemployment, and much more poverty.

The other segments of the rural economy where growing poverty is likely to have been concentrated are household industry, construction and services. Of these, NSS and GDP data permit verification of developments in construction and services only. In both these sectors output per usual principal status worker went down between 1987–88 and 1993–94, despite respectable rates of GDP growth. Labour productivity (at constant 1980–81 prices) declined precipitously from Rs 8252 in 1987–88 to only Rs 4796 in 1993–94 in the case of the construction industry, and from Rs 10,311 to Rs 9413, in the case of services. Both these terminal year productivity figures stand substantially below the corresponding ones for agriculture.

We have known for some time that in India construction workers suffer the highest incidence of poverty, next only to agricultural labourers (see Bhalla [1994]). When all else fails, underemployed workers gravitate to construction labour as a last resort. In Haryana, now, services has become the new 'residual sector'.

These events illustrate nicely Amit Bhaduri's [1993] observation that, in countries like India, when labour markets come under pressure, it is not wage rates (nor labour absorption in the aggregate) that adjusts, but rather labour productivity. To this date, in most parts of India, agriculture remains the residual sector, although construction employment, mining and quarrying, and even petty trade, to some extent play the same role in particular states [Bhalla, 1994]. In Haryana, the diversification of residual sector behaviour into services is something new. Even construction did not play that role a decade earlier.

VII. THE HARYANA STORY: (b) THE REACTION OF RURAL LABOUR AS A CLASS, A SURPRISING ACQUIESCENCE

In Haryana, how did rural labour, as a class, react to all this? By and large, it did so with a surprising degree of resignation, if not acquiescence. Historically, ever since the formation of Haryana as a separate state in November 1966, hired rural Haryana workers have been remarkably docile, despite the fact that, by the end of the 1970s, more than 90 per cent of them were landless and dependent almost entirely upon wage paid work. There seem to have been two major reasons for this. One of them is in the realm of control over labour processes, and the other is in the area of the organisation and political mobilisation of landless workers.

(a) Control over Labour Processes

In Haryana, the introduction of high yielding varieties of wheat in the late 1960s pushed up demand for hired labour substantially. Initially, there was no upward pressure on wages, largely because of the substantial pool of underemployed and unemployed labour available for work at prevailing wage rates. But this was a situation which could not last. Clearly the workers' inherent bargaining position had improved, especially at harvest time.

The introduction of new kinds of 'permanent' labour contracts[30] by the bigger cultivators was an innovative solution to two kinds of problems thrown up by this new situation. First, it provided an assured labour supply at peak seasons, at relatively low implicit wage rates; secondly it weakened the bargaining position of casual work seekers by reducing the number of casual days work available during the busy season as well as in the lean season. In short, it was a strategy which for some time was effective in dealing with the problem of rising labour costs, as seen from the cultivators' perspective. It also divided the hired farm workers into two camps: those with permanent labour jobs, who came largely from landed households, and the casual workers, who were more commonly landless and from Scheduled Castes. Not only did this deliberate segmentation of the labour market produce downward pressure on casual labour wage rates, it also nipped in the bud incipient efforts by the workers in the Green Revolution regions to organise themselves for purposes of wage bargaining.

When real wages finally went up in the second half of the 1970s, mostly in response to the growth of non-farm work opportunities, labour displacing mechanisation replaced the permanent labour contract as the chosen means of holding down the wage bill.

(b) Organisation of Political Mobilisation of Landless Workers

(i) No systematic efforts at organisation from the mid-1960s to the end of the 1980s: During this entire period, from the mid 1960s to the end of the 1980s, there were no systematic efforts[31] to mobilise hired agricultural workers as a class. This is significant because Haryana was a part of Punjab until 1966, and Punjab had been one of the two states which had pioneered the organisation of agricultural workers.

The Punjab Khet Mazdoor Sabha[32] was founded, and its inaugural session held at Khan Khanan in district Jullundur in December 1954[33] twenty four years before the first all India organisation of farm labourers – the Bharatiya Khet Mazdoor Union – was set up in 1968. Punjab also hosted the inaugural session of the all India body, which was held in Moga. (The first state level union was established in Andhra Pradesh in 1936–37).

The delegates to the initial meetings of the state level organisation all came from districts now in Punjab. None came from Haryana. From the union's inception until 1966 when Haryana became a separate state, none of the annual sessions was held at any place now within Haryana borders.[34] Evidently this CPI[35] led organisation had a weak base in the Haryana region. Although there are CPI units today in several districts, there have been no state level actions in recent years.

The rise of the CPM led agricultural workers' union is a relatively recent phenomenon. Even at the all India level, until the 1980s, the CPM had no separate agricultural workers' organisation.[36] Instead they operated under the umbrella of the All India Kisan Sabha (AIKS) which covered cultivators, large and small, as well as hired workers. In Haryana, the All India Agricultural Workers Union organisation (AIAWU) really got off the ground only after 1991, the unsatisfactory state of its earlier development frequently noted in the annual reports of the General Council of the AIAWU,[37] and vividly reflected in the on again, off again membership figures for the decade up to 1991–92.[38] Until then, among casual labourers, the organisation had enjoyed only a regional influence, concentrated in the districts of Karnal, Rohtak and Hissar. Moreover, although union activists took part in several successful struggles focussed on land redistribution, especially during 1988 and 1989 (usually jointly with the AIKS) dissatisfaction with the conduct of the Haryana unit's affairs was expressed pointedly, and repeatedly, at the annual meetings of the General Council of the AIAWU and at the third conference of the AIAWU, held in April 1992.[39] It was only from 1992 onwards that the Haryana state unit began to function as a democratically constituted regional organisation should.[40] In 1993, a union office was established in Rohtak, a place readily accessible from most parts of the state.

(ii) The 1990s and their roots: Today, there are active units in seven or eight districts, and agricultural workers have been mobilised from all over the state for meetings and demonstrations in Chandigargh, New Delhi and elsewhere. In 1996, eight representatives of the Haryana unit attended the Fourth All India Conference of the AIAWU, held at Khammam in Andhra Pradesh and two of the delegates were elected to the General Council of the AIAWU. The 1996 Documents of the IVth All India Conference of the AIAWU, along with the usual lines of criticism, now also contains some words of praise for the Haryana unit's efforts: '… states like Haryana have not only begun to function but are also maintaining contact with the all India Centre now' [*AIAWU*, 1996: 33].

The big question is: why did the Haryana AIAWU come of age just as the real pinch of the new economic policy was becoming felt in the rural labour markets of this otherwise eminently successful regional economy? Was it, at least partly, a coincidence? The answer to the second part of the question is, I think, yes. In fact, probably the most important lessons learnt by this fledgling all India agricultural workers' movement were drawn from organisational developments which took place before 1992. Of these, the success of certain initiatives taken by the national union produced the crucial advances.

The first was the decision to strengthen the AIAWU Central Office in New Delhi. This was, in effect, a precondition for the substantive developments on the organisational front which followed. For most of the first decade of its existence, the AIAWU Central Office had been manned by a lone functionary, the founder General Secretary, P.K. Kunjachan.[41] From mid-1992 onwards, in addition to the President and a new General Secretary, neither of whom could be present all the time, there were three Joint Secretaries. This not only provided a much needed base from which organisational forays could be launched into the hitherto relatively neglected Hindi speaking heartland of north and north western India, it also enhanced the Centre's capacity to undertake joint activities with the AIKS, and with other left-led peasant and workers' organisations. That these two kinds of activities provided the catalyst to the rise of the agricultural workers' union in Haryana was clearly recognised in the documents of the AIAWU.[42]

The eventual take off of the Haryana unit of the AIAWU was a centrally sponsored development. As early as 1983, it had been decided that one Joint Secretary of the union should be deputed to help Haryana and Rajasthan activists to build their unions, while another should go to help those in Karnataka.[43] Unfortunately the project did not really get off the ground until a series of organisational innovations of a rather different kind took effect in the late 1980s. These involved pulling a spectrum of like minded organisations into concerted actions.

The August 1987 Joint Meeting of the Central Working Committees of the AIKS and the AIAWU initiated the process of organising joint movements. This effort culminated in what became known as the 'September 1987 movement', in which 40 lakh (four million) peasants and agricultural workers are said to have participated in different parts of India. Their joint demands focussed on issues connected with land.

The enthusiasm generated by the September 1987 movement – the biggest mobilisation of its kind since Independence – inspired moves to undertake campaigns with even wider participation, extending to seven left-led peasant and agricultural workers' organisations.[44] Another, bigger joint mobilisation, involving the enlarged array of participating organisations followed in September 1988. In July 1989, a state level convention of left-led peasants and agricultural workers' organisations was held at Jind, in Haryana. Since then a coordinating committee of left-led peasant and agricultural workers' organisations has been meeting regularly to plan and carry out joint actions, conventions, campaigns and protest rallies, such as the 20 October 1993 demonstration in Delhi when GATT's Director General visited there. This rally included many activists from Haryana and Uttar Pradesh, mobilised at short notice for the demonstration. A few years earlier workers from both these states had been conspicuously absent from such events.

The September 1987 and 1988 agitations are officially credited with giving the momentum to the development of the AIAWU in Haryana, and in Rajasthan.[45] In short, these broad based mobilisations have turned out to be the most appropriate vehicle for getting agricultural labourers actively involved in the AIAWU. Given the confidence that these larger gatherings have given them, they have been able to conduct struggles at the district and village levels as well.

However, organisational factors are only one side of the story. The other is that circumstances and the agricultural workers involved in them had both changed. Haryana workers had gone through a phase, ending in the mid-1970s, during which there was a boom in demand for hired farm labour. This, fortunately for them, was followed immediately by a decade of expansion in rural and urban non-farm employment opportunities, associated with the rapid industrial development of the state. By 1989, wage expectations and some degree of confidence in the capacity of the system to generate acceptable jobs and incomes were probably at their peak. In rural areas, the chickens of under investment in infrastructure, in power generation and distribution in particular, had not yet come home to roost.

In the 1990s, the era of economic and political optimism came to an abrupt end. The absolute number of jobs in manufacturing industry declined, the prices of foodgrains soared, and the condition of public infrastructure in rural areas deteriorated visibly for want of maintenance expenditure, as well as for want of fresh investment. In Haryana, not only agricultural workers and small peasants, but also the medium-sized and larger capitalist cultivators, as well as unionised industrial workers, reacted with dismay, and increasingly with a sense of betrayal. A common development, one which took place among both Haryana's capitalist cultivators and also among existing industrial trade unions, was for hitherto competing groups to come together, in militant, and in the case of farmers' agitations, in violent confrontations with the police and state government authority.

(iii) Agitations and developments in the 1990s, and some lessons: Both the left-led peasant movements and Haryana's own 'new farmers' movement',[46] the Kisan Sangharsh Samiti,[47] organised *gheraos, bandhs,* and *rail roko, rasta roko*[48] campaigns. The Bharatiya Kisan Union (BKU) not only extended vigorous support to the agitations initiated by the Haryana Kisan Sangharsh Samiti in 1995, 1996 and 1997, it may have undertaken some of the most destructive actions on its own.[49] The AIKS and the AIAWU organised militant resistance to the ejectment of peasants from land they had been granted, as refugees, shortly after Partition in 1947. And the AIAWU got involved in mass actions, including gheraos, jointly with brick kiln workers, *anganwadi*[50] workers and village *chowkidars* (watchmen). Among Scheduled Caste workers, the Bahujan Samaj Party (BSP) made renewed efforts to establish a foothold, and in the industrial towns and cities, trade unions of diverse affiliation and ideology came together in common protests against the new economic policies of the 1990s.

An early sign that the times were changing in rural areas was the effective debut on the Haryana political stage of the BKU early in 1993.[51] Avowedly non-political, and claiming to speak for Haryana cultivators generally, the BKU succeeded in wresting substantial concessions from the then Congress Chief Minister, Bhajan Lal, in June of that year. Their demands had centred on the pricing and supply of electricity in rural areas, and compensation to relatives of those killed and injured in the violent demonstrations leading up to this settlement.

However, the very next year, in 1994, the Bhajan Lal government increased the power tariff, in effect going back on a part of the agreement of 1993. The cultivators of the south west plateau region[52] then formed a *sangharsh samiti* (an informal, unstructured organisation for struggle) and boycotted the payment of electricity bills. Their decision was supported by the Haryana Vikas Party (HVP) of Bansi Lal, whose constituency is in this area. Bhajan Lal then retaliated by cutting off the power supply from the Kadma power station. In reply, the cultivators, apparently now protesting under the banner of the BKU[53] gheraoed the power station. This eventually led, on August 23, 1995, to a police firing in which five peasants were killed and others injured.

At this stage, with Parliamentary and State Assembly elections in the offing, Bansi Lal, then in opposition, promised that, if voted to power, his party would create an additional, cheaper, fourth slab[54] to encourage tubewell irrigation in the region. He also promised a judicial inquiry into the Kadma killings, and the withdrawal of serious police cases against some peasants. After his election, in 1996, he instead scrapped the slab system altogether, and introduced a uniform tariff system. The farmers were outraged, revived the Kisan Sangarsh Samiti in December 1996, and began an agitation which got support from the entire spectrum of peasant organisations, including the AIKS and the BKU.

It is worth noting that a full month before this organisational resurrection, a joint convention of the two Kisan Sabhas, (the CPM's and the CPI's), held in Kurukshetra district of Haryana, condemned the Bansi Lal government for reneging on election promises, and set out a list of demands, many of them focused on precisely the rural electric power supply and tariff issues[55] which subsequently became the storm centres of the militant agitations of 1997. Thus the left-led peasant organisations were in on the 1997 agitations, at least in principle, from the beginning.

The level of violence peaked in October 1997, after the rainy season had ended, but before the paddy and other rainy season crops had been harvested. On 10 October, in the Nanwan area of Mahendragarh district, seven farmers were shot dead by police while squatting on the Delhi-Bikaner railway line.[56] Others were beaten up, including a farm couple who had provided the protesters with drinking water from their well. Many, including women, were arrested and taken to jails in other districts far from their homes. This led to widespread bandhs – in Mahendragarh, Narnaul, Atteli, Dadri, Rewari and Ambala – blockades of highways and processions against policy 'brutality', during the course of which at least one police inspector and two constables were injured.[57] In some areas the bandhs were described by the media as 'near total'.[58]

Into this political and organisational maelstrom, the CPI, CPM, the AIKS and the AIAWU all intervened. The Haryana CPM and the AIKS undertook an on-the-spot investigation into the Mahendragarh firings whose findings were widely reported in regional newspapers, such as *The Tribune* of Chandigarh, as well as in the party press. The CPM and CPI State Committees took out a joint protest demonstration in Panipat on 13 October. The CPM organised protest demonstrations at Hissar on 17 October, Fatehbad on 18 October and Sirsa on 19 October. Hannan Mollah, MP, and Joint Secretary of the AIAWU visited Satnali on 15 October. There he made a speech in which he 'extended the support of the AIAWU to the movement, and demanded that the government should immediately talk with the farmers, repair and replace the (burnt out) transformers and resume power supply so that cultivation could begin again'. He 'appealed to the farmers to remain united and continue the struggle, to spread the movement to other areas, and to organise a big mobilisation in Bhiwani town.'[59] Finally, he called on farmers to gherao the secretariat building at Chandigarh, if their demands were not met by the government. They were not. The Chief

Minister, Mr Bansi Lal, announced instead that the government would not replace burnt out transformers as demanded by the agitationists until after the farmers had paid their Haryana State Electricity Board dues. The media generally thought this statement ill-considered.[60]

In the end, in November 1997, the convenor of the Kisan Sangharsh Samiti, Ravinder Singh Sangwan, met the United Front Union Agricultural Minister, Chaturanan Mishra in New Delhi, to ask him to intervene. In a curious coalition of disparate interests the farmers movement delegation was accompanied by the Haryana State leaders of the CPI, the CPM and the Janata Dal. After this meeting, when Sangwan was accused of letting the agitation slip into the hands of political parties opposed to them, he is reported to have replied that the Kisan Sangharsh Samiti 'will accept support from any quarter.'[61]

Although appropriate oil was poured on troubled waters as a result of this meeting, the farmers' agitation of 1997 finally died a natural death, with the start of the new sowing season in November and the subsequent onset of winter rains. But if the financial resource crunch faced by the state government is allowed, once again, to affect rural power supply during critical periods in the growing season, and if future Chief Ministers are similarly intransigent, the same issues could lead to violent farmer-government confrontations again.

At this stage, a word about the left-led peasants and workers organisations' justification for associating themselves so closely with Haryana's 'new farmers' movement' would seem to be in order. In this justification, there are two distinct elements. The first is a matter of considered policy about what issues should be addressed by AIKS units in different parts of India. The second relates to what is seen as a commonality of interests on certain specific issues which were highlighted during the 1997 agitations.

The policy question was discussed in detail at the CPM's AIKS all-India conference held in Hissar (Haryana) in September 1992. In its assessment of the agrarian scene the 1992 conference concluded: 'The country can be divided into three broad categories on the basis of land reform measures as well as the nature and level of development of capitalism in agriculture.'[62]

States where peasant movements were strong and land reforms had been by and large carried out constituted the first category. West Bengal, Kerala and Tripura were described as belonging to this group. Haryana was placed firmly in category number two, areas belonging to the 'green revolution belt … where capitalist development is taking place by making use of irrigation facilities, chemical fertilisers, high yielding variety seeds, modern agricultural implements, etc.'[63] The third category was described as 'those areas where semi-feudal relations still dominate.'[64] The emphasis of AIKS activities was to differ from one kind of region to another.

It was noted that due to the capitalist development which had taken place in places like Haryana, 'peasant unity cannot be built up by taking up the land question alone.' The other issues which needed to be pursued included, at the head of the list, irrigation and power facilities.[65] The list goes on to cover, among other things, economic and commercial infrastructure facilities normally provided out of the public budget in India.

The documents of the AIAWU 1996 Conference, which repeat this broad regional categorisation, are, however, quite explicit about the contradictions between the new capitalist farmers and farm labour in states like Haryana, 'where capitalist development has transformed land relations, confronting labour with rich peasants and landlords.'[66]

Nevertheless, there are perceived points of common interest. To illustrate, when the AIAWU president Prakash Chander spoke to a large gathering of agricultural labourers, industrial workers and poor farmers in Rohtak in December 1997, he argued along the following lines. The intrusion of capitalism in the agricultural sector made it capital intensive, and by implication, more dependent on uninterrupted electricity supplies. Economic liberalisation had reduced government investment in agriculture generally, including the rural power sector. This was bad for everybody, including agricultural workers.[67] The other common rallying points seem to have been the insensitivity of elected political leaders who were seen to have gone back on their word, and the question of police highhandedness and brutality, a civil rights issue on which a wide spectrum of public opinion was agreed.

One awkward fact remains, however. The way the AIKS is developing in Haryana, its interests increasingly are diverging from those of its younger brother organisation, the AIAWU. This polarisation of interests in rural Haryana could in future make it more and more difficult for them to find issues for joint action at the village and district levels. The alternative would seem to be to focus AIKS energies on mobilising poor peasants whose economic and social concerns more nearly coincide with those of agricultural and other rural labour, in Haryana, as well as at the all India level. Even this may not be enough, to judge by the self critical assessments made in AIAWU documents published during the 1990s, about which more later.

Most of the other major mobilisations in which the AIKS and AIAWU members participated were of a more conventional kind, involving agricultural labourers and unorganised workers in the rural informal sector or peasants about to be ejected from their lands. An example of this last kind is the *Abadkar* (colonising settler) struggle of 1997.

During the dying weeks of 1996, a joint committee of the two Kisan Sabhas took up the cause of some 25,000 families spread over 25 villages, who had been asked to vacate land they had tilled since the time of Partition, when they came to India as refugees. In 1950–52, the government had given them 20-year *pattas* (official papers conferring cultivation rights for the stipulated period). Now they were asked to vacate. The joint agitation began with two mass protest rallies, one on 23 December 1996 at Pehawa and the other on 31 December at Kurukshetra. The agitation continued inconclusively for nearly a year. The high point of this campaign for proprietary rights on the land was the militant rally staged in Chandigarh on 18 March in which thousands of Haryana peasants took part. Subsequently the anti-eviction struggle continued in several districts, in the course of which one peasant was shot dead while working in the fields, reportedly by the men of the district BJP president.[68]

A more interesting alliance was that of the Haryana unit of the CPM-led industrial workers' union, CITU, (Centre of Indian Trade Unions), with the AIAWU. Following a rally organised jointly by CITU and the AIAWU on 14 December, whose demands focussed on improving the public distribution system and providing rations to the poor at half price,[69] the chits[70] of the agricultural labourers' union were accepted for the purposes of drawing rations at cheaper rates in some parts of the state. Brick kiln workers and some unorganised construction workers in Hissar city were among the beneficiaries.

A few months later, the AIAWU-CITU joint action committee held a mass demonstration of 10,000 agricultural workers, brick kiln workers, *anganwadi* workers, village watchmen, forest workers and other unorganised workers at Chandigarh, on 19 March 1997. They blocked the road to the Assembly and held a public meeting there. Speakers, aside from CITU and AIAWU activists, included representatives of the *Anganwadi* union, the leader of the Sarva Karmachari Sangh and the secretary of the brick kiln workers union. The list of demands which they presented to the State agricultural minister included: comprehensive central legislation for agricultural workers; land and housesites for the landless; special ration cards for the poorest sections; a resolution against privatisation of the Haryana State Electricity Board; minimum wages for unskilled labour; and 'regular wages for chowkidars (village watchmen), who are forced to collect feudal dues from families in the village to this day'.[71]

The Haryana government conceded the demand for regular wages for *chowkidars* on the spot. They were to be paid Rs 400 per month through the Block Development Officers and *panchayats* (village councils). This benefited some 6,000 *chowkidars*, all of them belonging to Scheduled Castes, who up to that time had no fixed remuneration. In addition to the modest salaries, they now got Rs 500 annually for uniforms as well.

Another of the more successful actions involving agricultural labourers took place in the Hissar Green Revolution belt, where the CPM has developed a good base. More than a hundred cases of bonded labour, sometimes involving whole households, came to the union for help. More than half were freed by the trade union, and others at the instance of the local administration under pressure from the union.[72]

Aside from issues of wages, prices and social oppression, the Haryana unit of the AIAWU has intervened in the interests of communal harmony in the Mewati Muslim area of southern Haryana, where group clashes took place in the months following the demolition of the Babri Masjid. A highly successful public rally there, at which the Union Minister for Social Welfare was the chief guest, was addressed by functionaries from CITU, and both the CPI and CPM, as well as by AIAWU activists. Their demands centred on issues of special interest to Muslims of this area, in particular employment and lack of education facilities. There was also a call to end the ban on buffalo slaughter (a potentially important source of income for these people) to complete a sanctioned but much delayed weavers' colony (planned to be built by the Haryana Urban Development Authority, HUDA); to allot land for a graveyard; and to end discrimination in the matter of ration cards and inclusion in voters' lists. At the end of it, the Union Minister announced a Rs 30 lakh grant to build a school and Rs 5.1 lakhs to buy land for a graveyard. The CPM member of Parliament, H.S. Surjeet, handed over the cheques.[73]

The most remarkable feature of this, and most other 'successful' actions, in which the AIAWU had a stake, is that whatever victories were won, were won through the intermediation of government, central, state or local. No major victories were recorded which emerged from direct confrontation between capitalist cultivators and agricultural labourers on either the economic or the social front. In Haryana, concessions are wrested directly from the employer mainly by trade unions active in the urban non-farm sector, and rarely by workers in rural areas.

In this connection, another potentially significant development on the joint action front in Haryana, was the establishment of a forum for joint action by a spectrum of industrial trade unions otherwise divided along lines of political affiliation. All the major trade unions, the Indian National Trade Union Congress (INTUC), the All India Trade Union Congress (AITUC), the Hind Mazdoor Sabha and CITU constituted the forum, which then organised one of the biggest industrial workers' demonstrations ever seen in the region, in Gurgaon, a Haryana industrial township adjacent to Delhi, in early March 1998. The common rallying point was the adverse impact of the new economic policy on industrial employment, on working conditions, on the prices of essential commodities and on the prospects for economic growth.[74]

In short, the fiscal stabilisation and structural adjustment programmes put in place in the early 1990s created conditions in which militant trade unionism flourished in Haryana[75] and workers with sometimes common, sometimes conflicting, class interests tended to come together on the same platforms. Rural areas were most affected.

In this context the AIAWU was chiefly concerned about 'unbridled encouragement to market controlled economic growth' and 'withdrawal of the State from its social commitments',[76] the decline in the number of days work available to casual farm labourers, new economic policy driven increases in foodgrains prices, and efforts to dilute or dismantle land ceiling legislation in the name of promoting agro-industrial growth. It was explicitly recognised also that the vast majority of unorganised labourers now faced the same problems as agricultural labourers did.[77]

There were, however, some second thoughts on the subject of joint actions by the AIAWU with the AIKS,[78] and within the AIKS about taking up issues of particular interest to the bigger capitalist farmers and landlords.[79] It was emphasised in the CPM's 1995 Political Organisational Report, that the peasant unity which is to be built must be based on the poor sections among the peasantry, who constitute the majority. The issues to be taken up most vigorously should be of special interest to them and should serve to isolate the landlords.[80] Further, it was argued that excessive dependence on joint actions with the AIKS had led to the relative neglect of the specific problems of agricultural labourers, especially in broad based campaigns, and failure to enhance the capacity of members of the AIAWU to take up independent activity.

Thus it had become recognised, by the middle of the 1990s, that while united actions helped in drawing people into the movement in the first instance, in order to make an organisational breakthrough, independent action under the banner of the AIAWU was essential. Unless this is done, there may continue to be what a 1992 document describes as 'some hesitation in taking up questions like wages and atrocities against Scheduled Castes and Tribes'.[81]

The longer-term limiting effects of joint actions may be one of the reasons why the leading figures in these efforts in Haryana now admit that the tangible gains for AIAWU supporters are few. Moreover, while large numbers may have participated in rallies and other joint actions, the growth in paid up membership has been modest. The main achievement, they say, is that these workers have developed self confidence. They have, for the first time, stood up individually and collectively in demonstrations and rallies. Not only this. By and large, even the workers who have benefited personally from union activities, do not vote in elections for the party which has organised and led them. The only CPM candidate from Haryana who contested in the 1998 parliamentary elections lost his deposit. So did the lone CPI candidate.[82]

Traditionally, in Haryana, rural labour and its large intersection set of Scheduled and backward class workers, have voted Congress. But after the late 1970s, they have behaved more as a large, detachable, voting block, difficult to mobilise for any particular party. But their negative votes have been an important factor in the defeat of governments in power.

The most striking illustration of this was the 1977, post Emergency, election which brought down the Indira Gandhi Congress government. Visits to Haryana villages after the election had been called, but before a group of opposition parties came together to form the Janata Party, revealed that the population of the Scheduled Caste neighbourhoods was going to vote solidly against Congress. At the time, when people back in Delhi were told about this, there was only a momentary suspension of disbelief; then the question: 'But who are they going to vote for?' There was, at this stage, no possible answer.

More recently, in 1996, the 14 per cent shift away from Congress is said to have been accounted for mainly by these votes. The list of issues, aside from non-fulfilment of promises by Congress, corruption and declining prestige, included prominently the following: price increases, especially of foodgrains, unemployment, and the sense that the weaker sections were being marginalised by the new economic policy.

It is of note that they did not vote for the Scheduled Caste party, the Bahujan Samaj Party, which contested more than 60 seats out of 90, and did not win one, although they did get more than seven per cent of the votes cast in the Assembly elections. At the same time there was an anti Chautala (Samta Party) vote based in part on the caste antagonisms of non-Jat, non-peasant cultivating castes. By and large, however, rural labour voted on non-caste, non-class lines.

Bansi Lal, who led the victorious Haryana Vikas Party (HVP) – Bhartiya Janta Party (BJP) alliance, best seen as a rural-urban combination, gained the votes the Congress lost in 1996. In this win Bansi Lal's personal reputation was an important factor. He was seen as less corrupt and more efficient than the available alternatives. Voters had 'forgotten' his association with the Emergency of 19 years before. What they remembered was his vigorous implementation of infrastructural and agricultural development programmes in the state during the Green Revolution years of the late 1960s and the 1970s. He also picked up the women's votes which had been mobilised by rural women's associations in a 'women against liquor' movement, under way since the early 1990s.

Having said all this, it may need to be reiterated that from the side of the agricultural labourers, it was still largely a negative vote, although a section of the cultivators voted for Bansi Lal who had wooed them with specific promises, in relation to electricity tariffs, for example, a subject on which there had been violent agitations only a few months before the elections.

By 1997, the situation, as compared to just one year earlier, had changed. Rural Haryana had lost faith in the Bansi Lal government's capacity and will to provide the basic economic and social infrastructural development which they considered their due. The charms of Prohibition had worn thin, and worries about the influence of local bootleggers and their links with the police came to the fore. On 1 April 1998, Prohibition was repealed. Today local opinion predicts that the next Assembly elections will see an anti Bansi Lal, anti BJP vote from rural labour. They are likely to return to Congress. The results of the 1998 parliamentary elections tend to support this assessment.[83]

In short, during the 1990s, there has been, for the first time, a significant awakening of Haryana wage workers as a class. But it is not clear how much this development has to do directly with the new economic policies of the 1990s. Much of it may be attributable to organisational decisions taken in the first instance, outside Haryana, including the decision to mount joint campaigns with other left-led peasant and rural labour organisations. Excessive reliance on joint mobilisations with the AIKS, however, may now have become counter productive, inhibiting the capacity of the AIAWU to take up issues and carry out actions independently. Campaigns conducted jointly with CITU may be more promising in the long run, because of the way recent economic and organisational events have changed circumstances. One development in Haryana which militates against the success of continued close tie-ups with the AIKS has been the tendency of the peasants' union to get drawn into agitations mounted by medium and large scale capitalist farmers and focussed on issues of particular interest to this class, to the relative neglect of the problems of poor peasants and landless workers. The development which favours increasing emphasis on tie-ups with CITU is the fact that in the most recent decade many workers from Haryana's agricultural labour households have diversified their activities. Some are now working full time, and others intermittently in a range of non-farm jobs. In addition, new elements have joined the agricultural labour contingent, including members of marginal farm households, erstwhile workers in household industry and in traditional crafts and services. In short, there are reasons to believe that Haryana agricultural workers, as a set, may have acquired a wider perspective. Many, in their regular or part time capacity as non-farm workers, in the construction industry, in brick kilns, in municipal services and elsewhere, have been exposed to the workings of better organised trade unions. It is indeed significant that some of the AIAWU's more concrete achievements, described earlier, have benefited a wide spectrum of otherwise unorganised rural workers. Thus joint action with rural, and small town, non-farm labour may be a part of the shape of things to come in this state where capitalism in agriculture is now well entrenched.

VII. CONCLUSION

On the larger labour market front, it is clear that the all-India statistics mask a great diversity of regional experience. The common denominators are increasing poverty, the expansion of old residual sectors or the emergence of new ones. The Haryana figures demonstrate that in economies where labour markets do not clear, and where landless casual workers suffer unequal access to existing work opportunities, rising wages and declining persondays unemployment rates can coexist with substantial increases in poverty. Falling output per worker in industries which absorb large numbers of unskilled workers identify them as new residual sectors.

Most important, what the Haryana case demonstrates is that the ultimate enemy of the poor in this context is the tendency of the new economic policy to generate gross inequality – not the straightforward kind where most people get better off, but the benefits of growth accrue more to the rich than the poor, but the really mean kind where the relatively rich get richer and the poor get poorer, not just in relative terms, but absolutely. No economic policy can be called efficient in third world countries if it does this to people, whatever else it may achieve in other areas.

NOTES

1. The average value of yield figures for the triennium 1992–95, and the output growth figures cited subsequently, are taken from Bhalla and Singh [1997: A-3 and A-4, Tables 1 and 2].
2. The growth figures are as follows:

Per cent Annual Compound Growth Rates

	1962–65 to 1970–73	1970–73 to 1980–83	1980–83 to 1992–95
A. Average value of output at 1990-93 constant prices			
Haryana	4.65	3.02	4.74
Punjab	6.63	4.74	3.87
B. Average value of yield at 1990-93 constant prices			
Haryana	3.30	2.04	4.13
Punjab	4.16	2.65	2.85

Source: Bhalla and Singh [1997: A-3 and A-4, tables 1 and 3 respectively].

3. The basic nominal wage data referred to here, up to 1992-93, come from Ozler, Datt and Ravallion [1996]. This was updated by Abhijit Sen [1997, computer printout] using information given in the Government of India's annual Economic Survey 1996–97, and converted to real wages using the official consumer price indices for agricultural labourers, 1960–61 = 100.

4. The relevant passage reads:

> It is not the actual greatness of national wealth, but its continual increase, which occasions a rise in the wages of labour. It is not, accordingly, in the richest countries, but in the most thriving, or in those which are growing rich the fastest, that the wages of labour are highest.

See Book I of Adam Smith's *The Wealth of Nations* [*Smith*, 1977: 61–2].

5. For an analysis in the rural Indian context, see Bhalla [1993].

6. In this study, the terms 'agriculture' and the 'farm sector' are used interchangeably. 'Agriculture' in the production data cited from Bhalla and Singh [1997] covers 42 field crops only and excludes plantation crops, horticulture and floriculture, animal husbandry and allied agricultural activities. In the National Sample Survey workforce data, and in the National Accounts Statistics gross domestic product data used later for purposes of calculating employment elasticities, 'agriculture' is defined more broadly to include field crop production, horticulture and floriculture, plantation crops, bee keeping, poultry and animal husbandry plus (at this level of aggregation) forestry, logging and fishing. The 'secondary sector' as defined here includes mining, as well as manufacturing, electricity, gas and water supply and construction. The 'tertiary sector', sometimes loosely referred to as the 'service sector' covers transport, storage and communication services, financial, insurance, real estate and business services, and community, social and personal services. The term 'non-agriculture' is used to refer to everything other than 'agriculture' as defined above. 'Agricultural workers' includes both those who are self-employed in the farm sector and those who work for wages there. The terminology used for rural and urban areas is identical.

7. The absolute figures were:

Haryana, Usual Principal Status Workers: Number (in 000)

Sector	1987–88 (R+U)	1993–94 (R+U)
Non-agriculture	2008	2559
Agriculture	2539	2272
Tertiary	1147	1685

Source: my work in progress, on NSS data.

In the official National Sample Survey terminology 'usual principal status' workers are people whose main activity is work. This distinguishes them from 'subsidiary status' workers, who may work intermittently or part time on a more or less regular basis, but whose main activity is something not counted as work.

8. The four states in question which have more than half of all 'principal status workers' in non-farm employment are Haryana, Kerala, Punjab and West Bengal. The figures for 1993-94, of usual principal status workers (rural plus urban) in non-agriculture are:

State	% Share
Haryana	53.34
Kerala	57.32
Punjab	51.40
West Bengal	54.88

Source: my work in progress, on NSS data.

9. Between 1987-88 and 1993-94 the situation with respect to states and farm workforce share was as follows:

Expanding	Contracting
1. Andhra Pradesh	1. Haryana
2. Assam	2. Himachal Pradesh
3. Bihar	3. Jammu and Kashmir
4. Gujarat	4. Karnataka
5. Madhya Pradesh	5. Kerala
6. Orissa	6. Maharashtra
7. Rajasthan	7. Punjab
8. Tamil Nadu	8. Uttar Pradesh
	9. West Bengal

Source: my work in progress, on NSS data.

10. As in Kuznets, *Modern Economic Growth: Rate, Structure and Spread* [1966].
11. An alternative measure of this process based on data on per capita net state domestic product from 1960 to 1995 (in constant 1960-61 prices) reveals that regional disparities declined from 1961–62 to 1981–82. Since then coefficients of variation have been rising steadily, with a steep increase after 1990-91. See Ghosh and Neogi [1998: 1627–8].
12. This phenomenon, described by the authors as the 'suction mechanism', was first documented and discussed by Alagh, Bhalla and Bhaduri [1978].
13. See especially: Mitra [1977], Chakravarty [1977, 1979], and Patnaik [1979].
14. Details are given in Bhalla [1994b].
15. On long term, and recent, trends in poverty in India, see especially Sen [1996] and Ravallion and Datt [1996].
16. The UK story is told in the Report of the Income and Wealth Inquiry Group [1995]. Reviews of the South Asia experience appear in Ghosh and Mukherjee [1995].
17. On wage rates in the most recent period, see especially Unni [1997] and Ozler, Datt and Ravallion [1996] and tables updated by Abhijit Sen using data from the GOI Economic Survey, 1996-97.
18. See Acharya and Papanek [1989] and Bhalla [1993].
19. On this see Bhalla [1992].
20. See especially page 143.
21. The term 'employment elasticity', as used here, is a measure of the impact of economic growth in a specified segment of the economy, on employment growth in that segment. It may be measured as the rate of growth of employment in a sector, divided by the rate of growth of the gross domestic product of that sector over the same period, as done here.
22. GOI, Ministry of Planning [1995: 3].
23. A J-curve describes the path of a typical restructuring economy, whereby growth rates first fall for a few years, then begin to rise again, reaching levels above the pre-restructuring growth rates.
24. For an analysis, see Papola [1989, 1991].
25. National Sample Survey 'Rounds' typically cover one full year of field work, divided into four 'sub-rounds' of three months each so that a representative sample is covered in each of the seasons of the year. The 'Rounds' of 1977–78, 1983, 1987–88 and 1993–94, also known as the 32nd, 38th, 43rd and 50th Rounds all had separate questionnaires on employment and unemployment, and on consumer expenditure, administered to the same sets of households. In addition to these full scale quinquennial surveys, from the 45th Round onward, the National Sample Survey Organisation collected information on key items on employment and unemployment from a limited set of households annually. The quinquennial surveys have become known as the 'full sample' Rounds, while the annual surveys for intervening years are the so-called 'thin sample' surveys. Doubts have been expressed about the reliability of the data generated by 'thin sample' surveys, especially at the state level.
26. All India Agricultural Workers' Union (AIAWU) activists vigorously dispute these NSS based results. For documentation, see, for example, page 16, General Secretary's Report, Documents, AIAWU IVth All India Conference (2–4 Nov 1996), which mentions Haryana

specifically, and in relation to mechanisation. There may be several good reasons for this. First of all, 1987-88 was a drought year in Haryana. Secondly, the NSS figures are rates per worker, but since the number or workers has come down over the past 10 years, the number of days work available could have declined without pushing up the recorded rates. Thirdly, the AIAWU focuses on the casual labour subset, whose unemployment rates may well have risen to levels much above those for all agricultural workers combined. Finally, a number of those whom the AIAWU counts as members of the agricultural workforce, will have been recorded by the NSS as belonging to other categories, such as construction, to which they have been forced to move recently because of lack of work in agriculture. In short, the AIAWU is, correctly, conscious above all, of the squeeze on agricultural labour markets in a period of workforce restructuring, while the NSS simply calculates a rate at a point of time, which fails to capture the employment uncertainties faced by workers caught up in the adjustment process.

27. The 1996 AIAWU General Secretary's Report notes (at the all India level) the 'steep decline in the proportion both of self employed rural households and those engaged in rural household industries ...' Moreover, 'village craft persons, washermen, *chowkidars'* (watchmen), 'and the like no longer have the support they used to get from the village community. They have turned to casual labour' (page 15, AIAWU (1996) Documents, AIAWU IVth All India Conference, (2-4 November). Some of these people would previously been working under the 'jajmani' system, under which certain categories of craftsmen and service workers used to be entitled to payment in kind out of the harvest, and many of them would have had cultivable plots.

28. The field work was carried out in 153 sample villages from October 1972 to October 1973, and covered 382 agricultural labour households and 1004 cultivating households. Most of the results which are relevant   here came out in Bhalla [1995].

29. The study was based on data for 3412 cultivating, 484 wage labour, and 485 other, non-cultivating households from 329 villages surveyed in 1975–76.

30. An account of these 'modern' long term contracts in Haryana is given in Bhalla [1976].

31. However, there were local, individual efforts. In the late 1970s, in the Samalka area, for example, a CPM worker, Cm. Sube Singh, worked to mobilise landless workers.

32. The Sabha was originally called the Punjab Dihati Mazdoor Sabha. The name was changed to Punjab Khet Mazdoor Sabha in 1971, at the twelfth session of the Sabha.

33. A carefully documented history of the Punjab Khet Mazdoor Sabha was written by Master Hari Singh in honour of the silver jubilee of the Sabha. See Singh [1980].

34. A brief account of successive sessions of the Sabha, and where they were held, is given in Chapter 3 of Singh [1980].

35. When the CPI split in 1964, so did the sabha organisation.

36. The all India Agricultural Workers Union (AIAWU) was formed at a meeting held October 12th and 13th, 1981, at Vijayawada in Andhra Pradesh. At this time, there were only five state units – in Kerala, Andhra Pradesh, Tamil Nadu, Punjab and Tripura. (The West Bengal membership was then, and continues now, under the umbrella of the All India Kisan Sabha, (AIKS). But as early as 1954, at the 12th session of the AIKS, held 24 September at Moga (Punjab), an organisation separate from the AIKS was mooted and a resolution passed, which reads: 'It is time that agricultural labourers are brought in large number into the organisation of agrarian movement. This can best be done by organising them in their separate agricultural labour union ...' (page 23 AIAWU, 1982, General Secretary's Report to 24th Session of the AIKS, held at Midnapore, West Bengal, 8–11 Nov.

37. See, for example, the AIAWU Report of the 2nd All India Conference, 1986, 9, 10, 11 and 12 December held at Palghat, Kerala, page 59, and page 14, *Proceedings, Report and Resolutions of the General Council of the AIAWU*, held at Khammam, Andhra Pradesh, 1 May 1989, which describe activities, in 'some pockets' and in 'three districts' respectively, but then go on to note, for example, that 'no meeting ... has yet been held to structure the organisation'.

38. Haryana's AIAWU membership figures were: 1981–82 – 1,400; 1982–83 – nil; 1983–84 – nil; 1984–85 – 400; 1985–86, 1986–87 and 1987–88 – all nil; 1988–89 – 1,500; 1989–90 – 5,000; 1990–91 – nil; 1991–92 – 5,000; 1992–93 – 6,640; 1993–94 – 5,900; 1994–95 –

6,854; 1995–96 – 8,600. The paid up membership figures are, of course, a small fraction of the numbers who participate in the demonstrations and other activities of the union, including local activities. It may be noted that at the all India level, the AIAWU membership was estimated at 2.94 per cent of the total population of agricultural labourers, and that roughly 60 percent of these are from Kerala, where 2 out of every 3 agricultural labourers is a member. For details on other states see tables on pages 43 and 44 of AIAWU, *Documents of the IVth All India Conference*, 2 –4 Nov., held at Khammam, Andhra Pradesh.

39. See, for example, page 27, *Proceedings, Report and Resolutions of the General Council of the AIAWU*, held at Saharanpur, Uttar Pradesh, in June 1990, and page 6 of the *Documents of the Third Conference of the AIAWU*, held 17–19 April 1992, in Samistipur, Bihar.

40. For information to help date the completion of this gradual metamorphosis, I am indebted to Com. Suneet Chopra, Joint Secretary of the national level AIAWU.

41. He was assisted by a Joint Secretary for a couple of years from the end of the 1980s, but then, in June 1991, the founder General Secretary died, leaving a single Joint Secretary to man the Central Office until the middle of 1992, when two more Joint Secretaries were appointed. For details see page 67, *Documents of the Third Conference of the AIAWU*, 1992, and page 33 of the *Documents of the IVth All India Conference*, 1996.

42. See especially page 36 *Proceedings, Report and Resolutions* of the General Council of the AIAWU meeting held at Khammam, Andhra Pradesh, on 1 May 1989.

43. The decision was taken at a Working Committee Meeting held in April 1983 in Delhi, but could not be implemented at that time. Com. Dhanpat Rai Nahar from Punjab was to be sent to help Haryana and Rajasthan, and Com. M.K. Krishnan to help Karnataka. See pages 43 and 44, *Proceedings of the Meeting of the All India Council of the AIAWU*, 25–27 Nov. 1983, held at Nellore, Andhra Pradesh.

44. The seven organisations were: the AIAWU, the AIKS (CPM led), the AIKS (CPI led), the CPI led Bharatiya Khet Mazdoor Union (BKMU), the Agrami Kisan Sabha, the Samyukta Kisan Sabha and the Krishi Mazdoor Union.

45. See page 36, *Proceedings, Report and Resolutions of the General Council of the AIAWU*, held at Khammam, Andhra Pradesh on 1 May 1989.

46. For a characterisation of such movements see the *The Journal of Peasant Studies*, Special Issue on New Farmers' Movements in India', edited by Tom Brass, Vol.21, Nos.3 and 4, April/July 1994. The Haryana Kisan Sangharsh Samiti, and its 1997 convenor, Ravinder Singh Sangwan, perhaps differs marginally from the BKU model of Mahendra Singh Tikait in its willingness to accept support from, and to rely on high level interventions by the CPI and CPM, and their Haryana state leaders.

47. The 'sangharsh samiti' is an informal, unstructured organisation for struggle, rather than a formal farmers' union.

48. A *gherao* is a demonstration in which entry to and exit from, for example, a government office, a power house or other place is blocked by substantial numbers of people. A *bandh* is a strike which closes down normal activities, usually in a given geographical area, rather than in the protesters' place of work. *Rail roko, rasta roko* translates roughly as 'block the rail lines, block the roads'.

49. In the press reports of the period, there was considerable confusion about who was leading (or 'instigating') this series of agitations. *The Tribune*, Chandigarh, for example, issues of 14 October and 2 November 1997, and *Peoples' Democracy*, various dates, both state that the Kisan Sangharsh Samiti was leading the farmers. *The Tribune* mentions also that the Congress party as well as the BKU were active. But on 17 October, 1997, *The Tribune* reports specifically that a 'mob' of the BKU ransacked and burnt the Uchana railway station, and on the day before *The Tribune* wrote that the BKU had torched another railway station near Narwana. Bansi Lal, the Chief Minister, is reported in *The Tribune* of 18 October 1997, to have blamed it on a 'conspiracy' of Mr. Bhajan Lal, a former Congress Chief Minister of Haryana, and Mr. Om Prakash Chautala, another political adversary. The truth of the matter seems to be that the Samiti attracted widespread sympathy and support among both Jats and non-Jats in rural Haryana, and that many groups tried to cash in on it.

50. An *anganwadi* is a creche-cum-day nursery, sometimes located in an open courtyard.

51. Gill [1994], and other contributions to the April/July 1994 (Vol.21, Nos.3/4) issue of the *The*

Journal of Peasant Studies, provide a perspective on the BKU.

52. The south west plateau region of Haryana includes districts Bhiwani, Mahendragarh, Loharu and parts of Gurgaon. All of them are characterised by a very deep water table. This makes tubewells costly to run as well as to install.
53. As reported in *The Pioneer*, New Delhi, 24 Oct. 1997, in a review of the on again, off again agitations of 1995, 1996 and 1997.
54. The 'slab system' is a tariff system under which the rate for tubewells depends on water table depth. The slab system was first introduced in 1977, revised in 1981 and 1994, and enhanced again in 1995. In 1996 (Sept.), Bansi Lal abolished the slab system, introducing instead a flat rate which smaller farmers in the plateau region would have found difficult to pay.
55. The list of demands included: the withdrawal of electricity rate increases; free electricity to poor peasants, six monthly bills for the rest; 'daily replacement of burnt-out transformers – preferably within 24 hours'; investment in specified power houses and canals, and in flood control projects; stern action against dealers in spurious fertilizers and pesticides; remunerative prices, for cotton particularly; revocation of the legal provision for imprisonment for loan repayment defaulters; comprehensive crop insurance; and a farm accident and death benefit scheme for farmers and agricultural workers (*Source: Peoples' Democracy*, 1 Dec. 1996.)
56. *Peoples' Democracy*, 26 Oct. 1997.
57. See *The Tribune*, 13 Oct. 1997.
58. *The Tribune*, 14 Oct. 1997.
59. All quotations from a report in *Peoples' Democracy*, 28 Dec. 1997.
60. See, for example, *The Pioneer*, New Delhi, 24 Oct. 1997.
61. Report in *The Tribune*, 2 Nov. 1997.
62. Page 93 of the Political Organisational Report of the 15th Congress of the CPI(M) held in Chandigarh, 3–8 April 1995.
63. Besides Haryana, they included: Punjab, Western Uttar Pradesh, delta areas of Andhra Pradesh, parts of Tamil Nadu, Karnataka, Maharashtra and Gujarat. See page 93 of the 1995 Political Organisation Report.
64. Listed under this category were: Bihar, Eastern and Central parts of Uttar Pradesh, Orissa, Madhya Pradesh, parts of Rajasthan, Gujurat, Maharashtra, Andhra Pradesh, Karnataka and Tamil Nadu.
65. The full list, given on page 95, ibid. includes: credit facilities, storage facilities, marketing facilities, promotion of cooperative cultivation, strengthening of public distribution system, remunerative prices for agricultural products and ends with 'wages and better service conditions for agricultural workers, public health facilities, public education facilities, etc.'
66. See page 6, Documents AIAWU IVth All India Conference, 2–4 Nov. 1996.
67. Reports in *Peoples' Democracy*, December 1997, on the Ninth State Conference of the Haryana CPM held in Rohtak, give the gist of his speech. See page 11.
68. *People's Democracy*, 5 Oct.1997.
69. *People's Democracy*, page 19, 2 Feb. 1997, for a report.
70. A 'chit' is a written note, in this case one vouching for the eligibility of the worker to draw rations at subsidised rates and attesting to his standing as a member of the agricultural workers' union.
71. As reported in *People's Democracy*, 30 March 1997, page 15.
72. A brief reference is made to this action on page 45 of the 1996 Documents of the AIAWU IVth All India Conference. The details were provided by Com. Inderjit Singh and other activists at the CPM office in Rohtak.
73. See the report on page 5 of *People's Democracy*, 19 Oct. 1997.
74. See report in the *Sunday Observer*, 5 March 1998.
75. In some other states, it may need to be noted, trade unions and left-led mass organisations went into retreat, and militant caste based, ethnic and communal organisations flourished instead.
76. Page 10, Presidential Address by Paturu Ramayya to the fourth all India conference of the AIAWU, 1996.
77. Page 30, Report of the IVth AIAWU Conference, 1996.

78. Especially page 104, CPI(M), (1995), Political Organisational Report, 15th Congress.
79. Revealed, for example, on page 94 of the 1995, CPM Political Organisational Report.
80. This critique is taken from page 94 of the 1995 Political Organisational Report.
81. Page 65, Documents of the Third Conference of the AIAWU, 1992.
82. There are ten parliamentary seats in Haryana. The CPI and the CPM together polled just under 0.5 per cent of the votes. Source: Election Commissioner of India (1998), Statistical Report, Vol.1 (Ver. 1), (National and State Abstracts), New Delhi.
83. In the 1998 Parliamentary elections, out of 10 Parliamentary seats, the Haryana Vikas Party and the BJP won only one seat each. The gainers were: the Congress, with 3 seats and just over 26 per cent of the vote; the Haryana Lok Dal (Rastriya), which won 4 seats with just under 26 per cent of the votes polled; and the BSP which gained a seat and 7.68 per cent of the vote. For more details see Election Commission of India [1998].

REFERENCES

Acharya, S. and G.F. Papanek, 1989, *Agricultural Wages and Poverty in India: a Model of Rural Labour Markets*, Asian Centre Discussion Paper No.39, Centre for Asian Development Studies, Boston University, Boston. July.

Alagh, Y.K., Bhalla, G.S. and Amit Bhaduri, 1978, 'Agricultural Growth and Labour Absorption In India', in Bardhan *et al.* (eds.) *Labour Absorption in Indian Agriculture*, Bangkok: ARTEP, ILO.

All India Agricultural Workers Union (AIAWU), 1983, *Proceedings of the Meeting of the All India Council of the AIAWU*, New Delhi.

All India Agricultural Workers Union, 1986, *Report of the Second All India Conference*, New Delhi.

All India Agricultural Workers Union, 1989, *Proceedings, Report and Resolutions of the General Council of the AIAWU*, New Delhi.

All India Agricultural Workers Union, 1990, *Proceedings, Report and Resolutions of the General Council of the AIAWU*, New Delhi.

All India Agricultural Workers Union, 1992, *Documents of the Third Conference of the AIAWU*, New Delhi.

All India Agricultural Workers Union, 1996, *Documents, AIAWU IVth All India Conference*, New Delhi.

All India Kisan Sabha, 1982, *General Secretary's Report to 24th Session of the AIKS*, New Delhi.

Bhaduri, Amit, 1993, *Structural Adjustment, Labour Market and Employment in India*, New Delhi: ARTEP Working Papers, Asian Regional Team for Employment Promotion, ILO.

Bhalla, Sheila, 1976, 'New Relations of Production in Haryana Agriculture', *Economic and Political Weekly*, Vol.11, No.13, 27 March.

Bhalla, Sheila, 1992, 'The Formation of Rural Labour Markets in India', in T.S. Papola and Gerry Rodgers (eds.) *Labour Institutions and Economic Development in India*, Research Series 97, Geneva: International Institute for Labour Studies.

Bhalla, Sheila, 1993, 'The Dynamics of Wage Determination and Employment Generation in Indian Agriculture', *Indian Journal of Agricultural Economics*, Vol.48, No.3, July–Sept.

Bhalla, Sheila, 1994a, 'Poverty, Workforce Development and Rural Labour Markets', *Indian Journal of Labour Economics*, Vol.37, No.4, Oct.–Dec.

Bhalla, Sheila, 1994b, 'Rural Industrialisation and Non-Farm Employment', laser printed report of an ILO sponsored study submitted to the ILO, Geneva, in Nov.

Bhalla, Sheila, 1995, 'Development, Poverty and Policy: The Haryana Experience', *Economic and Political Weekly*, Vol.30, Nos.41 and 42, 14–21 Oct.

Bhalla, G.S. and Gurmail Singh, 1997, 'Recent Developments in Indian Agriculture: A State Level Analysis', *Economic and Political Weekly*, Vol.32 No.13, 29 March.

Brass, Tom (ed.), 1994, 'New Farmers' Movements in India', The Journal of Peasant Studies, Vol.21, Nos.3 and 4, April–July (Special Issue).

Chakravarty, S., 1977, 'Reflections on the Growth Process in the Indian Economy', in C.P. Wadhwa (ed.), *Some Problems of India's Economic Policy* (2nd edn), New Delhi: Tata-Mcgraw Hill.

Chakravarty, S., 1979, 'On the Question of the Home Market and Prospects for Industrial Growth', *Economic and Political Weekly*, Vol.14, Nos.30–32, 9 Aug., Special Number.

Communist Party of India (Marxist), 1995, 'Political Organisational Report of the 15th Congress', held in Chandigarh, 3–8 April, New Delhi.

Election Commissioner of India, 1998, *Statistical Report, Vol.1 (Ver.1) (National and State Abstracts)*, New Delhi.

Ghosh, R., Marjit, S. and C. Neogi, 1998, 'Economic Growth and Regional Divergence in India; 1960 to 1995', *Economic and Political Weekly*, Vol.XXXIII, No.26, 27 June–3 July.

Ghosh, S. and S. Mukherjee (eds.), 1995, *Emerging South Asian Order: Hopes and Concerns*, Calcutta: Media South Asia.

Gill, Sucha Singh, 1994, 'The Farmers' Movements and Agrarian Change in the Green Revolution Belt of North West India', *The Journal of Peasant Studies*, Vol.21, Nos.3 and 4, April–July (Special Issue).

Government of India, Ministry of Finance, 1997, *Economic Survey 1996–97*, New Delhi.

Government of India, Ministry of Planning, 1995, *Employment Generation in the Eighth Plan*, New Delhi.

Kuznets, S., 1966, *Modern Economic Growth: Rate, Structure and Spread*, New Haven, CT: Yale University Press.

Mitra, Ashok, 1977, *Terms of Trade and Class Relations*, London: Frank Cass.

Ozler, R., Datt, Gaurav and Mark Ravallion, 1996, *A Data Base on Poverty and Growth in India*, Policy Research Department, World Bank.

Papola, T.S., 1989, 'Restructuring in Indian Industry: Implications for Employment and Industrial Relations', in Gus Edgren (ed.) *Restructuring, Employment and Industrial Relations*, New Delhi: ILO-ARTEP.

Papola, T.S. , 1991, 'Industry and Employment: Recent Indian Experience', laser printed ISID Foundation Day Lecture, Institute for Studies in Industrial Development, New Delhi.

Patnaik, Prabhat, 1979, 'Industrial Development in India since Independence', *Social Scientist*, Vol.7, No.11, June.

People's Democracy, New Delhi, various issues.

Ravallion, Martin and Datt, Gaurav, 1996, 'India's Chequered History in the Fight Against Poverty: Are There Lessons for the Future?', *Economic and Political Weekly*, Special Number, Vol.XXXI, Nos.35, 36 and 37, Sept.

Sen, Abhijit, 1996, 'Economic Reforms, Employment and Poverty', *Economic and Political Weekly*, Special Number, Vol.31, Nos.35, 36 and 37, Sept.

Sen, Abhijit, 1997, computer printout.

Sidhu, H.S., 1991, *Agricultural Development and Rural Labour: A Case Study of Punjab and Haryana*, New Delhi: Concept Publishers.

Singh, Jitender Pal, 1997, 'Employment, Wages and Poverty in Haryana: 1983 to 1993–94', unpublished M.Phil. dissertation, Jawaharlal Nehru University, New Delhi.

Singh, Master Hari, 1980, *Agricultural Workers' Struggle in Punjab*, New Delhi: People's Publishing House.

Smith, Adam, 1977, *The Wealth of Nations* (Everyman's Library), London and Toronto: Dent & Sons.

Tendulkar, S.D. and L.R. Jain, 1995, 'Economic Reforms and Poverty', *Economic and Political Weekly*, Vol.30, No.23, 10 June.

The Pioneer, New Delhi, various issues.

The Sunday Observer, New Delhi, various issues.

The Tribune, Chandigarh, various issues.

Unni, Jeemol, 1997, 'Employment and Wages Among Rural Labourers: Some Recent Trends', *Indian Journal of Agricultural Economics*, Vol.52, No.1, Jan.–March.

Unfree Relations and the Feminisation of Agricultural Labour in Andhra Pradesh, 1970–95

LUCIA DA CORTA and
DAVULURI VENKATESHWARLU

INTRODUCTION

This study examines the effects of 'green revolution' induced agricultural growth and state policies on labour and domestic gender relations in villages in Andhra Pradesh (AP) over the last 25 years. We focus on the phenomenon of women's rising share of agricultural wage employment *vis-à-vis* men, a trend occurring across this state [*Ravathi*, 1994].

Studies of the effect of technological change and associated growth on male and female agricultural labour tend to follow the marked ideological divisions between Marxist and Neo-liberal analyses which so characterised the debate on agrarian change in India. Early Marxist studies argued that capitalist development flooded the labour market as small farms lost their land to larger capitalist farms. The latter owned the resources necessary to take advantage of the new technology and enjoyed the advantages of superior economies of scale. The labour market was further flooded as artisans lost their market to urban manufactured goods. Capitalists' increased demand for labour under the new technology was not sufficient to overcome this vastly increased supply of labour and so labourers' employment opportunities were seen to suffer along with their wages [e.g., *Byres*, 1981; *Rahman*, 1986].

Lucia da Corta, Development Studies Institute, London School of Economics and Political Science, Houghton Street, London WC2A 2AE and Davuluri Venkateshwarlu, Department of Political Science, University of Hyderabad, Hyderabad, Andhra Pradesh, 500 041, India. The authors are indebted to Barbara Harriss-White, Judith Heyer, Wendy Olsen and Santa Sinha for advice during the course of their research and to Karin Kapadia for comments. They are also grateful to Tom Brass who commented extensively on earlier drafts and suggested some changes. This research was supported by St. Anne's College, Oxford and by the Overseas Development Administration. The views and opinions expressed in this contribution, however, do not reflect ODA's official policies or practices, but are those of the authors alone.

Writers concerned with female agricultural labourers suggested that as family farms or artisans' means of production became too small to be economic without outside income to supplement subsistence and to acquire cash for the purchase of expensive inputs, women were forced into the workforce at a faster rate than men [e.g., *Mies*, 1986]. Moreover, some traditional avenues for female employment were seen to decline.[1] Several writers note that according to census figures the percentage of rural women workers classified as agricultural labourers had almost doubled from 25.6 per cent to 49.6 per cent over the period 1961–81; by contrast male rural workers were primarily cultivators, with the percentage rise in agricultural labourers over the period rising from 16.2 per cent to 24.3 per cent [*Agarwal*, 1984: 203; *Duvvury*, 1989: 101]. Rural Labour Enquiries data over the years 1964/5 to 1974/5 also revealed a greater percentage increase for women than for men, that is, 57.5 per cent for women and 43.6 per cent for men (cited in Agarwal [1984: 203]). This rise in women's classification as agricultural labourers was seen to be 'supply driven' by the pauperisation of smallholders and artisans. Whereas some writers, such as Agarwal [1984], attributed this pauperisation to capitalist development, others, such as Duvvury [1989], argued that such pauperisation was also a result of rapid population growth coupled with land fragmentation. The overall result of this pauperisation for male and female labourers included falling annual days of employment, rising involuntary unemployment, falling annual wage earnings, wide disparities between male and female wages (widening in some states) and a rise in the percentage of female headed households dependent on wage labour [*Agarwal*, 1984, *Mies*, 1986; *Duvvury*, 1989].

While these writers may well have documented correctly the changing labour relations of the 1960s and 1970s, there are some difficulties with using the conclusions of these studies to understand labour relations in south India in recent decades.[2] Most importantly, these writings were concerned with an early 'labour surplus' stage of developing agrarian capitalism, that is, before competition from other capitalists and overproduction drove labour costs up and commodity prices down, forcing employers to change their accumulation strategies (see, for instance, Kautsky [1988] and Brass [1990; 1993]).

More recently a number of writers have attempted to challenge the conclusions of the early Marxists regarding the effects of the green revolution on male and female labourers. These Neo-liberal writers come mainly from the large development research institutions, including the World Bank, International Food Policy Research Institute (IFPRI) and International Crops Research Institute for the Semi-Arid Tropics (ICRISAT). They loosely follow Mellor [1976] in their suggestion that the benefits of the new technology, while initially slow, eventually trickled down to male and female labourers in various parts of India through the creation of agricultural employment and supplementary, off-farm employment resulting from growth linkages to both the rural and urban non-agricultural economies. The rise in employment opportunities led to a substantial reduction in oppressive conditions of employment, to sharply rising real wages and to a corresponding fall in deprivation [e.g., *Hazell and Ramasamy*, 1991; *Walker and Ryan*, 1990]. The labour market was not seen to be flooded by land dispossession among small farmers because, though there was an initial lag in the adoption of the new varieties by small farmers, the 'inverse relationship' between farm size and productivity held true and encouraged a relatively faster growth in smallholder yields compared to large farms [*Lipton and Longhurst*, 1989: 142–4; *Hazell and Ramasamy*, 1991: 240, *Singh*, 1990]. This inverse relationship, together with greater outside employment opportunities, actually enhanced the ability of small farmers to buy land and further tightened the labour market [*Walker and Ryan*, 1990; *Hazell and Ramasamy*, 1991]. Large landowners, by contrast, suffered downward mobility because of their total dependence on increasingly expensive hired labour, their increased spending on marriages and/or inferior skill in managing fertilisers or irrigation [*Walker and Ryan*, 1990: 159; *Hazell and Ramasamy*, 1991: 243]. What is noteworthy is that according to these writers the effects of growth did not merely trickle down to labourers as suggested by Mellor [1976], but that a process of 'equalisation' in land ownership took place.

Neo-liberal writers concerned with female labour suggest that women's employment opportunities in agriculture grew more rapidly than men's. The argument that there has been a clear trend of feminisation of the agricultural labour force in most of India in recent years is put forcefully in an influential report by Bennett [1992], who summarises the World Bank report [1991] *Gender and Poverty in India*. She argues there has been an increase in both the absolute numbers and proportion of women involved in agricultural wage work since 1961, finding that 'In every state but Uttar Pradesh and Bihar, the percentage increase for female agricultural labourers has been greater than that for males' [1992: 22]. This rise has been particularly marked in south India, where women have historically comprised a high proportion of the wage labour force. For instance, based on the Government of India Labour Bureau data, Bennett [1992: 84, Table 14] estimates that over the period 1971–81 the number of female wage labourers rose by 31.1 per cent in Andhra Pradesh and by 68.9 per cent in Tamil Nadu, compared to a 14.1 per cent and 11.0 per cent rise in male labourers respectively. Indeed, Bennett [1992: 22] concludes: 'In most of India south of the Ganges, there are more women than men in the agricultural labour force.'

Bennett suggests that the rise in women's share of agricultural labouring in South India was largely 'demand driven', a result of extended opportunities on a labour market characterised by rising wages and better conditions. Rather than being thrust onto the labour market as suggested by Agarwal and others, women were 'tempted out' of their homes to accept new work opportunities. The sharp rise in demand for female casual labour is seen to result from technical changes which greatly expanded the area devoted to those high yielding crops which require more work culturally deemed to be 'women's work' compared to traditional varieties [*Bennett*, 1992: 2–4]. A number of micro-studies conclude that there has been a greater demand for female hired labour under different high yielding crops in different Indian states [e.g., *Ray et al.*, 1985; *Joshi and Alshi*, 1985; *Chand, et al.*, 1985; *Gadre and Mahalle*, 1985; *Marothia and Sharma*, 1985].[3] As an example Walker and Ryan [1990: 115] observed that 'of the total female labour used in the Mahbubnagar and Akola villages [in Andhra Pradesh and Maharashtra] 80–90 per cent was hired ... the activities of paddy transplanting and weeding in Mahbubnagar and cotton picking in Akola create a high demand for hired female labour'. In sum these writers argue that the introduction of the HYV-fertiliser-irrigation package has increased the number of labour days needed in those particular agricultural operations (for example, transplanting, weeding, etc.) which just happen to be exclusively or primarily women's work. It is implied that the greater demand for women's work in agriculture – though not planned by the designers of the 'green revolution' – was an extremely fortuitous result of the adoption of the HYV package because such demand enhances women's employment and thereby reduces the sex bias which is so marked in the Indian subcontinent.

Bennett also suggests that the growth in agricultural production and the resulting rise in prosperity has pushed up the demand for non-agricultural goods and services and has encouraged mostly male worker migration into non-farm employment, thereby increasing further the demand for female agricultural workers. In order to provide evidence that the rise in women's share of the workforce is 'demand driven', Bennett cites studies where there is apparently evidence of declining male female wage differentials [e.g., *Jose*, 1988] and shorter working days [e.g., *Walker and Ryan*, 1990]. She also cites Duvvury's [1989] study which shows that the incidence of female agricultural labour is positively correlated with district level agricultural growth rates and share of gross cropped area planted to cash crops (that is, largely 'green revolution' parts of India).

The neo-liberal argument suggests a natural complementarity between growth and women's welfare, and that policy attempts to enhance growth can only enhance women's welfare. It is often concluded from these more recent analyses, together with the experience of the East Asian countries, that economic reforms based on liberalisation and the encouragement of private enterprise can only be beneficial for both male and female labourers.

We believe that villages in Andhra Pradesh would make an interesting case study to examine afresh the views of Bennett and other Neo-liberal writers. As Agarwal [1984] notes, it is the one state in which two otherwise divergent studies, Ahluwalia [1978] and Griffin and Ghosh [1979] agree that there has been a negative trend over time in the incidence of rural poverty. Moreover, published reports exhibit significant increases in real agricultural wages: men's wages rose 83.4 per cent and women's wages rose 81.0 per cent, based on three year averages between 1968/71 and 1988/91 [*Reddy*, 1991]. Finally, evidence of women's rising share of the agricultural labour market has been found in all three regions of Andhra Pradesh, that is, Rayalaseema, Telengana and Coastal Andhra [*Ravathi*, 1994]. It is commonly assumed that the women led anti-liquor movement in AP is a reflection of women's greater power in domestic relations emerging from this rising share of employment.

Indeed, since the introduction of the 'green revolution' technology to the survey villages there has been an important improvement in labourers' economic position in several ways, which *on the surface*, seem to confirm Neo-liberal conclusions regarding the effects of growth. For instance, since 1973, 35.3 per cent of landless labouring men gained land (2.3 acres on average).[4] Moreover, men's involvement in *traditional,* permanent bonded labour relations declined, off-farm employment opportunities grew and the labour marked tightened. Also, women's share of total agricultural wage employment *vis-à-vis* men has risen significantly since 1970.

Yet despite these changes two apparent paradoxes exist. The first is that despite a near doubling of real wages and greater landownership among labourers, the latter still depend on exploitative loans from employers and merchants for food and other essentials which act as downward pressures on their earnings. This paradox – which we label the 'Standard of Living Paradox' – was identified by Heyer [1997] with respect to villages in Coimbatore district, Tamil Nadu. She found that over the past 17 years real wages doubled, or even trebled (depending on the deflator used) but that there was not the corresponding improvement in standard of living one would expect from this doubling. Heyer observed workers living in poor, crowded housing, wearing tattered saris and some still relying heavily on children's paid labour rather than sending them to school. According to our own 1988/9 data, 46 per cent of labourers (including those with land) in the survey region still reduced their food consumption at each meal and reduced the number of meals from three to two during March, April, May (the hot season) and during October, November (just before the harvest). An additional 32 per cent switched to cheaper food (mixing more millet powder into broken rice) during these months. With a near doubling of *real* wages, the expectation would be that labourers were better fed and no longer dependent on employers for loans for food and other essentials.

A second paradox – which we label the 'Women's Empowerment Paradox' – is that women's greater share of agricultural employment did not herald a corresponding improvement in women's power *vis-à-vis* menfolk to influence domestic decisions.

In order to shed some light on these paradoxes in the villages studied, we first examine some major methodological difficulties with the more recent Neo-liberal writings and then describe our survey region and method of classifying rural men and women. We then move on to an analysis of changes in male labour relations since 1970 and examine both changes in electoral politics and state interventions and in capitalists' accumulation strategies. We then turn to changes in female labour relations and domestic (gender) relations, plus the feminisation of agricultural labour.

METHODOLOGICAL ISSUES

There are several major methodological difficulties with the more recent Neo-liberal studies that would affect the relevance of their conclusions to labourers in Andhra Pradesh. First, there is a tendency to confuse the effects of 'growth' with the cumulative impact of government anti-poverty policies on tightening the labour market [*Athreya et al.*, 1990; *Harriss*, 1992; *Sender*, 1995]. Strategic attempts of both Congress and the Telugu Desham Party in Andhra Pradesh to win the allegiance of rural male labourers have led to a series of ad hoc populist state welfare interventions.[5] It will be argued below that these 'vote-buying' interventions – despite many problems – supported male agricultural labourers' movement out of traditional permanent bonded labour relations and into employment on encroached government land and in government related non-agricultural work.

Second, Neo-liberal studies tend to neglect analyses of the ways in which capital, *in the later stages of agrarian capitalist development,* reacts to and develops methods to overcome competitive forces resulting in the falling price of commodities (through overproduction) and rising labour costs. In rural India, capitalists have responded to labour market tightening using their superior control in other markets, such as in land rental and credit markets. In the villages studied there were two main reactions to rising labour costs: commission trading based on 'tied harvest' arrangements and capitalist farming based on 'tied labour' relations.[6]

Under 'tied harvest' arrangements, commission traders extend credit or lease out small amounts of land to 'smallholders' on the basis that the latter pledge their harvests to lenders at commodity prices which are substantially less than what they could receive under competitive market conditions. Some writers analyse the exchange of harvest for loans as credit market transactions, where the reduced price paid for harvests is factored into the explicit interest rate. If the combined interest is unduly high or usurious, such relations are said to block or inhibit capitalist development [e.g., *Harriss*, 1982]. Yet more recently the existence of tied harvest relations – in modified forms – are seen to be compatible with capitalist development, a method whereby capitalists can secure reliable supplies of commodities for trade [e.g., *Harriss*, 1992]. Under circumstances of rising labour costs and falling prices for commodities, it may be more profitable for capitalists to appropriate surpluses indirectly through these tied harvest exchange relations (for example, marketing produce and credit) than through production relations based on hiring in labour. In this way, capitalists can take advantage of the nature of smallholders to work harder on their own land for lower returns (compared to hired in workers) and to underconsume in order to retain land and remain independent from large landowner employers [*Kautsky,* 1988; *Alavi and Shanin*, 1988; *Ellis,* 1988; *Patnaik,* 1979]. Thus commission agents can contribute to a form of capitalist development which is compatible with the proliferation of male operated smallholdings.

The existence of 'tied harvest' relations in our villages calls into question Neo-liberal views regarding: the source of smallholder survival in south India (that is, the inverse relation and agricultural productivity versus capitalists' ability, through tied harvest arrangements, to take advantage of smallholder's ability to self-exploit themselves);[7] the conceptualisation of smallholder/borrowers as 'independent' cultivators; and the actual benefit of new land ownership to labourers.

In 'tied labour' arrangements, agrarian capitalists extend credit and/or lease out garden plots of wet land to labourers on the basis that labourers pledge their labour (or the labour of kinsfolk) at wages which are much less then what they could receive under competitive market conditions (that is, prices less than going market prices published rates at time of sale). Tied labourers agree to work exclusively for the employer/creditor for the duration of the attachment and often perform additional, unpaid work.

A difficulty with the Neo-liberal treatment of attached labour arrangements in rural India (that is, the exchange of labour service for credit) is that either such arrangements are ignored altogether or they are conceptualised as 'free' arrangements where labourers voluntarily enter into and remain in such arrangements because conditions are good and wages are competitive. (for example, loans are often viewed simply as a cash advance on wages).[8] Another view is that such relations may be oppressive (that is, payment is lower than casual work and hours longer) but that they can disappear with economic growth through the creation of employment opportunities (especially non-agricultural work) which eliminate labourers' need to engage in exploitative arrangements [e.g., *Platteau*, 1995: scenario 2]. The notion that economic growth abolishes unfree/attached/bonded labour is paralleled in the Marxist semi-feudal view that such modern relations are pre-capitalist 'relics' destined, by definition, to disappear with the development of capitalism.[9]

More recently, it has been argued that non-permanent attached labour relations are compatible with capitalist development.[10] Brass [1993] de-links attached labour relations from situations of labour surplus (so common in the Indian literature) and forges a link instead with those economic crises characteristic of more advanced stages of agrarian capitalism (that is, the fall in commodity prices due to overproduction, labour cost rises and related class struggle). Such crises may force capitalists to respond by enforcing non-permanent attached labour relations and thereby to segment the labour market, secure cheaper and/or more disciplined workers and to re-establish profitability. He labels this process 'deproletarianisation'[11] and Brass [1993: 46–7] argues that:

> In contexts/periods where/when further accumulation is blocked by overproduction, economic crisis may force capital to restructure its labour process either by replacing free workers with unfree [and cheaper] equivalents or by converting the former into the latter. The economic advantage of deproletarianization is that such restructuring enables landholders/planters first to lower the cost of local workers by importing unfree, more easily regulated, and thus cheaper outside labour, and then to lower the cost of the latter if/when the original external/local wage differential has been eroded. In this way it is possible either to maintain wages at existing (low) levels or even to decrease pay and conditions of both components of the workforce, thereby restoring/enhancing profitability and with it the accumulation projection (or linked to) the capitalist labour process.

Brass [1993: 34–5] concludes that 'assaults by capital on the freedom of wage labour – the ability of workers to enter *and withdraw* from particular labour markets and labour processes – are a *general* feature of capitalism' [original emphasis].

The inability of a labourer to commodify his/her labour while in tied labour relations calls into question the Neo-liberal conceptualisation of attached labour as wholly free and as obtaining competitive wages. There is, however, an important debate between Marxists regarding the definition of modern attached labour relations in rural India as unfree or free (but economically constrained) and whether unfreedom is growing or abating.

A third major difficulty with the Neo-liberal literature on rural labour in India is the tendency to see gender inequalities as something to explain (for example, 'female unemployment creates sex bias') rather than as a causal process in itself affecting both the level of women's involvement in wage labour (feminisation) and both men's and women's labour relations. Men's and women's relations with employers are heavily and separately influenced by their domestic (gender) relations, namely the relative power of men and women to influence decisions, especially those regarding *who is responsible for family maintenance* (food, clothing and medication needs). This issue is particularly important in Andhra Pradesh where men's personal spending, especially on alcohol, is rising with men's rapid movement into the cash economy. Also, relations with employers are related to power to influence domestic decisions regarding *who is responsible for what work* within the home, on own assets or paid work [*Rogaly*, 1997: 63–5], with implications for status, remuneration and quantity of work performed.

Women's power in domestic relations regarding family provision and division of labour affects the conditions under which women enter the market for wage labour. As an example, their domestic relations can reduce their power to strike against low wages offered by employers by refusing work [*Kapadia*, 1993] and can diminish their power to 'choose' higher paid employment [*Rogaly*, 1997]. Together with class struggles between labour and capital regarding payment and conditions of employment, men's and women's power in class struggles regarding free/unfree relations of production in agriculture can be linked by their power in domestic relations.

It is in this context that we should re-examine the assumption that greater female employment – especially if that employment is unfree and low paid – necessarily leads to enhanced women's empowerment within the home (for example, regarding food/medical allocation among family members and domestic divisions of labour; see Miller [1981]). Moreover, if cash contribution to household income is relevant then one must consider contribution relative to men (for example, relative annual earnings) rather than merely as an increase in cash (versus other economic) contribution over time. It is equally important to consider the status of work performed by women (for example, inferior wage work as opposed to higher status work on own assets or non-farm work). Many feminists now suggest that economic contribution is often not directly relevant to women's position within the home [*Kabeer*, 1994]. Below we take these methodological considerations into account in our fresh attempt to examine the effects of green revolution induced growth on men's and women's labour relations.

THE SURVEY REGION AND CLASSIFICATION METHOD

Covering a 25-year period 1970–95, we conducted interviews for our study in two villages and 12 of their surrounding hamlets in Chittoor District in the Rayalaseema region of Andhra Pradesh. 1970 was the year when machine power pumping sets were first introduced into this dry land millet and paddy region. Pumping sets enabled the larger landowners to convert a substantial amount of dry land near dug wells into 'wet' land in order to cultivate high yielding varieties (HYV) of paddy. In the early 1980s, HYV groundnuts – a cash crop – replaced millet on dry land and larger farmers began cultivating some tomato on wet land (following the first HYV paddy crop). A few anti-poverty policies were introduced in the early 1970s, but most were implemented and intensified in their impact throughout the 1980s and early 1990s. These included a policy allowing the landless to encroach wasteland, a land ceiling, and subsidies on formal credit, on productive assets and on food.

We were well acquainted with the study region through Olsen's 1986/7 field research [*Olsen*, 1991] and through our own study of economic mobility and agrarian change [*da Corta*, 1993]. For the present study we spent an additional six months in the region (in several visits over the period July 1994 to June 1996), in the course of which we collected information from 99 women and 97 men and their children from 50 households selected randomly from a census population of 834 households. Based on the results of a cluster analysis [*da Corta, Tomlinson and Joseph*, 1992] the region was divided into two areas. The more developed *central region* includes a *mandal* revenue village and four nearby hamlets. This region has access to canal irrigation from a dam project, more off-farm employment opportunities (for example, in government offices, bus station, hotels, hospital, rice mills, shops, several temples and a mosque) and greater access to formal credit from a state bank. The less developed *remote region* includes a smaller village (about four kilometres from the *mandal* revenue village) and eight hamlets (the most outlying hamlet is a further six kilometres away).

In this contribution we classify rural men and women based on 'labour classes'; that is, the relative importance of (i) hiring out their labour (ii) self-employment on owned means of production and (iii) hiring in labour. This importance is measured by approximate time spent in each activity. This classification is not merely related to Marxist thought regarding prospects for surplus value appropriation, but is also deeply rooted in the Indian context where villagers identified themselves and neighbours as labourer (*kuulie*), farmer (*raitu*), or landlord (*bhuswami*) and where social status is strongly linked to the financial ability to withdraw from socially inferior wage labouring, and, at higher levels, to withdraw from manual work on one's own means of production [*Epstein*, 1973]. Thus this classification mirrors *social status* and, at best, such a classification may also reflect productive wealth ownership, opportunities for surplus value appropriation and for upward and downward social mobility [e.g., *Lenin*, 1977]. Based on data on the primary, secondary and tertiary activities in terms of time spent for men and women, a crude schema based on Roemer's [1982] system was developed which defines class position by how individuals relate to the buying and selling of labour power and to self-employment, as illustrated in the diagram below [*Bardhan*, 1984: 167–8].[12] However, we extend this schema to include hiring in/out and self-employment on *non-agricultural* means of production.

TABLE 1
LABOUR CLASS RANKS (REVISED VERSION OF ROEMER'S SCHEMA)

Labour Class	Name	Primary Activity	Secondary Activity
L	Pure Labourers	HO	—
L+	Labourers with PCP	HO	SE
SP	Small PCPs	SE	HO
MP	Middle PCPs	SE	—
BP	Big PCPs	SE	HIN
C	Capitalists	HIN	—

Where:

HO = Hires out – includes agricultural as well as non-agricultural paid labour work (e.g., salaried tank watchman, construction worker, rice mill labourer, crop weigher).

SE = Self-employed or petty commodity producers – includes working on one's own farm and/or as an artisan (e.g., weaver, mat maker, farrier, barber, potter) or petty trader (e.g., selling bangles and family run tea shops).

HIN = Hires in or Leases out – includes employment of agricultural and non-agricultural labour (e.g., in construction, rice mills, hotels). This group also includes merchants/commission traders, and educated professional white-collar workers who do not perform manual work.

— = negligible amounts of other activities.

In this contribution we also refer to three aggregated groups. The category 'labourers' refers to men and women from the L, L+ and SP classes; that is, all those involved in labouring as a primary or secondary activity. Labourers tend to be heavily involved in tied labour relations with employers. These attachments call into question their 'proletarian' status insofar as there are restrictions on their ability to commodify their labour [*Brass*, 1993]. Nevertheless, we retain the label 'labourers' and in the course of our analysis below discuss the relative freedom/unfreedom of different sub-groups of labourers. Men from the L and L+ groups own very little land, and what they do own is largely encroached government waste land (see Tables A1, A2, A3 in Appendix A for characteristics of land owned and leased in). Ls and L+s do not own ploughs, bulls, or bullock carts and as a consequence they are both (i) denied access to extremely high wage work involving own bulls (e.g., ploughing, bullock cart transport of grain, etc.) and (ii) are not freely given land to lease in (unless the they promise to perform tied labour). SP men by contrast tend to own bulls and bullock carts and are more likely to lease in larger amounts of land without tied labour conditions but still borrow on tied labour for credit.

The category 'smallholders' is composed of agrarian PCPs whose primary or secondary occupation is self-employment on own land but who do not hire in significant amounts of paid labour (that is, L+, SP and MP). This group tends to cultivate paddy on tiny plots of wet land and groundnuts and/or millet on dry land. Smallholders do require outside labour at peak periods. However, unlike BP and Cs they tend to rely on the unpaid labour of neighbours – what we label exchange labour- rather than on paid labour. Men in this group tend to be heavily dependent on merchant/commission traders for loans based on 'tied harvest' arrangements (especially SPs and remote region MPs). Their involvement in tied harvest arrangements calls into question their 'independent' PCP status insofar as there are restrictions on their ability to commodify the produce of their farms and ownership of farms can be tenuous (government land). Nevertheless, we will retain the labels 'smallholders' or 'agrarian PCPs' and reflect on the extent of their 'independence' in the course of our analysis. This 'smallholder' group overlaps with the 'labourer' group and thus we find that some men in this group are involved in both tied harvest and tied labour arrangements.

The category 'capitalists' (BPs and C) refers to those who rely heavily on hired-in labour and whose primary or secondary occupation is supervising such labour, or involvement in trade, moneylending or in non-agricultural accumulation. BPs and Cs are much more diversified in agriculture (growing fruit and vegetables) and have much more in the way of productive assets than smallholders, including tractors, power tillers, cars, mopeds, trucks, buildings and stores. This group extends credit/garden plots of wet land to labourers and smallholders on tied labour and tied harvest bases. More detail on these groups will be given in the course of our analysis below.

We classed women in our sample into labour classes even though there is the major methodological problem with identifying women's work on their menfolk's land as 'self-employment' or PCP work and women's supervision of labour on their menfolk's land as 'capitalist' (that is, to assume that women own/control their menfolk's means of production). We felt it was necessary to illustrate important comparisons between men and women's social (class) status and related levels of domestic empowerment. For instance, even when we classified women in this way we found that women lagged behind their husband's class standing, for example, approximately half of men whose class standing was L+ had wives who were pure labourers (L), approximately half of male SPs had wives whose primary occupation was labouring (L+) and two-thirds of MP men who withdrew their labour fully from paid labour altogether had wives who remained heavily involved in wage labouring as their secondary occupation (see Table A4 in Appendix A). Moreover, since 1970, the percentage of men in the sample in the labouring group fell from 74.0 per cent to 55.5 per cent, yet for women the percentage in labouring remained high and much more stable, falling merely from 80.0 per cent to 76.0 per cent (see Table A5 in Appendix A).

THE ROLE OF THE STATE

In much of the neo-liberal literature cited above, greater landownership by labourers, a rise in non-agricultural employment and decline in permanent labour relations is attributed largely to a growth in agricultural productivity. Yet in the state of Andhra Pradesh, the effects of agricultural growth on labour relations cannot be separated analytically from important changes in electoral politics and state interventions. The traditionally Brahmin based Congress Party and the Telugu Desham Party (TDP, representing the interests of Reddy and Kumma castes in AP) have competed to win the electoral allegiance of rural male labourers (that is, from the Scheduled Castes, Scheduled Tribes and Backward Castes) and this has resulted in a profusion of populist state interventions.

Some policies had a direct and fairly strong impact on male labourers' economic position, such as the 1969 policy of opening up formally restricted government wasteland for use by landless labourers. Labouring households in the study villages encroached 1.2 acres on average since 1969, while in Chittoor District as a whole the 66 per cent of workers who encroached land gained an average of 1.9 acres each [*Reddy*, 1987]. Moreover, 33 per cent of men acquired housing sites by seizing 0.03 acres on average thus enabling them to move off their employers land [ibid.]; together with distribution of houses in some areas, this weakened employers' claim on their labour. Another effective scheme was subsidised rice. Implemented in the early 1980s, this provided labouring households with roughly one-quarter of their rice needs each month at the highly subsidised price of Rs 2 per kilogram.[13] This scheme greatly reduced the dependence of labourers on employers for consumption and hence further weakened employers' claim on their labour. Moreover, there was some government related, non-agricultural employment creation focused in the mandal revenue village. This employment included (i) construction of government offices and homes for officials, (ii) road, bridge, dam construction and repair and maintaining government tanks and wells, and (iii) providing services (for example, cleaning, running messages, and other *kuulie* work) in the government hospital, schools, bank, post office, other government offices [*Sender,* 1995]. (By contrast, privately generated non-agricultural employment included private well repairs, crop weighing and some work in rice mills and hotels.)

It is well known that some policies had little *direct* effect, such as the practical non-enforcement of the policy to abolish bonded labour and the land-ceiling act.[14] Moreover, there have been well-documented problems of inadequate coverage and corruption with government schemes, such as Integrated Rural Development Programme (IRDP) which extends subsidised credit to acquire productive assets such as livestock, artisan tools, to dig wells and so on [*Copestake*, 1992].[15] Added to these commonly cited problems are: the fiscal pressure caused by the phenomenal cost of the non-targeted subsidised rice scheme (even capitalists received benefits); the end to land available for encroachment; the lack of non-agricultural employment creation in remote hamlets; the intensified divide between men's and women's asset ownership and corresponding empowerment.

For the most part these problems are the result of an ad hoc, vote-buying populist strategy by the TDP government. These policies did not seriously challenge the economic or political power of the dominant Reddy and Kamma castes. Indeed the policy which arguably had the greatest impact, that allowing waste land to be encroached for cultivation and house sites, was costless except for the assigning of pattas (ownership rights) at the village level ex-post. Nevertheless, the *cumulative* economic effects of public expenditure and public policies on labourers' position was strong, both tightening the male labour market (as men were drawn to work on their own encroached land, IRDP cattle and other assets and non-agricultural work) and weakening the dependence of labourers on employers for consumption loans and residence [*Robinson,* 1988; *Harriss,* 1992]. These antipoverty policies – together with Scheduled Caste reservations in government – had an even stronger impact on the political consciousness of men by encouraging them to emancipate themselves from the economic and symbolic humiliation of bondage and casteism as well as to vote independently from their employers [*Robinson,* 1988].[16] In sum, male agricultural labourers were the chief beneficiaries of AP state policies which – despite problems – diminished employers' control over male workers and enabled men to escape from traditional permanent bonded labour relations and to engage in petty commodity production on encroached land and enter non-agricultural employment. This decline in the availability of male labour power pushed labour costs up.

CHANGES IN CAPITALISTS' ACCUMULATION STRATEGIES

In this section we investigate the successive changes in capitalists' accumulation strategies in response to rising labour costs which resulted in downward pressures on smallholders' and labourers' earnings. We begin by asking the following question: 'Why didn't smallholders lose land (whether encroached or purchased) to capitalist farmers as capitalist farming became more profitable with the introduction of "green revolution" technology?'.

Since independence and up to the late 1960s, Reddy landlords and Muslim and Vaisya merchants were interested in obtaining as much land as possible, mostly in order to extend their political influence and to secure their claim on smallholders' labour rather than merely to acquire productive wealth [*Washbrook,* 1978: 78]. Some were truly involved in 'landgrabbing', the English word used by our respondents to refer to the practice of obtaining smallholders' land by foreclosing on land mortgaged or, more generally, tricking smallholders out of their land [*da Corta*, 1993: Ch.5].[17] Moreover, the labour market was flooded by the combined effects of distress sales, population growth on the partitioning of land and artisan's assets, and as artisans suffered competition from cheap urban manufactured goods. As a consequence, real wages grew slowly in the 1960s; in Andhra Pradesh, they rose 6.6 per cent for men and 11.0 per cent for women over the period 1958/61 to 1968/71 (see Table 2 below). Real wages plunged with each drought (for instance, wages in 1974/5 were 38.7 per cent lower than their wages in 1970/71). This rather gloomy picture is consistent with the findings of writers who carried out fieldwork in the mid-1970s [e.g., *Mies* 1986] or based their analyses on RLE data over the period 1964/5 to 1974/5 [e.g., *Agarwal,* 1984].

However, with the introduction of the new technologies in the early 1970s, the more entrepreneurial landowners – especially from the Reddy caste – were more interested in developing existing land than in acquiring additional land. They converted dry land near wells into wet land with machine powered pumping sets and intensified their use of chemical fertilisers and pesticides. Indeed, while some land was resumed from tenants for cultivation by hired-in labour, much more was *sold* to tenants, especially in the remote hamlets, in order to finance this land development. An earlier study revealed that between 1974 and 1988 'rich' households on average sold more than they purchased (14.7 acres sold versus 10.1 acres purchased).[18] Yet when land value gained through conversions to wet land is weighed in (8.5 acres on average) they are found to be *net gainers* on the land market. An examination of the reasons for land sales revealed that 91.5 per cent of the land sold by the rich was to finance the purchase of more desirable land, to acquire irrigation equipment and purchase other productive assets [*da Corta*, 1993: Chs. 4 and 6].[19] That capitalist farmers were more interested in maximising yield per acre rather than land acreage did not escape the notice of Lenin [1964: 38] who commented: 'owing to the technical peculiarities of agriculture, the process of its intensification frequently leads to a *reduction* in the improved acreage on the farm, and at the same time, expands it as an *economic unit*, increasing its *output*, and making it more and more of a *capitalist* enterprise' [original emphasis]. Large capitalist paddy farms profited massively in the 1970s, with low labour costs, a secure source of mostly permanent labour and a high price for paddy (see also Hazell and Ramasamy [1991: 17] who document a sharp jump in gross margins per hectare of paddy between 1973 and 1976).

However, real wages in AP began to creep up in the late 1970s (18.6 per cent for men and 23.8 per cent for women) and they rose very sharply in the 1980s (54.7 per cent for men and 60.6 per cent for women, see table below).

TABLE 2
REAL WAGES FOR AGRICULTURAL LABOUR IN ANDHRA PRADESH

Years	Average Male Real Real Wage (over 3 years)	Average Female Real Real Wage (over 3 years)	Average Female Wage as a Percentage of Males Wage
1958/59 to 1960/61	1.36	.93	69.1%
1968/69 to 1970/71	1.45 (6.6% rise)	1.05 (11% rise)	72.4%
1978/79 to 1980/81	1.72 (18.6% rise)	1.30 (23.8% rise)	75.6%
1988/89 to 1990/91	2.66 (54.7% rise)	1.9 (60.6% rise)	71.4%

Source: Calculated from S.S. Reddy [1991] – growth rates are calculated from his table of money wages deflated by the consumer price index for agricultural labourers in Andhra Pradesh.

The use of machine powered pumping sets actually reduced capitalists' requirements for permanently attached male labour to operate traditional lift irrigation. For the typical large farm employer these requirements fell from 25 traditional permanent bonded labourers in 1958 to 10 in 1973 and to 1 in 1995. However, this fall in demand for male labour was offset partly by increased demand for male labour with the double cropping of HYV paddy and further increase in area under paddy resulting from the use of irrigation pumps. Moreover, labour costs rose as some male labourers withdrew their labour to cultivate encroached government land, as off-farm employment opportunities increased and as employers' control of traditional permanent bonded labour waned. The competition for hired labour increased further with new entrants into capitalist farming from a few entrepreneurial MPs (who purchased land sold in the remote hamlets by Cs in the central region) becoming capitalist farmers in their own right.

Other input costs also rose (especially fertiliser costs and costs associated with the less dependable supply of ground water) and real paddy prices began to fall as a result of the vast rise in agricultural productivity. By the mid-1980s these factors contributed to a 'cost prices squeeze' which has been clearly documented in other studies of South Indian agriculture [*Harriss*, 1992; *Hazell and Ramasamy*, 1991: 21–2, 153; *Walker and Ryan*, 1990: 79; *Olsen*, 1991: 183]. Groundnut prices actually grew in the late 1970s and 1980s [*Olsen*, 1991; *Hazell and Ramasamy*, 1991: 153]. This growth encouraged some capitalist paddy farmers to cultivate groundnuts on land formerly used to grow paddy but which had suffered from unreliable water supplies (due to overuse of groundwater). Nevertheless, rising labour costs still cut deeply into the profits of those capitalist farms relying fully on hired labour – whether groundnut or paddy.

In response to rising labour costs capitalists once again altered their accumulation strategies by (i) diversifying out of paddy/groundnut farming, (ii) commission trading based on 'tied harvest' arrangements and (iii) capitalist farming based on 'tied labour' arrangements. We focus on these latter two responses.

Some wealthy capitalists moved into agricultural pursuits requiring more intensive application of capital (for example, sericulture, fruit and vegetables, poultry and pig farms). Others diversified out of agriculture and into food processing (for example, rice milling, rice flour mills, groundnut processing), construction (obtaining government and semi-government road and bridge construction contracts), residential and commercial building (locally and in nearby towns), transport (for example, bussing, trucking) and entertainment (for example, video cinemas). Most also invested in the education of sons, to train them for salaried positions in government and private banking/industry. This off-farm investment – together with public expenditure in rural areas – contributed to off-farm employment opportunities for labourers living in the central region. These capitalist landowners generally either sold land in order to invest in these areas or leased out their land.

COMMISSION TRADING AND TIED HARVEST ARRANGEMENTS

Capitalists also reacted to diminishing returns in agriculture by moving into commission trading, or doing so on a much larger scale. This involved buying up paddy and groundnuts at harvest, storing them and then reselling them later at a higher price to urban merchants. With the introduction of formal bank credit in 1973, Vaisya merchant moneylenders were forced to push down the interest rates that they charged on loans to larger farmers. Interest rates fell from between 36 per cent to 60 per cent per year in 1970 to 24 per cent in 1995. Moreover, the 1973 land-ceiling act discouraged flagrant 'land grabbing' from smallholders through foreclosures. Yet with the new surpluses of HYV paddy and groundnut in the 1970s and rising prices of groundnut in the 1980s, speculating on price rises became lucrative.

In order to secure reliable and cheap supplies of groundnut and paddy at harvest (a time when competition among traders for buying up smallholders' harvests is at its peak) merchants used their existing power in the credit and land rental markets to gain greater control in the commodities market through 'tied harvest' arrangements. Under such arrangements, merchants advanced cash loans to smallholders for consumption and working capital costs (especially for fertilisers) and/or leased out a garden plot (¼ acre of wet land) on a normal 50/50 share basis. In return borrowers must promise to repay *in kind* at harvest at a price determined by the lender. Smallholders feel compelled to agree to tied harvest conditions because of their continued need for access to *immediate* loans, often mid-season with none of the delay associated with formal bank or co-operative society procedures. Indeed, approximately one-quarter of SPs and MPs also took out bank loans, yet they still agree to tie their harvests for loans for additional working capital needs, consumption during the lean season, medical care and alcohol consumption. We found that the percentage of the population of smallholders engaged in tied harvest arrangements has *increased* since 1970, rising from 61.3 per cent to 82.8 per cent (see Table 3 below). Moreover the absolute number of smallholders engaged in tied harvest contracts has also increased, rising 26.3 per cent.

TABLE 3
INCIDENCE OF TIED HARVEST* ARRANGEMENTS AMONG LABOUR
CLASSES IN 1970 AND 1995

	1970	1995
L+	66.7%	87.5%
SP	53.8%	91.7%
MP	66.6%	66.7%
% of Total L+, SP, MP		
Population	61.3%	82.8%

* Through loans, leased land or both. By labour class of male, except for three cases in 1995 where the head is a woman.

By demanding that smallholders pledge their harvests, local commission agents could successfully counter threats to their established oligopolistic position from new local entrants to this trade and from larger, non-local merchants who, because of their size, could offer better prices to smallholders.[20] As an example, one *Vaisya* merchant alone controlled 27.3 per cent of *all* loans extended in the remote region in 1988/9 (this includes loans from other moneylenders, bank loans and loans from friends). Moreover, commission trading based on tied harvests secured cheaper supplies. Smallholders lost out from tying their harvests (and lenders gained) in several ways: while the explicit interest rate of Rs 2 per month is less than the rates prevailing in 1970, it is still Rs 1 above formal rates in 1995, the price paid for harvests is Rs 10 to Rs 30 per bag below the going rate (that is, what they could get by freely selling to another merchant or what the same commission trader pays to non-tied farmers) and smallholders are forced to sell their product to the lender in a depressed post-harvest market and forgo their right to store the product and sell it when prices improve [*Athreya et. al.*, 1990].[21]

As labour costs rose, capitalists took advantage of smallholder production through tied harvest arrangements, finding it more profitable to appropriate surpluses indirectly through exchange relations (e.g., marketing produce and credit) than through production relations based on hired-in 'free' labour. In this way capitalists could take advantage of the nature of smallholders – who desperately strive to remain independent from erstwhile traditional bonded labour employers – to work harder on their own land for lower returns (compared to hired in workers) and to underconsume in order to retain land [*Kautsky*, 1988: 110–20; *Ellis*, 1988: 52; *Patnaik*, 1979: 391, 405–6; *Alavi and Shanin*, 1988]. Under these circumstances the question becomes just whose work is being expended when commission traders, through tied harvest arrangements, are exploiting these smallholders? As we shall see below, work intensity on own land, unwaged reproductive work and wage employment falls disproportionately on the female members in smallholder families and thus women can be said to subsidise men's tied smallholder production.

It has been argued that the green revolution encouraged a rise in land owned by the landless, hence stimulating what amounts to a peasantisation of the landless (or in our area, a repeasantization of those who lost their land before the 1970s). Can smallholders in our villages be conceptualised as 'independent' cultivators? How far have they benefited from gaining land? It has been argued that tied harvest relations may be best characterised as disguised production relations, where the loan is a wage advance and covers production costs and where the payment received by the smallholder after deductions for explicit and implicit interest is equal to his/her necessary labour time [*Banaji,* 1977; *Alavi,* 1987]. Under this argument , tied harvest smallholders (including MPs in our remote region) would be considered to be 'disguised labourers', 'wage labour equivalents', or 'labourers who cultivate' rather than 'cultivators who labour'. On the other hand, Harriss [1982] claims that smallholders dependent on loans still *own* their own land and merchant moneylenders do not have full control over the management of smallholders' farms.

With respect to smallholders in our villages, we believe the answer lies somewhere in between. There is strong evidence that smallholders are 'not fully independent'. Their control of land is somewhat tenuous: encroached wasteland is legally owned only if the person has a *patta* and owners cannot sell the land for cash or exchange it and so it cannot be used as collateral on loans. Moreover, encroached reserved land is held illegally. Smallholder cultivation is contingent on moneylender's capital and thus the smallholder must cultivate the crop that the lender requires for his trade.

Smallholders are also involved in repeat tied harvest arrangements which dilute their independence as self-employed cultivators insofar as they are unable to commodify their harvest: most of smallholders' harvests (an average of 90 per cent of their groundnut crop and 70 per cent of their paddy crop) is rendered in kind immediately after harvest to commission traders as repayment for loans taken out earlier in the season. This reduces potential income from the free sale of the harvest and which could be conceptualised as a form of indirect surplus value accumulation by capitalists (that is, labour time). (Even if the whole SE element among L+, SP and MP smallholders is not conceptualised as 'labour time', involvement in tied harvest arrangements depresses the 'SE' element to some extent and raises the 'L' element, that is, the time embedded in the earnings lost to commission agents through interest and price fixing.)

Equally important is the fact that male smallholders cannot survive without significant amounts of wage labour (while SP men are significantly involved in labouring, it is the primary occupation of female family members). Taken together such factors raise the 'L' portion in smallholders' labour time, and hence tied SPs, in particular could be conceptualised as labourers who cultivate rather than cultivators who labour.[22] It is very difficult for tied smallholders to accumulate the surplus necessary to emancipate themselves from such relations through cultivation alone.

Nevertheless, it is still important to distinguish 'labourers with land' from landless labourers for two reasons. First, tied smallholders who own land have the *potential* of financing working capital needs from non-agricultural work (together with women's wage earnings) enabling them to escape tied harvest relations (as MPs in our central region have escaped). Secondly, compared to landless labourers, labourers who have gained encroached land have significantly greater bargaining power *vis-à-vis* employers of wage labour because owning land pushes up the reservation wage. *In sum, some smallholding men are now freer to commodify their labour but not to commodify their crops.*

CAPITALIST FARMING AND TIED LABOUR ARRANGEMENTS

In response to rising labour costs, those agrarian capitalists who remained in farming invested in machinery to replace expensive, labour intensive male work, such as irrigation and ploughing. They also used non-permanent attached (henceforth 'tied') labour arrangements where they lend cash and/or lease out wet land to labourers in return for labour service. These tied labour arrangements were enforced in order to secure cheaper male labour during peak periods of demand (as they were withdrawing from wage labour at a faster rate than women) and gain indirect access to the relatively cheaper, largely unfree, female labour of the attached male for the remainder of the season (see below).

Under 'tied labour through credit' arrangements labourers, in return for loans, are obliged to report to the lender's farm first, before other employers, and to work off the loan based on a prearranged 'tied' wage. The arrangement lasts as long as it takes for the labourer to pay off the loan. Often the amounts borrowed are small (that is, Rs 200–500) and are paid back within 10 and 15 days, usually less than one month. Nevertheless, this arrangement is frequently 'renewed' as labourers require more credit. Sometimes the amounts borrowed are large (for example, 500–2000 rupees), to meet lumpy expenditures associated with medical costs or ceremonial expenses, and here the arrangement is much longer term.

'Tied labour through lease' is a seasonal arrangement where an employer leases out about one quarter of an acre of wet land to a male labourer on a 50/50 share contract. Labourers intensely desire leased in garden land in order to cultivate paddy to cover family consumption needs during the lean season. In return for the 'privilege' of leasing in this small amount of land male labourers must agree to plough the lender's land (usually using the lender's bulls) at a pre-agreed wage or for free, depending on the terms set by the individual employer. The borrower must also water the lender's land daily for free. L and L+ men are usually denied the right to lease in land without ties because they do not own bulls and are otherwise considered too poor to cultivate the land. Another way employers tie labour for ploughing is by allowing a male labourer the 'privilege' of grazing their cattle on a 'pale' basis. Under this arrangement the labourer grazes the employers cattle for free, and, if the cow bears a calf, the labourer can keep it as payment. During the 'pale' period, labourers are obliged to plough employers' land free of charge.

In addition to these specific obligations, men borrowing on tied labour through lease, 'pale', and large loans, together with their families, are often *expected* to fulfil other demands, such as to perform unpaid, 'small works' when required (for example, cleaning his cattle shed, domestic work, chopping wood, delivering messages, etc.), and to report to the lender's farm first for other casual fieldwork throughout the season (for example, weeding, assisting transplantation, harvesting, etc.) and to accept the low wage offered by the lender. Often the tied labour through leasing land or cattle arrangements are combined with loans (for food and farm inputs) thereby intensifying the landlord's claim on the labour of the tenant cum borrower's family.

Labourers feel compelled to accept these oppressive tied labour conditions because of their pressing need to cover consumption costs, especially during the lean season, to cover medical costs (which are increasing with the growing unreliability of government health care provision), to meet expensive ceremonial costs and due to greater alcohol consumption.

It is sometimes assumed that tied arrangements are made by capitalists primarily in order to *secure* labour, not to *reduce* labour costs (for example, that 'tied labour through credit' is simply a wage advance). But in the villages we studied, (i) the actual wages received under these arrangements (ii) the possible contract gang and non-agricultural wages forfeited and (iii) the unpaid work performed, indicate that capitalists use such arrangements not merely to secure labour at peak periods but also in order to reduce labour costs of men and their families [*Brass*, 1990: 40-41and note 21; 59; *Banaji*, 1992). *Wages received under tied labour contracts were found to be universally lower than the 'going' market daily wage rates and substantially below the wages labourers could get if they were free to perform contract gang or non-agricultural work* (see Tables 6, 7, 8, 9 in Appendix 1). For instance, in the central region, in exclusively male work (without own bulls) for paddy cultivation, daily wages average 57.1 per cent higher than tied work, contract gang wages average 85.7 per cent higher, non-agricultural daily wages average 100 per cent higher, and non-agricultural contract wages average 152.6 per cent higher.

Tied labourers through credit are offered a pre-arranged daily wage rate used to calculate number of days spent working off the loan; hence the labourer does not receive a wage at the end of the day but rather a loan in advance. By contrast, under tied lease, labourers and their family are expected to report to the lender's farm first for other casual work throughout the season and to get paid a market wage at the end of the day. In practice, however, wages are low compared to payment offered by nearby employers, and labourers consider these lower wages 'tied' even if such wages do not go toward repayment of loans.

Not only are wages under tied arrangements low, but the unpaid work of tied labour through lease arrangements is time consuming, cutting down the period when labourers can otherwise be employed for a wage. For instance, non-tied labourers would ordinarily be paid 2 bags of paddy (Rs 800) per season for watering large farmers' fields. And while it is assumed that this work takes only one-and-a-half hours each morning, in practice it usually takes a full morning as labourers need to wait for electricity to be supplied. As a result, labourers usually forfeit a full days wage work elsewhere. It is generally agreed that labourers receive a wage from employers to whom they are tied if the 'small works' last more than half a day. Thus employers try to keep 'small works' down to half a day or less to avoid paying wages, yet these part days add up to significant wage forfeitures for labourers. For instance, by working two hours a morning cleaning her employer's cattle shed, a woman actually works 30 eight hour days in each season, which, when multiplied by the lowest daily wage for women in agricultural work (Rs 15), means that she forfeits at least Rs 450 per season as a consequence of her husband's tied labour agreement.

In this article, we distinguish between traditional, permanent bonded labour and modern non-permanent tied labour. Traditional permanent bonded labourers – labelled 'Jeethagallu' by respondents (Telugu for 'salary') – ordinarily entered into this agreement in order to obtain a big loan for ceremonies or to meet a crisis such as famine. These labourers agreed to work every day, from dawn to dusk, for a fixed period and a fixed payment. In 1970 this consisted of three bags of paddy, two pairs of clothes and pickles (women, usually domestic servants, received two bags). In general, these traditional permanent attached labour relations have features similar to the features of traditional debt bondage identified by others [e.g., *Breman*, 1985; *Rao*, 1997]: they were enforced by the traditional authority of Brahmins and Reddis and by frequent resort to physical force; were several years long, sometimes a lifetime;[23] debt repayment was transmissible to other family members, and agreements were informal and based on expectations of complete economic, social and political loyalty. Most permanent bonded labourers slept on the veranda of the employer's house and their families' homes were situated on the employer's land, which further increased employers claim on the labour of the bonded labourers' family.

By contrast, modern, non-permanent tied labour arrangements are shorter in duration, enforced much less by resort to violence and by the traditional authority of Reddis and Brahmins, and are relatively more formally specified (though open to much contestation over terms). Moreover, most labourers moved off their employers' land. Yet modern non-permanent relations remain based on expectations of loyalty of the family of the attached labour (such as performing unpaid work and reporting first to the lender's fields; see below).

In 1995, almost all capitalist farmers in the central region used tied labour through lease in order to secure one or two male labourers in order to perform the jobs that much larger numbers of traditional permanent labourers used to perform in 1970 (especially unmechanised, labour intensive lift irrigation and ploughing). This change is reflected in the table below which shows that while the percentage of the male population involved in traditional bonded labouring fell from 24.3 per cent to 0 per cent since 1970, the percentage of the male labouring population involved in tied lease actually *increased* from 32.4 per cent to 40.0 per cent.

TABLE 4
PERCENTAGE OF MALE LABOURING POPULATION INVOLVED
IN DIFFERENT LABOUR TIES IN 1970 AND 1995

	1970	1995
Traditional Permanent	24.3%	0%
Tied Through Lease	32.4%	40.0%
Tied by Loans	21.6%	12.0%
Tied by Influence*	5.4%	4.0%
No Ties	16.2%	44.0%
TOTAL	99.9%	100.0%

*Tied labour relations (without any debt or lease) to employers who happen to be very influential in village administration, especially the former 'Munsif' and 'Karanam'.

DECLINE IN UNFREEDOM?

Empirical observations of the decline in traditional permanent debt bondage across India are often associated with a decline in unfreedom in India because modern attachments appear to be free from extra-economic coercion and shorter in duration [e.g., *Breman*, 1985; *Jodhka*, 1995]. In the Indian literature, unfreedom is conventionally defined as the involuntary involvement of a worker in an attached labour arrangement and retention within an employment relation through extra–economic enforcement, which includes politico-juridical coercion, physical force, traditional authority of dominant castes, ideology of clientelism and custom [*Breman*, 1993: 1985; *Jodhka*, 1995; *Rao*, 1997] and/or permanent attachments rather than of seasonal duration [e.g. *Breman*, 1996; *Jodhka*, 1995].

Yet other writers subscribe to a less restrictive definition of unfreedom, that is, that inability to *exit* from a relationship is sufficient for a relation to be unfree [*Brass*, 1993; *Thorner and Thorner*, 1962].[24] For instance, labourers can 'voluntarily' enter agreements due to economic constraints, such as famine or poverty. Moreover, extra-economic enforcement of unfree relations does not need to be premised on the presence of politico-juridical sanctions or on physical force, but can operate through ideological pressure via kinship networks. The latter can operate independently of the law (e.g. *Brass*, personal communication).[25] Finally, it is argued that unfreedom is related to constraints on the ability to enter the free labour market rather than to duration, and hence seasonal attachments could be unfree [*Brass*, 1995: 1997] especially as labourers are left to fend for themselves during the unemployed slack season [*Rao*, 1997].

It is clear that even according to the conventional definition of unfreedom that the traditional, permanent bonded labour arrangements described above were unfree with the possible one exception that entry into such relations were often initiated by economic deprivation rather than by extra-economic coercion. However, defining modern tied labour relations as free or unfree is more difficult. There are features of these relations which, according the conventional view, suggest that they are not unfree. First, these arrangements are non-permanent in duration. Moreover, while men agree to perform ploughing and watering obligations, some are refusing to perform those informal obligations of tied relations which would otherwise stretch the duration of the agreement, such as unpaid half day work and reporting to the lender's farm first for other casual wage work throughout the season. Secondly, there is less use of physical force and caste authority deployed to enforce these relations.

On the other hand, it might be useful to invert the question and ask: how *far are attached men free?* There is evidence that suggests that men involved in tied labour for lease, 'pale' or big loans are not entirely free. First, regardless of duration, men involved in these tied relations surrender their right to commodify their labour, that is, to re-enter the labour market and obtain higher wages (such as during the peak season). Indeed, for some writers the right to choose one's employer is the most important element of freedom [*Lucassen*, 1993].[26] As a consequence of their inability to choose employers, labourers are found to obtain substantially lower wages. Thus, at the very least, the labour market is not the free one founded on competitive wages as assumed by Neo-liberal writers. Secondly, entry is involuntary insofar as it is subsistence-driven: indeed there is nothing voluntary about starvation or death of one's child due to inadequate medical provision. Moreover, that a reason for entry into attachments is non-economic bears little relation to the level of oppression suffered within the relation. Thirdly, while there is less extra economic coercion (violence, caste pressure, etc.) enforcing such relations, the wage differential between tied and free wages is so wide that it suggests the possible presence of additional ideological pressures which we need to examine through future field research.

In sum, in response to the question 'is unfreedom declining?' Table 4 shows some evidence of a decline in male unfreedom since 1970, with a clear decline in traditional permanent bonded relations; while tied through lease increased, overall the percentage of male labourers who are free rose from 16.2 per cent to 44.0 per cent, reflecting greater access to encroached land, to off farm employment and to state food and other subsidies; there has also been a major fall in the percentage of men involved in labouring altogether (by 32.4 per cent) as men have acquired land or non-farm assets. In short, as labourers acquired land they exchanged their labour ties to employers for harvest ties to commission agents (tied harvest male smallholders increased in both absolute and proportional terms).

On the other hand, while those 56.0 per cent of male labourers who remain in tied labouring are not unfree, neither do they appear to be 'wholly free'. Most importantly, the question 'has unfreedom declined?' cannot be answered without reference to the freedom/unfreedom of female labour who are found both to remain in agricultural labouring since 1970 and to perform more tied work than men throughout the year.

FEMALE LABOUR RELATIONS AND DOMESTIC RELATIONS

The feminisation of the agricultural wage labour force in India is, to some extent, reflected in all India census data. Over the period 1961–81 the percentage of female main workers classified as agricultural labourers doubled from 23.9 per cent to 46.3 per cent (with a corresponding fall in female workers in cultivation and in household industry). The equivalent figure for men increased more slowly from 13.4 per cent to 19.7 per cent. From 1981 to 1991, this figure for women stabilised at approximately 44.9 per cent and for men at 21.1 per cent. Census authors attribute this stability to the greater netting in of female cultivators, as enumerators were specially instructed to be more alert to unpaid female labourers [*Government of India*, 1991]. Despite these special instructions (and general tendency to under-represent female workers[27]) the percentage of women workers classified as agricultural labourers in 1991 is *double* the corresponding figure for men, or in broad terms *nearly half of women workers are agricultural labourers compared to only a quarter of male workers.*[28]

In some green revolution areas of North India a rise in women's involvement in agricultural wage employment is noted (see, for instance,

Chaudhry [1994: 174–5]). Yet the feminisation of agricultural wage employment is strongest in southern states, where women's participation in paid labour is traditionally higher. Duvvury's [1989] district wise data show that over the period 1961–81 there was a sharp rise in the number of districts *where female labourers are equal to or outnumber male labourers* (see Maps 1 and 2). The 1991 census reports that in most southern states about 50 per cent of agricultural labourers are women (e.g., in Andhra Pradesh, 51.7 per cent Maharashtra, 53.6 per cent, Karnataka, 50.4 per cent, Tamil Nadu, 47.8 per cent; see Government of India [1991]). For the following reasons, we believe that these figures underestimate the degree to which women dominate agricultural wage labouring in parts of southern India. First, there is a general tendency to under represent those female labourers who live in medium-sized landholding families but who are heavily involved in agricultural labouring (see Table A4 in Appendix A). We found that 62.9 per cent of those who had agricultural wage labouring as their primary occupation were women, a rise from 55.1 per cent in 1970. Secondly, classification by principal occupation obscures actual annual days worked. We found that those women performing agricultural labour worked more days annually than men, that is, working not merely at seasonal peaks (as was the norm for women) but on a continual basis. Indeed, we found that, on average, women perform 2.7 times as much outside agricultural labour as men (this includes paid field and cattle grazing and unpaid field exchange labour). If we exclude unpaid exchange labour, then women perform 2.5 times as much paid agricultural labour as men (see note to Table 5).

Why has women's involvement in wage labouring increased? One way to approach this question is to examine changes in men's and women's labour use on capitalist farms. Our survey data reveal that over the last 25 years, women's share of total agricultural wage employment has risen rather dramatically, superseding men's share in both paddy and groundnut. Women's share of the wage labour days needed to cultivate an acre crop of paddy rose from approximately 44.5 per cent to 56.9 per cent and in groundnut rose from 42.5 per cent to 60.8 per cent (see Table 6). Moreover, over this period the area under paddy and groundnut rose, largely the result of the increase in cultivable area through the extension of irrigation, HYVs and by developing wasteland.

In order to examine the reasons for women's rising share of wage employment since 1970, we separated out the changes associated with HYVs and bio-chemical inputs, labour saving machinery and non-technical reasons on work culturally regarded as exclusively male (EM), exclusively female (EF) and joint (J), that is, work ordinarily performed by both men and women. It is commonly assumed that 'feminisation' is the result of the switch from traditional crops to HYVs, because the latter require more

MAP 1
DISTRICTS WITH AS MANY OR MORE FEMALE AGRICULTURAL LABOURERS
AS MALE AGRICULTURAL LABOURERS, 1961

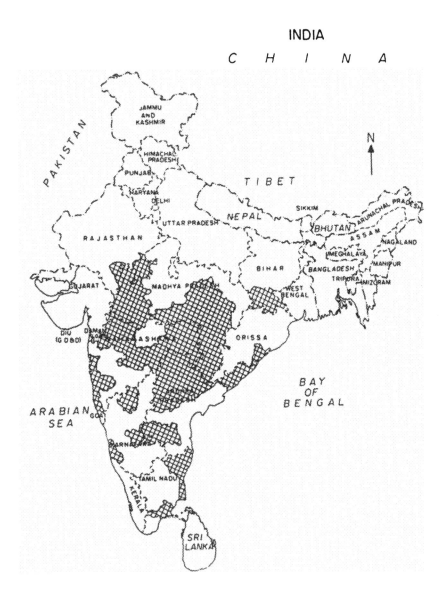

Source: Duvvury [1989: 104–5].

MAP 2
MAP OF DISTRICTS WITH AS MANY OR MORE FEMALE AGRICULTURAL
LABOURERS AS MALE AGRICULTURAL LABOURERS, 1981

Source: Duvvury [1989: 104–5].

TABLE 5

AVERAGE NON-DOMESTIC MINUTES SPENT ON DIFFERENT ACTIVITIES IN ONE
DAY AMONG MALE AND FEMALE LABOURERS (L, L+, SP)

Activity	Male	Female
Paid Agricultural Field Work and Exchange Labour	51.0 (14.7%)	213.4 (58.9%)
Paid Cattle Grazing	30.0 (8.7%)	2.5 (0.7%)
Non-Agricultural Wage Work	37.9 (11.0%)	10.4 (2.9%)
Tenancy	47.5 (13.8%)	19.6 (5.4%)
Work on Own Farm	71.3 (20.6%)	71.6 (19.7%)
Own Cattle (Grazing, Collecting Fodder, Milking)	67.3 (19.5%)	35.3 (9.7%)
Non-agricultural Self-Employed Work	40.3 (11.7%)	9.8 (2.7%)
Total work (minus unwaged reproductive work)	345.3 (100.0%)	362.6 (100.0%)

Note: An average over three days in each season, including days unemployed, for each member
in the sample. This table shows that the extent of women's involvement in agricultural
wage labour in 1995 is substantially higher than our per acre figures for paddy and
groundnut suggest (see Table 6). Besides being more rigorously collected, these labour use
data are much more inclusive. First, they also comprise all field work done on other crops,
including tomato (where female participation is higher than on paddy) and contract gang
work (where female participation higher than on daily wage work). In cash crops and
contract work the gender division of labour is less strict, women are able to perform what
is ordinarily considered exclusively male work on capitalist paddy farms. Second, we
included labour on reciprocal labour agreements among small farmers where women's
participation is much higher than men's. We included this under the category paid work
because villagers tended to consider it inferior 'outside work' and men tended to delegate
this work to women in their families in the same fashion that they delegated low wage
work. This work accounts for roughly 24.5 minutes or 11.5% of women's paid work and
3.5 minutes or 6.8% of men's paid work.

labour on female operations than on male tasks. Yet we found that the effect
of the switch from traditional to HYV crops on exclusively female
operations had a negligible effect on feminisation (see appendix 2). By
contrast, labour saving technology (especially pumpsets but also power
tillers and tractors) had a fairly substantial effect on reducing male working
days, accounting for 73.9 per cent of the days men lost in paddy cultivation
and about 16.5 per cent of the days men lost in groundnut cultivation. Yet

TABLE 6

APPROXIMATE NUMBER OF MALE & FEMALE WORK DAYS REQUIRED FOR CULTIVATION OF ONE ACRE OF PADDY AND OF GROUNDNUT IN BOTH PAID WORK AND FAMILY LABOUR IN 1970 AND 1995

	CROP	1970			1995			Abs. Ch. in Days	Ch. in Male Days	Ch. in Female Days	Ch. Due to Mech	Ch. Due to HYVs
		M	F	TOT	M	F	TOT					
Paid Work	Paddy	85 55.6%	68 44.5%	153	62 43.1%	82 56.9%	144	–9	–23	+14	–17	+8
	Ground nut	36.8 57.5%	27.2 45.2%	64	24.7 39.2%	38.3 60.8%	63	–1	–12.1	+11.1	–2	+1
Family Labour	Paddy 56.6%	79.2	60.8 42.4%	140	59.4 46.0%	69.6 54.0%	129	–11	–19.8	+8.8	–14	+3
	Ground nut	35 58.3%	25 41.7%	60		29.75 50.4%	59	–1	–5.75	+4.75	0	–1

by far the most significant impact on the women's share has been through non-technical, unexplained changes in the balance of male and female labour in *joint work* which accounts for 100 per cent of the working days women gained in paddy, 100 per cent of the days women gained in groundnut; 26.1 per cent of the days men lost in paddy, and 75.2 per cent of the days men lost in groundnut. Indeed, the gender division of labour in paid work – often regarded to be immutable in south Asia – changed over the period in question, with some exclusively male work becoming 'joint' (for example, as women move into threshing) and some formerly 'joint' work becoming exclusively female (for example, seed preparation).[29]

Why is such joint work becoming feminised? To some extent men are deterred from accepting offers of joint, daily wage work because the wages are so much lower compared to exclusively male work in agriculture (which, by involving the use of draught animals or machines, is seen as more productive and more highly valued) and contract gang work (where work is more intensive and free from labour ties). In the central region, compared to joint daily wage work, exclusively male work with bulls averages 141.8 per cent higher, exclusively male work without own bulls averages 27.3 per cent higher and contract gang joint work is 31.1 per cent higher. Indeed, because wage differences between these forms of work and joint work are so large, the latter is increasingly being seen as 'women's work'. In joint work, women's wages are just 15.3 per cent lower than men's wages.

TABLE 7
DAILY WAGES IN THE CENTRAL REGION (AVERAGED ACROSS
PADDY AND GROUNDNUT)

	Male Wages	Female Wages
Exclusively male work with bulls	60.6	–
Exclusively male work without bulls	27.5	–
Joint	21.6	18.3
Exclusively Female	–	16.1

Men are also deterred from accepting joint work in agriculture altogether because wages in off- farm work are so much higher – joint work wages for men off-farm average 27.3 per cent higher than joint work in agriculture and exclusively male work (without bulls) averages 62.0 per cent higher. Wages off-farm are higher partly because they are much freer of the partial ties characteristic of daily wage work in agriculture (see below).

It is often suggested that with the growth of the non-agricultural economy, men are moving into off-farm employment leaving women the opportunity to take on more labouring and self-employed work in agriculture [*Bennett,* 1992]. Some evidence for this view is found in 1991 Indian census data which shows that 78.5 per cent of the increase in female workers since 1981 were either agricultural labourers or cultivators compared to a 49.2 per cent rise among men [*Government of India,* 1991]. Moreover, evidence from our survey villages also seems to support the view that women are working more in agriculture, both as wage labourers and on the 'family' farm. Since 1970, women's share of the average annual number of working days required to cultivate an acre of paddy on family farms rose slightly, from 42.4 per cent to 54.0 per cent and from 41.7 per cent to 50.4 per cent on groundnut farms (see Table 6). We found that women are increasingly involved in joint work operations on the 'family' farm, despite the reduction in exclusively male work attributable to labour saving machines and the rise in women's paid agricultural work (see Appendix C). This evidence gives some weight to the view that women are working more in agriculture in general – paid work and work on 'family' farms – while men work more elsewhere.

While our data from capitalist farms give us a rough indicator of the direction and magnitude of changes in labour use on paddy and groundnut farms, to obtain a more precise measure of the balance of agricultural work and non-agricultural work among men and women we examined our time allocation data for the year 1994/5. The data indicate that women spend a total of 5.6 per cent of their time on non-agricultural work whereas men spend 22.7 per cent (see Table 5 above). In 1991 in Andhra Pradesh 10.7 per cent of women workers were involved in non-agricultural work compared to 20.1 per cent of male workers [*Government of India,* 1991]. Indeed, according to census data the percentage of women involved in agriculture as opposed to non-agriculture actually rose slightly since 1961, from 81.7 per cent to 87.8 per cent [*Government of Andhra Pradesh,* 1991: 5, based on census data in relevant years].

Men's movement into non-farm work is certainly part of the explanation for women's rising share of agricultural wage employment, as off-farm opportunities increase and off-farm wages rise. Because most available non-farm work is generated by public investment, such opportunities are highly concentrated in semi-urban villages (where it comprises an average of 21.5 per cent of men's non-unwaged reproductive time) and are relatively insignificant in the poorer, remote villages (5.4 per cent). And in the region as a whole, the growth of off-farm work has not expanded sufficiently to account fully for the feminisation of agricultural wage work (see Table 5 above).

The tendency to focus on the agricultural/non-agricultural distinction as an explanation for feminisation of the agricultural labour force can obscure an equally important distinction between self-employment and hired labour: 62.4 per cent of women's time is spent on wage work (both agriculture and non-agriculture) and 51.8 per cent of men's work is devoted to self-employed work on land, livestock and non-agricultural means of production (see Table 8). This gender divide extends to offspring of working age: unmarried daughters are delegated agricultural wage work and exchange labour and sons are groomed to avoid paid agricultural waged work, if possible, and to work instead on own assets, tenanted land and off-farm.

TABLE 8
AVERAGE PERCENTAGE OF NON-DOMESTIC TIME SPENT ON WAGE WORK,
TENANCY AND PCP WORK IN ONE DAY AMONG MALE FEMALE
LABOURERS (L, L+, SP)

Activity	Male	Female
Wage Work	34.4%	62.4%
Tenancy	13.8%	5.4%
PCP Work	51.8%	32.2%

Note: An average over three days in each season, including days unemployed, for each member in the sample.

As male labourers are moving into petty commodity production, women are replacing them as agricultural wage labour. Consequently, the gender divide corresponds, to some extent, to a class division between a non-propertied/ waged workforce composed of women (and largely unfree, see below) and self-employed men (though largely tied to commission agents). This gender based class division is also found in state-wide census figures for Andhra Pradesh in 1991, which show that 63.7 per cent of female rural workers are agricultural labourers compared to only 37.3 per cent of men; the bulk of male workers are to be found in cultivation (39.1 per cent) and off-farm work (20.1 per cent), which includes wage and self-employed work (Government of India [1991]; see also Table 10 in Appendix 1).

Over the past 25 years, women have remained in wage employment as men in their families have withdrawn their labour from agricultural employment in order to work on their own assets largely acquired as a result of a policy allowing landless to encroach waste land together with government subsidised credit for assets (such as livestock) and non-agricultural employment creation. In 1970, 80.0 per cent of women in our sample had performed wage labouring as their primary or secondary occupation, falling just to 76.0 per cent in 1995. Yet the decline for men was much steeper, from 74.0 per cent to 50.5 per cent as they moved into self-employment. Our study of individual mobility among the labour rankings (defined above: i.e. L, L+, SP etc.) revealed that women's mobility lagged behind men's, with 48.9 per cent of men experiencing upward mobility as opposed to only 28.0 per cent of women. As men acquired land or other non-agricultural productive assets they stopped working for a wage, but they still depended on their wives to perform wage labour for the survival of the family. Moreover, women experienced more downward mobility than men did (18 per cent of women versus merely 8.8 per cent of men). Women's downward mobility occurred as menfolk lost family assets and women were forced to work. Most of female downward mobility occurred among women who became heads of their families through the death or incapacitation of the male head, or through separation and divorce. Many of these women lost their land through appropriation by their husband's brothers – who had every incentive to acquire this land in order to reconstitute their father's holding – or through distress mortgages and sales. We found that nearly half of the cases of *household* downward mobility since our 1988/9 study were the result of the loss of the male head.

GENDER AND CLASS STRUGGLE

Male labourers' movement out of joint daily wage labour also has its basis in their fierce struggle conducted against higher caste employers for freedom from tied labour work obligations, for improved wages and for improved status. Among the obligations contested by men are low/unpaid ploughing/irrigation tasks, beck-and-call arrangements, and the denial of their right to seek better paid work elsewhere, in the process either shirking or refusing work. Moreover, daily wages in agricultural work under erstwhile employers of traditional, permanent bonded labour also tend to be low. Indeed, part of the reason joint daily wages are so low relative to other work is because of the 'partial tying' involved in much daily wage work (which is relatively absent in contract and off-farm work).

We found that not only 31.3 per cent of male labourers in our sample refused offers of agricultural wage work regularly, but also that each had been a traditional bonded labourer who had only recently come out of such arrangements. Our male respondents explained that they refuse offers of agricultural wage work in an attempt to express their contempt for employers who attempt to impose on them the same onerous conditions associated with traditional bondage, such as low/unpaid wages, insults and physical abuse while working the fields, etc. Not working for Reddy caste employers is indeed the ambition many parents have for their male children, and many young men are avoiding agricultural wage work altogether. Thus agricultural daily wage work supervised by Reddy employers is considered to be much more demeaning than other forms of wage work because of the deplorable way labourers are treated in the fields and the low wages received relative to other work. What is ironic is that as demeaning as agricultural wage work is, men do not mind their wives or daughters being increasingly involved in such work: men's own withdrawal from paid work appears to be much more important to their status than their womenfolk's withdrawal (the reverse is true of forward caste men in the region).

One consequence of men's struggle against low wage work, particularly in the remote region where off-farm employment opportunities are slim, is that, in the short term, it is undermining their families' ability to support themselves. We encountered instances of men refusing offers of agricultural wage work with no alternative work to do those days, either for a wage or self-employment. How can men sustain their struggle? One reason why men can refuse agricultural wage work is that they increasingly rely on their wives' earnings to pay for family essentials. They are, in fact, shifting responsibility for the latter onto women. Take the case of Yallamma, a female labourer who is married to Chandra and lives in one of the remote hamlets. On the day Chandra was interviewed he said that he turned down joint work in paddy cutting offered by a large Reddy farmer – his former master – on the basis that the wage offered was only Rs 15 and the other employers normally offered more, Rs 18 and Rs 20. But there was no other work offered to him that day. In fact, all the male labourers in this Mala (Dalit) part of the village refused work (except one 13-year-old boy and one 55-year-old man). However, several women from the village had agreed to work. Chandra's wife was one among them and she explained: 'It is true that the wage offered is low, but what do we get if we sit at home? Rs 15 at least helps us buy something. We have a baby and we can buy something for her.' She then turned to here husband and said angrily 'If we both sit at home who will feed us? Where will we get our food from?' Yallamma's complaint was a common one among female labourers interviewed. The aim of presenting this case study is not to argue that men are being 'callous' with regard to their children's nutrition but rather that men are involved in an acute form of class struggle with their current employers, a struggle sustained at the expense of women's own struggle.

We found that men conduct their struggles separately from their wives. In the Yallamma case men did not consult their wives nor include their womenfolk's wages in negotiations with the employer (for example, to raise women's wages to 17 rupees). From Chandra and his friends' point of view there are several advantages to waging a separate struggle from their womenfolk. First, women, by taking up such work, enable men to prolong their strike: their families do not forfeit a full day's wage. Moreover, men reported that they could usefully conserve their energy for better paid contract or non-agrarian work when it does come along. Second, that men's wages might have risen faster if women also chose not to take on the work men refused is less relevant than would be expected *because men are largely leaving low paid and demeaning joint work to women* in favour of higher paid work elsewhere (in the same way that men left domestic service to women in the West). Furthermore, men's freedom from tied labour obligations, their dignity and strike credibility are enhanced when that employer next offers them exclusively male work or contract work. Indeed, we did not find evidence of men trying to prevent their wives from taking up the work they refuse (as they might a 'strike-breaking' worker from another family). Quite opposite to the notion that women assist capital by undermining men's struggle by taking on the work that men refuse, we argue that men's decisions to exclude women from their wage struggle, with the aim of enhancing further their own struggle with capital, enforces women's low pay and unfreedom (see below).

The shift in the responsibility for family maintenance onto women through men's refusal of low paid, low status work is compounded by men's withdrawal of part of their own earnings from family provision to spend on alcohol and other personal expenditures. Male labourers in our sample devoted an average of 77 per cent of their wage earnings to family essentials in 1970, and by 1995 this figure had fallen to 55 per cent. By comparison, women's contribution was higher at 90 per cent in 1970 and fell merely to 85 per cent in 1995. Moreover, 46 per cent of men whose primary occupation is labouring (L, L+), devote less than half their earnings to family essentials, with about one-quarter devoting 16 per cent or less. Spending on alcohol comprises a large proportion of this spending (see also Desphande [1994]). As an example, a typical labourer spent approximately Rs 1200 annually on alcohol alone (25.9 per cent of his total yearly wage earnings). Yet alcoholism was not uncommon: for instance, one labourer in our sample spent Rs. 2400 on alcohol alone (71.7 per cent of his earnings). Male respondents also spend on tobacco, cinema, eating out and gambling (playing cards). Men's spending outside the home increases men's debt and the need for women's wages to finance this debt.

Why are men shifting the responsibility for family provision onto women? Men's personal spending has increased partly because of a change in the way they are paid, from a twice yearly payment in paddy (all of which goes directly to household consumption) under traditional bonded labour to intermittent and high daily cash wages (that is, during seasonal peaks in demand or occasional off-farm work) which are found to be more easily be squandered on liquor, tobacco, gambling, etc. And male labourers' movement into the public sphere recently has been rapid, no longer spending evenings doing odd jobs for employers and sleeping on the employers' veranda or cattle shed as they did in 1970 under traditional bonded labour arrangements, they now frequent tea stalls, arrack shops, gambling clubs, political meetings (where country liquor is supplied to buy votes) and make numerous trips to a nearby city.

Moreover, capitalists who benefit from tied male labour dependent on debt generated by alcohol consumption are found not to discourage the latter activity among their workers (and a few are even found to lend them money when drinking with them; see van Onselen [1976]).[30] Before prohibition, proximity to liquor supplies as a result of state policy contributed to men's drinking, as noted by Desphande [1994], who argues that since the early 1980s it has been the policy of the Andhra Pradesh government excise department to flood villages with liquor by promoting liquor shops in every village (often providing sachets which could be carried home in one's pocket). One state liquor shop opened in 1988 in the central region.[31]

In sum, men can carry out their rejection of agricultural daily wage work – despite their underemployment – because they increasingly rely on women's earnings to pay for family essentials. They either delegate this work directly, or indirectly, by refusing work offers or withdrawing their wage earnings from family provision. As a consequence of women's greater responsibility for feeding the family, they feel compelled to take up all offers of wage work, no matter how low paid and humiliating, which increases their unfreedom, reduces their actual wages received, increases real male female wage differentials and increases hours worked per day.

GENDER AND TIED LABOUR

When we compared male labourers and their wives we found that a higher percentage of women were tied: whereas 56 per cent of male labourers were tied, 68 per cent of their wives were tied. This figure for women rises to 76 per cent when we include female-headed households. And for female labourers as a whole, who greatly outnumber male labourers, the figure drops to 60.5 per cent of all women whose primary or secondary occupation is labouring. The latter figure falls because wives of MP men are not tied.

In 1970 the reverse was true: a higher percentage of male labourers were tied (83.8 per cent) compared to female labourers (77.5 per cent). If men were tied their wives were ordinarily also tied: however, wives of permanently bonded labourers were not attached permanently, with the exception of a few women involved in domestic service. Most wives of permanently bonded labourers were expected to turn up for all female and joint work over the one main growing season, and to accept tied (= low) wages as well as to be available on a beck and call basis for small unpaid tasks. Slightly more men than women were tied at this conjuncture, because wives of male permanent bonded labourers who worked outside the village generally remained on the family homestead and in fact managed small millet farms themselves and were not formally tied to local employers.

The decline in involvement in tied labour relations was sharper for men (falling from 83.8 per cent to 56.0 per cent) than for their wives (falling from 77.5 per cent to 68.0/60.5 per cent), both because of access by the former to state granted assets and non-agricultural employment, and also because men's emancipation from traditional bonded labour and non-permanent tied arrangements was facilitated by women's wage earnings. This subsidisation of men's freedom was direct – insofar as women's earnings, in many instances, went toward repayment of men's loans based on traditional permanent labour service – and indirect – insofar as some men could contest tied wages under contemporary non-permanent arrangements safe in the knowledge that the earnings of their wives would go towards family maintenance.

In 1995 we found that if men were tied then their wives were tied, but among free male labourers, nearly half of their wives were tied. We were rather surprised to find this, because it is generally argued that employers' primary reason for tying labour is to secure male labour. There were two main reasons for this phenomenon. Firstly, women were involved in their husband's tied relations. In tied labour for credit, women were involved directly in debt repayment, and women whose husbands were involved in tied labour for lease and by influence were found to be fulfilling employers' expectations that they turn up for daily wage work, work at lower tied wages, and also perform unpaid tasks. Second, women took out loans independently of their husbands by pledging their own labour. Sometimes these were relatively small loans to cover immediate consumption needs, as women's need for loans increased with their greater responsibility for family consumption. Often, however, women also took out large loans to cover ceremonial or medical expenses. One important reason women themselves took out large loans is that many male labourers who recently left traditional bonded relations alienated employer/creditors who then would lend only to women. As men increasingly withdrew their labour from low paid and tied employment, capitalists turned increasingly to the employment of cheaper, more hardworking women. Lending to women was seen by employers to be not merely 'safe' but also a good method to re-secure female labour which would more readily work for low wages, turn up for work promptly, work harder and generally was more disciplined than its male counterpart.

The figure 68 per cent of wives of male labourers (and 60.5 per cent of the sample of female labourers) underestimates both the intensity and duration of women's involvement in tied labour compared to men's involvement. While men on tied lease completed ploughing and irrigation work, they nevertheless contested the expectation that they also report to the lender's farm for other exclusively male and joint male/female fieldwork. By contrast, women were found to fulfil their portion of attached labour obligations by working at the wages stipulated for the rest of the season. For example, on capitalist farms men would agree to perform ploughing and irrigation work (approximately 23 days for one paddy crop and six days for one groundnut crop). Yet they were found to contest the additional EM work (23.7 days in paddy and 3 days in groundnut) and joint work (15.3 days in paddy and 15.7 days in groundnut). Women, by contrast, were found to work a minimum of 82 days in paddy and 38.3 days in groundnut and more if men refused to do their share of joint work (i.e. 15.3 days in paddy and 15.7 days in groundnut).

Women were also found to fulfil the unpaid tasks inherent in tied labour contracts, even when men contested these obligations. Additionally, women tended to perform unpaid work on a daily basis: for instance, cleaning employers' cattle sheds and toilets, and also performing domestic work. In return for this unpaid work, women would accept a 'saddi' breakfast: that is, employers' leftover food from the previous afternoon that they would normally either feed to animals or throw out. Men would ordinarily refuse 'saddi' because of its symbolic humiliation, reminiscent of the appalling treatment under traditional bondage.

One of the reasons why women discharged such obligations was to secure consumption loans for the future. As men were seen to be 'disloyal' by employers – either by recently breaking traditional bonded labour relations without fully repaying outstanding loans or contesting tied labour arrangements – women would attempt to regain their access to credit by performing unpaid and low paid, tied wage work. Indeed some men are increasingly choosing to leave small debts partly unpaid so that they can work elsewhere or as part of the struggle against low wages (for instance, in the belief that based on fair wages the loan should be paid of in ten days rather than the 15 required by the employer). This requires women to meet debt servicing labour obligations in order to secure access to consumption loans from employers in the future, in order to feed, clothe and provide health care for her family. Similarly, daughters are more likely than sons to fulfil tied labour obligations through the season.

Partly as a consequence of women's greater involvement in tied work, average female daily earnings as a percentage of male daily earnings is only

53.5 per cent, a substantially lower figure than the published daily wage differentials for Andhra Pradesh (71.0 per cent). Indeed, published wage differentials based on differences in joint work are becoming increasingly irrelevant when women dominate joint agricultural wage work, with only much older men and below working age boys coming forward to perform the male component of joint work. Moreover, women's daily earnings as a percentage of men's is found to fall as men's involvement in self-employment rises, from 74.8 per cent for L, 61.7 per cent for L+ to 38.4 per cent for SP. This fall reflects the influence of women's real lack of co-ownership of family land and inequalities in domestic relations on women's wages.

TABLE 9

DAILY WAGE EARNINGS FOR MEN AND WOMEN*

	Men's	Women's	Women's Wage as % of Men's Wage
L	23.8	17.8	74.8%
L+	29.8	18.4	61.7%
SP	50.0	18.5	38.4%
Average	34.5	18.5	53.5%

Note: Annual wage earnings divided by total days worked in paid labour, summary of case study material.

Based on the results of our time allocation study, we found that when unwaged domestic work – such as childcare, cleaning, cooking, fetching firewood and water – is included women work 1.5 times as long as men: women work an average of 9.5 hours compared with 6.5 hours for men. In recent years women have become more involved in wage labouring than men, doing more throughout the year as a result of double and treble cropping. It might be argued that a reduction in time spent on food processing has freed up time for women to perform wage work, but we have found no evidence for a *substantial* fall in women's unwaged domestic work. A fall in time allocated to processing food has been offset by more time spent procuring firewood (given the increase distance to forests) as well as greater time spent cooking food, especially given the decline in traditional permanent bonded labour (three cooked meals a day) and the rise in daily wage work (one meal) and contract labour (no meals).

Given that women work 1.5 times as much as men, it could be argued that, together with tied harvest arrangements, women's surplus labour underpins the survival of smallholdings in the region. Women not merely work more hours per day than men, they also tend to perform more arduous work, primarily manual labour (both paid, on family farm, and through reciprocal labour arrangements), while men do relatively less arduous work, such as herding cattle and machine-assisted labour (see Table 5 above).

WOMEN'S PROLETARIANISATION OR DEPROLETARIANISATION?

The deepening class divide between men and women is not confined to parts of south India. Prem Chaudhry [1994: 174–8] finds that among smallholders in green revolution villages in Harayana 'vast numbers' of women are being sent out for agricultural wage work on a regular basis as a consequence of land fragmentation and the greater need for cash for green revolution inputs. Yet she finds that men continue to operate their holdings and seek employment off-farm. Chaudhry [1994: 177–8] concludes:

> So while men participate in the dominant capitalist mode of production, this participation has important repercussions for women, whose proletarianization is distinctly visible. This also underlines the man's possession and control of land and other means of production rendering him a member of a different class from that of the women who is absorbed in the (capitalist) system as an agricultural wage labourer.

Although in our survey villages access by labourers to land was due largely to state intervention, in terms of the male/female division of labour the situation was much the same.

Chaudhry [1994] equates workforce 'feminisation' with women's proletarianisation, in concert with earlier studies [e.g., *Agarwal*, 1984]. Yet it in our villages women are not fully proletarianised but rather appear to be absorbed into the capitalist agricultural system as *unfree* labour. Suggesting that attached relations are unfree when those working off a debt do so involuntarily, due to the transmission of debt from parents to offspring upon the parents' death, Rao [1997: 7] argues:

> ... offspring (or other kin) obliged to work off their parents' unpaid debts seem to meet the criterion of unfreedom: their right to refuse to abide by the terms set by their employer-creditor has been surrendered under the force of law or custom that allows debtor and creditor to accept the labour-power of the debtor's offspring as collateral. That is, the relationship is founded no less on a coercive social rule (one's offspring are one's chattel) than is slavery.

He argues that this applies equally to the transmission of debt servicing labour obligations between family members when a debtor is still alive, and distinguishes between *actual* and *potential* heritability/transmission to kinsfolk, arguing that actual not potential transmission makes a relation unfree. For instance, if an indebted man's wife works off part of his debt, then he is free yet his wife is 'unfree'.

Based on Rao's definition, there is an *element* of unfreedom in women's attached labour relations in our villages, in so far as womenfolk obliged to provide debt servicing labour to their menfolk's lenders/landlords do not have the right to refuse terms set by their employer. This element of unfreedom is reinforced by the economic coercion placed on women by men, as the latter shift more of the responsibility for family provisioning onto females, either by refusing low paid agricultural work or by withdrawing part of their own wage earnings from the family budget. This shift enables capitalists to discipline the labour of women more easily because women are more *economically* dependent on creditors than men. These considerations – together with the fact that more women than men are involved in attached relations and their involvement is more intense and of a longer duration – suggest that women are both unfree and more controllable than are male labourers.

In this regard, Brass's deproletarianisation thesis may be somewhat more useful for conceptualising the basis of workforce feminisation in our villages in AP than arguments about women's proletarianisation (through pauperisation). As rising labour costs and falling commodity prices threaten the profitability of capitalist farming based on hired labour, capitalists were forced to restructure the labour process by intensifying non-permanent attached labour relations in order to segment the labour market and also to secure cheaper and more disciplined workers. In our AP villages capitalists took advantage of the gender gap in wages and power, which intensified as a result of state interventions targeted on men and also as a consequence of the shift in the responsibility for family maintenance on to women. The overall result was a conversion of male workers recently emancipated from traditional bonds into less free, tied and cheaper labourers for the few days needed on exclusively male work, and a replacement of male workers seeking to free themselves from non-permanent ties with cheaper, more economically dependent and thus more easily disciplined labour-power of unfree females employed in women's work and joint male/female work. In addition to men's movement into off-farm work and petty commodity production, therefore, this substitution of more free male labour with less free female labour is an important reason for workforce feminisation in our AP villages.

Brass [1993: 46–7] suggests that one economic advantage of deproletarianisation is that it enables employers to lower the cost of local workers by importing cheaper outside labour. This aspect of his thesis may have less relevance where the members of the workforce in question are from the same family and where gender/generational inequalities are wide (and may have more relevance to geographical and or racial differences between workers of the same gender, but different families). We found that while capital is enjoying lower wages through a straightforward substitution of free men with mostly unfree women, this substitution is not, in turn, substantially reducing free men's wages partly because men are receiving an income from female work enabling them to sustain their struggles over longer periods (particularly with respect to higher paid male work) and partly because higher paid opportunities are available elsewhere. Both enable men to leave low paid joint male/female work to women.

While Brass labels this substitution 'deproletarianisation', in AP changing labour relations in 1970 cannot be characterised entirely as 'diminished freedom' insofar as the incidence of unfree labour relations among men has fallen for male labour (83.8 per cent to 56.0 per cent). On the other hand, their wives involvement in attached labour relations has fallen much less (77.5 per cent to 68.0/60.5 per cent) and in some respects have increased in duration insofar as women are involved throughout the year, working more intensively and replacing men in what was traditionally considered male labour service. So, in many respects, the much more important issue with regard to unfreedom in our AP villages is not the shift from permanent to casual employment – so often reported in the Indian countryside – but rather a shift from a permanently employed workforce composed of men to a *near* permanently employed workforce composed of women. The latter work not merely at seasonal peaks (as they did in the past) but on a more continual basis over the season and throughout the year.

It is necessary to ask, therefore, is workforce feminisation in these circumstances empowering? As a result of state interventions targeted specifically at men and of capitalists' restructuring of the labour process, divisions within the home deepened: men became owners of assets and engaged in freer non-agricultural wage labour (though smallholders remained tied to commission agents) and women remained engaged in the most socially demeaning form of work, agricultural wage labouring, which was largely unfree. *In this context, we contend that feminisation was largely disempowering for women.*

Furthermore, any theoretical advantage of women's increased employment and cash contribution to their power in domestic relations was diluted significantly because of low earnings due to tied labour and because men's earnings from higher paid wage work and PCP employment are so much greater. Indeed the emphasis on 'cash contribution' in the literature on 'sex bias' in India can mask the fact that inequalities in gender power relations in South Asia are both profound and enduring. For instance, inequalities within the home are reflected in women's powerlessness to (i) direct more of her husband's earnings toward family essentials (ii) to choose to perform less tied, higher status, higher paid work and (iii) to share their much greater work burden with menfolk. Moreover, the ability of women in south Asia to influence domestic decisions is severely constrained by their general lack of negotiating power – for example, to divorce with some household assets upon disagreement with husbands. The effect of government policies on male labourers' economic status, political status (through changes in electoral politics) and in social status (through reservations for scheduled castes) has been to bring about a process of political and social 'individualisation', as they break with erstwhile masters and vote independently of them. Indeed men's status has grown tremendously, out of all proportion to their families' economic position, as men are able to refuse work in agriculture despite underemployment and to withdraw earnings from family maintenance.[32]

CONCLUSIONS

We began this article citing the arguments by neo-liberal writers that 'green revolution' induced agricultural growth in south India is largely responsible for rising wages, a reduction in oppressive conditions, increased land ownership among landless labourers and even some equalisation in land owned between rich and poor. This argument was extended to female labour, with green revolution growth seen to be responsible for a faster rise in women's employment relative to men, for declining wage differentials and for a rise in women's 'empowerment'. Attempting to refute the findings of earlier Marxist studies that reported pauperisation and proletarianization, particularly among women, these Neo-liberal writers insist that improving the market still further – through economic reforms based on liberalisation and encouragement of private enterprise – can only enhance the benefits received by labour even more.

We examined these views afresh in light of evidence gathered from villagers in Andhra Pradesh. We then identified two paradoxes in our survey data: the 'Standard of Living Paradox' – that despite a near doubling of real wages since 1970, food consumption levels and general standard of living were lower than expected and this is reflected in a heavy dependence on employers and merchants for exploitative loans; and the 'Empowerment Paradox' – that women's greater involvement in paid employment – the chief goal of policy makers concerned with 'sex bias' – has coincided with a decline in women's relative power in domestic relations, especially regarding who is responsible for family maintenance and who is responsible for what work in the family.

Several reasons were given for these paradoxes. First, we suggested that the effects of economic growth on labour relations could not be separated from strategic attempts of both Congress and the Telugu Desham Party to win the allegiance of rural labourers through a series of anti-poverty policies. Male agricultural labourers were the chief beneficiaries of policies encouraging the encroachment of government wasteland, subsidies on credit, productive assets and food, as well as non-agricultural employment generation. As a result, employers had less control over the consumption and residence of male workers, enabling men to escape from traditional bonded labour relations and to engage in petty commodity production and enter non-agricultural employment.

Second, the resulting decline in the availability of male labour power and rise in agricultural productivity due to the new technology occasioned a rise in labour costs and fall in profit margins. Agrarian capitalists responded to this crisis in profitability: partly by mechanising expensive male work; and partly by intensifying non-permanent (short-term and seasonal) forms of tied labour – specifically in order to secure control over and reduce costs of male labour power for the few days needed on exclusively male work and female labour power controlled by a indebted male for exclusively female and joint work as well as unpaid tasks over the season. Rural capitalists have also responded by commission trading, based on tied harvest arrangements, in order to secure the labour of smallholders indirectly. Both non-permanent tied labour and tied harvest arrangements pushed actual wage earnings and prices for harvests below market (and published) levels.

Third, the feminisation of agricultural wage labour was partly the result of men's movement into off-farm employment and into petty commodity production. Yet feminisation was also the result of capitalists' substitution of men attempting to emancipate themselves with cheaper – and to some extent unfree – female labour. That female labour was cheaper, more easily disciplined more economically dependent and ultimately less free than male labour was partly enforced by men themselves. Men delegated debt repayment to women directly (especially unpaid obligations) and indirectly, by shifting more of the responsibility for family provisioning onto women. The latter occurred as men refused to perform agricultural work in protest against the low level of tied wages and as men withdrew wage earnings from family provision. As a consequence, women felt compelled to take up agricultural work, at whatever wages and conditions this was offered. Women were also forced to take out tied loans themselves, to directly repay men's debts when they absconded from labour service debt repayment, and to satisfy employers' expectations of loyalty in order to assure access to consumption credit in the future. The latter included working on employer/creditors' farms at significantly lower tied wages as well as performing unpaid tasks throughout the season. Thus, to some extent, men's class struggle for emancipation was both subsidised by, and at the expense of, better wages and emancipation for women.

As capitalists turn increasingly to the employment of unfree female labour power through non-permanent attached labour relations, divisions within labouring households are deepening: between men as owners of assets or as holders of freer non-agricultural jobs, and women as agricultural labourers, mostly unfree. As a result, workforce feminisation has been largely a disempowering experience for the women concerned. Females are replacing males as the unfree agricultural workforce in these Indian villages.

NOTES

1. Some labour saving technology in agro-processing led to an overall decline in women's employment opportunities. For instance, new rice milling technology replaced the traditional foot operated mill, which used female labour. Moreover, factory produced vegetable ghee and other cooking oils partly replaced ghee produced at home by women [*Watson and Harriss*, 1986: 32–3]. The use of pesticides, herbicides and mechanical threshing were expected to displace female agricultural workers in parts of Southern India [e.g., *Mencher and Saradamoni*, 1982].

2. Both Agarwal and Duvvury refer to Rural Labour Enquiry data over the years 1964/65 to 1974/65 – a period before the new technology was even introduced to the more remote regions areas of India. Moreover, as Duvvury points out, 1974/75 was a drought year and hence the rise in unemployment since 1964/65 may have been overestimated.

3. Most of these studies have been published in a special edition of the *Indian Journal of Agricultural Economics*, Vol.40, No.3. Studies also report higher female labour participation in areas where irrigation has been extended [*Surayawanshi and Kapse*, 1985].

4. Total of land purchases, encroachments of wasteland and household mergers minus land sold, partitioned and gifted away.

5. Compared to other Indian states, AP State governments have been unique in their more rigorous implementation of central Government schemes, in their initiation of new policies and in devoting the largest proportion of its budget to social welfare schemes.

6. Tied harvest arrangements are also frequently referred to as 'rent in kind' or 'forward buying' arrangements. Similarly tied labour arrangements are also referred to as 'labour rent'.

7. The persistence of smallholdings could also be linked to the requirement on the part of capitalist farms for a permanent/local source of wage labour [*Kautsky*, 1988].

8. These writers describe relations as evidence of 'worker choice' [e.g., *Bardhan*, 1984]. Brass [1993] links the arguments of neo-classicals with those 'culturalist' arguments (derived from the literature on moral economy, survival strategies, resistance theory [e.g., *Scott*, 1985] and post-modern arguments) all of which concur that capitalism is present but reject or diminish the existence of unfreedom. It is assumed that what Marxists label unfree cannot be labelled exploitative (oppressive, unfree) since (i) attached labour arrangements are entered into voluntarily (freely) by labourers (ii) labourers benefit from such arrangements in the way of subsistence and/or employment guarantees and (iii) workers can chose to resist/make unoperational any arrangement (but generally choose not to) [*Brass*, 1993: 36–43].

9. According to this view, extra-economic coercion (i.e. the use of physical force or ideological pressure) prevents workers from personally commodifying their own labour power and

impedes the exchange between buyers and sellers of labour power. As a result, the supply of (and demand for) labour is not determined by economic criteria alone and the labour market does not function properly, which is seen to hinder the process of accumulation. Thus unfree labour – which prevents labour power from being a commodity – is non-market/pre-capitalist/feudal. The existence of unfree labour is motivated not by profit by the economically irrational behaviour (prestige, patronage) based on consumption rather than investment (Brass, personal communication). For these reasons, attached labour relations were theorised to be either pre-capitalist forms of accumulation [*Bhaduri*, 1973; *Patnaik*, 1990] or unproductive forms of conspicuous consumption [e.g., *Breman*, 1974] which result in economic backwardness. For some writers, these bonded relations constituted 'patronage' where employers provide subsistence/employment/protection guarantees to labourers. Insofar as capitalism annihilated these guarantees, 'depatronisation' was seen to make labourers worse off in some respects (e.g., Breman [1974] with regard to the historic *Hali* relationship, which binds permanent farm servants to employers in south Gujarat).

10. Earlier arguments that capitalists use loans/debt in order to accumulate surplus value in order to set capitalism in motion include Banaji, [1977] and Alavi *et al.* [1982].

11. According to Brass [1993: 46]: 'deproletarianization (or the economic and politico-ideological decommodification of labour-power) corresponds to workforce restructuring by means of introducing or reintroducing unfree relations, a process of class composition/decomposition which accompanies the struggle between capital and labour'.

12. This labour class rank is also a very crude approximation of Patnaik's [1976/1987] labour exploitation or 'E' criterion.

13. The subsidy price was recently raised to Rs 3.5 to account for inflation.

14. The land ceiling allowed a maximum of 54 'dry' acres per family of five (where one wet acre = 2.5 acres dry) with lands in surplus to this ceiling to be distributed to the landless. Of the six surplus landowners in the region, only two were 'caught', one of whom claims still to own 179.6 acres and the land he surrendered is unsuitable for cultivation. In Chittoor district as a whole the 'redistribution' of lands under the land ceiling act amounts to merely three per cent of land encroached by labourers.

15. In the study villages, 34.5 per cent of labouring households received a subsidised loan. Many of these received *several* loans by paying bribes to local officials, while the majority of labourers received none. Moreover, inability to repay loans was common, either because assets received were faulty in some way due to corruption (for example, receiving unhealthy livestock) or loans were used to finance pressing consumption needs.

16. Though the AP state government has implemented some recent pro-women legislation, it is too early to assess their full impact in the villages. These include extending reservations for woman in local bodies, offering property rights to Dalit women and implementing a scheme providing parents of girl children with money for education (the last two schemes being very small in coverage). The government has also had a relatively more rigorous implementation of the central government driven DWACRA programmes for women. In coastal Andhra NGOs following DWACRA guidelines in literacy and consciousness raising are reported to be having a powerful effect.

17. See also Sayana [1952] and Rajasekhar [1988] who observed similar trends in their studies of land transfers in dry districts of the Madras Presidency in the decades before independence.

18. Rich households here are defined as owning more than 20 acres of land where one acre of wet land is equivalent to between two and six dry land equivalent acres depending on quality·

19. All the land sold for distress was from one Brahmin landlord. Brahmins tended to lease out all land and took little interest in increasing production in the 1970s.

20. One merchant argued that the only reason he retains his otherwise unprofitable village clothing shop is in order to give him one additional method of tying smallholders to his commission trade compared to outside commission agents.

21. In 1986, farmers from all classes agreed that storing groundnut at harvest (usually December) and reselling them at sowing time (usually June) would lead to approximately a 28 per cent rise in sale price. A typical large farmer's stocks would bring him a Rs 2000 profit from storing his own produce for six months [*Olsen*, 1991: 120].

22. Indeed, this highlights a potential methodological problem with the identification of class simply in terms of time devoted to different activities versus the extent to which these different activities contribute to the economic reproduction of the subject concerned. For instance, among the category SP, that more time is devoted by men to production on owned land than to wage labouring does not mean that income generated from smallholding is greater than that from sale of labour-power, particularly smallholders in tied harvest relations which reduce their income from marketing produce substantially making them very similar to L+ both economically and in terms of class relations.

23. Usually about ten years, that is, between 16–26 years of age, an age when men were at their strongest for operation lift irrigation.

24. Brass [1993: 32] argues that 'Unlike a free labourer, who is able to enter or withdraw from the labour market at will, due to the operation of *ideological constraints or extra-economic coercion* an unfree worker is unable personally to sell his or her own labour-power (in other words, to commodify it)' regardless of duration of employment. This includes "forms of unfreedom where: [i] the labouring subject is prevented from entering the labour market under any circumstances (in which cases labour-power ceases to be a commodity, [ii] is prevented from entering the labour market in person (labour-power remaining a commodity in such circumstances, but is sold by someone other than its owner) and [iii] and is permitted to enter the labour market in person, but only with the consent and at the convenience of someone other than its owners .'

25. Brass states that: 'In the case of Harayana (and also Bihar), the ideological constraints on migrants to comply with debt-servicing labour obligations extend from pressure exercised indirectly on their kinsfolk by, e.g., a labour contractor or an employer, to pressure exercised directly on them by their kinsfolk. Labour contractors or employers (who frequently recruit their own workers) can of course exercise economic sanctions on an absconder's kinsfolk, with the intention that the latter then apply ideological pressure on the indebted worker in person. Hence the distinction between ideological and economic constraints is obviously not an absolute one: both may be combined to secure the desired effect (the return of a migrant to meet debt-servicing labour obligations), but may be effected separately at particular moments (contractor or employer exercises ideological or economic pressure indirectly, on kinsfolk of indebted migrant; kinsfolk then exercise ideological pressure directly, on the indebted migrant concerned).'

26. Lucassen [1993: 9] writes 'Probably the most important distinction between free and unfree labour is the freedom whether or not to choose one's own employer and therefore one's labour conditions, or to choose one's means of production.'

27. In 1991, merely 25.2 per cent of rural women were counted as rural main workers in India.

28. While the 1991 census reports that female agricultural labourers are still outnumbered by male labourers (women being merely 38.6 per cent of the agricultural wage labour force), since 1981 the absolute number of female agricultural labourers has been growing at a slightly faster rate than for men (36.2 per cent versus 31.2 per cent), both being more than the rise in population for both men and women (23.9 per cent).

29. We documented this loosening of the gender division of labour in paddy and in groundnut. According to our respondents, even more relaxation occurred in non-traditional cash crops (e.g., tomato) and non-traditional arrangements (for example, contract gang work) which we have not at this time fully quantified (yet Table 5 shows evidence of this).

30. Onselen [1976] argues that debt generated by alcohol consumption led to proletarianization and the creation of a mining workforce in the late 1800s in South Africa.

31. Another reason why men have shifted the onus of family provision onto women is that they are aware that women's paid employment has risen almost enough to cover bare subsistence (along with subsidised rice) and so they demand that their wives cover household expenses despite men's greater overall earnings and the possibility of improving family consumption patterns, for example, with more vegetables and milk. This is also a generational problem; older labourers who have much younger wives do not see the importance of vegetable and milk when they survived on a diet largely of millet when under traditional bondage.

32. In this regard, it is significant that Brass [1993: 50] links unfreedom with the type of class struggles that can occur in later stages of agrarian capitalism: 'when labour begins to act

individually or to organise collectively in defence of its own interests, by exercising freedom of movement to secure higher wages, better working conditions, shorter working hours, etc.' (p.50). Brass [1993: 49–50] thereby allows for a situation of capitalist restructuring under conditions where increased 'levels of political consciousness and organisation exhibited by workers' bid up wages even in labour surplus areas, such as in non-peak periods in our remote region.

REFERENCES

Agarwal, B., 1984, 'Women, Poverty and Agricultural Growth in India', *The Journal of Peasant Studies*, Vol.13, No.4.

Agarwal, B., 1994, *A Field of One's Own: Gender and Land Rights in South Asia*, Cambridge: Cambridge University Press.

Ahluwalia, 1978, 'Rural Poverty and Agricultural Performance in India', *The Journal of Development Studies*, Vol.4, No.3.

Alavi, H., 1987, ' Peasantry and Capitalism: A Marxist Discourse', in T. Shanin (ed.), *Peasants and Peasant Societies*, Oxford: Basil Blackwell.

Alavi, H. *et al.*, 1982, *Capitalism and Colonial Production*, London: Croom Helm.

Alavi, H. and T. Shanin, 1988, 'Introduction to the English Edition: Peasantry and Capitalism' in Kautsky [1899/1988].

Athreya, V., Djurfeldt, G. and S. Lindberg, 1990, *Barriers Broken: Production Relations and Agrarian Change in Tamil Nadu*, New Delhi: Sage Publications.

Banaji, J., 1977, ' Capitalist Domination and the Small Peasantry: Deccan District in the Late Nineteenth Century', *Economic and Political Weekly*, Vol.12, Nos.33–34.

Banaji, J., 1992, 'Historical Arguments for a "Logic of Deployment" in "Pre-Capitalist" Agriculture', mimeo, St John's College, Oxford.

Bardhan, P., 1984, *Land, Labor and Rural Poverty: Essays in Development Economics,* New Delhi: Oxford University Press.

Bennett, L, 1992, ' Women, Poverty and Productivity in India', Economic Development Institute Seminar Paper, No.43, The World Bank, Washington, DC.

Bhaduri, A., 1973, 'A Study in Agricultural Backwardness under Semi-Feudalism', *Economic Journal*, Vol.83, No.329.

Brass, T., 1990, 'Class Struggle and the Deproletarizanization of Agricultural Labour in Haryana (India)', *The Journal of Peasant Studies*, Vol.18, No.1, pp.36–67.

Brass, T., 1993, 'Some Observations on Unfree Labour, Capitalist Restructuring and Deproletarianization', in Brass, van der Linden and Lucassen [1993].

Brass, T., 1995, 'Unfree Labour and Agrarian Change: A Different View', *Economic and Political Weekly*, Vol.30, No.13.

Brass, T., 1997, 'Immobilised Workers, Footloose Theory', *The Journal of Peasant Studies*, Vol.24, No.4.

Brass, T., van der Linden, M. and Jan Lucassen (eds.), *Free and Unfree Labour*, Amsterdam: International Institute for Social History.

Breman, J., 1974, *Patronage and Exploitation: Changing Agrarian Relations in South Gujarat, India*, Berkeley, CA: University of California Press.

Breman, J., 1985, *Of Peasants, Migrant and Paupers: Rural Labour Circulation in Capitalist Production in West India*, Delhi: Oxford University Press.

Breman, J., 1993, *Beyond Patronage and Exploitation: Changing Agrarian Relations in South Gujarat,* Delhi: Oxford University Press.

Breman, J., 1996, *Footloose Labour,* Cambridge: Cambridge University Press.

Byres, T. J., 1981, ' The New Technology, Class Formation and Class Action in the Indian Countryside', *The Journal of Peasant Studies*, Vol.8, No.4.

Chand, R., Sidhu, D.S. and J.L. Kaul, 1985, 'Impact of Agricultural Modernisation in Labour Use Pattern in Punjab with Special Reference to Women Labour', *Indian Journal of Agricultural Economics*, Vol.40, No.3.

Chaudhry, P., 1994, *The Veiled Woman: Shifting Gender Equations in Rural Haryana, 1880–1990*, Delhi: Oxford University Press.

Copestake, J. G., 1992, 'The Integrated Rural Development Programme: Performance During the Sixth Plan, Policy Responses and Proposals for Reform', in B. Harriss, S. Guhan and R.H. Cassen (eds.) *Poverty in India: Research and Policy*, Bombay: Oxford University Press.

da Corta, L., 1993, 'Household Mobility and Class Differentiation in South Indian Villages 1950–88/9: A Comparative Study of Two Methodological Schools', draft prepared for D.Phil. thesis for the University of Oxford.

da Corta, L. and D. Venkateshwarlu, 1992, 'Field Methods for Economic Mobility' in S. Devereux and J. Hoddinott (eds.) *Fieldwork in Developing Countries*, Hemel Hempstead: Harvester Wheatsheaf.

da Corta, L., Tomlinson, M. and G. Joseph, 1992, 'Classification of Rural Households: A Cluster Analysis', *Economic Mobility in South India,* Report to the Leverhulme Trust, Department of Economics and Econometrics and Social Statistics, University of Manchester.

Deshpande, M., 1994, ' Reworking Gender Relations, Redefining Politics, NelloreVillage Women Against Arrack' in *The Status of Dalits in Contemporary India*, Mysore: Land Reforms Unit, Lal Bahaduri Shasti National Academy of Administration.

Dreze, J. and A. Sen, 1995, *Indian Economic Development and Social Opportunity*, Delhi: Oxford University Press.

Duvvury, N, 1989, 'Work Participation Of Women In India: A Study with Special Reference to Female Agricultural Labourers, 1961–1981', in *Limited Options: Women Workers In Rural India*, New Delhi: Asian Employment Programme (ARTEP), International Labour Organisation.

Ellis, F., 1988, *Peasant Economics: Farm Households and Agrarian Development*, Cambridge: Cambridge University Press.

Epstein, T.S.,1973, *South India: Yesterday, Today and Tomorrow*, London: Macmillan.

Gadre, N. A. and Y.P. Mahalle, 1985, 'Participation of Female Farm Labour Under Changing Agriculture in Vidarbha', *Indian Journal of Agricultural Economics*, Vol.40, No.3.

Government of Andhra Pradesh, 1991, *Women Work Force in Andhra Pradesh*, report published by Directorate of Economics and Statistics.

Government of India, 1991, *Census of India,* New Delhi (data taken from 'Series-1, Paper 2 of 1992, Final Population Totals: Brief Analysis of Primary Census Abstract', by Amulya Ratna Nanda, Registrar General and Census Commissioner, India, Ministry of Home Affairs).

Griffin, K. and A.K. Ghose, 1979, 'Growth and Impoverishment in the Rural Areas of Asia', *World Development*, Vol.7, Nos.4/5.Harriss, J., 1982, *Capitalism and Peasant Farming: Agrarian Structure and Ideology in Northern Tamil Nadu*, Bombay: Oxford University Press.

Harriss, J., 1992, 'Does the "Depressor" Still Work? Agrarian Structure and Development in India: A Review of Evidence and Argument', *The Journal of Peasant Studies*, Vol.19, No.2.

Hazell, P. and Ramasamy, C., 1991, *The Green Revolution Reconsidered: The Impact of High-Yielding Rice Varieties in South India*, Baltimore, MD and London: Johns Hopkins University Press.

Heyer, J., 1997, 'Intra-Household Conflicts in Labourer Households in Coimbatore Villages (Tamil Nadu)', Paper for South Asia Workshop, Queen Elizabeth House, University of Oxford, Jan.

Jodhka, 1995, 'Agrarian Changes, Unfreedom and Attached Labour', *Economic and Political Weekly*, Vol.30, Nos.30–31.

Jose, A.V., 1988, ' Agricultural Wages in India', *Economic and Political Weekly*, Vol.23, No.26.

Joshi, C.K and M.R. Alshi, 1985, 'Impact of High Yielding Varieties on Employment Potential of Female Labour – A Study in Akola District (Maharashtra)', *Indian Journal of Agricultural Economics*, Vol.40, No.3.

Kapadia, K., 1993, ' Mutuality and Competition: Female Landless Labour and Wage Rates in Tamil Nadu', *The Journal of Peasant Studies*, Vol.20, No.2

Kabeer, N., 1994, *Reversed Realities*, London: Verso.

Kautsky, K., 1899/1988, *The Agrarian Question* (2 vols.; trans. P. Burgess) London: Zwan Publications.

Lenin, V. I., 1899/1977, *The Development of Capitalism in Russia,* Moscow: Progress Publishers.

Lenin, V. I., 1915/1964, 'New Data on the Laws Governing the Development of Capitalism in Agriculture', in *Collected Works*, Vol.22, London: Lawrence & Wishart.

Lipton, M. and R. Longhurst, 1989, *New Seeds and Poor People*, London: Unwin Hyman.

Lucassen, J., 1993, 'Free and Unfree Labour Before the Twentieth Century: A Brief Overview', in Brass, van der Linden and Lucassen [1993].

Marothia, D.K and S.K. Sharma, 1985, 'Female Labour Participation in Rice Farming System of Chhattisgarh Region', *Indian Journal of Agricultural Economics*, Vol.40, No.3.

Mellor, J.W., 1976, *The New Economics of Growth: A Strategy for India and the Developing World*, Ithaca NY: Cornell University Press.

Mencher, J.P. and K. Saradamoni, 1982, 'Muddy Feet and Dirty Hands: Rice Production and Female Agricultural Labour, *Economic and Political Weekly*, Vol.17, No.52.

Miller, D.B., 1981, *The Endangered Sex: Neglect of Female Children in Rural North India*, Ithaca, NY: Cornell University Press.

Mies, M., 1986, *Indian Women in Subsistence and Agricultural Labour*, New Delhi: Vistaar Publications (Division of Sage Publications, India).

Olsen, W., 1991, 'Distress Sales and Exchange Relations in a Rural Area of Rayalaseema, Andhra Pradesh', D.Phil. thesis, University of Oxford.

Onselen, C. van, 1976, 'Randlords and Rotgut, 1886–1903: An Essay on The Role of Alcohol in The Development of European Imperialism and South African Capitalism', *History Workshop*, 2.

Patnaik, U., 1990, *Agrarian Relations and Accumulation: The 'Mode of Production' Debate in India*, Bombay: Oxford University Press for Sameeksha Trust.

Patnaik, U., 1987, *Peasant Class Differentiation: A Study in Method and Reference to Haryana*, Delhi: Oxford University Press.

Patnaik, U., 1979, 'Neo-Populism and Marxism: The Chayanovian View of the Agrarian Problem and its Fundamental Fallacy', *The Journal of Peasant Studies*, Vol.6, No.4.

Patnaik, U., 1976, 'Class Differentiation Within the Peasantry', *Economic and Political Weekly*, Vol.11, No.39.

Platteau, J.P., 1995, 'A Framework for the Analysis of Evolving Patron-Client Ties in Agrarian Economies', *World Development*, Vol.23, No.5.

Rahman, A., 1986, *Peasants and Classes: A Study of Differentiation in Bangladesh*, London: Zed Books.

Rajasekhar, D., 1988, *Land Transfers and Family Partitioning: An Historical Study of an Andhra Village*, New Delhi: Oxford and IBH Publishing.

Rao, J.M., 1997, 'Agrarian Power and Unfree Labour', draft paper prepared for the Workshop on 'Rural Labour Relations in India Today', 19–20 June, Development Studies Institute, London School of Economics.

Ravathi, E., 1994, 'Women, Work and Technology in Indian Agriculture: A Study in Andhra Pradesh', Ph.D thesis, Department of Economics, Karatiya University, Warangal.

Ray, A.K., Rangarao, I.V. and B.R. Attari, 1985, 'Impact of Technological Changes on Economic Status of Female Labour', *Indian Journal of Agricultural Economics*, Vol.40, No.3.

Reddy, S.S., 1991, 'Poverty Monograph No.2', Centre for Economic and Social Studies, Hyderabad.

Reddy, K.V., 1987, *Land Forms and the Emergence of New Agrarian Structure in Andhra Pradesh: A Case Study of Chittoor District*, Tirupati: L.V. Press.

Robinson, M.S., 1988, *Local Politics: The Law of the Fishes*, Delhi: Oxford University Press.

Roemer, J., 1982, *A General Theory of Exploitation and Class*, Cambridge MA: Harvard University Press.

Rogaly, B., 1997, 'Linking Home and Market: Towards a Gendered Analysis of Changing Labour Relations In Rural West Bengal', *IDS Bulletin*, Vol.28, No.3.

Sayana, V.V., 1952, *Land Sales, Land Values and Land Transfers*, Delhi: S. Chand.

Scott, J., 1985, *The Weapons of the Weak: Everyday Forms of Peasant Resistance*, New Haven, CT: Yale University Press.

Sender, J., 1995, 'Gender and Agriculture: with special reference to Bangladesh, Indonesia, Uganda and South Africa', UNRISD, Geneva, draft manuscript.

Singh, I., 1990, *The Great Ascent: The Rural Poor in South Asia*, Baltimore, MD: Johns Hopkins

University Press/World Bank.
Suryawanshi, D.D. and P.M. Kapse, 1985, 'Impact of Ghod Irrigation Project on Employment of Female Agricultural Labour', *Indian Journal of Agricultural Economics*, Vol.40, No.3., July–Sept., pp.240–44.
Thorner, D. and A. Thorner, 1962, *Land and Labour in India*, Bombay: Asia Publishing House.
Walker, T. and J. Ryan, 1990, *Village and Household Economies in India's Semi-Arid Tropics*, Baltimore, MD and London: Johns Hopkins University Press.
Washbrook, D.A., 1978, ' Economic Development and Social Stratification in Rural Madras: The Dry Region' 1878–1929' in G. Dewey and A.G. Hopkins (eds.) *The Imperial Impact: Studies in the Economic History of Africa and India*, London: Athlone Press.
Watson, E. and B. Harriss, 1986, 'The Sex Ratio in South Asia: A Review of Evidence and Explanations for Women's Welfare', mimeo, Nutrition Policy Unit, London School Of Hygiene and Tropical Medicine, July.
World Bank, 1991, *Gender and Poverty in India*, Washington, DC.

APPENDIX A: FIELD DATA COLLECTION AND TABLES

Two sets of data were gathered: (i) detailed data for the year 1994/5, (ii) retrospective data comparing the years 1970 and 1995. Data for the year 1994/5 included a labour time allocation study based on approximate minutes spent by each sample individual on the previous day's activities. This information was collected in one day in each of three seasons over the year. The activities included unwaged reproductive work (i.e. child care, cleaning, cooking, fetching water etc.), productive work (on 'family' farm, livestock and artisan means of production), work on leased in land and waged work (agricultural and non-farm).

This information was supported by very detailed case studies of a subset of labouring families with whom we had superb relations. These case studies included information on actual annual days of employment. Each member was interviewed regularly at intervals of one to two weeks throughout each season for days and partial days of employment in different activities. We used this information to test the validity of the data on approximate minutes in one day in each season. We also obtained information on wages earned for each activity from work on own means of production, on leased land and expenditure and savings patterns.

Quantitative information to cover changes over the period 1970–95 was gathered from one man and one woman in each sample household, normally a man and his wife. Each was asked to compare 1995 with 1970 on a variety of issues. If the respondent was not over 17 years old in 1970, we inquired about their parents or asked their parents directly.

There are two problems with this method that could affect our comparison of respondents' answers between the two years: (i) there is an age gap, though we tried to get as many as possible in the 25–45 age group (and if this was not possible, we compared father with son and mother with daughter closer to the same age group); and (ii) the class position for a particular individual in 1970 may not be the same in 1995. However, as da Corta's [1993] analysis shows, most economic mobility over the period 1973–88 was confined to classes within the labour group (L, L+ and SP) rather than the broad jumps to, for instance, MP, BP and C (which occurred only for a small number of households). Most individuals remained labourers despite small improvements in the landholding for some. For (ii) and (iii) the data for 1970 were collected using a special technique which we developed during our 1988/89 study to collect quantitative information and which was used in subsequent studies by da Corta and Venkateshwarlu. This technique involved periodisation/listing/comparing/ranking and finally constructing proportions when possible (see da Corta and Venkateshwarlu [1992] for a full explanation of this method).

For each respondent, we recorded changes in: (i) the primary, secondary and tertiary occupations in terms of time and income, (ii) labour and tied harvest arrangements and in the terms of these arrangements, (iii) power and decision making relations within the household and with employers, and (iv) proportion of earnings devoted to household essentials. We also used group interviews in order to gather quantitative estimates of changes in the gender division of labour in paid work and on 'family' farm, in labour requirements for the cultivation of paddy and groundnut, in wages for each type of labour arrangements and prevalence of different labour arrangements.

We also gathered retrospective qualitative data and much time went into conducting 48 interviews on reasons for changes in: employer-labour relations, domestic relations and class and gender ideologies as well as the impact of government policies since 1970. These interviews were taped, transcribed directly from Telugu into English and then analysed. Our field data results were compared with published data on employment and wages, both from the decennial Indian censuses (1961–91), as well as from various recent state and district level reports.

TABLE A1
CHARACTERISTICS OF LAND OWNED BY LABOUR CLASS
IN THE CENTRAL REGION

	Average Wet Acres Owned	Average Dry Acres Owned	Average % of Land which is Encroached	Average Land Value in 1988/89 Prices (rupees)
L	0.05	0	100%	1,245
L+	0.26	0.83	75%	13,025*
SP	0.18	2.13	29%	14,037
MP	0.85	7.20	18%	48,826
BP	1.93	3.38	0%	69,200
C	6.06	11.69	2%	572,747

*Labour classes are based on agrarian and non-agrarian means of production. Some central region SPs own more in the way of non-agrarian means of production than of land (e.g. barber shops, tea shops) which on average brings down the landownership in this category.

TABLE A2
CHARACTERISTICS OF LAND OWNED BY LABOUR CLASSES
IN THE REMOTE REGION

	Average Wet Acres Owned	Average Dry Acres Owned	Average % of Land which is Encroached	Average Land Value in 1988/89 Prices
L	0.03	0	100%	950
L+	0.06	1.23	40%	6,632
SP	0.56	2.57	21%	34,324
MP	0.71	5.99	24%	46,776
BP	3.75	20.45	0%	258,794

TABLE A3
AVERAGE LAND LEASED IN AND LEASED OUT IN ACRES BY
LABOUR CLASS IN THE WHOLE REGION

	Leased in Wet	Leased in Dry	Leased out Wet	Leased out Dry
L	0.11	0.11	0.02	–
L+	0.17	0.29	–	0.09
SP	0.78	0.25	–	0.42
MP	0.45	0.10	0.37	–
BP	0.50	–	0.62	1.75
C	–	–	5.37	7.56

Note: Women head all of the labouring families who lease out land.

TABLE A4
CLASS OF MEN IN 1995 AND AVERAGE CLASS OF THEIR WIVES

Class of Male	Average class of their Wives
L = 1	1.00 (=L)
L+ = 2	1.57 (between L and L+)
SP = 3	2.58 (between L+ and SP)
MP = 4	3.33 (between SP and MP)
BP = 5	3.85 (between SP and MP)
C = 6	5.5 (between BP and C)

Note: Sample = 45 households. For the five female headed households, there were two L, two L+ and one SP.

TABLE A5
NUMBER (PERCENTAGE) OF MEN AND WOMEN IN EACH LABOUR
CLASS IN 1970 AND 1995

	1970		1995	
Labour Class	Men	Women	Men	Women
L	10 (20.0)	11 (22.0)	6 (13.3)	11 (22.0)
L+	12 (24.0)	16 (32.0)	7 (15.5)	11 (22.0)
SP	15 (30.0)	13 (26.0)	12 (26.7)	16 (32.0)
MP	7 (14.0)	6 (12.0)	9 (20.0)	7 (14.0)
BP	3 (6.0)	2 (4.0)	7 (15.5)	3 (6.0)
C	3 (6.0)	2 (4.0)	4 (8.9)	2 (4.0)
Total	50 (100.0)	50 (100.0)	45 (99.9)	50 (100.0)

TABLE A6
AVERAGE WAGES IN TIED, DAILY WAGE AND CONTRACT WORKS IN PADDY,
GROUNDNUT AND NON-AGRARIAN WORKS IN THE CENTRAL REGION (1995)

	Tied Daily Wage		Daily Wage		Contract Wage*	
	Men	Women	Men	Women	Men	Women
PADDY						
Exclusively Male Tasks[1] (with own bulls)	47.5	–	56.2	–	77.5	–
Exclusively Male Tasks[2] (without own bulls)	17.5	–	27.5	–	32.5	–
Exclusively Female Tasks[3]	–	13.5	–	16.2	–	21.5
Joint Tasks[4]	18.3	16.8	22.5	18.5	28.7	26.9
GROUNDNUT						
Exclusively Male Tasks[5] (with own bulls)	55.0	–	65.0	–	93.3	–
Exclusively Male Tasks[6] (without own bulls)	18.7	–	27.5	–	35.0	–
Exclusively Female Tasks[7]	–	15.0	–	16.0	–	21.0
Joint Tasks[8]	16.8	15.6	20.7	18.1	27.9	26.2
NON-AGRARIAN						
Exclusively Male Tasks[9] (with own bulls)	50.0	–	65.0	–	90.0	–
Exclusively Male Tasks[10] (without own bulls)	29.2	–	35.0	–	44.2	–
Exclusively Female Tasks[11]	–	–	–	–	–	–
Joint Tasks[12]	25.0	17.7	27.5	20.5	38.7	33.7

Notes:
* calculated on an eight hour day, the full wage for a contract 'day' is much higher as days are often 9+ hours long.
  [1] ploughing and transporting grain and fodder
  [2] ploughing, building ridges, assisting transplanting, applying fertilisers
  [3] transplanting, weeding
  [4] cutting paddy, threshing. winnowing, applying natural fertilisers (manure)
  [5] ploughing, sowing, transporting harvests
  [6] ploughing, transporting
  [7] shelling groundnut (seed preparation)
  [8] clearing fields, sowing, weeding, plucking groundnut, collecting yield together, separating groundnut
  [9] carrying loads with bullock cart
  [10] roof covering, construction (Tapi work), cutting wood
  [11] no exclusively female tasks
  [12] construction work, well repair, road work, tamarind collection

TABLE A7
PERCENTAGE DIFFERENCE BETWEEN TIED WAGE AND DAILY AND
CONTRACT GANG WAGES IN CENTRAL REGION

	Ex. Male With Bulls	Ex. Male Without Bulls	Joint Male	Ex. Female	Joint Female
PADDY					
Daily	18.3	57.1	23.0	20.0	10.1
Contract	63.2	85.7	56.8	59.3	60.1
GROUNDNUT					
Daily	18.1	47.1	23.2	6.7	16.0
Contract	69.6	87.2	66.1	40.0	67.9
NON-AGRARIAN					
Daily	30.0	19.9	10.0	–	15.8
Contract	80.0	51.4	54.8	–	90.4

TABLE A8
AVERAGE WAGES IN TIED, DAILY WAGE AND CONTRACT WORKS IN PADDY,
GROUNDNUT AND NON-AGRARIAN WORKS IN REMOTE REGION (1995)

	Tied Daily Wage		Daily Wage		Contract Wage*	
	Men	Women	Men	Women	Men	Women
PADDY						
Exclusively Male Tasks (With Own Bulls)	45.0	–	48.7	–	68.7	–
Exclusively Male Tasks (Without Own Bulls)	16.5	–	22.5	–	29.5	–
Exclusively Female Tasks	–	13.0	–	15.2	–	18.7
Joint Tasks	16.8	16.0	19.5	16.5	30.6	29.0
GROUNDNUT						
Exclusively Male Tasks (With Own Bulls)	50.0	–	55.0	–	81.6	–
Exclusively Male Tasks (Without Own Bulls)	17.5	–	25.0	–	32.5	–
Exclusively Female Tasks	–	14.0	–	15.0	–	19.0
Joint Tasks	15.6	14.5	18.8	17.0	24.2	23.4
NON AGRARIAN WORK						
Exclusively Male Tasks (With Own Bulls)	45.0	–	55.0	–	80.0	–
Exclusively Male Tasks (Without Own Bulls)	25.0	–	30.8	–	38.3	–
Exclusively Female Tasks	–	–	–	–	–	–
Joint Tasks	20.7	16.7	23.7	18.3	33.1	30.0

*Calculated on an 8 hr day.

TABLE A9
PERCENTAGE DIFFERENCE BETWEEN TIED WAGE AND DAILY AND
CONTRACT WAGES IN REMOTE REGION

	Ex. Male With Bulls	Ex. Male Without Bulls	Joint Male	Ex. Female	Joint Female
PADDY					
Daily	8.2	36.4	16.8	16.9	3.1
Contract	52.6	78.8	82.1	43.8	81.3
GROUNDNUT					
Daily	10.0	42.9	20.5	7.1	17.2
Contract	63.2	85.7	55.1	35.7	61.4
NON-AGRARIAN					
Daily	22.2	23.2	14.5	–	9.6
Contract	77.8	53.2	59.4		79.6

TABLE A10
PERCENTAGE DISTRIBUTION OF RURAL MAIN WORKERS IN
ANDHRA PRADESH IN 1991

Category	Men	Women
Agricultural labour	37.3	63.7
Cultivators	39.1	24.5
Livestock, Forestry, Fishing and allied, etc.	2.6	0.7
Mining	0.8	0.4
Non-Agrarian*	20.1	10.7

*Government of India [1991]. Combines the remaining census categories of manufacturing, processing, servicing and repairs, construction, trade and commerce, transport, storage and communications and other services.

APPENDIX B:
CHANGES IN MALE AND FEMALE WORK
DAYS IN PAID WORK

It is commonly assumed that 'feminisation' is the result of the switch from traditional crops to HYVs, because higher yielding crops require more labour on female operations than on male tasks (see section 1). While HYVs contributed to the greater annual demand for labour in general, we found that the switch from traditional varieties of paddy and groundnut to HYV varieties had no impact on women's growing share of agricultural employment vis-à-vis men. For instance, in paddy cultivation there was an absolute fall in 9 days of employment per acre of paddy cultivated, with men losing 23 days and women gaining 14 days. Yet the direct HYV/chemical input effect on EF and EM operations was opposite to the trend of women's rising share. In EF work, the increase demand in paddy transplanting (+2 days) was outweighed by a fall in 4 days weeding (with the shorter duration of the HYV crop). EM work actually rose by two days because of the greater time needed applying chemical and pesticides (see Tables B1 and B2). Similarly, the switch to HYV groundnut had little effect on women's rising share. In groundnut, while there was an absolute fall in 1 day of employment: men lost 12.1 days and women gained 11.1 days. HYVs had no effect on EF work and EM work fell by one day (a fall in two days needed applying natural fertilisers and increase in one day applying chemical inputs, see Tables B3 and B4).

Changes relating to labour saving machinery had a more direct effect on women's rising share by replacing male labour. In paddy, machine operated pumping sets reduced 15 days in the EM operation of irrigation (formerly an extremely labour intensive task performed by lifting huge buckets from wells with the help of bulls). Moreover, power tillers reduced EM ploughing days by an average of two days. Thus labour-displacing machines led to 73.9 per cent of the days men lost in paddy cultivation. In groundnut, tractors reduced ploughing needs by about two days, resulting in about 16.5 per cent of the days men lost in groundnut cultivation. Ploughing is about 20 per cent mechanised in the region, but it is likely to increase as male labour costs rise and as the tractor industry targets south India for its market.

The major location for feminisation, however, is a spectacular rise in women's share of work in joint operations, which cannot be explained by technical reasons. The distinction made between gender specific and joint work is rarely made in the literature. Yet this distinction is of crucial analytical importance because there is no a priori reason why any changes in the number of days needed on a particular joint task induced by the switch to HYVs should go to one sex or the other. We found that changes as a result of the switch to HYVs/chemical inputs rarely led to a balanced distribution of days between men and women. Even when the new crops did not change days required on particular operations, women were found assuming a greater share. For instance, as a result of improved yields under HYV paddy cultivation, 8 additional days are needed on joint harvesting activities (including cutting paddy, +5, threshing, +2, winnowing +1). Yet men lost 8 days and women gained 16 days. Moreover, women assumed an additional eight days from men in joint (four days paddy cutting, 1.3 threshing, one applying natural fertiliser, one from winnowing and 1.7 from other activities). Indeed, in paddy cutting alone HYVs increased labour need by five days, but men lost four and women gained nine (see Tables B1 and B2). In groundnut cultivation women also assumed a greater share of joint work. The switch to HYVs led to a fall in weeding requirements (−2 days) and rise in four days needed in joint harvesting (plucking groundnut, +1, collecting yield together, +1, separating groundnut, +2). Of this net gain of two days in joint work, women gained 11.1 days and men lost 9.1 (see Tables B3 and B4).

TABLE B1
AVERAGE NUMBER OF MALE AND FEMALE WORK DAYS SPENT
FOR THE CULTIVATION OF ONE ACRE OF PADDY THROUGH PAID
LABOUR IN 1970 AND 1995

Task	Male Work Days 1970	1995	Fem. Work Days 1970	1995	Tot. Days 1970	1995	Abs. Loss Due to Mech.	Ch. Due to HYVs	Ch in Male Days	Ch in Fem. Days	Ch. in Gender Ratio
Exclusively Male Tasks:											
Ploughing	10	8	0	0	10	8	−2	0	−2	0	none
Building Ridges	8	8	0	0	8	8	0	0	0	0	none
Assisting Trans-plantation by Providing Saplings	2	2	0	0	2	2	0	0	0	0	none
Carrying Bundles of Paddy to 1 place	3	3	0	0	3	3	0	0	0	0	none
Applying Chem. Fertilizer and Pesticides*	0	2	0	0	0	2	0	+2	+2	0	none
Threshing**	8	6.7	0	3.3	8	10	0	+2	−1.3	+3.3	1:0-2:1
Watering	30	15	0	0	30	15	−15	0	0	0	none
Transporting Grain & Fodder	2	2	0	0	2	2	0	0	0	0	none
Exclusively Female Tasks:											
Transplanting	0	0	21	23	21	23	0	+2	0	+2	none
Weeding	0	0	22	18	22	18	0	−4	0	−4	none
Joint Tasks:											
Seeding	1	1	1	1	2	2	0	0	0	0	none
Applying Natural Fertiliser	4	3	2	3	6	6	0	0	−1	+1	2:1-1:1
Cutting Paddy	10	6	15	24	25	30	0	+5	−4	+9	2:3-1:4
Threshing (see above)											
Winnowing	2	2	2	3	4	5	0	+1	0	+1	1:1-2:3
Other	5	3.3	5	6.7	10	10	0	0	−1.7	+1.7	1:1-1:2
TOTAL (% of total days)	85	62	68	82	153	144 (−9 days)	−17	+8	−23	+14	

* Using chemical fertilisers and pesticides was not prevalent in 1970.
** Threshing was exclusively male in 1970 and was joint work by 1995.

TABLE B2

SUMMARY TABLE: DETAILS REGARDING THE CHANGE IN THE NUMBER OF
EXCLUSIVELY MALE, EXCLUSIVELY FEMALE AND JOINT WORK DAYS SPENT
FOR CULTIVATION OF ONE ACRE OF PADDY THROUGH PAID LABOUR OVER
THE PERIOD 1970–95

		EM	EF	JOINT Overall Change	Change for Men in Joint	Change for Women in Joint
Days lost due to Mechanisation	Ploughing	−2				
	Watering	−15				
Days lost due to HYVs	Weeding		−4			
Additional days due to HYVs	Applying chem. fertiliser and pesticides	+2				
	Transplanting		+2			
	Threshing (H)*			+2	−1.3	+3.3
	Cutting Paddy (H)*			+5	−4	+9
	Winnowing (H)*			+1	0	+1
No loss or gain in absolute days (but change in gender ratio)	Applying natural fertiliser*				−1	+1
	Other misc. tasks*				−1.7	+1.7
Overall changes		−15	−2	+8	−8	+16

* Tasks where there was a change in the gender ratio.
(H) Harvesting activity.

TABLE B3
AVERAGE NUMBER OF MALE AND FEMALE WORK DAYS SPENT FOR THE
CULTIVATION OF ONE ACRE OF GROUNDNUT THROUGH PAID LABOUR
IN 1970 AND 1995

Task	Male Work Days 1970	1995	Fem. Work Days 1970	1995	Tot. Days 1970	1995	Abs. Loss Due to Mech.	Ch. Due to HYVs	Ch. in Male Days	Ch. in Fem. Days	Ch. in Gender Ratio
Exclusively Male Tasks:											
Ploughing	8	6	0	0	8	6	−2	0	−2	0	none
Applying Natural Fertiliser	2	0	0	0	2	0	0	−2	−2	0	none
Applying Chemical Fertiliser	0	1	0	0	0	1	0	+1	+1	0	none
Transporting Yield	2	2	0	0	2	2	0	0	0	0	none
Exclusively Female Tasks:											
None	–	–	–	–	–	–	–	–	–	–	none
Joint Tasks:											
Seed Preparation*	1	0	4	5	5	5	0	0	−1	+1	1:4-F
Clearing Fields	1	1	1	1	2	2	0	0	0	0	none
Sowing	3	2	1	2	4	4	0	0	−1	+1	3:1-1:1
Weeding	10	4.5	10	13.5	20	18	0	−2	−5.5	+3.5	1:1-1:3
Plucking Groundnut	3.3	3	1.7	3	5	6	0	+1	−0.3	+1.3	2:1-1:1
Collecting Yield Together	1	1.5	1	1.5	2	3	0	+1	+0.5	+0.5	none
Separating Groundnut from Plants	1.5	1	4.5	7	6	8	0	+2	−0.5	+2.5	1:3-1:7
Other	4	2.7	4	5.3	8	8	0	0	−1.3	+1.3	1:1-1:2
TOTAL (% of total days)	36.8	24.7	27.2	38.3	64	63	−2	+1	−12.1	+11.1	

* Seed preparation (shelling groundnut) became exclusively female by 1995.

TABLE B4
SUMMARY TABLE: DETAILS REGARDING THE CHANGE IN THE NUMBER OF
EXCLUSIVELY MALE, EXCLUSIVELY FEMALE AND JOINT WORK DAYS SPENT
FOR CULTIVATION OF ONE ACRE OF GROUNDNUT THROUGH PAID LABOUR
OVER THE PERIOD 1970–95

		EM	EF	Joint Overall Change	Change for Men in Joint	Change for Women in Joint
Days lost due to Mechanisation	Ploughing	−2				
Days lost due to HYVs	Natural Fertilising	−2				
	Weeding*			−2	−5.5	+3.5
Additional days due to HYVs	Applying chem. fertiliser and pesticides	+1				
	Plucking Groundnut (H)			+1	−0.3	+1.3
	Collecting Yield Together (H)			+1	+0.5	+0.5
	Separating Groundnut from Plants (H)			+2	−0.5	+2.5
No loss or gain in absolute days (but change in gender ratio)	Seeding Preparation				−1	+1
	Sowing				−1	+1
	Other misc. tasks*				−1.3	+1.3
Overall changes		−3	0	+2	−9.1	+11.1

*Tasks where there was a change in the gender ratio.
(H) = Harvesting activity.

APPENDIX C:
CHANGES IN MALE AND FEMALE WORK DAYS ON
THE 'FAMILY' FARM

Evidence from our survey villages also seems to support the view that women are working more in agriculture, both paid work and work on the 'family' farm. Estimating days on own farm work was more difficult than for paid work because (i) own farm activities are often performed in partial rather than full days and are interwoven with other household chores and (ii) use outside labour during peak periods, usually through reciprocal labour arrangements with other farmers. Our estimates suggest that since 1970, women's share of the labour days required to cultivate an acre of paddy on family farms on average rose slightly, from 42.4 per cent to 54.0 per cent and from 41.7 per cent to 50.4 per cent on groundnut farms. On family farms there are no exclusively female tasks and fewer exclusively male tasks (see Tables B1, B2, B3 and B4). In paddy, labour displacing machines reduced exclusively male days by 14 (less than in paid work because of a general tendency for family farmers to work more intensively on their own farms). All other changes associated with the switch to HYV paddy were in joint work, loosely following the changes in paid work with a fall in days weeding (−5), rise in days applying chemical inputs (+2), transplanting (+2) and harvesting (+4). Overall, there were 11 days lost per paddy crop, but men lost 19.8 (14 due to labour displacing machines, 5.8 in joint) and women gained 8.8. Notably, women acquired days in what are considered EM tasks in paid work, e.g., watering, building ridges, applying fertilisers and carrying bundles. Indeed, paddy cutting is nearly becoming exclusively female.

In groundnut, HYVs led to a net loss of one day in employment. Tractors had no effect on displacing male labour in ploughing on family farms, and most changes occurred in joint work (a fall in days weeding, −3, applying natural fertiliser, −1 and increase in days applying chemical fertilisers, +0.5) and harvesting (+3). But men lost 5.75 days and women gained 4.75 days in joint work. In sum, women are increasingly assuming male days in joint operations on the family farm despite the reduction in exclusively male work and rise in women's wage agricultural work. This evidence gives some weight to the view that women are working more in agriculture in general – paid work and work on 'family' farms – while men work more elsewhere.

TABLE C1
AVERAGE NUMBER OF MALE AND FEMALE WORK DAYS SPENT FOR THE
CULTIVATION OF ONE ACRE OF PADDY THROUGH FAMILY LABOUR
IN 1970 AND 1995

Task	Male Work Days 1970	1995	Fem. Work Days 1970	1995	Tot. Days 1970	1995	Abs. Loss Due to Mech.	Ch. Due to HYVs	Ch. in Male Days	Ch. in Fem. Days	Ch. in Gender Ratio
Exclusively Male Tasks:											
Ploughing	10	8	0	0	10	8	−2	0	−2	0	none
Watering*	25	10.4	0	2.6	25	13	−12	0	−14.6	+2.6	EM:4:1
Transporting Grain & Fodder	2	2	0	0	2	2	0	0	0	0	none
Exclusively Female Tasks:											
None	–	–	–	–	–	–	–	–	–	–	–
Joint Tasks:											
Seeding	1	1	1	1	2	2	0	0	0	0	none
Building Ridges	7	6	1	2	8	8	0	0	−1	+1	7:1-3:1
Assisting Trans- plantation by Providing Saplings	1	1.5	1	0.5	2	2	0	0	+0.5	−0.5	1:1-3:1
Transplanting	1.8	1	16.2	19	18	20	0	+2	−0.8	+2.8	1:9-1:19
Applying Natural Fertiliser	4	3	2	3	6	6	0	0	−1	+1	2:1-1:1
Applying Chemical Fertilisers and Pesticides	0	1	0	1	0	2	0	+2	+1	+1	none
Weeding	5	3	15	12	20	15	0	−5	−2	−3	1:3-1:4
Cutting Paddy	9.2	6.25	13.8	18.75	23	25	0	+2	−2.95	+4.95	2:3-1:3
Carrying Bundles to One Place	2	2.25	1	0.75	3	3	0	0	+0.25	−0.25	2:1-3:1
Threshing	5.2	5.3	1.8	2.7	7	8	0	+1	+0.1	+0.9	3:1-2:1
Winnowing	1	2	3	3	4	5	0	+1	+1	0	1:3-2:3
Other	5	6.7	5	3.3	10	10	0	0	+1.7	−1.7	1:1-2:1
TOTAL	79.2	59.4	60.8	69.6	140	129 (−11 days)	−14	+3	−19.8	+8.8	
(% of total days)											

* Watering became joint work by 1995.

TABLE C2
SUMMARY TABLE: DETAILS REGARDING THE CHANGE IN THE NUMBER OF
EXCLUSIVELY MALE, EXCLUSIVELY FEMALE AND JOINT WORK DAYS SPENT
FOR CULTIVATION OF ONE ACRE OF PADDY THROUGH FAMILY LABOUR OVER
THE PERIOD 1970–95

		EM	EF	Joint Overall Change	Change for Men in Joint	Change for Women in Joint
Days lost due to Mechanisation	Ploughing	–2		0		
	Watering**	–12		0	–2.6	+2.6
Days lost due to HYVs	Weeding*			–5	–2	–3
Additional days due to HYVs	Applying chem. fertiliser and pesticides			+2	+1	+1
	Transplanting			+2	–0.8	+2.8
	Threshing (H)*			+1	+0.1	+0.9
	Cutting Paddy (H)*			+2	–2.95	+4.95
	Winnowing (H)*			+1	+1	0
No loss or gain in absolute days (but change in gender ratio)	Applying Natural Fertiliser*			0	–1	+1
	Building Ridges*			0	–1	+1
	Assisting Transplantation*			0	+0.5	–0.5
	Carrying Bundles to One Place*			0	+0.25	–0.25
	Other misc. tasks*			0	+1.7	–1.7
Overall changes		–14	0	+3	–5.8	+8.8

* Tasks where there was a change in the gender ratio.
** Watering became joint work by 1995.
(H) = Harvesting activity.

TABLE C3
AVERAGE NUMBER OF MALE AND FEMALE WORK DAYS SPENT FOR THE
CULTIVATION OF ONE ACRE OF GROUNDNUT THROUGH FAMILY LABOUR
IN 1970 AND 1995

Task	Male Work Days 1970	1995	Fem. Work Days 1970	1995	Tot. Days 1970	1995	Abs. Loss Due to Mech.	Ch. Due to HYVs	Ch. in Male Days	Ch. in Fem. Days	Ch. in Gender Ratio
Exclusively Male Tasks:											
Ploughing	6	6	0	0	6	6	0	0	0	0	none
Transporting Yield	2	2	0	0	2	2	0	0	0	0	none
Exclusively Female Tasks:											
None	–	–	–	–	–	–	–	–	–	–	–
Joint Tasks:											
Seed Preparation	2	1	2	3	4	4	0	0	–1	+1	1:1-1:3
Clearing Fields	1	1	1	1	2	2	0	0	0	0	none
Sowing	3	2	1	2	4	4	0	0	–1	+1	3:1-1:1
Weeding	9	6	9	9	18	15	0	–3	–3	0	1:1-2:3
Applying Natural Fertiliser	1	0	1	0	2	0	0	–2	–1	–1	none
Applying Chemical Fertilisers and Pesticides	0	0.5	0	0.5	0	1	0	+1	+0.5	+0.5	none
Plucking Groundnut Plants	3	2.5	2	2.5	5	5	0	0	–0.5	+0.5	3:2-1:1
Collecting Yield Together	1	1.5	1	1.5	2	3	0	+1	+0.5	+0.5	none
Separating Groundnut from Plants	2	1.75	3	5.25	5	7	0	+2	–0.25	+2.25	2:3-1:3
Other	5	5	5	5	10	10	0	0	0	0	none
TOTAL	35	29.25	25	29.75	60	59	0	–1	–5.75	+4.75	

TABLE C4
SUMMARY TABLE: DETAILS REGARDING THE CHANGE IN THE NUMBER OF
EXCLUSIVELY MALE, EXCLUSIVELY FEMALE AND JOINT WORK DAYS SPENT
FOR CULTIVATION OF ONE ACRE OF GROUNDNUT THROUGH FAMILY LABOUR
OVER THE PERIOD 1970–95

		EM	EF	Joint Overall Change	Change for Men in Joint	Change for Women in Joint
Days lost due to Mechanisation	None					
Days lost due to HYVs	Natural Fertilising			–2	–1	–1
	Weeding*			–3	–3	0
Additional days due to HYVs	Applying chem. fertiliser and pesticides			+1	+0.5	+0.5
	Collecting Yield Together (H)*			+1	+0.5	+0.5
	Separating Groundnut from Plants (H)*			+2	–0.25	+2.25
No loss or gain in absolute days (but change in gender ratio)	Seed Preparation*			0	–1	+1
	Plucking Groundnut Plants*			0	–0.5	+0.5
	Sowing*			0	–1	+1
Overall changes		0	0	–1	–5.75	+4.75

* Tasks where there was a change in the gender ratio.
(H) = Harvesting activity.

APPENDIX D:
POLICY IMPLICATIONS

Since state interventions have been an important reason for tightening the labour market and upward land mobility of labourers, anti-poverty policies need to be sustained rather than cut through liberalisation policies. In the remote region the policy having the strongest effect, that enabling landless to encroach, has effectively ended, with the drying up of land contributing to rising land inequality. This region – and others like it in the state – need more public investment, as off-farm employment possibilities are slim.

In the context of such profound and enduring inequalities in class and domestic (gender) relations, reforms based purely on liberalisation and on market-led growth would be inadequate. The powerful argument that the basis of fast economic growth is a prior, heavy state investment in health, education and social security [Drèze and Sen, 1995] is much more relevant to the needs of labourers. Such interventions would go far to reduce the consumption crises that force labourers to tie their labour and harvest and accept unequal terms. However, these universal interventions, while sorely needed, might be insufficient unless there is also a more direct attack on the material basis of unequal class and gender relations – inequalities in the ownership of the means of production. Both a proper rural land reform based on the redistribution of good quality irrigated land together with minimum wages legislation would be desirable, but difficult to enforce. Nevertheless, there are several things the Andhra Pradesh government could to do increase the wages and asset ownership of labourers through direct redistribution of assets together with some 'welfare' based interventions which would result in a redistribution.

(i) Increasing investment in government health care and increasing the provision of rice to labourers under the rice subsidy scheme in the lean season can help prevent the consumption crises which force labourers to take loans and thereby enable them to get a fairer price for their labour. Such investment would also allow labour costs to rise to their natural, market based level. As labour costs rise, more capitalist employers will be inclined to give their land over to better paid contract works and more favourable fixed rate tenancies or to move out of farming and sell their land to farmers using family labour (where the land will be cultivated more productively). Indeed, the government could then come in at this stage, buy up land as it comes onto the market, and then ensure that it goes to labourers, preferably female labourers.

(ii) Women's lack of real possession of the 'family' land and assets reduces their power in domestic relations and diminishes their power to protest successfully for fair wages on the basis of such holdings. The state government should enforce existing legislation regarding women's legal rights to family land [Agarwal, 1994]. A government-sponsored scheme in Andhra Pradesh, which gives landless women both (a) distributions of all surplus waste land as well as (b) land purchased from market sales meeting with some success in many districts. Other government asset subsidies (such as upon livestock, houses, rice subsidy cards and fair price shops) should also be put in women's names. Government sponsorship of women's literacy, consciousness raising efforts and savings schemes should continue (but given cultural constraints on men selling rice for alcohol, it might be helpful to make the matching government subsidy portion in rice, not cash, and be distributed through the existing 'fair price' rice subsidy shops). (First implemented in Guntur district and now extended to other districts of AP, for example, Rangareddy, Nalgonda, the AP Scheduled Caste Finance Corporation offers credit to poor families to buy land. However, coverage of families in each district is limited by the small budget of this corporation.)

Rural Labour Relations and Development Dilemmas in Kerala: Reflections on the Dilemmas of a Socially Transforming Labour Force in a Slowly Growing Economy

K.P. KANNAN

I. INTRODUCTION

Ever since the publication of *Poverty, Unemployment and Development Policy: A Case Study of Selected Issues with Reference to Kerala* by the United Nations [1975], the southern state of Kerala has become well-known in international development literature for its high level of social development and rapid decline in the rate of growth of population.[1] Distributive issues have been central to the question of development in Kerala, and its achievements – especially in the spheres of land reform, education, health care and public distribution of food grains – had set it apart from the rest of India by the early 1970s. A feature which had attracted the attention of social scientists earlier was the early emergence of radical left-wing politics, culminating in the election of a provincial government led by the then undivided Communist Party of India. This was in 1957, a year after the State of Kerala was formed by the merging of the two formerly princely States of Travancore and Cochin with the Malabar District of the state of Madras. Less well known, but very important, is the continuing economic backwardness manifested in low per capita income, high unemployment and an almost unchanging employment structure dependent on low productivity occupations in rural areas. The highly contested nature of distributive issues in a regime of low accumulation has given rise to a number of development dilemmas for Kerala. Without resolving these dilemmas, Kerala's quest for all-round development will

K.P. Kannan is a Fellow, Centre for Development Studies, Trivandrum, Kerala, India. This study was written on the basis of a presentation made by the author at an international workshop on Rural Labour Relations in India Today held at The London School of Economics and Politics, London, during 19 and 20 June 1997. The author would like to thank Terry Byres, Karin Kapadia and Jens Lerche for their comments on an earlier draft and Jan Breman and Ashwani Saith for their encouragement.

remain incomplete. This study is an attempt to relate the emergence of these dilemmas to the dynamics of rural labour relations.

An important question that one might raise is: how are rural labour relations related to the development dilemmas in Kerala? Because of the highly politicised and militant nature of labour struggles until the recent past, Kerala has acquired a certain kind of notoriety, especially among the investing class but also among the middle class, who shape public opinion in India, that it is a 'problem state' as far as labour relations are concerned and that 'labour is not cooperative'. Therefore, Kerala is unable to attract investment, which it badly needs, because of the seriousness of the problem of unemployment especially among its educated population. Capital, therefore, does not migrate to Kerala but labour from Kerala migrates to not only other parts of India but overseas – especially to the countries in the Gulf region – and is known for its skill, diligence and intelligence. So the message is that labour relations have become a fetter upon economic development especially with respect to overall economic growth through accumulation. Since rural labour accounts for more than 70 per cent of the total workforce, and is highly organised as a class, rural labour relations are intimately linked to the emergence of the development dilemmas. It is not the preponderance of rural labour that makes it an active player in the development process, but its emergence and positioning as a class that stands in contradiction to the interests of capital that has brought it to the centre of the development discourse in Kerala. In what follows, when discussing rural labour relations we will refer to labour and capital as the two main actors.

Kerala is unique among Indian states in that labour, including rural labour, has acquired a dominant position both in the development discourse and in the development process. This is due to its historical role in national as well as radical political movements, and subsequent organisation in terms of trade unions closely linked with political parties.

Moreover, capital is much less powerful in Kerala than in the rest of India. While wage labour is the predominant form of employment, not all those who hire labour can be characterised as capitalist, although that is the name – *Mudalali*, one who owns capital – by which workers refer, in their common parlance, to their employers, including small farmers, small scale industrialists and traders. Since the formation of the state of Kerala the influence of capital over the government has been at best marginal. The land reform measures did away with the emergence of any powerful agrarian capital in much of agriculture. Because of the tiny size of the private modern manufacturing sector, industrial capital was negligible. Capital in Kerala was, and continues to be, mostly mercantile in character, engaged in such small-scale agro-processing activities as coir, cashew, fisheries, wood, vegetable oil, etc. The strategy of such a capitalist class was confined to extraction of absolute surplus value until that was effectively countered by the emergent organised power of labourers. A shift to a strategy of extraction of relative surplus value via the introduction of technological change was partly thwarted by the organised power of labour and became unattractive: producing a stalemate in the commodity producing sectors of the economy. The state could neither induce such a change nor take up the role of producing it directly.

That, then, brings us to the role of the third player in the development discourse – that of the state. The state in Kerala, as represented by the state government, has limited degrees of freedom. It is critically dependent on the central government in New Delhi for finance. Most investment decisions in the public sector are taken by the central government and thus fall outside the realm of the state government. That does not mean that it is powerless to decide on the direction of development or to intervene effectively when it so desires. However, in Kerala, the state has not been able to exercise a decisive role in determining the course of economic development in general and investment decisions in particular. The coming to power of political parties strongly supported by the labouring poor in general and organised labour in particular has meant that the government has had to address distributive issues first. Given the dependence on wage labour of the majority of the population, important political parties sought to create their own political constituencies among the working class. Organised labour, because of its political clout, may be seen to exercise a hegemonic role whether or not the political party – or, rather, parties – in power is dependent on their support. Coalition politics and governments have had to reckon with the power and demands of labour. Much of the energy of the state has been directed at mediating disputes between labour and capital and/or labour and the state. Given the influential positioning of organised labour and the limited autonomy of the government, the state in Kerala may be characterised as a 'soft' institution. Such a situation of limited autonomy has to be seen in the context of two other limitations. One is the limited nature of fiscal power of the states under the Indian Constitution and the other is the limitation imposed by the nature of coalition politics.[2]

II. WHAT ARE THE DEVELOPMENT DILEMMAS?

We discuss here three major development dilemmas that are closely related to the dynamics of labour relations in general and rural labour relations in particular. The first one may be identified as 'wage gain but job loss'. While the organised power of labour enabled real increases in wage rates as well as securing better conditions of work, the employers resorted to a strategy of technological change to increase productivity and to prevent increases in the share of wages. Faced with a situation of displacement of labour in a context of labour surplus in the economy, trade unions opposed such technological change. This resulted in employers seeking strategies to reduce the quantum of employment in an effort to reduce, or prevent, further increase, in wage cost. In agriculture, this led to crop substitution in favour of low labour-absorbing crops. In a number of rural industries, this meant the migration of capital to low-wage areas in neighbouring states where the organised power of labour is quite weak. The decade of the 1970s witnessed this phenomenon.

The second dilemma emerged in the context of rapid social development that included rural poor households, in which rural labour is located, and may be summed as 'a mismatch between labour supply and labour demand'. The likelihood of immiserisation of rural labour, that could have followed the decline in employment for rural labour, was partly thwarted by a series of government poverty alleviation programmes. An equally important part in preventing immiserisation of rural labour was played by large- scale migration of labour, mostly from rural areas, to countries in the Middle East as a result of the economic boom following the rise in incomes of those countries from higher prices for oil. For rural labour, this also created conditions for securing higher wages despite the continuing high incidence of unemployment in the economy. The higher social development of the rural population, especially of the younger age group, gave rise to a change in expectations with respect to the nature of and duration of employment. Younger members expected, and wherever feasible opted for, more regular and 'clean' jobs as opposed to the casual employment in agriculture and rural industries involving much drudgery and low social status. The second dilemma, which unfolded by the second half of the 1980s, therefore, was the existence of a vast reservoir of reasonably educated, young, socially conscious unemployed labour in a technologically stagnant economy reporting labour shortages for unskilled manual labour on a casual basis.

The third dilemma relates to the role of the state. This may be summed up as a failure of the state to promote technological change and enhance investment despite the emergence of favourable conditions. It is the inability of the state to resolve the contradiction between rising wage costs and stagnant technology through a technological breakthrough in existing agricultural and rural industrial activities that led to the second dilemma. The key to this was its failure to provide critical infrastructure. The dilemma deepened as a result of the country-wide economic reforms which liberalised trade and investment from the early 1990s. On the one hand, Kerala found itself unable to attract investment from outside the state, as a result of its image as a 'labour problem state', and, on the other, unable to convert the considerable loanable funds in the domestic banking system – as a result of remittances – into domestic investment.

The dynamics of labour relations and the emergence of the abovementioned dilemmas are closely related and have become a general phenomenon in Kerala and not confined to a particular sector. However, we need to demonstrate the working out of this dynamic in concrete terms. This we do in relation to rural labour relations in the basic sector of the economy, that is, agriculture. Our discussion will be focussed on agricultural labour relations in the rice producing sector, where these dilemmas have pushed the trade unions, the state and the farmers to reconsider their earlier strategies. To emphasise our point about the generalised nature of the nexus between labour relations and developmental dilemmas, we shall bring into the discussion examples from other labour situations – especially rural labour situations – wherever appropriate.

III. A BRIEF BUT NECESSARY OVERVIEW OF RURAL CLASS FORMATION

While the concrete situation discussed here is that of agricultural labour relations, it is important to keep in mind the generalised process of the formation of a rural proletariat as a class-in-itself and its subsequent emergence as a class-for-itself. In an earlier study, *Of Rural Proletarian Struggles*, published in 1988, I dealt in detail with the historical process of the 'making of a rural proletariat' in Kerala as well as its political mobilisation and organisation. The emergence of a market for rural labour in Kerala needs to be located in the historical context of the penetration of capitalism under conditions of colonialism in an agrarian society. The traditional labour institutions under the caste system, with social stratification as its main distinguishing feature, gave way to the emergence of wage labour as a result of the commercialisation of the economy. While caste identity remained as a segmenting force even in the emerging labour market, the process of expanding the sphere of wage employment continued.

A major reason for the widening wage employment relations of the Kerala economy was the 'commercial' nature of its output (perennial cash crops and their processing) as well as the 'commercial' potential of its natural resources (e.g. forests). The process of rural proletarianisation began in the second half of the nineteenth century and continued well into the second half of this century. Initially the process started with trade and related economic activities and the beginnings of capitalist enterprises in plantations and agro-processing sectors. The opening up of plantations (for tea, coffee, rubber, and spices) attracted labour from the lower castes to work in the public works programmes engaged in opening up the forests, and to work in plantation estates and processing factories.[3] The setting up of factories to manufacture coir products out of yarn, spun by women in households, was another. Other 'large-scale' manufactories included the introduction of tile factories, using the locally available fine clay and saw mills for processing wood, etc. To this should be added those workers who were in small-scale production units under wage employment. Prominent among these were workers in coir processing (defibring, spinning), toddy tapping (extraction of an alcoholic beverage from coconut trees) and beedi (country cigarette)-making. Even those who were classified in the census reports as 'household workers' were dependent on the market for the sale of their labour power through the sale of their products. These were the handloom weavers, blacksmiths, potters, etc. To this should be added workers in such services as transport (for example, country boat workers), loading and unloading of agricultural products, workers in repairing roads and canals and workers grouped under 'those without a definite occupation' in the census reports. The significance of the commercial nature of the agrarian economy can be gauged from the fact that all kinds of workers in the non-agricultural sector varied, as per census reports of 1901 and 1931, between 52 to 62 per cent of the total workers in Travancore which was then the most commercialised part of present-day Kerala. In Cochin, a smaller region, the figures were 51 to 53 per cent; while in Malabar, the least-commercialised part directly under the British, they were 37 to 41 per cent.

The single largest group of workers, however, was that of agricultural labourers. In Malabar, their proportion to total workers was higher than in Cochin and Travancore – varying from 35 to 40 per cent between 1901 and 1931; while Travancore accounted for the lowest per centage – between 7 to 15 per cent – as a result of the higher share of cultivating owners, mostly small peasants. Cochin was in-between, accounting for 24 to 29 per cent.

The process of the formation of a 'class-for-itself' of rural workers was the direct result of an active strategy of political mobilisation of all types of workers undertaken first by the Congress Socialist Party, a left-wing group within the Indian National Congress which was at the helm of the movement for independence, and later by the Communist Party, which was a successor to the Congress Socialist Party in Kerala. Historical factors played an important role in this process of, what I called in my 1988 study, 'political mobilization under conditions of accelerated social change'. These factors were: the early proletarianisation of a large segment of the traditional workforce; the emergence of social reform movements for attaining social dignity for the poor and those considered socially backward; and the coming of nationalist politics, quickly accompanied by a radical political movement which sought to incorporate all sections of the labouring poor, irrespective of their status as peasants, wage labour, or self-employed in non-agricultural occupations. This was made possible at a time of deep economic hardship (during the Depression of the 1930s). I have referred to this context as a 'historical conjuncture' facilitating early and rapid radicalisation of rural workers in Kerala (see Kannan [1988: Ch.3]). Political mobilisation sought to bring workers and non-workers (students, women, intellectuals, etc.) under the fold of the Communist Party while trade unions were formed for specific groups of workers to fight for their rights as workers against employers and/or the state. Though the process of unionisation *per se* was greatly facilitated by the radical political movement, the unions soon realised that they had to function, in part, in the context of capitalist labour relations. However, the objective situation was such that there was only a small segment of the economy which could approximate to capitalist enterprises (for example, plantations, large coir manufacturing factories, etc.). Given the strong anti-capitalist ideology (in the non-agricultural sector) and the strategy of peasant-worker alliance in agriculture (against a relatively small landlord class), all situations characterised by relations of labour exploitation were considered appropriate for unionisation. Hence the rapid extension of the process of unionisation to the so called 'unorganised' or 'informal' sectors (see Kannan [1992]).

Caste initially provided a framework for protest movements aimed at the destruction of feudal domination in social and cultural spheres but caste did not prevent the process of class polarisation and the emergence of class-based organisations such as trade unions. The role of the state, given the explicitly political nature of the mobilisation and organisation of workers, was one of confrontation and suppression but it was unable to prevent the growth of a working class movement. Increasing literacy and education of the poorer sections played a catalytic role right from the early stages of social reform to the emergence of secular, nationalist and socialist movements.

Two features, specific to the ecological situation of Kerala, which seem to have favoured the process of mobilisation and organisation of rural workers should also be noted here. The first is the spatial concentration of large groups of workers as a result of specialisation in, and export of, a variety of comercial crops and their processing as rural industrial activities. The second is the absence of sharp rural-urban distinctions. The implication of this was that while the workers' movement was originally confined to the tiny 'urban surroundings' activists soon realised the limitations imposed by the small size of 'urban workers'. They, therefore, looked further afield to the large number of rural proletarians and began to incorporate them. Geographical proximity and relative ease of transport and communication combined with the spread of education facilitated the mobility of both people and ideas.

It is against such a background that I place the emergence of a class of agricultural labourers. The evolution of agrarian labour relations in Kerala is rooted in the history of its land tenure system. Ownership of land, tenurial conditions and the employment of labour were marked by layers of rights and characterised by a complex system of infeudation and sub-infeudation. Agricultural labourers who were agrestic slaves, with no ownership or tenancy rights, stood at the bottom while the absentee landlord, receiving rent, stood at the top. Differentiation in Kerala immediately after independence and preceding the formation of the state (in 1956) can be classified in terms of rent receivers, cultivating landowners, tenants and agricultural labourers. Because of the abolition of tenancy and conferment of proprietary rights on cultivators as early as the second half of the nineteenth century, cultivating landowners constituted more than 53 per cent of the agricultural population in Travancore but with a significant proportion of agricultural labours at 34 per cent. Tenants constituted only around 10 per cent. Cochin and Malabar presented a different picture because of the widespread nature of tenancy. In Cochin tenants constituted around 28 per cent and in Malabar it was as high as 39 per cent. But agricultural labourers constituted the single largest group in both these regions at around 49 per cent and 44 per cent respectively [*United Nations*, 1975: 57].

Tenancy reform was the most important goal on the agenda of the radical peasant movement in Malabar. In Travancore the working-class movement, including the movement of agricultural labourers, occupied a prominent place in the radical political movement. When the Communist Party formed its first government in Kerala in 1957, land reform assumed the focus of attention of both its supporters and opponents. The intention was to abolish tenancy and introduce a ceiling on land and redistribute the surplus to landless agricultural labourers. The Kerala Agrarian Relations Bill was passed in June, 1959. The land reform question remained alive on the political agenda of Kerala for more than a decade, during which further legislation was passed. It was a tortuous process, and the dilution of the original provisions and several compromises have been well documented [*Varghese, 1970; United Nations* , *1975*: Ch.V; *Raj and Tharakan, 1983*]. While the objective of tenancy abolition was achieved, the implementation of a land ceiling and redistribution of surplus land were far less effective. However, the agrarian situation was transformed radically.

We may usefully identify a differentiated peasantry in terms, broadly, of marginal, small and big cultivators. There emerged a class of big cultivators throughout Kerala. In rice cultivation, they were already present in the low-

TABLE 1

SIZE DISTRIBUTION OF OPERATIONAL HOLDINGS IN KERALA

Size class	1966–67			1990–91		
	No.of holdings (000)	Area operated (000 acres)	Av. size of holding (cents)	No.of holdings (000)	Area Operated (000 acres)	Av. size of holding (cents)
Marginal [< 1 acre]	1480 [60]	561 [12]	38	4548 [84]	1342 [30]	30
Small [1-5 acres]	798 [32]	1730 [39]	217	748 [14]	1772 [39]	237
Large [>5 acres]	201 [8]	2225 [49]	1107	123 [2]	1411 [31]	1147
All	2479 [100]	4516 [100]	182	5419 [100]	4525 [100]	84

Note: Figures in brackets indicate per centages.
Source: Nair [1997] based on Government of Kerala [1968] for 1966–67 and Census of
          Agriculture: Kerala [1991].

lying wetland regions in the districts of Alleppey and Kottayam in the south
(formerly in Travancore). A similar class emerged in the midland region in
the north in the district of Palghat (formerly in Malabar) and in the low-land
areas in Trichur (formerly in Cochin). The relevant details are given in
Table 1 but it should be noted that this is for all crops. What is significant
in these figures is the preponderance of marginal and small cultivators,
accounting for 92 per cent of the total in 1961. But the remaining eight per
cent of big cultivators, assuming that a holding is equivalent to a household,
operated almost half of the total area. For our purposes the first group of
'marginal' farmers are mostly household plots with such garden crops as
coconut and banana in the homestead land. The categories of 'small' and
'large' farmers are the relevant ones as far as rice cultivation is concerned.
The predominance of 'small' holders is evident here and they account for
39 per cent of the area in both the 1960s and the 1990s. It is against such a
background that we should examine the size and growth of the class of
agricultural labourers. We have already noted that agricultural labourers as
a group accounted for a significant part of the agricultural population in the
Malabar and Cochin regions of Kerala even before Independence. Taking
Kerala as a whole the overall ratio was in favour of cultivators (owners and
tenants) *vis-à-vis* agricultural labourers. But such a situation continued only
until the 1960s. The Census of 1961 reported that for every ten cultivators

in Kerala there were eight agricultural labourers. By 1971 the situation was reversed; for every ten cultivators there were 17 agricultural labourers. By 1981, there were 22 agricultural labourers for every ten cultivators. A marginal decline was seen in 1991 with 20 agricultural labourers for every ten cultivators, the reasons for which will be evident in our subsequent discussion. This is in sharp contrast to the situation in India as a whole where, even in 1981, cultivators outnumbered agricultural labourers; for every ten cultivators there were only six agricultural labourers. Rice cultivation, which absorbed more labour than any other crop in Kerala, provided much of the employment. The two regions of Kuttanad (comprising the whole of Alleppey district and part of Kottayam district) and Palghat accounted for about one-third of the area and around 37 per cent of the output of rice in the mid-1970s, the peak period of rice cultivation in Kerala.

IV. CLASS ACTION BY AGRICULTURAL LABOURERS

The political mobilisation and consequent organisation of agricultural labourers in trade unions first started in the thirties in Kuttanad, a low-lying water-logged area. Here rice cultivation had already assumed several of the characteristics of capitalistic agriculture. It was mostly owner-cultivated, large scale and spatially spread over blocks of 100 to 150 acres of land. Production was largely for the market and scarcity of foodgrains resulting in higher prices for paddy, especially during the Second World War, due to disruption of imports, had created conditions favourable to cultivators. One such was active state help in reclaiming land from waterlogged areas and improving lands which were vulnerable to floods (for details see Pillai and Panikar [1965]). The organisation of agricultural labourers received considerable support, in the initial stages, from the organisation of coir factory workers in Alleppey, who were at the forefront of the political and economic struggles of the working class in Kerala in the thirties and forties. A union of agricultural labourers was formed (called the Travancore Agricultural Workers Union) as early as 1938. Initially demands centred around changing the traditional social code of conduct emphasising subservient behaviour from agricultural labourers who belonged to lower castes. Agricultural labourers, for example, were not allowed to sport a moustache or wear headgear using their towels. They had to address farmers as 'master' and had to keep a distance while dealing with them. Trade union organisation backed by radical political activism helped them to eliminate these behavioural norms one by one. In addition, they started demanding a proper lunch break during work, an increase in daily wages and an increase in harvest wages (paid as a share of output). Strikes and sit-ins followed these demands and the labourers could hold on for days only because of the economic assistance and political backing from trade unions of other workers. Trade unions were careful in the timing of their demands in that they chose critical periods in the labour process such as during harvesting or dewatering the flooded fields. Farmers had to choose between accepting the demands or losing the crop. (For details see Alexander [1975]; Jose [1979]; Tharamangalam [1981: Ch.5]; Kannan [1988: Ch.6]).

The emergence of a separate organisation for agricultural labourers in Palghat in 1968, as in the case of Kuttanad in 1938–39, was due to the convergence of economic and political factors. Tenurial reforms, coupled with the political strength of the tenants, had already contributed to the emergence of a class of independent and rich farmers in Palghat. Although agricultural labourers lent considerable support to the struggles in securing tenancy reforms, the new owner cultivators were not eager to share their benefits. This situation coincided with the split in the Communist Party into two separate parties. The stronger one, the Communist Party of India (Marxist), referred to as CPI(M), was eager to bring the organised workers in Kerala into its fold and extend organisation to new groups. Thus a new state-wide organisation called the *Kerala State Karshaka Thozhilali Union* (KSKTU), or the Kerala State Agricultural Workers Union, was formed with Kuttanad (mainly Alleppey district) and Palghat as the two strong bases. Going by the membership figures, it appears that tremendous progress was made in recruiting large numbers of agricultural workers. By 1985 KSKTU alone accounted for 35 per cent of total agricultural labourers in Kerala; in the district of Alleppey more than 70 per cent of agricultural labourers were members of this union [*Kannan*, 1995a: 470].

The split in the main political party and the activity of other parties in forming trade unions among rural workers brought about the emergence of several unions for the same category of workers. Among agricultural labourers, the KSKTU was the biggest and strongest followed by the *Kerala State Karshaka Thozhilali Federation* (KSKTF) of the Communist Party of India (the CPI). When the Indian National Congress split in 1969, the new party led by Indira Gandhi formed a union of agricultural labourers in Kerala which is now known as the *Kerala Karshaka Thozhilali Union* (the Kerala Agricultural Workers Union). A number of regional parties, most with only local influence, formed their own agricultural workers unions. My own tally is that there are at least four to five unions in a given area with the total number of agricultural labourers unions in Kerala as a whole going up to eight. The abovementioned three unions are present throughout Kerala.

The emergence of a number of unions complicated the situation of labour relations in agriculture, as it did in other sectors. Unions competed with one another in putting forward new demands, a strategy supported by political parties to gain electoral support. The period from the mid-1960s also witnessed the introduction of the Green Revolution strategy by the central government to enhance food production and to eliminate dependence on food imports. Alleppy and Palghat were the two districts selected from Kerala under this strategy.

The demands and the militant posture of trade unions, especially led by the CPI(M), led to a generalised atmosphere of tension in the rice fields of Kerala between the mid-1960s and the late 1970s. Farmers responded by retrenching workers, often those who had been in long-term employment with them. They resorted to casualisation of employment and a policy of hire and fire. Physical violence broke out in several rice fields especially during harvest time. Several instances of workers forcibly harvesting rice were reported. Farmers tried strong-arm tactics by hiring mercenaries but it did not last long since the government was not always behind them. When pro-labour governments were in power, the scales tilted in favour of unions since the police would not be used to interfere in what was called 'labour disputes'. The attempt to introduce tractors as a means to reduce dependence on labour for some critical operations was met with strong resistance. In Kuttanad, some tractors were broken up, a Luddite strategy resorted to by the unions with a view to protect employment and retain their bargaining power. A similar strategy of blocking technological changes in the coir industry and demands for wage increases in many other industries had led to a situation of declining employment. This in fact added to the pressure in agriculture as such displaced workers, especially women, joined the ranks of agricultural labourers. Farmers gradually lost control over selecting labour. Unions would send in labour for harvests and sometimes the numbers were so large that they could finish harvesting in a matter of a few hours. Farmers often sought police protection to prevent more labourers joining in. A kind of order was brought in as unions decided to issue 'work cards' for those selected for particular agricultural operations. The situation symbolised union power not just in organising and bargaining but in the very functioning of the market for agricultural labourers: selection of workers, work enforcement, work rationing, and worker control. The following observation by a scholar, based on his field visits during the late 1970s, is pertinent here to convey the nature of union power. It also provides a sharp contrast to the current situation of labour shortage discussed later in the study.

> A typical harvesting operation proceeds as follows. The land owner is required by law to obtain the permission from the revenue office before harvesting. He announces the date of his harvest and requests police protection in advance. In addition, he approaches the local

KSKTU leader or leaders and reaches a prior understanding that no trouble will be caused. He would very likely have made a 'contribution' to the labour union. The morning of the harvest arrives with the police on the scene and about 2000 workers instead of the 250 that are supposed to be accommodated. (The I.R.C. [Industrial Relations Committee] had decided that the number of workers be restricted to 125 per hectare.) When the first 225 have been let into the field, respecting the rights of the workers of the vicinity, the landlord, the Police Officer and the local union leader would hold a brief discussion. The union leader suggests that another 400 workers could be accommodated. The police officer then says to the landlord "Sir, don't you think we could allow another 200 into the field?" Almost certainly the landlord accepts the suggestion. The officer then asks the remaining crowd to look for work elsewhere. In fact many will already have left for another harvest site [*Tharamangalam*, 1981: 86]

It was during these tumultuous years that a system of industrial relations was introduced and accepted by unions and farmers. The 1957 Communist government had already made it a policy not to use police in 'labour disputes' thus taking away a major instrument of coercion available to the farmers. Later Industrial Relations Committees were set up for agricultural labourers, as they were in several other rural industries (such as coir, cashew processing, toddy tapping, etc.). Demands for wages and non-wage benefits would be followed by long negotiations in the IRC before a settlement was reached. This would be disseminated far and wide by unions so that agricultural labourers in every village were made aware of them.

V. FARMERS' RESPONSE TO LOSS OF LABOUR CONTROL AND DECLINING PROFITABILITY

To begin with, farmers had to agree to better conditions of work as times were changing in Kerala. No more social indignities were tolerated. Behavioural changes were accepted gradually, though reluctantly. Command and control gave way to more impersonal behaviour (devoid of demeaning action) and patron–client relations replaced by contractual arrangements. In some cases, farmers lost out completely because of the loss of any bargaining power. This may be illustrated by the compromise on the introduction of tractors. When trade unions opposed the introduction of tractors, to the extent of breaking up of some of them, the farmers were not willing to give in. The new Green Revolution strategy, in the context of food shortage in the country, had made rice production attractive until the mid-1970s (see Table 2). So they persisted with their resolve to introduce tractors

TABLE 2
FARM PRICE INDEX OF RICE AND COCONUT
BASE 1962 TO 1964–65=100)

Year	Price index		Ratio of
	Rice	Coconut	2 to 3
1962–63	82	98	0.84
1963–64	86	95	0.91
1964–65	132	106	1.25
1965–66	176	155	1.14
1966–67	214	146	1.47
1967–68	281	180	1.56
1968–69	224	156	1.44
1969–70	201	198	1.02
1970–71	181	228	0.79
1971–72	199	167	1.19
1972–73	238	209	1.14
1973–74	375	373	1.06
1974–75	492	338	1.46
1975–76	365	265	1.38
1976–77	285	362	0.79
1977–78	261	392	0.67
1978–79	252	405	0.62
1979–80	266	453	0.59
1980–81	304	548	0.55
1981–82	358	452	0.79
1982–83	416	573	0.73
1983–84	503	963	0.52
1984–85	450	691	0.65
1985–86	485	769	0.63
1986–87	496	1028	0.48
1987–88	555	1128	0.49
1988–89	606	847	0.72
1989–90	581	809	0.72
1990–91	599	1195	0.50
1991–92	750	1561	0.48
1992–93	842	1667	0.51
1993–94	829	1292	0.64
1994–95	990	1222	0.81
1995–96	1094	1313	0.84

Source: Computed from price data given in Government of Kerala, *Statistics for Planning* and *Economic Review*, various issues.

that would reduce critical labour time and also enable double cropping wherever feasible. Unions also did not relent. Ultimately the issue was resolved by the farmers agreeing to pay wages to the traditional ploughmen for ploughing the fields and the unions agreeing to let the farmers use tractors. This meant that farmers would be free to use tractors for ploughing after they have paid the wages to the ploughmen. So the ploughmen would come and plough the field, take his wage and go away. Farmers would then prepare the land with tractors in whatever way they wanted. Over time, the ploughing by ploughmen became a ritual and gradually they stopped ploughing. But they would come and collect their 'wages'. This system continues even today in Kuttanad although most ploughmen or their successors ceased to be ploughmen. The initial compromise was attractive to the farmers since the price of rice was high enough to make it acceptable. With the decline in the relative price of rice from mid-1970s (see Table 2), this has become a source of complaint by the farmers.

The situation changed radically with the gradual decline in the relative price of rice leading to a decline in the profitability in rice cultivation. This started by the middle of the 1970s by which time food grain production in India had increased impressively and the zonal restrictions in movement was lifted. Cheaper rice from nearby states such as Tamil Nad and Andhra Pradesh as well as from more distant states such as Punjab and Haryana started coming into the Kerala market. Given the same price for such inputs as fertilisers, pesticides, machinery, etc. in all states, a higher wage rate in Kerala made it less profitable for farmers there to continue with rice cultivation. Initially their strategy was to reduce employment. In Kuttanad, it was found that farmers reduced labour input per crop area by 20 per cent between 1971 and 1979. In Palghat, there was no reduction. Palghat still enjoyed relatively lower wage rates and a double cropping system. However, labour became less cheap per unit of output. Thus a kg. of paddy commanded 2.36 hours of labour in 1971, which reduced to 1.32 by 1979, but this was still higher than the 0.75 hours commanded by farmers in Kuttanad in both 1971 and 1979 [Natarajan, 1982]. The farmers of Kuttanad could maintain this relatively high price of labour constant only by reducing employment.

The decline in profitability in rice cultivation cannot be deduced merely by considering the increase in money wage rates or in real wage rates. Real wages did show a sustained increase, as shown in Table 3, where the growth rates in money wages are greater than growth rates in the consumer price index for agricultural labourers.

From the point of view of the profitability to the farmer, however, we need to examine this in relation to the price received for the product. Assuming that farmers face the same or similar prices for non-labour inputs, an increase in money wages can be neutralised by a proportionate increase in labour productivity. This means that the product wage, that is, the share of wages in value added per worker, remains the same even if there is no increase in price of the product. I have subjected this question to a detailed analysis covering the major crops in Kerala across regions (see Kannan and Pushpangadan [1990]). What was found in that study was a generalised phenomenon of agricultural stagnation in Kerala between the mid-1970s and the mid-1980s. But the situation was acute in the case of rice

TABLE 3
GROWTH RATES IN MONEY WAGES OF RURAL LABOUR IN KERALA
1963–64 TO 1995–96

Category	Period I	Period II	Period III	Whole Period
Paddy field labour – men	10.13	15.48	14.30	10.11
Paddy field labour – women	13.47	12.04	16.95	10.42
Rural construction – unskilled men	10.49	14.13	13.13	10.28
Rural construction – unskilled women	10.66	14.40	14.17	10.94
Consumer Price Index for agr labrs	10.56	8.99	10.15	7.26

Note: For period-wise estimates, a linear function seemed to fit better than compound growth and exponential functions. For the whole period, an exponential function seemed to be the more appropriate one. Period I refers to 1963–64 to 1974–75; II to 1975–76 to 1987–88; and III to 1988–89 to 1995–96.

TABLE 4
GROWTH RATES IN YIELD (Y) AND PRODUCT WAGE(W)

				(y – w)	
Crop		Period I	Period II	Period I	Period II
Rice	y	1.0	1.2		
	w	–0.1	7.7	1.1	–6.5
Tapioca	y	4.0	NS		
	w	0.5	2.2	3.5	–2.2
Banana	y	NS	–2.3		
	w	NS	2.3	No change	–4.6
Coconut	y	-2.4	NS		
	w	-0.8	0.5	–1.6	-0.5
Rubber	y	9.0	NS		
	w	3.3	–0.5	5.7	0.5

Source: Kannan and Pushpangadan [1990: 2000].

cultivation. During the sixties and up to the mid-1970s, faced with militant trade unionism in agricultural labour relations, rice farmers could absorb the increases in money wages because the product price was increasing faster than money wages. The situation reversed from the mid-1970s because the product wage was increasing at a high rate. Thus the differential between the growth rate in labour productivity and the product wage was +1.1 during

1962–74, which meant that farmers were more than compensated through an increase in labour productivity as well as an increase in the product price, whereas this turned to –6.5 during 1975–85. This was solely the result of the faster rate of growth in money wages compared to the produce price despite a continuing increase in labour productivity. This was the case for most crops (except rubber and a few minor crops), indicating the severity of the crisis in Kerala's agriculture (see Table 4).

The response of the farmers in rice cultivation was one of crop substitution. The area under paddy started declining from 1977–78 although the gross area under all crops remained the same and even showed a marginal increase during the 1990s. Farmers were shifting to less labour absorbing perennial and cash crops like coconut. There was also a shift to rubber which remained an attractive crop till recently. The decline in area under rice has been truly alarming in a state which is deficient in rice to the extent of 50 to 70 per cent of its requirements. By the mid-1980s area declined to 77 per cent of the peak year of 1975–76. The decline continued uninterrupted thereafter and by 1995 the gross cropped area under rice was 470,000 hectares, that is, 53 per cent of the area in the peak year (see Table 5).

This decline in gross cropped area has been analysed in an independent study, carried out in 1992–93, on the nature of conversion of lands originally registered as 'rice field' (*nilam*) in the basic land tax register [*Kerala Statistical Institute*, 1994]. The results of this study strengthen our argument that crop substitution was resorted to as a strategy to counter the declining profitability in rice cultivation induced by a faster increase in money wages than the product price. In 1992–93, only 58 per cent of area classified as 'rice field' in the tax register was cultivating rice. Only six per cent of the area was converted for constructing buildings, roads and similar purposes as a result of the boom in construction. Twenty-four per cent of the area had already been converted to grow perennial crops like coconut and rubber, indicating that the farmers had taken an 'irreversible' decision. 8.5 per cent of the area was under annual or seasonal crops such as banana, roots, vegetables, etc. indicating that it could revert to rice cultivation once conditions became favourable. 3.5 per cent of the area was kept fallow which I reckon is a 'transitional' situation before the land is committed to permanent conversion.

Given the continuing trend in the decline of area under rice, it has already lost its prominent place in the cropping pattern of Kerala. In 1975–76 the area under rice accounted for 30 per cent of the gross cropped area, it declined to 24 per cent in 1985–86 and to just 15 per cent in 1995–96 (see Table 5). From the viewpoint of labour, the crucial impact has been on the decline in employment. Using the labour absorption figures of rice cultivation in Palghat for 1979,[4] which would represent most of area under

TABLE 5
DECLINE OF AREA UNDER RICE CULTIVATION

Year	Area under rice (000 ha)	Gross cropped area (000 ha)	(2) as % of 3
1	2	3	4
1962–63	803	2447	33
1963–64	805	2462	33
1964–65	801	2489	32
1965–66	802	2551	31
1966–67	799	2622	31
1967–68	810	2757	29
1968–69	874	2853	31
1969–70	874	2916	30
1970–71	875	2933	30
1971–72	875	2958	30
1972–73	874	2986	29
1973–74	875	2999	29
1974–75	882	3028	29
1975–76	885	2981	30
1976–77	·854	2933	29
1977–78	840	2923	29
1978–79	799	2949	27
1979–80	793	2854	28
1980–81	802	2884	28
1981–82	807	2905	28
1982–83	779	2862	27
1983–84	740	2861	26
1984–85	730	2874	25
1985–86	678	2866	24
1986–87	664	2870	23
1987–88	604	2899	21
1988–89	578	2963	20
1989–90	583	3019	19
1990–91	560	3020	19
1991–92	541	3021	18
1992–93	538	3046	18
1993–94	508	3042	17
1994–95	503	3048	17
1995–96	471	3048	15

Source: Government of Kerala, *Statistics for Planning* and *Economic Review*, various issues.

rice, the decline in employment would be equivalent to 31.3 million man days between 1975 and 1985 and 62.6 million man days between 1975 and 1995. This is assuming that labour absorption per hectare has remained the same. We have reason to doubt this assumption because data provided by farmers during an investigation in 1998 showed that labour absorption is only three-fourths of that in 1979.[5] Given the low labour absorbing nature of perennial crops, the net decline is likely to be in the range of 60 to 70 per cent of the total decline in employment.

This decline in area under rice as part of a broader strategy of crop substitution has had a direct impact on the economic condition of agricultural labourers. The absence of alternative employment opportunities in the sixties and 1970s, coupled with a decline in employment in agro-processing industries, resulted in an increase in the number of agricultural labourers. This was in addition to the natural increase due to population growth. Thus per capita employment of agricultural labourers declined sharply. Average annual days of employment for agricultural labourers in Kerala[6] in 1964–65 was 194 for men and 143 for women compared to 273 and 180 respectively for all India. This difference is mainly due to the predominance of perennial crops in Kerala's agriculture. By 1974–75 this declined to 160 for men in Kerala with no decline for women, the result of a strategy of substituting female labour for male labour during the initial period of wage bargaining. This was 245 and 173 for men and women at the all India level. In 1983–84 per capita employment declined to 147 and 115 for men and women respectively in Kerala. So the decline in men's employment was 18 per cent between the mid-1960s and the mid-1970s and eight per cent between the mid-1970s and the mid-1980s.

Therefore the decline in per capita employment proved to be the price that agricultural labourers as a class had to pay for their 'class action' through trade unions to increase wages and non-wage benefits. That the agricultural labourers as a class could not improve their economic condition (despite marked improvement in their social condition and institutionalisation of reasonable norms for conditions of work) has been borne out by a number of studies (see, for example, Mencher [1978; 1980]; Panikar [1978]). Even the cautious judgement of modest improvements is not based on their ability to increase income from employment but from a number of welfare programmes wrested from the state (see, for example, Raj and Tharakan [1983]; Kannan [1988]). Some improvement in the economic condition of agricultural labour households occurred during the 1980s as a result of the continuing increase in real wage rates. But the crucial element in preventing immiserisation of agricultural labourers, in securing, indeed, a modest improvement in their economic condition, was, as we shall see later, the combined impact of 'poor-relief' programmes implemented by the state.

This dilemma of 'wage gain but job loss' has not been confined to agricultural labourers. In fact, every major segment of rural labourers experienced it. In the coir manufacturing industry, demand for increased wages and better conditions of work led to the closure of factories by the employers as early as the 1950s. Later, employers set up small workshops in rural areas, in a process that has been termed a 'retrogression in the coir industry' [*Isaac*, 1982.). When labourers in these workshops were also brought into the fold of unions, employers sought technological change. More capital intensive technologies were available in coir defibring, spinning and manufacturing operations, making it possible to set up integrated plants. Unions opposed such technological change, which the government supported. Meanwhile, employers introduced technological change outside Kerala. Coir factories, mainly employing men, and coir processing units, mainly employing women in household units as well as small rural workshops, experienced a decline in employment over a period of time, thereby leading to a severe crisis in the industry in Kerala (for details see Isaac *et al.* [1992: Ch.2]).[7] In the handloom weaving industry, absence of modernisation (including technological change) in the Schumpetarian sense led to the decline of the industry in Kerala. This was despite the demonstrated ability of workers to innovate products and capture foreign markets for a short span of time. At the same time, in neighbouring states there was the introduction of powerlooms and an increase in the output of textiles. In the Coimbatore and Salem districts of the neighbouring state of Tamil Nadu there was an emergence of the hosiery industry followed by a technologically sophisticated garments industry. The emergence of Tirupur in Coimbatore district as a centre for woven cloth and garments with a turnover of over Rs 20 billion per annum by the 1990s and employing nearly 250,000 workers is in sharp contrast to the archaic state of the handloom textile industry in the nearby state of Kerala with its high quality labour force. Industries such as tile manufacturing, long established in Kerala, also grew in neighbouring states.

In those labour-intensive industries where technological change *per se* was not on the cards, there was a stronger tendency to migrate to low wage areas rather than embark on a programme of modernisation to enhance labour productivity. For employers, who were largely mercantile in nature, the easier option was to migrate to low wage areas not far from the borders of Kerala. A prominent example is that of the cashew processing industry employing around 100,000 workers, 95 per cent of whom were women. Introduction of minimum wages arising out of the demand of labour unions resulted in large- scale migration of the industry to Tamil Nadu and a sharp decline in employment in the industry in Kerala [*Kannan*, 1983: Ch.8]. In the registered factory sector, the number of workers employed declined by more than half (56 per cent) between 1975 and 1988, although per capita employment remained steady at a low level of around 130 days [*Deepa*, 1994: 46]. A similar situation arose in the beedi making industry concentrated in the northern part of Kerala in the late sixties [*Kannan*, 1988: Ch.5; *Raghavan*, 1986).

The opposition to technological change was a generalised one arising out of the well-known trade union strategy of protecting current employment. Thus, in the context of the organised power of labour unions in Kerala, it was not confined to agriculture and labour-intensive manufacturing. Labour unions in the organised sector – both public and private – opposed technological change. Unions in such public sector organisations as commercial banks and insurance companies as well as those in public administration opposed, for example, the introduction of computers in the 1970s. In Cochin Port, a critical infrastructure facility in the public domain, containerisation and related technological changes were initially opposed and later strongly contested resulting in considerable delay. Here payment of wages to port workers even when labour was not required for a specific job (subsequent to the introduction of new technology) was ensured. The precedent was the case of ploughmen in Kuttanad who successfully negotiated to continue receiving wages even when tractors were used for ploughing. A similar strategy was also adopted by the 'headload workers' who in the late 1970s emerged as one of the most powerful labour unions in Kerala. They insisted on employing union members in the respective localities to perform the loading and unloading of goods and enforced wages over which employers had very little control. A system of payment of 'wages' even when such labour was not actually employed was also successfully enforced. Although the majority of rural labour unions could not resort to such tactics, this did contribute significantly to an unfavourable image of labour in Kerala, especially among prospective investors.

The first dilemma may therefore be summed up as one where increases in wage rates as well as an improvement in formal conditions of work (for example, the eight hour day) were secured but resulted in a sharp decline in employment. Opposition to technological change with a view to protect current employment failed. Crop-substitution was the strategy adopted by farmers in rice cultivation while agroprocessing industries migrated to neighbouring states.

VI. THE RESPONSE OF THE STATE: POOR-RELIEF AND WELFARE

The growth in the class of agricultural labourers between 1961 and 1981 and the decline in their per capita employment should have led to a process of immiserisation. In fact, it did lead to a situation of immiserisation in the 1970s, in the form of an increase in the intensity of poverty among agricultural labour households. While the income (both wage and non-wage) of agricultural labour households was around 55 per cent of the income required to cross the officially determined poverty line in 1964–65, it declined to 49 per cent by 1974–75 [*Kannan*, 1995b: 717], lending support to the conclusions of earlier studies of a decline in economic condition. This situation turned around and by 1983–84 the family income of agricultural labourers was around 89 per cent of the required income to cross the poverty line [ibid.]. This has to do with some of the major developments in Kerala including the expansion in economic circulation as a result of remittances of workers from the Gulf leading to a higher demand for unskilled labour in construction and related activities (stone and sand quarrying, brick-making) and in service sector jobs such as transport. This, backed up by the organised power of labourers through trade unions, made it possible to realise an increase in real wages (see Table 3). However, as noted above, this was not sufficient to overcome a situation of poverty. It is here that the role of the state in initiating a number of welfare, or what I choose to call 'poor-relief', programmes, becomes important. As far as agricultural labourers were concerned this had two important dimensions. One was the realisation of some marginal benefits as a result of their struggles directed against the state and the other was the benefits derived from 'poor-relief' programmes of a generalised nature.

The first arose out of the struggles of agricultural labourers in the context of the inability of the state to redistribute land by imposing a ceiling on ownership as part of the Kerala Land Reforms Act of 1971. Since the better organised KSKTU belonging to the CPI(M) was in opposition, with the CPI leading a coalition government between 1969 and 1977, the former launched a vigorous struggle to secure land for hutment dwelling. The immediate action was to 'enclose' ten cents (one-tenth of an acre) of land around the hutments of agricultural labour families, which was in excess of the 7.5 cents stipulated for distribution as 'hutment dwelling' in the Kerala Land Reforms Bill, then awaiting the assent of the President of India. The mass agitational tactics led to several clashes with the police. By 1975, when a national State of Emergency was declared throughout the country, the struggle had gone through several phases. Subsequently, the struggle tapered off with the reshuffling of political alliances whereby both the communist parties became part of a left-wing coalition. By then, 62 per cent of the estimated 400,000 hutment dwellers, mostly agricultural labourers, secured ownership rights.

There were nearly 300,000 agricultural and other rural labour households who could not benefit by the above programme of securing a piece of land because they had no access to land and basic housing facilities. As a measure of relief for these households, the government launched a massive programme of distributing 200 square yards of land (two per cent of an acre) and a house with an area of 250 square feet for around 100,000 households. This was about one-third of the total landless households in the early 1970s. It was a massive programme in the sense that houses were to be built in all panchayats, and the government was to supply such material as timber and mobilise part of the labour as voluntary labour. The programme was launched in 1972 and closed in 1976. Only 56 per cent of the total intended houses were actually built. Though it fell short of the target, the achievement was significant and it served the larger purpose of focusing public attention on the minimum housing needs of the poorest sections in the society.[8]

These two concrete achievements along with the psychological changes brought about by political mobilisation helped accelerate the demise of the patron-client relationship and the consolidation of impersonal contractual relations in the agricultural labour market. Once the threat of eviction had gone, labourers became more forceful in demanding higher wages. Land owners responded by giving up their traditional obligation to provide for regular employment. The process of casualisation of the labour market became much stronger. Therefore, it is in the arena of the labour market that securing of ownership rights to hutment land was mostly felt.

Another struggle to push forward the agenda of land redistribution was also launched around this time. This was a joint agitation by peasants' organisations and the agricultural labour unions launched by the CPI(M). However, with the enactment of land reforms, the tenant-peasants had become land owners and were less enthusiastic about participating in this struggle. Over time, this became a symbolic struggle and by the end of the 1970s it had tapered off. The figures of actual redistribution of land were also no more than symbolic. By 1980 the government could suggest a figure of 0.11 million acres as the estimate of 'surplus' land. This was a mere six per cent of the estimate made in 1957 when the then communist government introduced a land reform bill. The implementation of take over and distribution was much more modest. Only 63 per cent of the land intended for expropriation was actually taken over and only 41 per cent actually distributed. Around 76,000 persons benefited with an average size of just 63 cents of land [*Kannan*, 1988: 268].

It was against such a background of meagre benefits to agricultural labourers and the new insecurity arising out of the casualisation of the labour market that the government sought to introduce legislative measures to guarantee payment of minimum wages, security of employment, and such non-wage benefits as a provident fund, and so on. Although a law was enacted, it failed completely in its implementation because of problems in enforcement (see Kannan [1988: 281–5]). Realising that, the government introduced a welfare scheme by which old-age agricultural labourers were entitled to a pension from the state. The amount was quite small but I consider it equivalent to one frugal meal a day.[9]

These 'poor-relief' programmes were clearly not sufficient to make up for the gap between actual family income and the required income to cross the poverty line. That was provided by other 'poor-relief' programmes from which agricultural labour households stood to benefit, being one of the main constituents of the rural poor. These programmes were the PDS which covered the entire population of Kerala to provide rice and a few other essential items (such as sugar and kerosene) at subsidised prices. Since poorer households depended on the PDS for two-thirds of their rice purchase, the system provided them significant relief: significant because this was the single most important programme among all the 'poor-relief' programmes examined (see Kannan [1995b: 722]). The other was the provision of a free lunch to schoolchildren up to the primary level (the first five years). Since primary school enrolment in Kerala was more or less complete for the relevant age-group by the mid-1970s, a free meal for poor children, who were mostly from agricultural labour households, was significant. There were other programmes. These included the programme for pregnant women and children below five years in terms of supplementary nutrition. Programmes like the Integrated Rural Development Programme and Rural Employment did not constitute a major share of benefits but a few households did benefit from these as well as from a variety of other small programmes such as scholarships for children from Scheduled Castes and Tribes (whose members were mostly agricultural labourers). Using the available figures for 1983–84, I made a rough estimate in which the money equivalent of all these 'poor-relief' programmes worked out at 21 per cent of the per capita consumption expenditure of rural labour households. Given a family size of around five, this meant that one in five persons in rural labour households was supported by the 'poor-relief' programmes of the state [1995b: 722].

The impact of the 'poor-relief' programmes was not confined to agricultural labour households alone. In fact it was part of a wider impact resulting in a decline in the incidence of rural poverty in Kerala in the 1980s [ibid.].

VII. THE EMERGENCE OF THE SECOND DILEMMA: MISMATCH BETWEEN LABOUR SUPPLY AND LABOUR DEMAND

The impact of these 'poor-relief' measures cannot be examined in isolation. It has to be judged in the context of an overall process of accelerated social development in Kerala marked by a demographic transition attaining replacement level fertility by the end of the 1980s, an increase in the rate of literacy which now covers practically all the younger generation, an increase in the average years of schooling, enhanced health status such as in increased life expectancy and low infant mortality (see Table 6). Given the expansion of the service sector as a result of the flow of remittances, there seems to have taken place a shift in the social expectations of the younger generation. This was also the case of youth in agricultural labour households. Younger members of agricultural labour households preferred to work in non-agricultural employment or to wait until they (hopefully) secured such employment. This was not an isolated phemenon. By the second half of the 1980s, farmers reported shortage of labour for agricultural operations as opposed to a situation of surplus labour and the problems associated with limiting the entry of such labour a decade previously. A study of this phenomenon, conducted in the rice-growing region of Kuttanad [*Francis*, 1990), has given us an idea of this emerging phenomenon.

The study, conducted in 1987, was prompted by the reported shortage of labour for critical agricultural operations in the rice fields. Ninety-one per cent of the farmers in the study area reported shortage of labour for harvesting, 69 per cent reported shortage for weeding and around 25 per cent for transplanting. This was happening during a period of decline in the area under rice, in, for example, the districts of Alleppey and Kottayam which come under the Kuttanad region. Wages continued to rise and one of the major achievements of trade unionism among agricultural labourers in this area was an impressive increase in harvest wages, paid as a share of the harvested rice. In 1952 the harvest wage was 1/12th or 8.3 per cent of the produce. That gradually increased to 1/6th or close to 17 per cent by the mid-1980s; and that continues even today.

The main findings of this study was that the younger members of agricultural labour households, especially those with better education, show a distinct preference to seek work outside agriculture. Thus only 52 per cent of the members of the agricultural labour households[10] in the 16–30 years age group reported as working as agricultural wage labour whereas more than 73 per cent of those in the age group of 31 and above worked as agricultural wage labour. Nearly half (48 per cent) of these younger members had attained an educational level of successful completion of 10 years of school education (known as the Secondary School Leaving Certificate or SSLC for short) and above including nine per cent with either a bachelor level degree or a technical diploma. I am not aware of any other part of India where younger members of agricultural labour households have attained such levels of education.

This however did not mean that the younger members were successful in finding a suitable job; only eight per cent had either a salaried job or 'technical work' (such as electricians or vehicle mechanics). Nearly 24 per cent reported as unemployed and were looking for a job outside agriculture.

Securing non-agricultural work, even in rural Kerala, is not easy since the strong trade unions had resorted to an 'insider' strategy to restrict entry into the labour market. Thus only a family member or relative of a toddy tapper could become a tapper, or membership of a union was a prerequisite for entry into such jobs as a headload worker or sand/limeshell worker.[11] That higher educational attainment was a major factor in moving away from agricultural wage work was revealed by the fact that 85 per cent of the unemployed had an educational level of SSLC and above. Men had a stronger motive to go out of agricultural wage work than women. This, I believe, arose out of greater freedom for spatial mobility as well as greater options in the labour market. Only 39 per cent of younger men – in the 16–30 age group – were agricultural labourers, whereas the figure was 64 per cent for women.

How could agricultural labour households afford such high unemployment of their younger members? A variety of factors contributed to this. A reduction in the dependency ratio arising out of the demographic transition, that has been characteristic of Kerala, was one such factor. The average size of agricultural labour households in the Kuttanad region in 1983 varied from 5.4 to 5.7 [*Government of Kerala* , 1985: 17]; Francis's study found this to be between 4.9 and 5.0 in 1987 [1990: 76]. The change in age-structure resulted in an increase in the average number of earners from 1.9 to 2.4 in 1983 to 2.5 to 2.7 in 1987. But it is our contention here that the combined impact of all 'poor-relief' programmes, equivalent to the consumption of one out of five members in the family, played a significant role in the ability of the younger generation to remain unemployed until employment could be secured in the non-agricultural sector. The preference for moving out of agriculture was so strong that parents expressed their desire to see their children move out of agricultural wage work.[12] This has certainly to do with the 'low status' of the agricultural labourer and the drudgery involved in such manual work in the casual labour market. Francis's observation would seem to sum up the dilemma of the younger members of the agricultural labour households:

> We feel that the lower participation of the youth in Kuttanad in agricultural activities could be the result of the broader socio-economic and cultural changes that the population has been going through since the break up of the feudal social system. As a latent effect of the dissolution of the feudal social relations, a vast section of the population have been emancipated from the caste based division of labour and cultural captivity. The experience of the long established nexus between agricultural work and low economic and social status makes the younger generation look for work in other sectors. In our

study we found that the youth have a clear preference for non-agricultural activities especially blue collar or service sector work. The higher levels of education achieved by the youth further strengthens their aspirations on these lines. Although we found only a very small section in Kuttanad now engaged in such activities, a shift of a sizeable section of the workforce from agricultural to non-agricultural sectors seems quite probable in future, if the economic milieu makes such changes viable. [1990: 142]

While Francis's study area was in the low-land region of Kuttanad, another study conducted in 1989 in five villages in the midland/highland region and reported recently [*Nair*, 1997] confirms the above findings. This study did not examine the labour supply characteristics in terms of age-groups but reports that 'workers are simply unwilling to do agricultural work and more particularly paddy cultivation' [ibid.: L-52]. This has resulted in farmers keeping as much as ten per cent of the crop area as fallow. Forty per cent of farmers reported 'clear shortage of workers'. They also reported increased transaction costs in terms of recruiting costs, supervision costs, not keeping contractual obligations, and so on. The evidence from the labour supply side seems to support the author's contention that there is a distinct preference for moving out of agricultural work. The unemployment rate among adults (excluding the aged) in rural labour households was around 36 per cent. Unemployment among the educated (SSLC and above) was 27 per cent and they all reported as not available for manual work. Even for all adults employment in manual work accounted for only 43 per cent [ibid.: L-50].[13]

The changes in the supply conditions of agricultural labour arising out of the kind of social development achieved by labour households has also to be seen in the wider context of social development in Kerala. The period of widespread unionisation and the organised profile of labour in general and rural labour in particular, that is, from the early 1960s to the mid-1980s, coincided with a demographic transition and sustained social development that affected the labour suppply.[14] That the demographic transition was evident even among agricultural labour households has been suggested by a recent study [*James*, 1997]. Agricultural labour households in the Alleppey district with a higher degree of political mobilisation and social development were found to have gone through a demographic transition earlier than the relatively backward district of Palghat. Refuting an earlier thesis [*Mencher*, 1980; *Basu*, 1986] of poverty-induced fertility transition, the author concludes that 'even without substantial improvement in the material well-being or modernisation fertility decline can take place in a population with a higher awareness and organisation' [ibid.: 153]. For

Kerala as a whole, the high population growth rate (around 2.2 per cent) between 1951 and 1971 and its subsequent decline contributed to an increase in the share of the labour force (economically active population in the age group of 15–59 years) in the total population. Projections suggest that such a tendency will continue till the turn of this century [*Rajan et al.*, 1993]. In 1961 the economically active population for males was 51 per cent of the total and this increased to 62 per cent in 1991. For females this ratio increased from 52 to 63 per cent. This has meant a greater pressure in the labour market. The increase in labour supply has been accompanied by an improvement in social development indicators in Kerala. These include a continuous increase in literacy and schooling, increase in age at marriage for women, a reduction in the number of children, increase in life expectancy that is greater for women than men, a sharp reduction in infant mortality and better access to such collective goods as transport and communications (Table 6).

The quest for better conditions of work, wages, non-wage benefits and such other arrangements as would approximate to formal employment status could therefore be better appreciated if we take into account such an underlying process of qualitative change. However, in the absence of increasing investment in the non-agricultural sector, the strategies of labour unions in terms of protecting current employment by opposing technological change and an insider strategy of restricting entry into specific occupations did not lead to either output growth or employment protection. This was manifested in an increase in the incidence of unemployment especially among the younger and educated groups and a deceleration in the growth of output in the productive sectors between the mid-1970s and late 1980s (see Tables 7, 8, 9 and 10). The most affected was the agricultural sector where output declined in absolute terms largely via the crop cultivating sector which we have illustrated here through the experience in rice cultivation.

It is important for our discussion here to place this second dilemma of a labour shortage in agriculture representing the casual labour market for unskilled workers in the context of an increase in overall labour supply and a distinct preference for formal employment status in terms of regularity and security. As mentioned earlier, the outward manifestation of this was the increasing incidence of unemployment among the younger age group especially those who are 'educated' (see Table 8). Although labour supply, as measured by the size of the labour force, increased the work participation rate in Kerala declined overall, and more for women than men.[15] Estimates of unemployment for men in Kerala varied between 14 per cent (Usual Status, meaning long-term unemployment) and 25 per cent (Current Daily Status, meaning short term unemployment)[16] in 1977 for rural as well as

TABLE 6
SOME INDICATORS OF SOCIO-ECONOMIC CHANGE IN KERALA AND INDIA

Indicator		Kerala	India
Sex ratio (females/1000 males)	1961	1022	941
	1991	1036	929
Crude birth rate	1961	43.9	47.1
	1991	19.8	30.5
Crude death rate	1961	19.7	28.2
	1991	5.8	10.2
Infant mortality rate	1961	128	140
	1991	17	91
Life expectancy at birth – Male	1961	44	42
	1991	71	60
Female	1961	45	41
	1991	74	61
Literacy (% of population) – Male	1991	94	64
Female	1991	87	39
Literacy among Scheduled – Castes (mostly agricultural labourers) – Male	1991	85	50
Female	1991	74	24
Proportion of readers among agricultural labourers (any publication) – Male	1989	46	3
Female	1989	12	1
Incidence of poverty (as % of population)	1993	27	36
Per centage of women work-seekers registered with Employment Exchanges	1993	50	22

Source: Compiled from various sources.

total population which increased to 13 per cent and 17 per cent respectively by 1987 (see Table 9). The rates for women were considerably higher: 30 and 27 per cent in 1977 to 25–26 to 27–29 per cent in 1987. There is hardly any difference between rural and urban areas. Detailed analysis of unemployment data reveals the gravity of the situation among the younger and educated labour force [*Mathew*, 1996). The incidence of unemployment was more acutely felt in the younger age-group (15–29 years) than any

TABLE 7
GROWTH RATES OF SECTORAL AND AGGREGATE INCOME IN KERALA AT
CONSTANT PRICES

Sector	Growth rate		
	Period I	Period II	Period III
Aggregate income	3.21	2.52	6.85
Primary	2.23	–0.33	3.83
(Agriculture)	(na)	(–0.52)	3.70
Secondary	4.71	2.39	8.14
(Manufacturing)	(Na)	0.63	5.74
Tertiary	4.24	5.81	8.59

Note: Growth rates have been calculated by fitting a linear function. Period I refers to 1960–61 to 1974–74; II to 1975–76 to 1987–88; and III to 1988–89 to 1995–96. 1975 marks the beginning of significant remittances into Kerala and 1988 marks the first major shift in national economic policy in favour of economic liberalisation.

TABLE 8
WORK SEEKERS IN EMPLOYMENT EXCHANGES

Year	No.of work seekers (in Million)	Share of 'Educated' (In %)
1981	1.90	48
1985	2.57	53
1991	3.64	64
1995	3.23	71

Note: 'Educated' means those with a secondary school pass (SSLC) and above.
Source: Government of Kerala, *Economic Review*, various issues.

other. Twenty-three per cent of males in this group were unemployed (Usual Status) in 1983 and that increased to 26 per cent in 1987-88. For women, the increase was from 36 to 47 per cent. Those with lesser education showed a relatively low incidence of unemployment whereas those with school education up to the secondary level showed the highest incidence. Here again, women suffered the most. In 1983, 27 per cent of rural males with secondary education were unemployed and it rose to 29 per cent in 1988,

TABLE 9
ESTIMATES OF UNEMPLOYMENT RATES IN KERALA 1977–78 TO 1987–88

Year/Age	Rural			Total		
Group	M	F	P	M	F	P
1977–78						
Usual Status	13.6	29.2	19.2	14.0	30.6	19.8
Current Daily Status	25.0	27.4	25.8	25.0	27.2	25.7
1983						
Usual Principal Status						
15–29	22.5	33.3	26.1	22.9	35.5	27.1
30–44	4.0	5.3	4.4	4.1	6.3	4.7
45–59	1.5	1.8	1.5	1.5	1.5	1.5
Total	10.6	17.0	12.6	10.8	18.4	13.1
Current Daily Status	24.3	31.0	26.2	24.0	30.7	25.9
1987—88						
Usual Principal Status						
15–29	25.7	44.9	32.4	26.1	47.1	33.3
30–44	4.7	11.8	7.1	4.9	11.8	7.1
45–59	3.0	5.5	3.7	3.1	4.9	3.6
Total	12.5	25.0	16.6	12.8	26.3	17.1
Current Daily Status	16.7	27.4	20.0	17.8	29.4	21.2

Note: M=male; F=female; P=persons.
Source: Abridged from Mathew [1996: 209 and 211] based on NSS data of 32nd, 38th and 43rd rounds.

whereas the ratios for women were 51 per cent and 60 per cent respectively. Mathew's observation that unemployment rates in Kerala 'are generally three to five times the all-India levels' and when it comes to the female labour force 'the disparity is still more pronounced' points to the seriousness of the situation in Kerala [ibid.: 208]. Kerala's share of the educated unemployed labour force rose from 12 to 16 per cent of the national total between 1983 and 1988. I should mention here that Kerala accounts for only around 3.5 per cent of the population in India. In short, the unemployment rates are disproportionately high in Kerala compared to all-India in whatever way they are measured.

We may recapitulate. Within Kerala, the unemployment rate is higher among the educated particularly those with middle level and up to secondary level. Unemployment is higher in rural areas than in urban areas and it is acute among the younger generation. Women have higher rates of unemployment with rural, young, school-educated women showing the highest incidence. As the general education level of the population has

TABLE 10
UNEMPLOYMENT RATES (USUAL PRINCIPAL STATUS) OF EDUCATED LABOUR
FORCE IN KERALA AND INDIA, 1983 AND 1987–88

Category	Kerala		India	
	Male	Female	Male	Female
1983				
Rural				
Secondary	26.6	50.5	10.5	33.5
Graduate and above	10.5	43.4	12.8	41.5
Total	10.9	49.1	10.9	35.0
Urban				
Secondary	15.1	40.5	9.1	23.0
Graduate and above	15.1	25.7	7.3	21.1
Total	14.0	35.7	8.5	22.2
1987–88				
Rural				
Secondary	28.9	59.9	10.6	33.8
Graduate and above	18.9	45.1	14.7	40.3
Total	27.0	56.9	11.5	34.9
Urban				
Secondary	23.6	52.7	8.7	22.6
Graduate and above	7.3	19.6	7.4	21.1
Total	17.9	41.7	8.3	21.9

Source: Abridged from Mathew [1996: 214] based on NSS 38th and 43rd rounds.

increased over time, the problem of unemployment has tended to become one of educated unemployment.

We have seen earlier that such a high and growing incidence of unemployment did not result in growing immiserisation. On the contrary, the incidence of rural poverty declined, demographic changes resulted in a reduction of the dependency ratio, and there have been remarkable achivements in such social development indicators as education and health for all strata of society in Kerala. This resulted in the second dilemma, namely, labour shortage in the casual labour market, especially in the primary sector; along with an increase in the unemployed, a disproportionate amount of whom were educated. This should have created conditions favourable to the emergence of a regime of accummulation and increase in the output of the productive sectors through appropriate technological change. The contribution of labour relations in general and rural labour relations in particular has so far inhibited the emergence of such a situation through a concerted opposition to technological change in an attempt to protect current employment. The impact of this dilemma of an increasing mismatch between labour supply and labour demand in the context of increasing wages and technological stagnation could be seen in the deceleratiaon in the growth of output of the productive sectors for as long a period as around 15 years beginning in the mid-1970s (see Table 7).

VIII. A DIFFERENT DILEMMA IN THE CONTEXT OF ECONOMIC LIBERALISATION

By the late 1980s, successive governments in Kerala realised the need for technological change in various economic activities across the board. They also realised the need to attract sufficient investment to generate new jobs and give a push to the growth of the productive sectors. But they found themselves in another dilemma. There was inadequate development of critical infrastructure (such as water control measures for agriculture and electrical power generation for industry) in which the state could not undertake additional investment. But there was an inability to attract private investment in these and directly productive sectors. Here the state has been burdened with its image of a 'high wage cost' as well as a 'labour problem' state with the result that it has been unable to convert the domestically available financial surplus in the banking system into investible resources. Bank deposits have increased at a compound rate of growth of 19 per cent during the last decade, largely contributed by remittances of Kerala workers from Gulf countries. Nearly 40 per cent of the bank deposits in Kerala are accounted for by 'non-resident' Keralaites. However, the credit-deposit ratio in Kerala has been only around 43 to 45 per cent for the past several years [*Government of Kerala*, 1998]. Let us first look at what happened in the rice growing sector.

By the early 1990s the farmers' complaint about labour shortage became widespread. Government recognised the gravity of the problem and announced measures for the mechanisation of farming. Agricultural labour unions, which hitherto had opposed any mechanisation, recognised the problem and let it be known that they were not opposed to mechanisation. But the unions stuck to their earlier strategy (when tractors were introduced) of demanding payment of wages to the same number of workers at the prevailing rate when machines are to be introduced. This in effect meant payment of double wages to an operation. For example, attempts were made in the early 1990s, when farmers faced shortage of labourers for harvest, to introduce mechanical threshers. This became worthy of reporting in the newspapers as it led to controversies between farmers' organisations and agricultural labourers' unions reminiscent of the situation in the 1970s. A prominent newspaper reported that agricultural labour unions did not object to the introduction of such machines but demanded the same rate of payment 'even when the job is done with the aid of the threshing machine to which the farmers are far from agreeable. The farmers aver that when the machine is introduced, the manual labour involved would be considerably reduced and then there is no justification for paying the labour at the old rates' [*Venogopal*, 1990: 3]. Of course, this did put a brake on introducing mechanisation in post-harvest operations. However, there were also other structural constraints in extending mechanisation. The fact that rice cultivation was dominated by small holdings, especially outside Kuttanad, meant that economies of scale could not be realised.

Despite opposition to the introduction of tractors, and later on power-tillers, these have now been widely accepted. It would appear that this was largely due to the versatility of these machines. First of all, they could be used for more than ploughing and other soil preparation operations. They could also be employed to transport a variety of materials in the rural context (such as fertilizers, cement, harvested paddy, milled rice, other agricultural products, etc.) as well as for pumping water. Along with this versatility, the speed with which soil preparation tasks were completed enabled timely starting of a second crop wherever feasible. Such multiple use of tractors and power tillers overcame the constraints imposed by the dominance of small-holding cultivation. A market for the services of these machines developed over a period, whereby a large number of small farmers rented these machines for their agricultural operations. Machines for other rice cultivation operations do not have this characteristic of tractors and tillers. Such large-scale machines as harvest combines, which are used widely in the states of Punjab and Haryana, are not feasible in the small-holding wetland rice fields of Kerala. Smaller and less costly machines were difficult to come by. In recent times, such small machines have been tried on a trial basis for such operations as transplanting, harvesting, threshing, winnowing and so on. Some innovative farmers in Kuttanad have fabricated less expensive threshing and winnowing machines to suit local conditions. From the industrially and entrepreneurially vibrant city of Coimbatore in the state of Tamil Nadu, adjacent to the Kerala borders in the Palghat district, a whole new range of small-sized and low priced machines are being introduced in the market and this could perhaps accelerate the process of mechanisation of rice cultivation in Kerala in years to come. However, for as long as the economics of rice cultivation continues to be less attractive, *vis-à-vis* substitutable crops, the pace of mechanisation is unlikely to take off .

Realising the increasing cost of cultivation, the government responded by initiating, during 1987–88, a new institutional mechanism of Group Farming, which essentially meant collective decision-making for various agricultural operations, collective purchase of inputs and better group management. It was first and foremost aimed at protecting rice production by reducing the cost of cultivation. Agricultural extension offices, known as *Krishi Bhavans*, were established in every Village Panchayat (an administrative and now the first-tier local government unit consisting of 10 to 15 villages). Financial and other assistance to farmers were streamlined. Around 30 per cent of the area under rice cultivation was brought under this innovative programme. The results were however mixed in that cost reduction was achieved only partially. In those 'group farming areas' where the programme was judged successful it was largely due to a reduction in cost of labour and not as a result of more efficient use of other inputs (see Jose [1991]). However, the enthusiasm lasted only as long as the Left Ministry (LDF) lasted (1987–91) and the subsequent government did not follow it up with equal vigour, for party-political reasons. Such narrow-mindedness in implementing development programmes is not unknown to Kerala; in fact, one of the major constraints in implementing any development programme in the state is its partisan character, arising out of a coalition system of government, in which a ruling political party (or parties) is all too eager to consolidate and enhance its electoral support through 'its own' development programmes. When an opposition political party, or parties, subsequently come to power such programmes suffer a 'political death'.

The efforts to enhance productivity in agriculture, especially in rice cultivation, also faced constraints other than an absence of mechanisation. This was the inadequate system of water control, mainly irrigation. In fact, appropriate technological change in water control would not only have been labour-augmenting, it could also have helped increase labour productivity in rice cultivation because of its role as a 'leading input'. Not more than 16 per cent of the gross cropped area was irrigated in Kerala even by the early 1990s. A major reason for such a dismal record was the incomplete nature of the many major and medium irrigation projects whose time and cost overruns are unlikely to have many parallels. There are projects which have been in a state of construction for more than 30 years with such cost overruns as 20 times the initial estimate for several of the projects. This is a clear case of 'government failure' in providing as critical a collective good as water control for the agricultural development of the state.

In the meantime, the decline in area under rice continued uninterrupted. Agricultural labour unions, already in a state of dormancy, woke up to the situation and decided to make it a political issue. They knew that they could not get a better place to launch their new 'struggle' than the legendary region of Kuttanad. In early August 1997, in a show of strength scores of agricultural labourers, led by union leaders of the KSKTU belonging to the CPI(M), gate-crashed into lands converted from rice to other crops and destroyed the new crops as a protest against the farmers' decision to move out of rice cultivation. They raised the question of decline in employment and demanded that the government enforce an existing law banning conversion of rice lands for other purposes. Suddenly it looked as if agricultural labour unions at last had found an answer to the long-term strategy of farmers moving out of rice cultivation! They knew that it was no more profitable to engage in rice cultivation (or that it was less profitable than growing other competing crops) . They demanded that government create such conditions as are necessary for the farmers to continue with rice cultivation. Farmers demanded protection from such 'acts of vandalism' and insisted that farmers have the right to use their land in any manner they deemed fit. The government, led by the CPI(M), was in a log-jam and was clearly not inclined to to go back to an earlier era of the politics of confrontation in labour relations (see *Economic and Political Weekly* [1997]). As a strategy to wriggle out of the immediate crisis, it appointed an Expert Committee to examine issues arising out of the declining area under rice. Only in this way could the government could buy some time.

Interestingly, the Kerala economy seems to have recovered, since the late 1980s, from the slow growth that prevailed from the mid-1970s to the late 1980s (see Table 7). This recovery coincided with the beginning of the economic liberalisation process in India, starting in the late 1980s and accelerating in the early 1990s. This is a significant development with an average annual growth rate of close to seven per cent, which exceeds the national average. However, it should be noted that this enhanced growth has been made possible by the growth in the tertiary sector (as a result of the continuing flow of remittances) and the secondary sector in which the non-manufacturing segment has performed better than the manufacturing segment. However, the situation seems to offer little hope for the unemployed as employment growth is dismal and unemployment rates remain high. Employment in the formal sector (both public and private) has stagnated at around 1.1 million jobs since the late 1980s [*Government of Kerala*, 1998: S18].

The economic liberalisation process seems to have aggravated the current development dilemma of Kerala. The relative price advantage for cash crops is accentuating the shift of land from rice to other crops. The agricultural sector as a whole seem to have enhanced its value of output through the farmers' strategy of crop substitution (see Table 7). To counter such a trend, the government is unable to increase its investment in critical inputs to enhance productivity in the foodgrain sector. Growth does not seem to be job creating; however, an increasing proportion of the unemployed are now classified as educated unemployed, clearly indicating their preference to move away from agriculture (see Table 8). Although states in India are free to attract investment into their regions by offering incentives and formulating clearer policies, the Kerala government has not been particularly distinguished in this sphere.

IX. SOME REFLECTIONS ON THE OLD AND NEW DILEMMAS

From the perspective of labour in general and rural labour in particular, Kerala's record in achieving a measure of human dignity and social progress is remarkable, viewed especially from an all-India perspective. The oppressive and degrading conditions, still prevalent in many parts of rural India, involving organised violence by landowning classes, indignities to women workers, and degrading conditions of work are no longer prevalent in Kerala. The emergence of trade unions as a strong labour institution and the overall social progress have led to a remarkable decline in the incidence of child labour (around one per cent as against eight per cent in all India), social acceptance of such work norms as an eight-hour day, intervals and formal labour relations as against patron-client relations. It has also witnessed a sustained increase in wages and the securing of non-wage benefits in several occupations which are not officially categorised as 'formal' or 'organised'.

But this measure of success, remarkable by all-India standards, has led to the kind of dilemmas discussed above. From a broader developmental point of view Kerala has reached a stage, socially speaking, where the labour force is ready to move into more skilled, technologically superior, high value-adding occupations with better wages and conditions of employment. But the dilemma is the inability of the state to meet this challenge. The government is unable to give a strong push towards the economic environment in which such a shift will occur. Although the policy regime has been a favourable one since the late 1980s, the inflow of investment is too small to make a perceptible dent. One reason for this is the inability of the state to provide necessary, and sometimes critical, infrastructure facilities such as electrical power and better transport conditions. The fiscal position of the government is too weak to develop the infrastructure, not to speak of the inability of the system to check leakages and time/cost overruns. In addition, Kerala's image as a 'labour problem' state has stuck in the minds of prospective investors (including those from within the state) and this has added a new dimension of 'psychic costs' that normally translates into high risk premiums. The labour situation as a problem for prospective investors has changed for the better in recent times, although the ability of organised labour to disrupt work and life for the mass of the common people is still considerable.

It should however be noted that the kind of resistance by labour unions to technological change that existed till the mid-1980s has given way to a silent acceptance as a sign of the changing preferences of the younger labour force as well as the failure of the earlier strategies. In the process, it would appear that Kerala has lost close to a generation's time (say 25 years) by not adopting a long-term developmental view in upgrading and modernising its labour-intensive occupations. A greater effort, *vis-à-vis* its neighbours, is now needed to catch up with those who have moved ahead in order to utilise its vast reservoir of a socially developed labour force. This has also thrown up its own dilemmas, especially in the new context of economic liberalisation.

The catching up time is one of transition. And that involves protecting those who may lose their current employment. When the earlier strategy of protecting current employment failed and the economy could not generate adequate new employment, the government resorted to extensive 'poor-relief' programmes. Some of these were part of 'poor-relief' of a general character, such as PDS and 'Free Noon Meals' for school-going children. Others were introduced either as part of nationally sponsored programmes (such as rural works programmes) or introduced by the state government, such as unemployment assistance and an old age pension. In the new context of economic liberalisation, the rationale of these programmes is being increasingly questioned mainly due to the fiscal crisis of both the central and state governments. In the event of any decline in funding of these programmes, poor labour households will be especially adversely affected. The PDS has already witnessed a partial withdrawal, making subsidised distribution of food grains to only 'eligible' households.

The new regime is also experiencing a crisis in the management of social sector programmes, particularly in education and health. The fiscal crisis of the state government has already led to a qualitative deterioration of these services and the withdrawal of the better-off sections of the society from access to such services. The argument is now in favour of introducing 'user fees' which will put a price tag on these services to the poor as well.

The withdrawal of the state from a number of public services will lead to an increase in the cost of living, thereby exerting added pressure to demand higher wages. In the absence of corresponding increases in labour productivity, the situation could lead to another round of economic crisis for Kerala. Such a prospect will further intensify the Kerala economy's dependence on remittances and, concomitantly, its vulnerability to external shocks.

This scenario does not necessarily mean that there are no alternatives. But one notes the gravity of the situation and the imperative need for a strategy that will, at the minimum, retain Kerala's distributive gains while launching it on a path of long-term economic growth. A recent study on this theme underlines the possibility of pursuing a broad-based strategy of growth in Kerala without giving up its distributive gains because 'the collective power of the working class has been incorporated within the state [and] militant mobilisation has made way to mediated corporatist arrangements' [Heller, 1995: 666]. The burden of our argument here is not to deny such a possibility but to focus on the continuing dilemmas facing Kerala, deservedly noted for its high social development, within the span of a generation.

NOTES

1. See, for example, Drèze and Sen [1989: 221–5]; Drèze and Sen [1995], Frankie and Chasin [1989].
2. It is important here to give an idea of the emergence of coalition governments in Kerala. Because of the inability of any single party to secure an absolute majority, Kerala has witnessed the gradual institutionalisation of coalition governments since its formation in 1956. The only exception was the first state assembly elections in 1957 when the undivided Communist Party of India secured an absolute majority with the help of a few independents. Following its controversial programmes of land reform and educational reform, this government was dismissed by the central government in 1959. A new government led by the Indian National Congress and inclusive of a few other parties was formed in 1961 and lasted till 1964 when President's (i.e. central government) rule was imposed following a split in the Indian National Congress and the inability of other parties to form a government. Since then parties have fought elections on the basis of coalitions. A new coalition led by the larger of the two Communist Parties, the CPI(M), and inclusive of the other communist party, the CPI, and a few other regional parties came to power in 1967 and lasted till 1969. The Indian National Congress was in opposition. Following differences of views between the two communist parties, a realignment took place. A new coalition with the Indian National Congress as the major partner but with the CPI heading a coalition government and inclusive of regional parties came to power in 1969 and lasted till 1977. The CPI(M), though the biggest single party, had to contend with sitting in opposition. This period witnessed a sharp political contest between the CPI(M) and the coalition led by the CPI to secure the electoral support of the mass of people. This situation gave way to another realignment following the imposition of a State of Emergency in the country by the then Prime Minister, Indira Gandhi, and suppression of civil rights. In the elections following the lifting of the Emergency, two coalitions emerged which continue till today. One is called the Left Democratic Front (LDF) led by the CPI(M) and inclusive of CPI, and a few other small parties called the Revolutionary Socialist Party, the Janata Party (now defunct) and Congress (S), a breakaway group of the Indian National Congress.. The other coalition was the United Democratic Front (UDF) led by the Indian National Congress and inclusive of all regional parties. This arrangement has continued to this day. Following a period of shuffling and reshuffling in alignments, the LDF came to power in 1980 but resigned in 1982; the following elections were won by the UDF; the LDF was back in power in 1987; the UDF was back in power in the next elections conducted in 1991; however, the LDF came back to power in the 1996 elections. The Kerala electorate has not given two consecutive terms in government to either the LDF or the UDF.
3. For a detailed treatment of labour recruitment in plantations, both from within and outside Kerala, and their social and gender characteristics see Raman [1997: Ch.4].
4. Labour absorption estimates through Cost of Cultivation Studies revealed that around 1211 labour hours per hectare per crop (that is, 151.4 days @ 8 hours per day) were needed for rice cultivation in Palghat district which represents the midland area in Kerala. This was around 162 days in water-logged areas such as Kuttanad (comprising the whole of Alleppey

district and a portion of Kottayam district) accounting for about seven per cent of the area under rice in Kerala in 1979. These estimates are exclusive of the labour time required for harvesting.

5. Data provided by around 400 farmers on the labour input in rice cultivation work out to a figure of 112 days per hectare per crop excluding harvesting. This is around 25 per cent less than the 1979 estimate of 151 days. These estimates are not strictly comparable as the methodologies differ. The latter information was provided by farmers in response to a questionnaire sent by an Expert Committee on Paddy Cultivation appointed by the Government of Kerala in 1997.

6. These figures refer to per capita employment of agricultural labourers in agricultural labour households. The figures are not different for agricultural labourers in 'Other Rural Labour Households'. The estimates are from the Rural Labour Enquiries (later known as Survey of Employment Unemployment) conducted by the National Sample Survey Organisation of the Government of India.

7. 'The highly labour-intensive technology, predominantly self-employed petty production structure and miserably low wages had enabled this export-oriented industry to flourish and become the main source of non-agricultural employment in the region. The emergence of militant trade unions and their success in raising wages resulted in further fragmentation of the production process and later on, in attempts to introduce labour-saving machinery. These moves were resolutely opposed by the unions. They demanded a ban on mechanisation, in order to protect employment, and the elimination of middlemen through a programme of cooperativisation in order to improve earnings. Vigorous intervention by the state in the raw material and product markets in support of the workers' cooperatives was also called for. Industrial circles and experts have been very critical of these policies, partly because of the ban on mechanisation and the nature of government intervention in the raw material market. However, given the political climate of the state, the policies pursued by successive state governments have been broadly in accordance with the policies advocated by the unions. Notwithstanding serious lapses in implementation, the above strategy of development seems to have exhausted its potential as is evidence by the acute crisis in the industry. Our analysis shows that if new policy initiatives are not forthcoming the crisis in the industry will probably be aggravated in the future.' [Isaac et al., 1992: 192–3].

8. For a quick evaluation of this scheme up to 1974 see United Nations [1975: 196–200].

9. This frugal meal cannot be more than a bowl of rice gruel with a few ounces of curry.

10. In this study, carried out under the supervision of this author, agricultural labour households were identified as those with at least one member working as wage labour in agriculture. This had the drawback of including those households where the proportion of non-agricultural labourers was more than half. However, it was found that 65 per cent of the total workers plus unemployed were agricultural labourers. This worked out to two agricultural labourers per households in a sample size of 380.

11. This was a deliberate strategy of unions to protect the interest of 'insiders' by restricting entry. Over time this led to a 'market' for union membership. Thus a headload worker could 'sell' his membership to an aspirant for a price. This worked out to the equivalent of two years' earnings in the case of headload workers (see Nambiar [1995: 738]). Such a phenomenon of 'rentier income' in the labour market was no doubt a manifestation of acute unemployment and the preference for a non-agricultural and regular work.

12. In the course of my recent meetings with agricultural labourers, as part of the work of the Expert Committee on Paddy Cultivation, several parents told me that they would not like to see their children grow up as agricultural wage labourers.

13. These figures were obtained by recalculating the figures provided by the author in terms of the distribution of total family members in various activities.

14. The relationship between social development, especially in education and health, and the demographic transition in Kerala has been subjected to considerable research since the publication of the CDS study (see UN [1975]). Some of the subsequent studies are Krishnan [1976], Nair [1981] and Bhat and Rajan [1990]. For studies on the impact of demographic transition on labour supply see Rajan et al. [1993].

15. According to population census reports, the male labour force in Kerala in 1961 was 51 per

cent of the population while women's around 52 per cent. The male labour force increased to 57 per cent and female labour force to 58 per cent in 1981. By 1991 the these ratios increased to 62 and 63 per cent respectively. The work participation rate for men remained around 47 per cent between 1961 and 1991 whereas it declined from around 20 per cent to 16 per cent for women.

16. The definition of Usual Status of unemployed is one having no work for at least 181 days in a year. Current Daily Status refers to unemployment during the previous day of the survey.

REFERENCES

Alexander, K.C., 1975, 'Nature and Background of the Agrarian Unrest in Kuttanad, Kerala', *Journal of Kerala Studies,* June, Part II.

Basu, A.M., 1986, 'Birth Control by Assetless Workers in Kerala: The Possibility of a Poverty Induced Fertility Transition, *Development and Change,* Vol.17, No.2.

Bhat, Mari, P.M. and S. Irudaya Rajan, (1990), 'Demographic Transition in Kerala Revisited', *Economic and Political Weekly,* Vol.XXV, No.36, 1–8 Sept.

Deepa, G.L., 1994, 'Industrial Crisis and Women Workers: A Study of Cashew Processing Industry in Kerala', Thiruvananthapuram: Centre for Development Studies (M.Phil. thesis submitted to the Jawaharlal Nehru University, New Delhi).

Drèze, Jean and Sen, Amartya, 1989, *Hunger and Public Action,* Oxford: Clarendon Press.

Drèze, Jean and Sen, Amartya, 1995, *India:Economic Development and Social Opportunity,* New Delhi: Oxford University Press.

Economic and Political Weekly, 1997, 'Kerala: Farm Workers' Agitation – Return to Politics of Confrontation?', Vol.32, Nos.33–34, 16–23 Aug.

Francis, Shaji, 1990, *Dynamics of Rural Labour Markets: An Analysis of Emerging Agricultural Labour Shortage in a Kerala Region,* Trivandrum: Centre for Development Studies (M.Phil. thesis submitted to Jawaharlal Nehru University, New Delhi).

Frankie, Richard and Chassin, Barbara, 1989, *Kerala: Radical Reform as Development in an Indian State,* San Fransisco, CA:Institute for Food and Development Policy.

Government of Kerala, 1985, *Report of the Survey on Socio-Economic Conditions of Agricultural and Other Rural Labourers in Kerala,* Trivandrum: Bureau of Economics and Statistics.

Government of Kerala, 1998, *Economic Review 1997,* Thiruvananthapuram:State Planning Board.

Heller, Patrick, 1995, 'From Class Struggle to Class Compromise: Redistribution and Growth in a South Indian State', *The Journal of Development Studies,*Vol.31, No.5, June.

Isaac, Thomas, T.M., 1982, 'Class Struggle and Structural Changes in the Coir Mat and Matting Industry in Kerala', *Economic and Political Weekly,* Vol.XVII, No.31.

Isaac, Thomas, T.M., Van Stuijvenberg, P.A. and K.N. Nair, 1992, *Modernisation and Employment: The Coir Industry in Kerala,* New Delhi: Sage Publications India.

James, K.S., 1997, 'Can Poverty Determine Fertility: Agricultural Labourers and Their Fertility Decisions', in K.C. Zachariah and I.S. Rajan, *Kerala's Demographic Transition: Determinants and Consequences,* New Delhi:Sage Publications.

Jose, A.V., 1979, *Trade Union Movement Among Agricultural Labourers in Kerala: The Case of Kuttanad Region,* Working Paper No.93, Trivandrum:Centre for Development Studies.

Jose, Sunny, 1991, 'Group Farming in Kerala: An Illustrative Study', M.Phil. thesis submitted to the Jawaharlal Nehru University, Trivandrum: Centre for Development Studies.

Kannan, K.P., 1983, *Cashew Development in India: Potentialities and Constraints,* New Delhi: Agricole Publishing Academy.

Kannan, K.P., 1988, *Of Rural Proletarian Struggles: Mobilisation and Organisation of Rural Workers in South-West India,* Delhi: Oxford University Press.

Kannan, K.P., 1992, 'Labour institutions and the development process in Kerala' in Papola, T.S. and Gerry Rodgers (eds.), *Labour Institutions and Economic Development in India,* Geneva: International Institute for Labour Studies.

Kannan, K.P., 1995a, 'State and Union Intervention in Rural Labour: A Study of Kerala', *Indian Journal of Labour Economics,* Vol.38, No.3, July–Sept.

Kannan, K.P., 1995b, 'Public Intervention and Poverty Alleviation: A Study of the Declining Incidence of Rural Poverty in Kerala, India', *Development and Change*, Vol.26, No.4, Oct.

Kannan, K.P. and K. Pushpangadan, 1990, 'Dissecting Agricultural Stagnation: An Analysis across Seasons, Crops and Regions', *Economic and Political Weekly*, Vol.25, No.36, 1–8 Sept.

Kerala Statistical Institute, 1994, *Conversion of Paddy Land in Kerala*, Thiruvananthapuram: Kerala Statistical Institute.

Krishnan, T.N., 1976, 'Demographic Transition in Kerala: Facts and Factors', *Economic and Political Weekly*, Vol.11, Special Number, Aug.

Mathew, E.T., 1996, 'Employment and Unemployment Trends in Kerala: A Study Based on National Sample Survey Data', *Review of Development and Change*, Vol.1, No.2, July–Dec.

Mencher, Joan, 1978, 'Agrarian Relations in Two Rice Regions of Kerala', *Economic and Political Weekly*, Vol.15, Annual Number, Feb.

Mencher, Joan, 1980, 'Lessons and Non-Lessons of Kerala: Agricultural Labourers and Poverty', *Economic and Political Weekly*, Special Number, Aug.

Nair, Gopinathan, P.R., 1981, *Primary Education, Population Growth and Socioeconomic Change: A Comparative Study with Particular Reference to Kerala*, New Delhi: Allied Publishers.

Nair, Somasekharan G., 1998, 'Redistribution of Land in Kerala: Facts and Fallacy' (mimeo), a note prepared for the Expert Committee on Paddy Cultivation, Government of Kerala.

Nair, Sukumaran M.K., 1997, 'Rural Labour Market in Kerala: Small Holder Agriculture and Labour Market Dynamics', *Economic and Political Weekly*, Vol.32, No.35, 30 Aug..

Nambiar, A.C.K., 1995, 'Unorganised Labour Unionism: The Case of Headload Workers in Kerala', *The Indian Journal of Labour Economics*, Vol.38, No.4, Oct.–Dec.

Natarajan, S., 1982, 'Labour Input in Rice Farming in Kerala – An Inter-Regional, Inter-Temporal Analysis', P.P. Pillai (ed.), *Agricultural Development in Kerala*, New Delhi:Agricole Publishing Academy.

Panikar, P.G.K., 1978, 'Employment, Income and Food Intake Among Selected Agricultural Labour Households', *Economic and Political Weekly*, Special Number, Aug.

Pillai, V.R. and P.G.K. Panikar, 1965, *Land Reclamation in Kerala*, Madras: Asia Publishing House.

Raghavan, Pyarelal, 1986, 'Organisation of Production in the Beedi Industry: A Study of Cannanore District, 1920-1985', Trivandrum: Centre for Development Studies (M.Phil. thesis submitted to the Jawaharlal Nehru University, New Delhi).

Raj, K.N. and Michael P.K. Tharakan, 1983, 'Agrarian Reform in Kerala and Its Impact on the Rural Economy – A Preliminary Assessment', A.K. Ghose (ed.), *Agrarian Reform in Contemporary Developing Countries*, London: Croom Helm.

Rajan, Irudaya, S., Misra, U.S. and P.S. Sarma, 1993, 'Demographic Transition and Labour Supply in India', *Productivity*, Vol.34, April–June, No.1.

Raman, Ravi, 1997, 'Global Capital and Peripheral Labour: Political Economy of Tea Plantations in Southern India c.1850–1950', Ph.D. thesis submitted to the University of Kerala, Thiruvananthapuram: Centre for Development Studies.

Tharamangalam, Jose, 1981, *Agrarian Class Conflict: The Political Mobilization of Agricultural Labourers in Kuttanad, South India, Vancour:* University of British Columbia Press.

United Nations, 1975, *Poverty, Unemployment and Development Policy: A Case Study of Selected Issues with Special Reference to Kerala* (prepared by Centre for Development Studies, Trivandrum), New York: United Nations.

Varghese, T.C., 1970, *Agrarian Change and Economic Consequences: Land Tenures in Kerala, 1850-1960*, New Delhi: Allied publishers.

Venugopal, P., 1990, 'Move to Mechanise Paddy Threshing Evokes Mixed Response in Kuttanad', *Indian Express*, 15 Sept., Cochin.

Politics of the Poor: Agricultural Labourers and Political Transformations in Uttar Pradesh

JENS LERCHE

This study addresses the question of how local level agrarian labour relations and labour struggles, and class and caste based emancipatory processes, relate to the wider political development of the north Indian state of Uttar Pradesh (UP). This agenda springs directly from UP state politics, specifically from the important (and dramatic) turn of events of the 1990s. In 1993, for the first time in India a party headed by, run by and voted for by the lowly 'untouchable' castes formed part of the winning coalition in a state election. Since then, the low-caste Bahujan Samaj Party (BSP) party has been in government thrice, often in alliances that cut across both the left-right and the caste political spectrum. As part of this, it has twice been able to see its own charismatic leader, a woman from the untouchable Chamar caste, occupying the position of Chief Minister of the state government.

This has taken the political establishment as well as academics by surprise, not least because it is happening in a state where violent local level oppression has been the stitching in the social fabric for decades. When academic commentators recovered from the 1993 election shock, some hastened to hail the result as 'the beginning of a new chapter in the political history of independent India', a 'move beyond the political discursive confines of contemporary India' [Srinivasulu, 1994: 159–60], and to pronounce the BSP leader Kanshi Ram 'as a harbinger of a new paradigm in social science discourse' [Ilaiah, 1994: 668].'

The main argument behind these claims is that not only has a coalition of low caste and religious minorities won state elections for the first time, but also that this has taken place against the background of a clear-cut caste based ideology. Caste has replaced class, and political categories such as left

Jens Lerche, Department of Development Studies, School of Oriental and African Studies, University of London, London WC1H 0XG. The author would like to thank the JPS editors, and the participants in the 'Rural Labour Relations In India Today' and 'U.P. 2000' workshops for comments on earlier drafts.

and right have lost their importance [*Srinivasulu*, 1994: 159; *Ilaiah*, 1994: 668; *Kothari*, 1994: 1589].[1]

This study agrees that the emergence of the BSP on to the political scene is important but for different reasons: namely because of its influence on rural class struggles. Although the BSP has not raised major class issues such as land reforms it has, nevertheless, influenced local agrarian struggles and labour relations through changes in how the local state apparatuses relate to them, and also through its concerted efforts to politicise the untouchables and mobilise them around a specific low caste agenda.

This raises a number of questions regarding the 'politics' of rural labourers and low caste people. This study examines the role of 'class' and 'caste'-based organisations in the local politics of rural labourers and low caste people, and how broader economic and political transformations interact with their local level conditions.

A major question is why a caste based party rather than a party of the left has become the vehicle of the rural labourers and low caste population. Why has no mobilisation on a class platform led by a communist party taken place? Why have agricultural labourers voted along caste lines and not class lines? More generally, how do we best understand mobilisation and emancipatory processes among agricultural labourers in UP, including their effects for the conditions of agricultural labourers ? How do class and caste relate to each other, both locally and in the wider political arena? And, not least, can a mobilisation on a caste based platform lead to improved class positions, or does it represent a 'derailment' of the class struggle? What is the impact of a caste-based emancipatory development on class consciousness?

These questions are pursued through a focus on emancipatory processes among low caste agricultural workers and their actions; the role of class and caste-based organisations in these processes; how these organisations relate to capitalist development in UP agriculture, and to present political developments in UP.

According to some authors, an important aspect of rural class struggle and labour relations in India since Independence is that rural labourers have gone through a major emancipatory process. The introduction of universal franchise, anti-discriminatory legislation, the abolition of the zamindari landlord system, the disintegration of personalised patron–client relations, and the breakdown of the village as the focus of labour relations, are factors cited, for example, for the Halapatis of South Gujarat [*Breman*, 1993: 352–65] and for India more generally [*Mendelsohn*, 1993].

However, any celebration of emancipatory development from 'below' must be tempered by analysis of the extent to which politicisation of rural labour has improved their positions. Thus, for example, Tom Brass argues that emancipatory developments in India have been more than matched by increased class struggle from 'above' [*Brass*, 1994a].[2] Capitalist development, intensified class struggle and increased oppression seem to have gone hand in hand.[3]

This analysis argues that in UP, rural labourers have experienced a number of important positive changes since Independence, and are increasingly able to assert what they now perceive to be their rights. Rural labour struggles have intensified and, in spite of counter actions by middle and big peasants, the position of labourers has improved. The low-caste BSP governments of UP in the 1990s have acted as a catalyst for some of these developments, but the changes on which the BSP has been able to build have deeper origins. The first two sections of the study will examine the development of rural class relations in UP since Independence, through an analysis of sharecropping and labour relations, local labour struggles and the overall position of rural labourers up until the early 1990s. The remaining sections will concentrate on the issue of caste and class-based policies and mobilisation among the rural labourers in the 1990s, including a discussion of why the BSP has been more successful than the communist parties in mobilising rural labourers.

The account draws on my own fieldwork in east and west UP as well as other field based studies. Comparisons of different regions of UP are relevant because economic and social development within this vast state (with a population of 139 million in 1991) has followed regionally different trajectories. Analytically, UP is commonly divided into east, west and central UP, and it is commonly accepted that the east-west divide represents two extremes regarding economic development, poverty and so on.[4]

AGRARIAN DEVELOPMENT IN UP

In a recent book, Zoya Hasan has summarised a broadly accepted understanding of agrarian development in UP [*Hasan*, 1998]. Historically, while landlords and sharecroppers dominated in the east, mixed owner and tenant cultivation was more common in the west. When the colonial government started investing in improving agricultural production in west UP during the latter half of the 19th century, most notably through irrigation facilities, producers there were not overly constrained by the social organisation of agrarian society, and could improve productivity to levels well above those prevalent in east UP.[5]

The UP Zamindari Abolition Act became law in 1951. Following from the mobilisation of peasants by the nationalist movement, the main effects of the reforms were the abolition of large-scale absentee landlordism. Smaller landlords could, in many cases, continue to cultivate at least parts of their land with the help of labourers, or within 'disguised' or unofficial tenancy relations, while better off sections of cultivating tenants became a prosperous peasantry [*Byres*, 1981: 423]. In west UP, relatively prosperous and politically strong peasant communities were in a position to take over zamindari land in many cases, while 'inferior' social groups such as low-caste agricultural labourers generally lost even those minuscule tenancy rights they had. In central and eastern parts, on the other hand, it was more common that village-based and politically stronger landlords held on to large parts of their land. Nevertheless, the upper layers of the old tenantry did generally emerge as minor peasant proprietors here as well, while, as in the west, 'inferior' social groups did not gain from the reforms. Thus, after Independence, rich and middle peasants dominated the western countryside, while in the central and eastern areas, landlords often maintained a strong position [*Hasan*, 1998: 72–8].

This laid the foundation for further regional differences in development. When the major post-Independence state-induced drive for increased agricultural production, the Green Revolution, began in the late 1960s it was only logical that west UP should play a major role. As stated by Hasan, the western part of UP, together with the neighbouring states of Punjab and Haryana, 'experienced the largest increase in rural capital investment, processing and small-scale industries in the Green Revolution era. By virtually all indices of growth and modernisation, western UP achieved considerable progress, and by the early 1980s this region was substantially ahead of others in the state' [*Hasan*, 1998: 88]. A class of surplus producing middle and big peasants, tilling their land with family labour as well as with agricultural labourers, and investing in modern agricultural inputs and machinery, developed. East UP, on the other hand, lagged behind.

However, the east–west dichotomy seems to have receded since the mid-1970s as agrarian growth has gained pace in most parts of east UP. District-wise data show that only districts in the north-western and south-eastern corners of east UP have remained stagnant [*Bhalla and Tyagi*, 1989; *Sharma and Poleman*, 1994: 38–55], and that the overall growth rate for east UP's agriculture from 1970–73 to 1980–83 was above four per cent [*Sharma and Poleman*, 1994: 240]. For the period 1968–71 to 1988–91, data compiled by S. Mahendra Dev and Ajit K. Renade shows high agricultural output growth rates in all three main regions of UP (see Table 1). While the western region outpaced the rest of UP regarding sugarcane (its main cash crop), central and east UP had output growth rates similar to those of west UP regarding rice, and higher output growth rates regarding wheat.

TABLE 1
REGION-WISE GROWTH RATE OF OUTPUT OF MAJOR CROPS IN UTTAR
PRADESH 1968–71 TO 1988–91, PER CENT PER ANNUM

Crop	Western Region	Central Region	Eastern Region	UP
Wheat	4.5	6.3	7.4	5.2
Rice	6.0	6.1	5.8	5.7
Pulses	–1.9	–1.2	–1.0	–1.1
Total Foodgrains	3.4	3.6	4.1	3.5
Sugarcane	3.0	2.9	0.5	2.8

Source: Dev and Renade [1997: 350]. Computed from Bulletin of Agricultural Statistics, Uttar Pradesh (Annual).

Sharma and Poleman see this output growth as a result of increased government investment in agrarian infrastructure in the east. Ravi Srivastava has argued that it is due to the fact that the small peasant proprietors created by the land reform process now pursue highly productive agriculture in the east [*Sharma and Poleman*, 1994: 36–8; *Srivastava*, 1994: 168, 170; 1995: 230]. My own fieldwork in Jaunpur district of east UP from 1993 onwards shows that even the old landlords had increased their productivity considerably. Through land reform, sale of land, and its partition through inheritance they have become a class of mainly medium-sized landowners each owning, on average, around five acres of land and working their land with family labour and agricultural labourers. In fact, they used even more machinery in the production than did smaller peasants, as they could better afford to invest in threshers, tube wells and (mainly rented) tractors.

However, as pointed out by Hasan, the agrarian sector is still far more developed in west than in east UP. While a transformation of what has been basically a landlord based economy is taking place in parts of east UP, the evidence suggests that a class of surplus producing peasants driven by a capitalist rationale of accumulation is firmly in charge in west UP.

Evidence from Village Studies

In 1993, I conducted fieldwork comparing agricultural labour relations and labour conflicts in a village in east UP with a village in west UP. During revisits in 1995/96 and 1998, the fieldwork material was updated, and the influence of outside political forces on local social and economic relations investigated in more detail.[6] The west UP fieldwork location was a village in Muzaffarnagar district north-east of Delhi, and the east UP location a village in Jaunpur district north of Varanasi.[7] I have discussed labour relations and, in particular, labour struggles in the villages up to 1993 in some detail elsewhere [Lerche, 1995]. Here, I concentrate on what I term the transformation of agricultural labourers into rural labourers, on the extent to which a move towards capitalist labour relations has taken place within agriculture and the consequences of these developments for the balance of power between labourers and landowners.

Muzaffarnagar district forms part of the Upper Doab region of west UP. The Muzaffarnagar fieldwork village was fully irrigated. Practically all ploughing was done by the 40 (1993) tractors of the village.[8] Sugarcane was the main crop, and only when the cane had been harvested were paddy, wheat and other crops grown.[9] The Jat caste was the dominant landowning group of the village, as of the region in general.[10] In the village in 1993, the landholdings of the Jats averaged around five acres, with no very large landowners present. Two-thirds of the Jat households had one or more members employed as government servants or in business.[11] Chamars formed the most important section of the agricultural labourers in the village (as well as in the region), with other low ranking castes such as Jhimars and Jogis.[12]

Within east UP, Jaunpur is one of the more agriculturally developed districts. The upper caste Thakurs (Rajputs) were the main landowning group of the district and of the fieldwork village.[13] In the Jaunpur fieldwork village, in 1993 the landholdings of the Thakurs also averaged around five acres, and no very big landowners stood out. 90 per cent of the Thakur households had members employed as government servants or in business, reflecting the general reputation that Jaunpur upper castes have for success in obtaining government jobs.[14] The Thakurs' ex-tenants, primarily from the middle ranking Yadav caste had, from the zamindari abolition onwards, managed to take control of around half of the village's land, previously under the control of the Thakurs.[15] The labourers were mainly from the Chamar caste, and worked primarily for the upper caste landowners. By the 1990s, the village had been fully irrigated bar a few plots owned by low caste people. In 1993, half of the land owned by the Thakurs and Brahmins was ploughed by four tractors owned by locals. By 1998, there were six tractors and all upper-caste farmers made at least partial use of them.[16] The main cash crops were wheat and potatoes, while paddy and sugarcane were mainly grown for own consumption.

In both villages, employment of labourers in agriculture has fallen dramatically since Independence. In the west, investment in motor driven tube wells from the 1960s onwards did away with the large number of labourers engaged in mechanical irrigation, while tractors (introduced in 1964) rendered most classical 'ploughmen' superfluous. Finally, the taking over by farmers of most farmyard work did away with most classical farm servants. The progressively smaller holdings also made it easier for landowners to manage primarily with family labour. In 1998, labourers were mainly employed for the wheat harvest and, in a few cases, also in paddy cultivation. The proportion of landowners who did wheat harvesting solely with family labour had reached around 50 per cent; and threshing was done solely with power driven threshers (first introduced in the early 1970s), most often also worked with family labour.

In the eastern village, the main thrust of development was similar, although it started later and had not gone as far regarding mechanisation and the amount of work done by peasants themselves. In 1993, the Jaunpur villagers estimated that, compared to the 1950s, their use of agricultural labourers had fallen by around a half, due to the introduction of motor driven tube wells (from the mid-1960s), tractors (from 1970) and motor driven threshers (from the mid-1970s), combined with smaller landholdings and the increased participation of landowners in production. In 1998, agricultural labourers were employed primarily during the peak seasons of paddy transplantation and wheat harvesting. In between, casual labour was also needed for irrigation jobs, sowing and harvesting of other crops, and weeding.

Yearly sharecropping had also lost its importance. In the Muzaffarnagar village, sharecropping on a yearly basis had become near-extinct and had been so since the mid-1960s while in the Jaunpur village, the proportion of farmers leasing out land throughout the year had fallen considerably, to around 15 per cent in 1993.[17]

However, in both villages, it had become common to lease out labour-intensive, non-mechanised paddy cultivation to the agricultural labourers. In Muzaffarnagar, this seasonal lease bore many similarities to piece-rate work, even though it was couched in sharecropping terminology. The balance between lessor and lessee regarding investments and risks, and the control of the labour process, was significantly changed. The lessee did not provide any means of production other than simple tools; the pair of oxen and plough, which used to be a prerequisite for a sharecropper, were not required as the landowner provided all inputs, including tractorised ploughing. Thus, the landowner retained control over inputs and production, while the 'sharecropper' only provided his (and often his household's) labour-power.[18] This system had existed for as long as people could remember, but had only become a common way of growing paddy since the late 1980s.[19] Landowners found that this was a cheaper and more efficient way of organising the labour process compared to employing daily wage labourers. It also required no day-to-day supervision and gave them fewer labour problems.

In Jaunpur, in 1998, around 75 per cent of all upper caste landowners leased at least part of the paddy land out during the *kharif* season. This was mainly done on a *'tiseri'* ('one-third') basis. The landowner supplied two-thirds of expenditure for fertiliser and seeds, and provided irrigation, while the sharecropper provided all labour as well as the remaining share of the inputs, and received one-third of the harvest.[20] Moreover, and opposed to the case of the Muzaffarnagar seasonal lease system, ploughing did form part of the lessee's duties. However, it was no longer necessary for the lessee to own a pair of bullocks (or to have access to bullocks from relatives etc.) as now, the renting in a tractor for ploughing was an option.

This *tiseri* system had gained in prominence since the 1960s and received an extra boost in the 1990s as agricultural wages increased. Thus, the main reasons for its popularity among landowners were, first, that it was less 'difficult' for them than paddy cultivation with wage labour, because strikes and other labour conflicts were averted. Secondly, it was nearly as profitable or, according to some landowners, just as profitable as cultivating paddy with wage labour.[21]

In both villages it was also important for landowners that they could tie labourers to them throughout the year through these forms of sharecropping. In order to gain access to sharecropping and the most remunerative labour tasks, workers had to accept that members of their household who did not migrate seasonally (women, old men) worked for the landowner on a priority basis at any time during the year, and performed a certain amount of unpaid labour (*begar*) for the landowner as well. I will return to this shortly.

From the labourers' point of view, since Independence, agricultural wage labour and sharecropping had lost their position as the most important sources of income. Non-agricultural work had become the main source of income for most labourers. In the west, the better paid brick kiln work in Punjab and Haryana was especially important for Chamar workers from the mid-1960s, when agricultural employment opportunities started to become scarce. This provided full-time work throughout the year, except during the rainy season when the kilns closed down. Another important non-agricultural occupation was working on sugar cane crushers (*kolhu*) in the villages, which provided full-time employment during the *rabi* (spring) season, and became the most prevalent occupation for the low caste Jhimars. For the labourers of the eastern village, migrant work in the factories and streets of Bombay became especially important from the early 1970s.[22]

By 1998, able-bodied adult men were rarely available for agricultural employment throughout the year.[23] Daily labour is now carried out by women and old men. Migrant workers do return to work in agriculture during the peak seasons, but even so, there has been a falling off in wage labour participation in agriculture (a development which cannot, to any great degree, be accounted for by their growing participation in seasonal sharecropping).[24]

Several other major changes have taken place in agrarian labour relations. Most importantly, there has been a transformation of wholly unfree labour relations into relations involving various degrees of unfreedom.[25] The labourers' ties to specific masters and to specific working conditions have changed and, in many cases, become looser. Another major development relates to the duration of labour contracts.

According to the landowners of both the fieldwork villages, practically all of them had employed one or more permanent labourers in the 1950s, who did the ploughing, irrigation and other fieldwork, and worked in the landowners' courtyard tending cattle and helping out in general.[26] The Muzaffarnagar labourers pointed to debt bondage as having been the core of this relationship.

While the Jaunpur labourers also stated that permanent labourers did normally take loans from their employers, they saw this as only one aspect of a much more encompassing relationship. According to both labourers and landowners, each landowner originally brought his permanent labour households to the area and settled them on his land; the worker therefore 'belonged' to this landowner.[27] This was seen as the core of the dependency relation. Thus, in both villages, debt bondage and, in Jaunpur, also other ties hindered the permanent labourers from leaving any job once the period contracted for was over: the permanent labourers were unfree labourers.

Since then, mechanical irrigation, tractors, smaller holdings and the taking over by farmers of most farmyard work, have done away with almost all of the permanent labourers. However, the sharp decrease in permanent unfree labour relations in both villages did not lead to the emergence of generalised free labour relations. Instead, new types of labour relations emerged. Today, the labour relations are as follows.

Very few permanent labourers remain. In 1998, in the Jaunpur village there were five, constituting only nine per cent of the agricultural workforce.[28] They were either elderly local men who could not find other occupations, or outsiders. Most had taken loans from their employer.

In Muzaffarnagar, long-term employment relations were different. Here, only the biggest farmers who needed to employ labourers at least throughout the sugarcane harvesting season had engaged one or two permanent labourers each: a total of around 20 labourers, all but one from Bihar and Nepal.[29] They thus constituted around 12 per cent of the agricultural work force. They were generally hired on three-to-four-month contracts; and three or four were employed on yearly contracts. They were, in principle, paid at least Rs 400 per month plus food.[30] Oppression and control during their stay was harsh, and could include the withholding or even non-payment of wages. However, some were paid properly, and there were cases of labourers returning for more than one year.[31]

Whereas the (few) Jaunpur permanent labourers are 'classical' unfree labourers, the seasonal labourers in Muzaffarnagar, however oppressed, are not unfree. The landowner may not keep his contractual obligations, and treat them extremely harshly, but the labour relation is entered into freely with no debt bondage or other ties hindering labourers from leaving once the period of their contract is over.

Importantly, however, most local labourers are not involved in 'permanent' and seasonal labour relations. Instead, in both villages, in the 1990s, all but two or three labour households worked for specific landowners on a priority basis. These priority arrangements encompassed a range of labour relations. One-third of the priority labour households in Jaunpur, and between half and two-thirds in Muzaffarnagar[32] had also taken loans from the employer. These labourers, while not permanently working for their employer-cum-moneylender, were tied into beck-and-call relations to him, and had to work for him whenever he required.[33]

The labour households who had not taken loans only worked for their priority employer when and if they had time, that is, if they had not got other work planned, and they were free to leave the priority work relation if they so wished. However, even these households experienced unfree elements within this priority relation. In Jaunpur, there were two reasons why labourers not tied by loans entered into the priority work relationship. It was either part of a sharecropping arrangement where landowners demanded it as a condition. Or, for those not engaged in sharecropping, it was simply because landowners were, generally, in a position to restrict employment only to those who accepted the priority arrangement. In Muzaffarnagar, an additional reason was to secure fodder from the employer's fields for the cattle; only households accepting a priority relation were permitted to take fodder from the employer's fields.

In both villages, all workers in priority relations had to perform *begar* (labour service) during the year. In Muzaffarnagar, this primarily related to the sugarcane growing (planting, weeding, harvesting), while in Jaunpur, the *begar* tasks were sugarcane and potato planting. In addition, those who had taken loans were also expected to perform some additional *begar* when and if the landowner needed it. In Muzaffarnagar, *begar* had become very significant: most work on sugarcane was done without labourers receiving a regular wage.[34] As outlined elsewhere [*Lerche*, 1995], it had become common for labour family members who stayed in the village (women, old men, and sometimes children) to rear a few head of milch cattle that provided them with an extra income but, in return for access to landowners' fields for fodder (weeds and sugar cane tops), and access to the relatively remunerative peak season jobs of paddy cultivation and wheat harvesting, they were obliged to weed the fields and harvest the cane without any direct payment.[35]

The landowners' restriction of employment to those who accept the priority labour relation, and their enforcement of *begar* as part of it, show that this is not a free labour relation. However, compared to the bonds that follow on from debt relations, labourers in general priority relations but who are not debt bonded possess an important degree of freedom, particularly that to choose to reject an offer of work from their priority employer, and to limit *begar* to certain specific tasks. There are also important variations in degrees of unfreedom between different types of non-debt priority labour relations, with the ties relating to cattle raising (in Muzaffarnagar) more rigid than those mainly relating to access to work.

The transformation over time of draconian permanent unfree labour relations into labour relations involving various degrees of unfreedom, as well as the decrease in and transformation of sharecropping, are important aspects of the overall development of labour relations in the two villages. So is the stronger reliance on debt bondage as well as other interlinked relations, by the Muzaffarnagar landowners, resulting in higher degrees of unfreedom for labourers there than in the Jaunpur village. It should not be forgotten, however, that today the majority of labourers have their main employment and main income source outside the villages. While the landed groups might still be capable of enforcing certain (weakened) dominance, the resulting unfreedom occupies a relatively small part of most labour households' employment relations. Also important in this respect is that a partially gendered division of labour has developed: in many households, the unfree aspects of labour relations prevalent during the slack season are taken care of by women (plus elderly men and sometimes children), whereas male labour migrants reappear in the village only during the peak seasons when better paid work is available.

Looking at the reasons why the number of labourers employed in agriculture has declined so sharply, one important factor not yet mentioned is the considerably higher wages outside agriculture.[36] While this drew labourers away from agriculture, the landowners found the local agricultural wages too high. In Muzaffarnagar, landowners accordingly applied extreme pressure to keep wages down [*Lerche*, 1995]. Here it is sufficient to note that the Jats have kept the village in an iron grip till quite recently, drawing strong support from their farmers union, the BKU. However, in spite of a successful lock-out action to lower wages in the mid-1980s, they were soon forced to increase wages gradually in order to attract labourers.[37] The farmers saw present wage levels as a strong incentive to manage without much paid labour - or to hire contract labourers from Bihar and Nepal.

In the Jaunpur village the availability of better paid work outside agriculture also influenced local labour relations.[38] Here, however, landowners had been less successful in keeping wages down. Labourers have gone on strike approximately every third year since 1972.[39] Wages increased sharply through these actions as well as through individual bargaining to a level which, in the 1990s, was similar if not slightly higher than in the Muzaffarnagar village.[40] The relative strength of the Jaunpur labourers was partly because landowners in the Jaunpur village were split into two factions: the old landlords from the high castes, and the old core tenants (the middle caste Yadavs) who had now become very productive peasants. This situation, which is not uncommon in east UP, gave rise to a very different power equation. Moreover, and at least partially linked to this, the Jaunpur Chamar labourers also became much more politicised during the last twenty years than their fellows in the west UP village. They were well aware of their own fighting capability.

Other Studies of Labour Relations in UP

I now compare the above cases with other case studies, with a focus on issues relevant to understanding the development of the landowners' attempt to maintain a docile work force and minimise their labour costs, and the labourers' attempt to free themselves from the most exploitative and oppressive mechanisms. First, a number of important material aspects of labour relations are discussed. This leads to a more general assessment of the development of agrarian labour relations and labour struggles. The focus is on post-Green Revolution case studies based on fieldwork since 1980, although older material is included where relevant.[41]

Non-agricultural labour: The tendency towards a substantial decrease in the amount of agricultural labour performed by rural labourers and a corresponding increase in non-agricultural rural employment has been noted by several studies. In west UP, a case study of four villages of the Upper Doab district of Meerut conducted in 1988/89 by Rita Sharma and Thomas Poleman showed that the number of man-days of agricultural labour available to each landless or marginal farmer household was only 44, 77, 86 and 146 respectively in each of the villages [*Sharma and Poleman*, 1994: 236]. Sharma and Poleman also detail the income sources of a sample of landless households of the villages. Between 59 per cent and 70 per cent of the average income came from non-agricultural employment, while only between 7 per cent and 24 per cent came from agricultural labour [*Sharma and Poleman*, 1994: 94, 172, 208, 237].[42]

Ravi Srivastava's study (included in this volume) also confirms the overwhelming importance of non-agricultural occupations in Muzaffarnagar. In 1993–94, in the two villages he studied in this district, 80 per cent and 90 per cent respectively of casual labour days were taken up by non-agricultural occupations. Srivastava's study also covered four other villages: two in Rae Barelly of central UP and two in Jaunpur district of east UP. The figures for these villages were between 45 per cent and 65 per cent. Moreover, in all six villages, the average number of days of agricultural employment available per agricultural labourer was between 43 and 71 (Srivastava, this volume).

A number of other case studies also show an increase in non-agricultural employment for those groups who used to be agricultural workers, without quantifying precisely its extent. Dipankar Gupta studied three villages in Meerut and Muzaffarnagar districts in the 1980s and 1990s.[43] His census of one of the villages shows that in two-thirds of the landless households, the head of household was engaged in non-agricultural employment. Among the remaining one-third working as agricultural labourers, a common complaint was that this type of employment was not available for more than three months a year [*Gupta*, 1997: 29].[44] Still in west UP, a study by Ashwani Saith and Ajay Tankha of a village in Aligarh district from 1970 to 1987 reports that, during this period, poor households especially took up migrant non-agricultural work [*Saith and Tankha*, 1997: 113].[45] In another village in the same district, surveyed in 1994, 95 per cent of all agricultural labourers worked between 120 and 180 days in agriculture, which represents an unspecified fall in agrarian employment (while more prevalent than in the other studies discussed here) [*Singh et al.*, 1996: 18]. From fieldwork in 1975 and 1984 in a west UP village of Mainpuri district, Susan Wadley reports that the number of labourers whose primary occupation was wage labour outside the village (cycle rickshaw driving, coolie work, construction work) increased between 1975 and 1984 from two to 84 [*Wadley*, 1996: 217].[46] Finally, in the village of Palanpur studied by, among others, Jean Drèze, it was found that the Jatabs [or Jatavs, that is, Chamars], the principal agricultural workers, had begun to work as casual labourers in the nearby town between 1983/84 and 1993 [*Drèze*, 1997: 160–61].

Thus, all these case studies point towards the growing importance of non-agricultural employment for rural labourers, a development which is particularly well documented for the Upper Doab region, while only my own and Srivastava's study provide evidence from parts of UP other than the west. The exact levels and regional variations of this tendency cannot be established from the existing material, but the few village studies which have assessed the question in detail all conclude, as does my own study, that non-agricultural work is now at least as important economically as agricultural work, and perhaps more so.

Sharecropping: Regarding sharecropping, one of the most detailed sets of studies in UP has been done by Ravi Srivastava, based on his survey of three villages in Muzaffarnagar district, Allahabad and Deoria districts of east UP during 1985–87. The Muzaffarnagar and Allahabad villages were revisited in 1989–90 but no major changes regarding shareropping had taken place [*Srivastava*, 1989a; 1997].[48] Srivastava's main conclusion regarding sharecropping was that '[t]here has been a progressive, though uneven, shift – as we move from Mangalpur to Chaukra [i.e., from the east to the west UP village] – from leasing out as a means of rental appropriation, to leasing out as a form of control over labour power, the appropriation of its produce and a means for furthering accumulation' [*Srivastava*, 1989a: 382]. This conclusion is in accordance with my own findings. The proportion of village land involved in tenancy relations (including mortgage of land) was, in Srivastava's study, going from east to west, 27 per cent, 34 per cent and 24 per cent. In all villages, the yearly tenancies were mainly given to landowning peasants (poor peasants in the central UP village and middle peasants in the Muzaffarnagar village), while seasonal tenancies, common only in the Muzaffarnagar village, were mainly given to labourers and, secondly, poor peasants.

Importantly, lessors dominated decision making about crops and inputs in both the Allahabad and the Muzaffarnagar villages studied in the most detail. The extent of their control was highest in the west. Similarly, while tenancies were mainly drawn up on a yearly half-share basis in the east, more than half of the tenancy contracts in the west were now seasonal 3/4 share arrangements on labour intensive crops such as paddy, with the sharecroppers supplying their labour as well as a quarter of the input costs. Seasonal leasing had also begun in the Allahabad district village, if not yet as widely practised as in the west [*Srivastava*, 1996: 234–8; 1997: 210–15]. Srivastava concludes that '[a]t the margin, such arrangements tend to reduce tenants to piece-rated workers with the added proviso that they must share the risk' [*Srivastava*, 1996: 237]. Srivastava's recent study (included in this volume) shows a similar pattern of development in sharecropping (Srivastava, this volume).

Concerning the Upper Doab region of west UP, Jagpal Singh's study from Meerut district shows a lower level of tenancy, but similar types of sharecropping to that of Srivastava's and my own studies. His 1984–85 survey of eight villages distributed throughout all four *tahsils* of Meerut district shows that here 1.32 per cent households leased land out while 4.84 per cent leased in, and that half of the leases were only for one crop, the potato crop [*Singh*, 1992: 45].

Still in west UP, Saith and Tankha's study from Aligarh district points out that while the level of tenancy was constant from 1970 to 1987 (*rabi* crop, 1970: 32 per cent, 1987: 31.5 per cent), rich peasants had changed from net leasing out to net leasing in of land. This common change is seen as related to the Green Revolution, especially to 'tractorisation' by rich peasants which enables them to cultivate more land themselves, with the help of agricultural workers; and it is also, in this specific case, related to the leasing in of land from other villages. However, the study does not distinguish between seasonal and yearly sharecropping [*Saith and Tankha*, 1997: 96–9].

A somewhat similar conclusion was reached by Susan Wadley in Mainpuri district [*Wadley*, 1996: 214].[49] Other studies point in various directions. A set of studies, based on fieldwork in Palanpur in Moradabad district of west UP from 1957/8 onwards, shows that while sharecropping increased until 1983–84 (28 per cent of the cultivated land), it had fallen a bit by 1993 (26 per cent). This sharecropping was mainly on a half-share basis even though fixed rent leasing also occurred [*Drèze, Lanjouw and Stern*, 1992: 6; *Drèze*, 1997]. On the other hand, Judy Whitehead's study from a village in central UP tells us that here, 'in 1965 there were approximately 125 sharecroppers while in 1983 there were 25' (no other details are presented) [*Whitehead*, 1991: 25].

So, it seems clear that tendencies towards a decrease in and/or transformation of sharecropping relations into labour controlling and accumulation oriented relations, with some important similarities to piece rate contracts, do exist. However, it is unclear how strong these trends are, especially outside the Upper Doab region of west UP.

Free and unfree labour relations: Statistical data on unfree labour relations is generally not reliable.[50] Looking at the UP case study evidence, pre-Green Revolution studies show a high incidence. In a village in Jaunpur district studied by Bernard Cohn in 1952–53, household members from 70 per cent of the 126 Camar (Chamar) households were engaged on annual contracts as ploughmen-cum-general agricultural servants. The ploughmen were recruited from among each Thakur's Camar tenants, often somewhat unwillingly but, as tenants, they could not refuse if chosen. While the point is not spelled out in detail, it seems that debt did not bond the ploughmen who, in some cases, changed 'almost yearly' [*Cohn*, 1954: 63–70, 74–5].[51] This might be because they were, at any rate, all tenants of the same Thakur and thus still depended on him to make a living. Daily labourers were also drawn from the ranks of the tenants [*Cohn*, 1954: 77].[52]

Other pre-Green Revolution studies simply assume that landowners employ at least one permanent labourer each but provide no detailed evidence on the relationship.[53] One exception is a study of agricultural labour in 100 villages in Meerut district in 1965 which found that 39 per cent of agricultural labourers were on regular contracts.[54] Contrary to what might have been expected, only 37 per cent of these labourers worked for more than three years for the same landowner, and only five per cent were in the same relationship for more than 20 years. The study suggests, seemingly based on discussions with the labourers, that long-term relations used to be more common 'a few decades' ago [*Saxena*, 1969: 99].[55] Asked for the reasons for entering into the relationship, only 20 per cent mentioned debt, while 74 per cent saw the main reason as being 'necessity of employment', presumably meaning that this was the only way to secure employment with the landowners [*Saxena*, 1969: 94–8].

Of more recent case studies, Srivastava found, from data collection in 1984/85 and 1989/90 that both in the Allahabad east UP and in the Muzaffarnagar villages the proportion of yearly farm servants had fallen since pre-Green Revolution days. In both villages, till the mid-1960s, agriculture had been based on various types of farm servant relations. In the Allahabad village, yearly farm servants constituted 15 per cent of agricultural labourers in 1963/64 but only 'a handful' in the 1980s. In the Muzaffarnagar village, there were 40 farm servants and ploughmen in 1951/52, a number which had fallen to 'more than 20' by the late 1980s. In both villages, a high proportion of daily labourers also worked for specific landed households on a priority basis in the 1980s. Both these types of labour relations were based on interlinkages between tenancy, credit and labour relations [*Srivastava*, 1989b: 500–504, 517–18; 1997: 216, 221–2].[56] Such interlinkages were most common in the Muzaffarnagar village where tied labour relations were 'more contractual' but, nevertheless, the 'more adverse forms' such as priority labour relations, labour service and underpayment were more common in the Allahabad village where they were underpinned by traditional patron-client relations [*Srivastava*, 1996: 242–3].[57] Interestingly, Srivastava argues that the monetized unfree relations in the west only 'place a relative constraint on the mobility of labourers' as farm servants can become priority labourers and labourers can repay loans and take up non-agricultural occupations. It seems that such mobility does not exist in the Allahabad village [*Srivastava*, 1996: 244–5]. In the Deoria village of east UP also included in the study, interlinked relations had broken down as a result of the political struggles of the labourers against debt and *begar* commitments [*Srivastava*, 1989b: 515].

Regarding the six other villages studied in 1993/94, Srivastava states that permanent, mainly migrant labourers were most prevalent in the two

Muzaffarnagar villages, and least common in the central UP villages. In all villages, harsh oppression plays an important role in maintaining these relations. It is also noted that the implications of the lease markets are similar to those of the earlier study (Srivastava, this volume).

In Palanpur village of Moradabad district of west UP, there were no 'bonded labourers' in 1983/84, nor any credit–labour or tenancy–labour interlinkages or interseasonal labour-tying [*Drèze and Mukherjee*, 1989: 238, 244].[58] The Aligarh and Mainpuri studies mentioned earlier show a marked decline in the number of permanent / bonded labour relations but do not look into other types of unfree relations, while the other Meerut studies referred do not consider unfree or permanent labour at all.[59]

Finally, an option taken up by some landowners in Meerut and Muzaffarnagar district is to cultivate less labour intensive crops. Fruit orchards in particular require very little labour input, and both Srivastava [1997] and Sharma and Poleman [1994] report that some landowners have moved in this direction. Based on field visits to villages in most parts of Muzaffarnagar district I would argue that this still seems to be a rare development, undertaken only by a few very big farmers.

Thus, judging from available pre- and post-Green Revolution case studies, including my own, the incidence of permanent labour relations has generally been declining in UP agriculture during the last 30 years or more. As part of that development, the incidence of unfree permanent labour relations has also gone down. The decline in the number of unfree permanent labourers seems to be least steep in the developed western Upper Doab region. Here, a number of case studies showed a shift towards seasonal contracts as opposed to yearly contracts, as well as a shift towards the employment of migrant labourers. However, although migrant labourers were treated very harshly and sometimes cheated of their pay, they could not be characterised as unfree.

While unfree permanent labour relations thus seem to have lost their previous importance in UP, a number of case studies point towards the importance of landowners' enforcement of priority work relations. This type of relation fulfils many of the same roles as unfree permanent labour relations with regard to maintaining a cheap and reliable workforce.

Interestingly, debt relations are not always the primary means of securing this workforce. In several cases, the main tool of the landowners seems to be their control of the amount of work available and/or their general oppression, which they attempt to use to dictate the allocation of work, working conditions and wages. My own case study confirmed the classic viewpoint that debt relations allow for greater dominance of the labourer than do relations relying solely on the general strength of the landowners. Also, together with Srivastava's study it points to a higher incidence of monetized and other interlinked contractual relations in west UP where capitalist farming is most developed. Opposed to this, classical dominance relations play a more important role in underpinning priority work relations in the east. Crucially, at least in the villages I studied, non-debt bonded priority work relations allowed labourers to refuse to take up work for their employer at his will; but this kind of work relation still involved labour services (*begar*). Equally important, whilst resorting to unfree labour relations can rightly be seen as a means of creating a cheaper and more docile labour force, landowners also make use of other means, such as restricting access to employment to certain types of priority labourers only, and also routinely breaching their contracts with labourers regarding wage payment.

In sum, the labourers' direct economic dependency on landowners, entailed by the old personalised, rather all-encompassing labour relations, has been somewhat relaxed. Most labour households now have other, possibly more important, income sources than working for the landowner. They depend on him in fewer areas than was the case earlier when borrowing, sharecropping, yearly labour contracts and traditional duties created a powerful cocktail of dependency and generalised unfree labour relations.

However, this also means that the landowners of the 1990s are forced to use quite harsh and direct means of oppression to maintain a cheap, reliable and docile labour force. Otherwise they must accept that the past is gone, and either pay the going rate or minimise their expenses by employing as few labourers as possible. Depending on the strategy chosen by landowners, the struggle around the labour process may take very violent forms as landowners commonly use physical violence as well as boycotts to press their point, while strikes are quite commonly used by labourers.

LABOUR POLITICISATION AND LABOUR ACTIONS

Part of the problem for the employers, I would argue, is that the efficacy of their classical means of oppression has been blunted during this century. As pointed out already, an important reason for employers to tie labourers into unfree relations is to curtail their bargaining power. In spite of this widely accepted viewpoint, I would argue that even unfree labourers may take action against their employers or engage in other kinds of collective bargaining process. This certainly happened from the 1970s onwards in the Jaunpur village I studied. Here, all labourers (and all but two to three agricultural labour households are in priority relations with specific landowners) participated in strike actions. Those who were in debt relations also took part, even though they did not wish to take lead of the actions. The local landowners acknowledged that debt could not stop labour actions nowadays. According to them, it was not even possible to use the threat of reclaiming the full loan against striking labourers, as they might then take the lender to court for usurious moneylending and illegal debt bondage. In the Muzaffarnagar village I studied, all local workers, irrespective of debt relations, were involved in the only strike that had taken place there (in 1979); and lock-out actions of the landowners (more common here than strikes) had been directed towards all labourers, be they free, unfree or debt bonded. Only migrant permanent labourers were not involved in any conflicts (see further below).

I see this failure to stop labourers' actions as part of a general development, in which local level oppression and reactions to it have changed considerably. Village level studies point towards increased emancipation of agricultural labourers and the lowest castes, and an improvement in their position. This has been an uneven process, with major regional variation within UP. The timing of labourers' first actions, and the events that trigger it, vary, but the common picture is that sometime between the 1920s and the 1990s, in most villages, they have collectively confronted the landowners on one or several issues. These issues not only relate directly to the labour process but also to the more general dominance by landed groups, which labour relations also rely on heavily.

There is little evidence of agricultural labourers engaging in direct confrontational action against the landed groups in UP before the 1920s.[60] However, it seems that from the 1920s onwards, a climate was created where such events could take place. This was due to a number of developments, such as the emergence of small low caste urban working and middle classes, and the creation, and activities, of various low caste organisations, or organisations also working with low caste people.[61]

Low-caste agricultural labourers were also politicised as part of the general struggle against landlordism and the colonial regime. The Left's strategy was to unite agricultural labourers and tenants (who often employed agricultural labourers) against the landlords. Agricultural labourers' demands for land, higher wages and the abolition of *begar* were articulated and fought for as part of, but subordinated to, the general anti-landlord struggle [*A. Gupta*, 1996; *Sen*, 1982: 161–4].[62] Thus, when these peasant- and tenant-led campaigns were stopped after Independence, having benefited mainly the 'occupancy tenants' (often from the middle castes), untouchable agricultural labourers were left with no allies and no autonomous organisations [*Omvedt*, 1986: 182].

A detailed early example of politicisation of untouchable labourers is provided by Bernard Cohn who reports that in a village in Jaunpur district in the 1920s, agricultural labourers from the Chamar untouchable caste carried out and won their first strike, against carrying 'manure' [presumably night soil – JL] to the fields for the landowners. They took this action in the context of increasing engagement in urban migratory work, and the influence by the ideology of caste upliftment which pervaded this part of the Jaunpur countryside at the time.[63] These agricultural labourers were all in tenancy relations to the landowners, the majority of them worked as permanent ploughmen (halwah), and all but a few borrowed grain from the landowners during the lean season. This, however, did not stop them embarking on the strike action [Cohn, 1954: 28, 64, 74, 124].[64] Some years later, the more general political changes that took place as part of the nationalist struggle created, for the first time, the opportunity for the Chamars of the village to ally themselves with other tenant groups against the Thakur landlords. The Chamars supported a low caste candidate against a Thakur candidate in the 1937 Legislative Assembly election, which led the Thakurs to retaliate by preventing them from sowing their next crop and by ripping down the thatched roofs on their houses. After Independence the low castes organised themselves in the Praja Party which led to the murder of their local political leader, and to the Chamars' attempt to involve the outside government machinery in local conflicts on their side for the first time [Cohn, 1954: 143–59].

More generally in UP, from the 1930s onwards, Leftist organisations raised demands on behalf of tenants and labourers, such as abolition of begar, debt annulment and rent reduction. Campaigns against landlords' large-scale evictions of tenants in the late 1930s represented an intensification of the struggle, especially in east UP. Direct action against landlordism culminated in widespread communist-led struggles around and just after Independence in many parts of India, including some incidents in UP [A. Gupta, 1996: 28, 71–4, 159, 444–7].

Rajendra Singh provides us with a case study of peasant struggles in Basti District of east UP during this period [Singh, 1979]. He states that prior to 1930, no organised actions by untouchable agricultural labourers had been recorded. From then on, the middle caste tenants' struggle against the landlords also came to involve the labourers. From 1935 to 1946, politicisation related to issues such as eviction of tenants, begar, sexual exploitation of tenants and labourers' womenfolk, etc. led to violent rebellions including several killings of oppressive and brutal landlords and landlords' henchmen. These actions were often carried out by groups consisting of several hundred tenants and labourers. From 1946–48, this led to the 'Nijai Bol' movement: a campaign for self-declaration of possession of land by tenants. In the end, some take-overs of land by the middle peasants were legalised, whereas untouchable labourers did not acquire land [Singh, 1979: 117–36].

In other parts of UP, politicisation of labourers did not lead to similar armed actions, and conflicts were less bold in the sense that they did not attack the overall dominance of landlords. In west UP, in the village I studied in Muzaffarnagar district, the first conflict involving agricultural labourers that local informants can recall took place at around the time of Independence, when the labourers took a group of Jats to court over a homestead plot that another Jat had given them.[65] Elsewhere in west UP, in the Mainpuri district village studies by Wadley, several confrontational actions regarding issues of payment were initiated by various groups, including agricultural labourers, from the 1920s onwards, including a six-month strike which took place around the late 1930s [*Wadley*, 1996: 229].

In Aligarh district of West UP, in the late 1950s, untouchables held protest meetings against *begar*, landowners' attempts to stop them cutting fodder and grass, and for land redistribution and better fair price shops. This mobilisation was furthered by the fact that several Jatav [Chamar] organisations existed before Independence which 'played a crucial role in mobilising the Jatavs' [*Brass*, 1985: 219–20; *Hasan*, 1989: 113, 116]. Local strike action is reported from a village in Muzaffarnagar in 1958, by Michael Mahar. He does not specify the exact type of labour relations, but the workers in question were not casual labourers as they were paid monthly [*Mahar*, 1972: 30].

During the 1970s and 1980s, more studies of conflicts appear. Most conflicts reported are strikes regarding higher wages, refusal of labourers to do *begar* and to work as ploughmen, reactions against social oppression, attempts by low caste groups to bring beatings and atrocities to court, and attempts to assert their right to vote, which are then followed by retaliation by the dominant landowning groups. The one major attempt at a general mobilisation of labourers and poor peasants was the 'land grab' movement of 1970, led by the communist parties [*'Mankind'*, 1986]. It did not, however, gain sufficient mass support and was, in most cases, easily beaten back by the landowners. In Basti district of east UP, for example, the 'uprising' only led to seven face-to-face encounters, and the united landowning group of ex-zamindars and their former tenants easily crushed it [*Singh*, 1979: 136–7].

According to a study by S.N. Pathak based on fieldwork in 1978–79 in four villages in each of the eastern districts of Basti and Gonda (both among the least developed eastern districts), the most common reason for tension between upper and lower castes was the latter's refusal to work as ploughmen. The second most common reason was their refusal to work as casual labourers at low wage rates, and other conflicts arose from their refusal to do *begar* or accept the rules of untouchability. Also, the increased political awareness of lower caste people and the election of some non-upper caste people to *panchayats* and in general elections created tensions [*Pathak*, 1987: 198–209]. From a village in Jaunpur, Masaaki Fukunaga describes how in 1982–83 Chamar labourers employed on long-term contracts 'took leave' from work in a group of Thakur households, which paid them a lower rate than agreed by the rest of the Thakurs [*Fukunaga*, 1993: 148–9, 163]. Srivastava similarly points to labourers taking action against *begar* and debt relations in the early 1970s in a village of Deoria district of east UP [*Srivastava*, 1989b: 505].

My own study of a Jaunpur village recorded that the first conflict the villagers remembered took place in 1971, over high caste disruption of the Chamars' yearly politico-religious celebration of their saint Ravidas, but led to fairly regular wage strikes from then on. Srivastava's recent study of six villages in west, central and east UP, included in this volume, shows that conflicts and actions took place from the mid-1980s to mid-1990s in all but one of the Muzaffarnagar villages. While wage issues were often on the agenda, many conflicts expressed untouchable and low-caste workers' increasingly strong reactions to acts of social discrimination and general oppression (Srivastava, this volume). This supports Susan Wadley's observation in her study from Mainpuri district that direct attacks on the acts and symbols of high caste landowners' dominance is a fairly recent phenomenon, related to the breakdown of classical patron–client relations from the 1960s onwards [*Wadley*, 1996: 226–34].

A different aspect is highlighted in Jagpal Singh's study from Meerut district. He mentions major reprisals in a village in 1971 after the rural poor tried to vote - the rural rich boycotted them for eight months, and their action was only stopped after intervention by the police. In another Meerut village, landowners boycotted labourers until they were forced to accept *begar* and to work as agricultural labourers on the conditions on offer [*Singh*, 1992: 80–81]. The landowners of the village I studied in Muzaffarnagar were in a similarly strong position, boycotting labourers and imposing behavioural rules and regulations more or less as they wished. As Craig Jeffrey quotes a Meerut Jat landowner: 'the Chamar became "cheeky" so we punched out his teeth' [*Jeffrey*, 1998: 1].

There are also villages where no open labour conflicts seem to have occurred. The Palanpur study from Moradabad district explicitly states that no labour conflicts had taken place, at least not before 1983 [*Drèze and Mukherjee*, 1989: 245], and some other studies do not mention conflicts in all the villages they cover. Not to mention conflicts, however, is not the same as stating that no conflicts have taken place.

To conclude this part of the study: while it is clear that politicisation among labourers has increased, the same applies, in some cases, to the oppressive responses by landowners. While unfree labour relations still exist, especially in parts of Upper Doab, they have changed in form, become less encompassing and given way to a variety of labour relations. An important reason for this is that, as shown, personalised oppressive relations have lost some of their efficiency: they do not in themselves hold the power to stop collective labour action.

That traditional oppressive means such as local patron–client relations no longer suffices to contain labourers' opposition is a point also suggested by Ronald Herring for South Asia in general. Herring argues further that the rural elite instead makes use of the powers of the state, which are easily available to them [Herring, 1984]. It is correct that the influence of outside authorities is an important aspect of local conflicts and the enforcement of oppressive labour relations.[66] In UP, leading landowning groups and other elites have close connections to the local state administration, including the police [Duncan, 1988: 45; Brass, 1997b: 54–6]. It is commonplace for village landowners to try to solve labour disputes by using the police to beat up unruly or striking labourers, or to have them jailed on trumped up charges (which will also involve a good beating), or to file court cases against striking labourers (i.e. accusations of theft) supported by false witness statements. Police and court actions on behalf of labourers are, in contrast, few and far between.

Nevertheless, the influence of outside authorities not only benefits the landed classes. In a number of ways, the present politicisation of low caste agricultural labourers is also linked with state interventions. Thus, as pointed out by several of the case studies mentioned above, Independence and the institutionalisation of universal franchise gave these groups new means of struggle.

Moreover, from Independence onwards, positive discrimination legislation aimed at untouchables furthered their belief in support in higher places. While most of these initiatives have more symbolic than practical value [Hasan, 1989: 147],[67] in the villages that I studied low caste people did refer to them when explaining why they took action or organised themselves.[68] Similarly, Whitehead notes Indira Gandhi's image as defender of the poor in the village she studied, and Hasan refers to Congress success in acquiring a pro-poor, pro-untouchable image in UP [Whitehead, 1991].

The bargaining position of labourers at village level has also, not surprisingly, been strengthened by the increased availability of better paid (though by no means well-paid) non-agricultural employment since the 1970s. As observed by a number of studies, protest actions are more easily undertaken by those with a degree of independent economic means, whether a small plot of land or access to non-agricultural sources of income [Sharma, 1978: 177–8; Pathak, 1987:192–7]. More specifically, landowners and agricultural labourers agree that non-agricultural wages put pressure on landowners to increase the wages they pay, whether through strike actions of labourers or simply to be able to attract sufficient labourers. It is therefore no surprise that the labourers of the villages I studied find that their standard of living has improved during the last decades, including the 1990s. The same is the case in the other recent case study of six villages by Srivastava included in the present volume.[69]

More generally, low caste workers are now aware of their legitimate social rights, such as the right to live according to the generally accepted norms of rural society as they perceive them. These include the right to protect the household (the male head, his wife and their children) against physical, psychological and sexual abuse, and to abstain from performing certain tasks which are considered polluting, hence ostracising. They also include the right to a decent material existence.

CASTE, CLASS AND POLITICS IN UP

In the 1990s, the emergence of a low caste party, the Bahujan Samaj Party ('Majority of Society Party') or BSP, at the centre stage of UP politics has added an important dimension to the economic and political actions of low-caste rural workers. This part of the study focuses on (i) how the rise of the BSP has influenced labour relations in the countryside, (ii) how, at local level, this caste-based party deals with class-based issues, and (iii) why the BSP has been much more successful in mobilising rural labourers than the class based policies of the communist parties have been. Before this, however, I outline some issues of the categories of class and caste, and the political background of the emergence of the BSP as a major political player.

Gail Omvedt argues that while agrarian capitalist development in India has remoulded the pre-capitalist correlation between caste and class in a more complex relationship where class crosses caste categories, there is still a certain basic correlation between caste groups and class [Omvedt, 1985: 134–9]. In UP, important overlaps certainly exist between caste and class hierarchies. In broad terms, the old landlord class belonged mainly to the upper castes, their ex-tenants who now constitute the majority of the landowning peasants are from the middle-ranking castes, and agricultural labourers are primarily from untouchable and other very low-ranking castes. However, the caste-class fit is far from perfect. The most important aspect of this in the present context is that around one-third of all agricultural labourers in Uttar Pradesh belong to other low castes than the untouchable castes [Omvedt, 1985: 128][70] and that, among the untouchables, a new small petty bourgeoisie has emerged. One reason for this is the reservation policy in education and government jobs. In the late 1980s, around 1.5 million untouchables nationwide had found government employment through this scheme [*Mendelsohn and Vicziany*, 1998: 137–8].[71] However, even earlier, a small untouchable petty bourgeoisie had developed in several towns in UP, the best known example being the Jatavs in the shoe and leather industry of the west UP town of Agra [*Lynch*, 1969: 32–66].[72] The fact that it is mainly better-off groups among the untouchables that have been able to take advantage of the reservation schemes has encouraged this development of a petty bourgeoisie separated from the untouchable majority [*Shah*, 1990: 363].

Caste is also an important category in rural workers' perceptions of their social and economic relations with others. Rural workers' class consciousness is often tempered by caste consciousness, not only due to cultural traditions but also because social oppression at village level, justified through 'Brahminical' Hinduism, generally follows caste lines, thus hitting all lower caste people, irrespective of class.[73]

There is, however, nothing 'natural' or inevitable about the present strength of caste. 'Caste' as it has emerged in politics is a fairly recent creation. It is an oft repeated point that ethnic/ religious / caste identities are constructs, created by elite groups or social and political movements which, in the process, make use of and transform inherited symbols to meet new ends.[74] Hence, without going into detail, 'the untouchables' as a *political* category is best understood as created through the contest between the colonial state, the Ambedkar movement and the Congress party and several cultural movements in the period leading up to Independence [*Omvedt*, 1994a].

PRESENT POLITICAL DEVELOPMENTS

Until the late 1980s, the Congress party was the dominant political force in UP. Expressed in caste terms, in UP as well as in the rest of India, Congress based its electoral strength on an alliance led by high caste upper classes and supported by untouchables and religious and ethnic minorities. However, already in the 1950s and early 1960s, a successful attempt to organise untouchables in a politically radical organisation was made by the Ambedkar movement, the major political movement of untouchables in India. It gained a particularly strong foothold among the politically radical Chamars of west UP who called themselves Jatavs. Whilst the movement and its party, the Republican Party of India (RPI), was strongest in towns such as Agra where it had major electoral success in the 1960s [*Lynch*, 1969], it also sent activists to the west UP countryside and gained support among rural untouchables, especially Jatavs, in districts such as Aligarh [*Brass*, 1985: 233–6] and Meerut [*Singh*, 1992: 94] in west UP.

The RPI, however, declined rapidly as an electoral force in UP when the minority alliance on which its electoral successes was built fell apart.[75] Thus, it was not the RPI but a party representing the interests of the rich and middle peasantry, the BKD (and various later incarnations such as BKL and Lok Dal) that challenged Congress hegemony in UP from the late 1960s onwards, as these peasant groups emerged as a major political force in UP with the onset of the Green Revolution.

The Green Revolution and related changes in agricultural labour relations also led to a rise in the political profile of the mainly untouchable rural labour group, and, in reaction to this, increasing atrocities against them. In this context of sharpening class-based contradictions (which were often expressed in caste terms), the patronage structures of the UP Congress party began to fall apart. Instead of consolidating the alliance on which its electoral success was based, for example, by attempting to absorb the political aspirations of the untouchables, (as Congress in Gujarat did through a realignment of forces within the party), the UP Congress developed a non-committal populist profile throughout the 1970s, resorting more and more blatantly to appeals to Hindu communal anti-minority interests to stay in power.

With the Congress party in structural crisis, a number of parties which combined a more forthright class-based policy with an even stronger caste and religious profile gained ground in the 1980s. These parties were the Bharatiya Janata Party (BJP), the leading Hindu nationalist party which has at its core high caste and business groups, and the Samajwadi Party (SP), led by the farming groups and middle castes. The two Indian Communist parties, on the other hand, saw their already small following decrease even further.[76]

These economic and political developments formed part of the background to a political development unique to UP: the BSP, a low-caste party led by an untouchable and projecting itself as a party for untouchables and other low castes, emerged as a major political player from the late 1980s onwards. The elections of 1989 saw the UP Congress party crumble. Since then, a turbulent power struggle has unfolded between the BJP, SP and BSP. Each has held office for a while, through a number of different coalitions and minority governments [P. Brass, 1990: 208–9; Hasan, 1989, 1998; Duncan, 1997].

The BSP gained prominence when it formed part of a winning coalition (with the SP), based on low and middle caste support in 1993. In 1995, it formed a minority government, supported by Congress and the BJP, which lasted four-and-a-half months. In 1997, it entered a formal powersharing arrangement with the BJP. This meant it held the Chief Minister post for six months, whereafter the arrangement broke down and the BJP took over the government.

The BSP was founded in 1984 by Kanshi Ram. Belonging to an untouchable caste, Kanshi Ram had been associated with the Republican Party since 1965, but in 1978 he created his own organisation, the Backward and Minority Group Community Employees Federation (BAMCEF), and in 1981 the Dalit Shoshit Samaj Sangharsh Samiti (DS-4) followed. DS-4 was more agitational and more oriented towards rural dalits than the 'middle-class' BAMCEF had been [*Mendelsohn and Vicziany,* 1998: 221–2; *Omvedt,* 1994b: 162–4].[77] It succeeded in rapidly gaining influence among the rural untouchables, much to the dismay of the existing communist labour unions. From 1985 onwards, the All India Agricultural Workers Union (AIAWU) singled out DS-4 as the major 'disruptive' or 'divisive' force among agricultural labourers in UP, and found it necessary to campaign actively against it [*AIAWU,* 1985: 44; 1986: 57, 61].

The BSP shot to prominence on the backs of DS-4 and BAMCEF, which provided the social and physical infrastructure for the party in UP [*Omvedt,* 1994b: 162–4]. In the 1989 election, it gained nine per cent of the UP votes, which increased to 21 per cent in 1996, a level it sustained in the 1998 election to the all Indian parliament [*Election Commission,* 1998].

The BSP's central thrust is to fight against the hegemony of the high caste minority, and for the emancipation and rule of the dalits[78] (untouchables), backward castes and other minorities who together constitute around 85 per cent of the population [*Kumar,* 1995: 342].[79] The 'Bahujan' or 'majority' element is stressed continuously by the party.[80] Nevertheless, the party's core constituency is the untouchables, and the BSP is generally seen as the untouchables' party, the inheritor of the Ambedkarite movement's mantle.[81] In fact, even among the untouchable castes, certain groups are closer to the party than others. The core support is drawn from the Chamar caste [*Brass,* 1997a: 2415; *Pai and Singh,* 1997: 1357–8; *Prashad,* 1995: 1357]. The Chamars are by far the largest and most politicised untouchable caste in UP. A small, educated and relatively well off class of Chamar government officials seems to have been at the forefront of their development into an independent political force [*Omvedt,* 1994b: 163; *Prashad,* 1996: 552]. The Chamars also formed the backbone of the RPI in the 1960s, but whereas the RPI had its main support base among the politicised Jatav Chamar group from west UP, the BSP has as much support in the east as in the west UP [*Brass,* 1997a].

There is nothing unusual in the fact that a single caste is the 'foundation caste' of a party in India; Gail Omvedt even sees this as inevitable. According to her, a more important question is whether or not the foundation caste 'can help a movement move beyond its limitations and draw in oppressed/exploited sectors or other castes' [*Omvedt,* 1994b: 156]. Till now, it seems that most untouchable groups support the BSP, but there are exceptions. This was to be expected as there are 66 registered untouchable castes in UP, with different statuses and different levels of political and economic autonomy [Pai, 1997: 2813]. For example, many from the sweeper castes do not support the BSP.[82]

The BSP has yet to spell out its goals and strategy in detail. The following section therefore relies mainly on secondary sources and on my interview with the UP president of the BSP, Mr Daryam Pal. A detailed assessment of the BSP's influence on local realities has yet to be undertaken, to my knowledge. The attempt made here is mainly based on my own fieldwork material and journalistic or semi-journalistic reports, and a single more detailed assessment of the role of BSP in four Meerut villages by Sudha Pai and Jagpal Singh [Pai and Singh, 1997].

BSP's overall aim is to 'transform the social system of India', or 'the structure of society', from upper caste domination to a society with caste equality (Pal, interview, 1998). It puts the direct fight against caste discrimination first, to the extent that other policies have not been formulated. It has no economic programme and claims not to follow any ideology. Everything other than the direct fight against caste discrimination must wait - according to Kanshi Ram, until after the annihilation of caste, when a seminar in Delhi with broad-based participation will seek to decide on a consensual way forward [Omvedt, 1994b: 164–5]!

Statements such as this serve to highlight the BSP's claim to transcend the left-right political spectrum. The BSP views the left parties as dangerous because they claim to offer a solution for the untouchable workers, while in reality failing to challenge high caste hegemony.[83] The right-wing high caste parties are perceived as less of a threat as their pro-high caste agenda is out in the open for all to see.

However, BSP's non-ideological stance is, not surprisingly, belied by its politics and practice since Kanshi Ram made the above statement. Regarding our main concern, the BSP's line on untouchable agricultural labourers is clear. According to the BSP UP president, untouchables should avoid all work for others. The BSP therefore focuses on enabling labourers to take up independent means of earning a livelihood. When asked specifically about BSP's stand on agricultural labourers' wage struggles, the BSP president did not endorse nor offer support to struggling labourers but reiterated that dalits should withdraw from such work. This process could be helped through the government's provision of education to the untouchables and, apart from education, a BSP government would stress a redistribution of government land and excess land belonging to landlords to dalits, thereby enabling the creation of self-employed as well as salaried dalits (Pal, interview, 1998).[84]

This policy towards rural labourers can be seen as an extreme version of a theme familiar from the classical movements for social upliftment of untouchables, namely that of the untouchables' withdrawal from demeaning labour tasks. However, the political direction expressed in this policy has even deeper roots. The BSP seems to be striving towards a typical populist ideal: to transform the working classes into a petty bourgeoisie.

More generally, BSP's strategy is centred around the politicisation of dalits on issues relating to caste-based oppression and discrimination, and using state powers to fight upper caste dominance, and improve the position of the lower castes. From its inception, the BSP has sought to mobilise dalits via campaigns against the high caste establishment, and for empowerment and self-respect among dalits [*Pai*, 1997: 2313]. As part of this it runs a fierce and, for the high castes, extremely provocative anti-high caste propaganda. However, it is not militant mass mobilisation but rather capturing state power via elections that is the centre of the party's strategy. 'Power is the key by which all doors can be opened. Power is the masterkey' (Pal, interview, 1998). In accordance with this focus, the party is adamant that it is prepared to ally itself with anyone to help it gain access to power. It has proved this in practice through the rather extreme caste- and class crossing alliances it has entered into in the UP parliament since 1995, in order to form a government.

The party's proclaimed achievements, when it was in government, can be considered under four headings: it claims to have

(i)   intensified its emancipatory campaigns among untouchables,
(ii) challenged the existing high caste bias of the state apparatus to make way for a low caste bias,
(iii) dramatically speeded up channelling of funds to untouchable communities via government programmes,
(iv) ensured dalits' access to some government land.

It has indeed been quite efficient in these four areas. The emancipatory campaigns and fierce anti-upper caste rhetoric gained credibility and substance through BSP's attempt to change the staffing of the state by unprecedented transfers of government officials, placing dalit cadres in key posts within the public administration [*India Today*, Sept. 1997: 46–8; *Frontline*, 1 Dec. 1995: 30–31; 18 April 1997: 18].[86] Moreover, the implementation of pro-untouchable administrative measures against caste-based atrocities and caste-based discrimination, such as special fast track investigation of any claims of crimes under the 'Scheduled Castes and Scheduled Tribes (Prevention of Atrocities) Act' of 1989, jailing of anyone accused of such crimes while cases are investigated, and the award of Rs 6,000 to any victim of such crimes to enable them to fight the case in court, showed the seriousness of the pro-untouchable bias of the government (Fieldwork notes). Previously, such cases would rarely have been brought to court, and most often the perpetrators would not go to jail. The local state apparatus was also made more accessible and thereby more under the control of 'ordinary people', that is, especially for low-caste people.[87]

The new dalit imprint on the government machinery and the BSP government's extreme outspokenness against caste oppression and high caste dominance, had a strong politicising effect. The assertiveness of untouchables increased dramatically in many parts of the state after the 1993 election, and even more when Mayawati became Chief Minister. Since the BSP–SP coalition government was formed in 1993, dalits have gone on strike for higher wages, and asserted whatever unimplemented land rights they had to a much greater extent than previously. Such activities often seem to have taken place with no stimulus other than increased government backing of justice for dalits [*Frontline*, 11 March 1994: 8–10], although in some parts of east UP left-wing organisations, especially the CPI(M) and CPI(ML), have utilised the new situation to organise land and wage struggles [*Misra*, 1993: 2059; 1995: 2911; 1996: 586; 1997: 2384; *AIAWU*, 1996: 25; *CPI(ML)*, 1997: 48]. Such organised struggles are, however, the exception. Landowners' response in cases where they have not been ready to accept the increased assertiveness and demands of their dalit workers, has been to resort to their classical violent means of oppression: rape, beatings, burning down hamlets and murders [*Frontline*, 11 March 1994: 4–10; 2 May 1997: 35; 31 Oct. 1997: 119–21].

BSP's politicisation campaign took as its symbolic core the installation of Ambedkar statues all over UP. During their six month stint in office in 1997 15,000 statues were raised. Libraries, schools, etc. have also been named after Ambedkar [*Pai*, 1997: 2313–14]. These symbolic demonstrations of their newly won position were meant as a challenge to the upper castes' political and cultural hegemony, and both the installation of and attempts to desecrate the statues have been flashpoints for violent clashes, such as the Meerut incidence as early as 1994 [*Indian Express*, April 2 1994; *Frontline*, 31 Oct. 1997: 119, *Misra*, 1994b: 1054–5].

However, the BSP slogan 'All government land is our land' [*Indian Express*, April 2 1994] also showed its limits. Redistributive land reforms were not part of its policy [*Misra*, 1994a: 723-4]. It limited itself to cases of enabling dalits to take possession of land they had already been allotted, and initiated only minor new allotments of government land [*Brass*, 1997a: 2415; *Government of UP*, 1997: 8; *Pai and Singh*, 1997: 1358; *Pinto*, 1995: 350].

The BSP government provided tangible improvements for some untouchable groups through channelling of government funds to

programmes primarily benefiting the untouchables. The focus of these
programmes were the 15,000 so-called Ambedkar villages, selected for
their high proportions of untouchable population.[88] While it has been argued
that non-dalit contractors were the main beneficiaries of the programmes
[*Pai*, 1997: 2314], it has also been reported that the untouchables of the
selected villages see these programmes as one of the biggest achievements
of the BSP government [*Pai and Singh*, 1997: 1358; *Brass*, 1997a: 2216].

BSP AND THE TWO FIELDWORK VILLAGES

Till now, there is no detailed study of how BSP politics have influenced
village labour struggles, with the partial exception of a study in Meerut
district by Sudha Pai and Jagpal Singh [*Pai and Singh*, 1997], but their
focus is on general caste relations rather than labour relations. In the two
villages of east and west UP where I conducted fieldwork in 1993 and
revisited in 1995/96 and again in 1998, the following pictures emerge.

In the east UP village of Jaunpur district, the 1993 BSP election gave a
very strong confidence boost to local agricultural labourers, with certain
direct practical consequences. For the first time, Chamar agricultural
labourers could anticipate that the local police and court system would not
act directly against their interests, at least if the civil servants wanted to
avoid the wrath of, and sanctions by, their political superiors.[89] This changed
the local balance of power. Hence, when agricultural labourers went on an
all-out strike for a considerable wage increase at paddy transplanting time
in 1994, they and not the landowners made use of the legal system, pressing
charges of assault and caste discrimination against a number of landowners
(charges which they told me were as false as the ones the Thakurs used to
press against them). The Chamars' charges were accepted by the police for
investigation and, even more unusually, the strike was finally settled by the
intervention of the police officer in charge (from a middle-ranking caste)
who convinced the landowners to increase wages by 33 per cent, apparently
impressing on them that times had changed and that they broke the law by
not paying the legally stipulated minimum wage.[90]

This kind of involvement by government officials in local labour
disputes in the village was entirely new. Previously, government officials
had, occasionally, reacted to atrocities against low caste labourers in the
area.[91] However, the direct intervention in labour conflicts on the side of
untouchable workers such as that in 1994 had never occurred before. Active
government intervention also occurred for the first time in the area of land
reform implementation, that is, supporting possession of previously
allocated land. Nine households of the second biggest Chamar hamlet had
not been in a position to take possession of plots (of between 0.08 and 0.17

acre each) allocated to them previously. However, during the Mayawati government of 1997, they complained to the District Magistrate, the highest ranking civil servant of the district. This led to a show of official strength in support of the Chamars, as the land record keeper (*legpal*) remeasured the plots under police protection, which enabled the Chamars to cultivate the plots that year. However, after the fall of the BSP government, some of the high-caste landowners have re-encroached on their plots, while others have filed court cases against the take-over. (Government land reform activities in the village also showed the futility of a strategy for social change based on redistribution of government land: there was only sufficient government land available for redistribution in the village for one household to receive a new plot!).

However, it was neither labour conflicts nor the land question that Chamars and Thakurs themselves focused on in 1995/96 and 1998, when asked about recent developments in their relations with each other. Instead, it was the politicisation of untouchables that was stressed. Chamars commonly said that they had acquired 'courage' and 'self-esteem', or that they were 'not afraid any longer', that they now dared to stand up for what they perceived as their rights. This change was encapsulated symbolically in the change that many Thakurs pointed to as central: that Chamars no longer showed them respect. Most Chamars would no longer participate in various festivals and rituals which, among other things, emphasised their inferiority, and they would answer the Thakurs back.

The Chamars' new non-deferential stand has also changed a number of aspects of labour relations. One is the priority work relation and how it is executed. Whereas a generation before, Thakurs could summon their Chamar workers for duty by yelling at them from the outskirts of the Thakur hamlet (a distance of 500 metres), this changed during the 1970s and 1980s when it became common for Thakurs to go to their labourers' homesteads in the Chamar hamlet to call them when needed. However, since 1995–96 they have even stopped doing this as they might now suffer the humiliation that Chamar workers would not stand up straight away when they arrived; the workers might ask the Thakur to sit down on the same *charpoy* (string-bed) as them, or even offer tea, thereby emphasising the egalitarian relationship between them. They might also claim not to be available for work, so that the landowners would have to go to several labour households to procure workers. To avoid such humiliations, Thakurs now send their children to call the Chamars instead.

This development is closely related to the effects of the BSP governments. The tightening up of the procedures for punishing caste discrimination offences, and not least the implementation of these procedures during the BSP regime, meant that verbal abuse and physical violence towards Chamars, and high caste men's sexual assaults of Chamar women, practically disappeared in the village. As it is put by Chamars and Thakurs, Thakurs now have to take care not to touch a Chamar labourer, even by chance, as the labourer might then file a caste discrimination charge straight away. One such case in a neighbouring village, where the accused was jailed for a couple of weeks, served as a warning to the Thakurs.

Hence, Thakurs have lost important means of enforcing their dominance over Chamars, and as a result found it harder to enforce obedience within labour relations. Even the duty of labourers to accept work within the priority work relation, a duty already under challenge, was now being contested to the point where Chamars did not consider it to limit their choice of employment at all.[92] These present developments should be seen against the background of the already strong position of Chamars in the village, where Chamar agricultural labourers had taken strike action against the landowners regularly since 1971. What was new was the role of the state apparatus and further politicisation since the BSP, and the results that followed.

Also the Chamars of the village have close connections with the BSP. A local Chamar widow who had come into contact with various organisations in the nearby town in the early 1990s became an outspoken BSP activist, moulding herself in the image of Mayawati. She both handled negotiations with the local landowners during the 1994 strike (previously the realm of the jati association) and kept in close touch with local government bureaucrats.[93] Moreover, it is probably significant that the village was named an Ambedkar village, as a result of which the Chamar hamlet received development programmes on an unprecedented scale during 1997. According to local Chamars and the *Gram Vikas* (a local civil servant involved in identifying beneficiaries for government programmes), the hamlet received more than it was legally entitled to – for example, all eighteen eligible and two non-eligible households received Rs 16,600 each in house construction grants,[94] all school-going Chamar children from 1st to 7th standard received scholarships (Rs 25 to Rs 40 per child per month), and most Chamars above 60 years of age received old-age pensions (Rs 125 per month). Unusually, the government official had come to the Chamar hamlet to register the beneficiaries (whereas normally they would have had to go to him) and, even more exceptionally, the funds actually reached the beneficiaries.

However, very little public construction (for example, road building) took place as part of the Ambedkar programme in this revenue village, hence local labour relations were not affected by the availability of better paid government work. Moreover, in spite of the BSP's focus on education as a means to gain salaried jobs, no such jobs were created for the local unemployed, educated Chamar youth. In the main Chamar hamlet, of the six unemployed youths with BA degrees, only one got a government job between 1995 and 1998, and this was achieved in time-honoured fashion – through bribing the relevant officials - and had little to do with BSP and its policies.

The backlash since the BJP assumed government in late 1997 has been felt in a number of areas. Funding of Ambedkar programmes in the village has become erratic or dried up. Caste discrimination crimes are still dealt with speedily, but the accused is no longer jailed while the case is investigated, and the plaintiff no longer receives Rs 6,000 to fight the case in court. Also, during the 1998 all Indian parliamentary elections, old routines reappeared: while Chamars from the main hamlet, which had led all labour conflicts since 1971, could not be prevented from voting, Chamars from outlying hamlets were 'persuaded' not to vote, and 500 (or an extra 25 per cent) extra false votes for the BJP were added by a group of young Thakurs, according to their own account.

Nevertheless, the improved position of agricultural labourers in the local labour relations has not been rolled back. Chamars stated that their standard of living had improved during the 1990s, both up to my first visit in 1993, and from 1993 to 1998, and workers have not been forced to revert to old practices *vis-à-vis* landowners or government officials.

Interestingly, in 1998 local support for the BSP encompassed most of the non-landed service castes, both untouchables and touchables, even though the material gains from government programmes during Mayawati's office were heavily tilted towards the Chamar group. Basing itself on widespread anti-upper caste sentiment, Chamars and 'their' political party had emerged as the undisputed leader of the non-landed low caste groups in the locality.[95] It must also be noted that all Chamars are backing the BSP, notwithstanding that the Chamar group encompasses both agricultural labourers, migrant workers, a few government servants and a few small landowners.

When assessing the role of BSP locally, one of its most tangible successes was in the one area where its central leaders claim it has no role to play, namely agrarian labour relations. On the other hand, the BSP has made very little progress locally in its proclaimed goals of establishing the Chamars as independent producers or as government officials. The important politicisation achieved might thus point in a somewhat different direction to that intended by the party. This said, it must be reiterated that the economic importance of agricultural work is less for most Chamar households than the importance of other employment. Therefore, the BSP line of untouchables minimising their contact with upper castes may hold some resonance for the Chamars of this village.[96]

In west UP fieldwork village in Muzaffarnagar district, the Jats had maintained an extremely harsh regime of oppression. They had managed to maintain a strong position of regional dominance in parts of west UP through, among other things, the Jat dominated farmers' union, the BKU, which had its headquarters near the Muzaffarnagar fieldwork village. One effect was to exclude the UP government from local influence and ability to intervene in local issues [*Rana*, 1994: 178–9]. In this village, agricultural labourers could not rely on any support from the state. The Jats had simply cut any direct forms of connection between local oppressed groups and the state machinery [*Lerche*, 1995].

This changed as the BKU disintegrated during the mid-1990s. Already by 1993, its political clout outside its heartland in Muzaffarnagar had diminished. In 1996 it also officially gave up its 'village republic' policy for this area, but it was not until the election of 1997 that government officials entered the village without first obtaining permission from the BKU.

Landowning Jats had, at least for the moment, given up their dominance over all aspects of low caste life, and had found ways of managing without much of their labour. In the 1995 local *panchayat* elections, one Jat candidate for the post of *Pradhan* (Mayor) won against another Jat by canvassing the support of one of the Chamar hamlets, the first time that Jats had broken ranks in this way.[97] The new *Pradhan* has maintained the inclusion of untouchables in his political base by implementing projects which benefit Chamars.[98] Moreover, during the last all India election, the low castes were actually allowed to vote, a rare event in this village. This was due both to internal political divisions within Jats which made it difficult for them to impose their will on others, and to unusually strong political pressure for free and fair elections from the district authorities, including the posting of extra election guards and a visit by the District Magistrate to the area on election day.

As in the east UP village, a politicisation process has also taken place among the low caste labourers of this village. In 1993 they talked about having to 'shamefacedly accept defeat' and accept the oppression of the Jat landowners. In 1995/96, typical comments from them were 'we have gained self-respect/self-confidence' and that the Jats now 'hesitated' before engaging in oppressive action – but such remarks were only relayed to us when the Jats were not around. Since then, issues such as the implementation of the 'Harijan Act'[99] bolstered low-caste people's self confidence even more. As one Chamar commented in 1998 with a laugh, ' We are like 11,000 Volts electrical wire – so everybody has become scared to burn their hands'.

The Jats view the ascendance of the untouchables as irreversible. They complain that Chamars would no longer work for them as they prefer employment in the brick kilns. They also resent the decline of permanent labour relations, which reduces their capacity to exercise full dominance over the low castes, and see their own oppressive actions, not least during the BKU years, as just attempts to re-establish the proper social order of before. They argue that nowadays some Chamars are better off than themselves, and as educated; and that these Chamars flaunt their new-found position by dressing improperly in town clothes in the village, drinking and being cheeky. Worst of all is that progress of low caste people has been achieved, not by merit but through the political patronage of first Congress Party and then the BSP.

While these sentiments reflect real change in the lower castes' position, the Jat perception of such change is clearly exaggerated. This may reflect the Jats' more general problem of losing ground overall, and especially to the political movement of the so-called Other Backward Castes (OBCs) which has managed to institutionalise government job quotas for OBCs, at the expense of the Jats among others. The Jats' attempt to improve their own position has, for the first time since the Green Revolution, or maybe even since Independence, been turned into a defensive struggle, but it is not really the low caste labourers who are threatening them.

The Chamars of the fieldwork village cannot challenge the Jat hegemony effectively. In spite of the demise of the Jat 'village republic', low caste people cannot expect direct government intervention in their labour relations with the Jats, as took place in the eastern village. Instead of confrontations over labour relations, their strategy seems to be to delink themselves as much as possible from the Jats, both economically and socially. This, however, mainly affects the heads of Chamar households, as the gendered division of labour leaves it to women to fulfil the obligations of priority labour relations throughout the year, while men are engaged in various non-agricultural occupations mainly outside the village. As part of this development, low caste workers found that their material standard of living had improved during the 1990s, but only marginally. Moreover, they saw this as being solely a result of the (relatively small) increase in migratory work; agricultural real wages had not improved.

Reflecting this complex situation, the issues of dominance and oppression in this district seem to have lost some of their importance among low caste people in the second half of the 1990s. During our fieldwork of 1998, the main issue for rural workers was not their relations to the Jats. For the first time we were not met with narratives of dominance and oppression, but issues such as access to jobs and the importance of better education were what they wanted to discuss with us. Similarly, while we were told in 1996 how Mayawati's government meant that they could 'keep their heads high' for the first time, the low castes did not discuss the BSP government at all in 1998. They perceived the emergence of the BSP as a powerful factor in

UP politics, a major ingredient in the decline of the political strength of the Jats, and in the cessation of the Jats' violent oppression of them. But to most low caste groups, this was a closed chapter now. What mattered were more mundane issues of improving their lot within the existing social order, though education, access to government officials and so on. Now the BSP was considered one of many ways to access the local state. Other political parties as well as personal contacts, sometimes even though Jats, were seen as equally important. In fact, several of the castes which supported BSP earlier had voted BJP during the last election as they saw it as the best provider of law and order. Earlier, low caste people had perceived the BJP solely as the landowners' party.

Hence, while the combined effect of the emergence of the BSP and the decline of the political influence of the Jats had led to a near collapse of the previous extremely oppressive regime of the Jat landowners and politicisation of low caste workers, this seems to have resulted in a new *modus operandi* between the two. Part of this was the split within the ranks of the Jats, with certain groups now accepting to form political alliances with the lower castes. Moreover, the increased economic delinking between the two seems to make it possible for low caste workers to live with exploitative labour relations in the village rather than embarking on risky direct confrontation with the Jats. So, in this west UP village, the improvement in the position of the lower castes was not as much a result of their own struggles as of the overall economic and political development of which they were part.

BSP AND CLASS STRUGGLE

I turn now to a more general discussion of why BSP has achieved its present levels of success in UP, and what the consequences of this are for the position of low caste labourers in the class struggle. This will be done by comparing the role of BSP and other parties.

BSP is an openly populist party. Drawing on classical ideals and methods from the Indian untouchable movement, it propagates a petty bourgeois utopia where the ideal is for low caste people to become independent petty commodity producers or well educated civil servants. Thereby it also stays well within the confines of existing capitalist property relations, its main aim being to carve out a better position for low castes within the existing structures of society.

BSP has been highly successful at achieving and maintaining the backing of the lowest castes, which owes much to its radical focus on caste oppression. It has increased political awareness among the untouchables, and made them part of the political process as never before. The untouchables now support their own party and no longer constitute a 'vote bank' for other parties. Most of them are now fairly openly mobilised in what they perceive as their own interests.

It is questionable, however, whether the BSP has succeeded in establishing a connection between its populist utopia and the social realities of low caste workers. On the surface, that part of its self-employment strategy recommending untouchable labourers' total withdrawal from agricultural wage labour relation seems to gain some credibility from the fact that agricultural work is now losing some of its importance for (male) untouchable groups all over UP. However, judging from the two fieldwork villages, this is qualified by the tying of female household members to landowners instead. Moreover, the alternative to agricultural wage labour is not to become self-employed, but rather to take up wage labour elsewhere, for example, as migrant workers in brick kilns or in large cities, as is the case for workers in the fieldwork areas. The credibility of the self-employment perspective was also not much enhanced through the BSP government's very limited land distribution.

It is therefore hardly surprising that not all BSP grass-roots organisations followed this political line, including the BSP UP leader's advice not to engage in agrarian labour conflicts. In the one fieldwork village where the BSP is active it took a leading role in agrarian wage struggles; labour conflicts were even reported to the BSP district unit which publicised them and attempted to get public and state support for the labourers' demands. Hence, while the party at the state level follows a populist strategy, its local units may in some cases take a rather different strong trade union stand.

The BSP emerged at a time of ferment among the untouchable groups in North India. Green Revolution, changes in labour relations, increase in non-agricultural occupations and thus a relative decrease in economic dependency on the landowners, the politicisation of groups of untouchables, and the increased class struggle from above, created a new situation. To its credit the BSP succeeded in expressing and enhancing this movement among low caste people, which it was able to do mainly because of its clear-cut anti-high caste agenda. However, an important reason why the BSP has been so successful in becoming the overwhelmingly dominant party for untouchables in UP is that the other parties vying for their support have failed them. That the Congress Party did not accommodate politicised untouchables was important, as were the failings of the communist parties, an issue I now turn to.

There are several isolated examples of successful communist-led rural labour struggles in UP,[100] but the communists never achieved a strong position in agricultural labour struggles in UP which remain predominantly unorganised. They were not able to mobilise the rural workers around a class-based agenda following the political ferment of the 1970s and 1980s. Furthermore, with the emergence of the BSP they have lost what local mass support they did have, as well as votes and allegedly also cadres.[101] A thorough investigation of the reasons for this is outside the scope of this study. However, a partial answer can be found by looking into the communist organisations' strategy and practice in relation to agricultural labourers in UP. Linked with the two main communist parties in India are two communist agricultural workers unions: BKMU (Bhartiya Khet Mazdoor Union) formed by the CPI in 1968, and AIAWU (All India Agricultural Workers Union) formed by the CPI(M) in 1981 and which is the stronger of the two now in UP.[102] The analysis here concentrates on AIAWU.

CPI(M)'s assessment of the class character of the Indian state as well as its rural mobilisation strategy has been analysed in some detail by Sudhanshu Ranade [1989]. Here, it suffices to note that CPI(M), according to its party programme, sees the Indian state as representing the 'big bourgeois leadership which has allied itself with landlordism' [CPI(M), 1993: 3]. In order to topple this alliance, it is necessary to build a broad People's Democratic Front. Its core in the countryside consists of agricultural workers and poor peasants, but the front also includes the middle and even rich peasantry. While the peasantry has its contradictions, all peasant classes, to a varying degree, come up 'against the oppressive policies pursued by the bourgeois landlord government' [CPI(M), 1993: 4]. The unity 'of the entire peasantry' is viewed as absolutely necessary for 'a victorious agrarian revolution' [AIAWU, 1982a: 3].

This broad alliance, according to the CPI(M), should not lead to a neglect of the specific demands of agricultural labourers and poor peasants which might, at least partially, be directed against the middle and rich peasantry, especially in the case of wage demands. Since 1966 when the Central Committee accepted that it had failed to raise such demands for fear of disrupting peasant unity, the CPI(M) has returned to this problematic time and time again [CPI(M), 1993: 5]. For example, at AIAWU's second conference in 1986, the General Secretary suggested that resolving conflicts of interest within the peasantry over issues such as wages should be sought through peasants and agricultural workers mutually supporting each others' demands, with the AIAWU and the communist peasant organisations as arbitrators [AIAWU, 1986: 61]. Confrontational labour action against peasant employers is not seen as the best way forward for the agricultural labourers, presumably because it would undermine building the broad Democratic Front. Such an approach fits well with Ranade's suggestion that various CPI(M) organisations 'soft-peddle' the wage issue [Ranade, 1989: 555].

During its first years, AIAWU did not engage in many grassroots struggles, as reflected in the 'immediate demands' listed in its constitutional document which are all demands for new legislation or implementation of existing legislation. A demand for central government minimum wage legislation tops the list, followed by demands for distribution of surplus and waste land to agricultural workers and poor peasants. Support to local struggles for higher wages, or local take-overs of land illegally held by landlords were not included in the list [*AIAWU*, 1982a: 5].

Throughout the 1980s, the weakness of AIAWU in most states of India was acknowledged. In UP, in 1989, AIAWU only existed in 30 of 62 districts, and its organisation was characterised as weak [*AIAWU*, 1989: 4-5]. It was precisely at this time that DS-4 and BSP gained strength in UP, watched by the UP AIAWU with clear hostility. As mentioned, DS-4 was seen as divisive and disruptive. In 1988, its threat was considered so strong that the AIAWU General Secretary considered that its 'mushrooming growth' could seriously hamper the worker–peasant alliance [*AIAWU*, 1988: 20]. However, from 1989 onwards the proceedings of the AIAWU Conferences and CPI(M) statements increasingly acknowledged that DS-4 and the BSP had read the situation of untouchable workers better than CPI(M), and had provided them with popular leadership.[103] In 1993, the progressive potential of the untouchables' struggle was strongly endorsed, as part of the CPI(M) Central Committee's analysis of 'the meaning of caste appeal':

> One aspect of this phenomenon is the growing consciousness and urge of the dalit and backward classes to shake off social oppression and to assert their rights in a caste-ridden society. The slogan of social justice exercises a strong appeal and has been successful in mobilising large sections of dalits and downtrodden sections in the rural areas. Whether it is the question of upper caste oppression or the demand for reservation of jobs, these sections are coming forward to challenge the old order. This awakening has a democratic content reflecting the aspirations of the most oppressed sections of society [*CPI(M)*, 1995: 32].

However, the flip side of caste appeal was still the negative aspect of 'caste polarisation affec[ting] the unity of the working people', which communists have to fight against [*CPI(M)*, 1995: 33]. The urgency of battling the caste based organisations, principally the BSP, has since been emphasised further. At the AIAWU 1996 Conference, the resolution 'Against Casteism' argues that 'To save and extend the organisations of the rural and urban working class, we have to fight this menace tooth and nail. If people like Kanshi Ram are allowed to divide the working class on caste lines and weaken its unity the fight against exploitation will become a dream' [*AIAWU*, 1996: 62]. So, while the mobilisation of the untouchables against social oppression is progressive, its locking into a caste based framework by the BSP is seen as serving reactionary forces, partly because it gives priority to caste over class, and partly because it jeopardises the creation of a broad democratic front of the peasantry.

In the mid-1990s, CPI(M) and AIAWU faced up to the difficult question of why BSP had managed to mobilise untouchable workers when they had failed. Their reaction was to carry out a self-critique on a number of important issues, and to make a number of changes in their policy towards low caste agricultural labourers. Firstly, that CPI(M) and AIAWU should now engage in, and attempt to take the lead in the fight for social justice, against social oppression and caste atrocities, and provide a class perspective to this struggle [*CPI(M)*, 1995: 33]. To give higher priority to such issues was now seen as necessary to any breakthrough [*AIAWU*, 1996: 22]. The fight for social justice was already on the agenda but, at least since 1989, the AIAWU's General Secretary had criticised the organisation for not taking this issue seriously enough [*AIAWU*, 1989: 31; *AIAWU*, 1996: 22].

The second self-critique related to organisational issues. In short, 'Our leading activists are reluctant to take up the difficult task of building movements and struggle and confronting our opponents in the rural areas, the landlords, or the police and other authorities' [*AIAWU*, 1996: 34]. The activists were bluntly told to visit the villages regularly, and to organise spontaneous actions already occurring there [*ibid.*, 34–5]. Again, this was a self-criticism already raised in 1993 [*CPI(M)*, 1995: 104]. A last criticism was that there had been little response by AIAWU units to the organisation's call 'take up wage issues in all seriousness' in 1993 [*AIAWU*, 1996: 23].

This amounts to a damning catalogue of criticism: social justice issues ignored, organisational weakness and failure to engage properly with village level issues; wage struggles not taken seriously enough. Moreover, it seemed that it was difficult to rectify these problems. This self-critique was also strongly expressed by district level organisers from both leading communist parties in the two fieldwork districts.[104]

In my judgement, the critique does pinpoint some important reasons why CPI(M) and its front organisation had left the political initiative to the BSP. The question, however, is whether the party and union can change their policy to the extent needed. The CPI(M) conclusion seems to be that while their overall strategy of uniting all sections of the peasantry in a broad front was correct, its transformation into a strategy for agricultural workers' struggle was flawed. Following on from its overall strategy, it was logical for the CPI(M) to focus on issues which pointed directly to the landlords or the government as the enemy. This was also why 'land struggles' focusing on seizures of land held illegally by big landlords came to be seen as central to the movement [*CPI(M)*, 1993: 19–20].[105] According to this logic, the problem of prioritising social injustice and caste atrocities is that such acts are as often committed by middle and rich peasants as by landlords, and could therefore hamper building the strategic alliance of all sections of the peasantry. A similar problem exists regarding wage struggles as low wage employers may also be middle or rich peasants.

Opposed to this logic, the decision to engage with the spontaneous actions of agricultural labourers, to take wage issues seriously, and to focus on social justice points towards a higher degree of acceptance of the tension between objective class relations and the subjective consciousness of the agricultural labourers. On a day-to-day level, the changes also involve grappling with the party cadres' subjective disinclination to engage directly with low caste rural labourers. However, this assumes that it is not the Party's analysis that is wrong, only its implementation. But what if there also are problems with CPI(M)'s overall analysis?

The UP communists' close alliance with the well-off peasantry is in fact a phenomenon of long standing. For example, Paul Brass notes that the main constituency of the UP communists in the 1960s was middle and rich peasants [*Brass*, 1980a: 414; 1980b: 23]. What is interesting is that the CPI(M)'s basic analysis of the class struggle has not changed since the 1960s, in spite of major changes within the agrarian sector where a productive capitalist agriculture seems to be replacing the old landlord dominated rural economy, particularly in the west but also in parts of east and central UP, while pre-capitalist labour relations are slowly on the wane.'

The party is not oblivious to these changes. It acknowledges capitalist development in west UP, while it sees the rest of the UP countryside as dominated by semi-feudal relations. Peasants in west UP will therefore have to be mobilised around different demands than the peasantry elsewhere in the state [*CPI(M)*, 1995: 93–5]. However, seen in the light of the present article, this understanding underestimates the degree of capitalist development that has begun to take place outside the west UP region. Moreover, and maybe because of this, changes in the rural areas have not led the party to alter its general rural class analysis or its policy of building an all-encompassing strategic alliance of the peasantry.

A critique of the CPI(M) analysis has, in fact, been given by a smaller, radical communist party in India, the CPI(ML) which argues that a class of capitalist farmers, consisting of kulaks and landlords engaged in capitalist farming, has emerged from the old peasantry and old landlord class respectively. This class has not only come to the fore in the Green Revolution regions of Punjab, Haryana and west UP, but also in parts of the

more generally semi-feudal areas of, for example, central and east UP
Importantly, the class interests of capitalist farmers exclude them from any
broad democratic front in the countryside; unity is only possible between
agricultural workers and the poor and middle peasantry. This means, among
other things, that rural class struggle against employers of agricultural
labour is not constrained by viewing them as progressive classes [*CPI(ML)*,
1997: 26–8, 37–9] .

While CPI(ML)'s analysis leaves a number of questions unanswered,
and without assessing the merits of the different Communist parties in
general, it appears to me that the developments highlighted by the
CPI(ML)'s analysis, as well as by the present article, are too important to be
discarded. If this is correct, it goes a long way towards explaining the
problems of CPI(M) antipathy to the caste-based mobilisation of the
untouchable labourers: mobilisation along caste lines has been able to point
the finger firmly and directly at specific exploiters and oppressors,
something CPI(M), given its overall class alliance policy, has found hard to
foreground in its analysis and practical policies.

CONCLUDING REMARKS

It is clear that rural labour relations in UP have changed since the Green
Revolution. The traditional economic ties between agricultural labourers
and landowners have lost importance as non-agricultural wage labour has
become the core income source of many, if not most, rural labourers.

The transformation of what agricultural labour and tenancy relations
remain has in many cases included a 'modernisation' of the existing
elements of unfreedom through credit relations or other interlinkages, as
opposed to a general development of free labour relations. Nevertheless, the
pervasiveness of the landowners' dominance has been diluted, both as the
rural labourers have become less economically dependent on them and as
the unfree elements of the labour relations have loosened.

This, however, has not been a smooth process. It has been closely
connected with the growing assertiveness of the rural labour groups from
the 1920s on, and has also involved an intensification of the class struggle
from above as landowners have resorted to village level collective
oppression, the use of the local government machinery against rebellious
labourers and open violence to maintain their position. The Jat's oppressive
'village republic' in parts of Muzaffarnagar district in the early 1990s is a
case in point.

The late 1980s and the 1990s saw rural workers respond politically to
the transformation that had taken place in rural economic and social
relations. The breakdown of traditional ties and the failure of these

transformed labour relations to maintain the level of all-encompassing dominance that had existed earlier made it possible for rural untouchable workers to mobilise in support of their own radical political party. This politicisation happened all over UP, and, judging from the regional voting patterns of the 1990s, to a similar extent throughout the different regions [*Brass*, 1997a: 2408]. This may be a reflection of the fact that the general social processes taking place in the rural areas, and the development of the labour relations in particular, now follow a largely similar pattern throughout the UP regions. The important regional differences that do exist in class composition, the extent to which a capitalist rationale of accumulation is dominant and the relative strength of the various classes do seem to be of relevance to the direction and intensity of the local struggles. However, such differences have no influence on the political aspirations of rural labourers in general to oppose their old masters at the level of party politics. That the new party of the rural untouchables is caste based rather than class based, does not alter the fact that this shift in the untouchable labourers' classical political loyalties strikes a landmark in the development of their political position, independent of their masters.

One reason why the BSP and not a communist party emerged as the harbinger of change has been the absence of adequate communist practical policies and a problematic communist strategy based on very broad-based rural alliances. This meant that the core issues for rural labour households (i.e.: social justice, wage struggles and redistributive land reform) were not given priority by the communists as they thus would have risked alienating the middle and rich peasantry from the alliance. By contrast, the BSP's radical anti high caste agenda and their dalit-isation of the public administration, including the police, met the immediate demands of the untouchable labourers a good deal better, especially (but not only) in the cases where local BSP units did support wage struggles, despite their leaderships' stated policy of non-interference.

To date, there is little evidence regarding the extent to which the caste based mobilisation has led to further development in free labour relations. The evidence from the two fieldwork villages does point to an erosion of the unfree elements of the priority relations in Jaunpur but not in Muzaffarnagar. However, this issue was seen as subservient to that of the general rolling back of the oppressive regime of the landowners. The improved position of untouchables has put an end to the classical violent means by which the landowners have enforced their authority in all types of labour relations and in social relations in general. This is an important point, given the often harsh regime enforced even on free labourers, and given that it is more difficult to enforce unfree labour relations without such means. The fact that landowners have managed to oppose labourers forcefully and taken out violent reprisals against them in precisely those areas of the state where there is no collusion between the local government structure and the untouchable labourers only serves to demonstrate the importance of this collusion.

It is also important to consider what has here somewhat imprecisely been termed a progressive feminisation of the unfree labour relations. In the fieldwork villages the main male breadwinners had de-linked themselves from all but the most profitable peak season processes in agriculture, and it might be that they were not particularly concerned about the unfree character of many of the slack season labour relations, as these relations did not involve them personally. If this is the case, then any further struggle against unfree labour relations awaits initiatives by or on the part of the female labourers.

Let us now return to a final assessment of the BSP. Its populist utopian perspective of the creation of a large untouchable petty bourgeoisie, and its refusal to tackle core class issues such as land reforms do hamper the development of a class-based alternative. But then so does the communists' strategic goal of creating a broad democratic front.

For how long can the mobilisation of the low castes take place on a populist agenda? The present mobilisation does not seem to have been fully separated from class based issues. The loosening of the landed caste groups' hold over government has, at least in some places, led to successful collective actions by agricultural labourers, and is also reported to have led to local pressure building up on the land issue. But this is an unstable balance. Involvement in local interest conflicts (most importantly relating to wages and land) could easily take BSP activists back to a basis the petty bourgeois party prefers to neglect: to a class-based policy. On the other hand, to avoid such a development, the party would have to modify its anti-upper caste policies in order to secure itself against unintended class-based consequences.

To date, the BSP has served a number of important purposes: it has highlighted weaknesses in the Indian left bringing the issue of social discrimination firmly onto the political agenda. It has played a vital role in the politicisation of untouchable groups, even though the exact strategic direction of this politicisation is still being fought over; and it has shown that state power can alter local power equations to the benefit of the oppressed. It may also be on its way to showing the limitations of a caste-based approach to class-based problems. However, the question of whether the left has yet developed a viable class based political alternative for the low caste rural labourers still remains in the air.

NOTES

1. This point of view is presented with varying degrees of sophistication, and so are the political implications. For Ilaiah, inherent in this development is the potential for a democratic revolution which can be likened to the great French revolution of 1789 [*Ilaiah*, 1994]. Kothari is more hesitant in specifying the end-goal of the low caste movement, but he also stresses that it holds the potential to emerge as the future main force for 'genuine emancipation' [*Kothari*, 1994: 1594].

2. Brass also argues that the direction of most emancipatory processes has been populist, based on caste mobilisation as opposed to class mobilisation, which might have important negative long-term consequences. This is an important criticism that will be discussed later [*Brass*, 1994a].

3. A somewhat similar position is taken by Ronald Herring. Concerned with the influence of the state on local agrarian relations, Herring has argued that, in South Asia in general, capitalist development of agriculture might favour 'labour-repressive and extremely exploitative social organisations of production' [*Herring*, 1984: 237].

4. Even the east–west–central regionalisation is a generalisation for the five regions of UP, the two remaining regions being Bundelkhand (south-west), and Hills (north-west). Certain subregions, such as the Upper Doab (far west of the western region) are also often specified.

5. Historically, the fertile plains of eastern UP provided the ground for a well organised surplus producing agriculture, and a hierarchical social order with a strong 'landlord' class at the apex. West UP was more of an agrarian frontier, with strong farming communities presiding over a less elaborately hierarchical rural order. These differences were reinforced by the colonial tax regime, which was predominantly *zamindari* in the east whereas *bhaiachara* and *zamindari* coexisted in the west. See Eric Stokes [1978] for the 'classic' discussion of *zamindari* and *bhaiachari* tax regimes in UP and the historical reasons for the differentiated development of east and west UP, and Zoya Hasan and Jagpal Singh for a discussion of the economic and social development of west UP in general, and the west UP Aligarh and Meerut districts in particular, from the 1830s to the 1980s [*Hasan*, 1989; *Singh*, 1992: 8–23].

6. During a 12-month stay in India in 1992–93, two assistants and I conducted six months' fieldwork in two villages, backed up by extensive touring of the districts where the villages were located. The research assistants were two sociologists: Mr Prakash Deo Singh and Ms Rajashree Ghosh. Mr Indu Shekhar (also a sociologist) joined the research team during the last two months. The follow-up visits in 1995/96 and in 1998 were both of a month's duration. During these visits, Prakash Deo Singh joined in again as a research fellow.

7. In both cases, the villages were chosen because they represented important conditions for which the district was known and which we wished to highlight. Thus, both villages were economically well developed and had a colonial revenue history common for the area. Moreover, the villages were dominated by landowners belonging to the district's strongest landowning group, and the main agricultural labour caste of UP, the Chamars, were well represented.

8. In 1998, the number of tractors had increased to 48.

9. The most common crop cycle stretched over two years and consisted of two consecutive crops of sugarcane followed by one paddy or wheat crop.

10. Forty-six per cent of the village's households are Jat. According to local informants, at Independence two Bania caste households held the tax rights for around one-third of the land, whereas the rest was held by Jat farmers. The post-Independence land reforms gave the Jats ownership rights to practically all land in the village. My village survey in 1993 showed they possessed 95 per cent of the land, and that this share had been constant since the 1950s.

11. In 1998, the number of households with one or several members of the household in government service or business had increased to around three-quarters. The issue of non-agricultural occupations is important for assessing the overall accumulation strategies of the landowners but is not pursued further here.

12. As most west UP Chamars, the Chamars of the fieldwork village see themselves as belonging to the Jatav Chamar sub-caste. However, when asked their caste (*jati, biradari*), most of them classify themselves as Harijan and, if pressed further, as Chamars. As the term Harijan in other contexts covers all untouchable groups, I have chosen to use the classical caste name Chamar here - even though the term 'Chamar' is also a commonly used derogative. Of the 84 households engaged in agricultural labour throughout the year, 25 are Chamar, 31 are Jhimar, 17 are Jogi and 11 are from other low castes. The villagers consider the Chamars to be the 'classical' agricultural labourers. 23 per cent of the village households are Chamar.

13. The revenue village studied consisted of 740 households. However, the main hamlets contained 212 households: 40 Thakur, 25 Brahmin, 36 Yadav, 86 Chamar and 56 of other castes.

14. In 1998, all Thakur households had members employed outside agriculture.

15. Before Independence, Thakurs and Brahmins were the only landholders. Their old tenants, especially the numerous Yadav group, gained in influence at Independence. Zamindari abolition, followed by the upper castes' sale of land situated at some distance from the high caste hamlet, and therefore difficult to control, amounts for Yadav acquisitions.

16. In 1998, ten upper caste households employed labourers for ploughing too, but even these households rented tractors to do part of the ploughing. Tenants, on the other hand, as a rule ploughed with bullocks, and so did many Yadav landowners.

17. In the Muzaffarnagar village in 1993, only one Jat household whose members were wholly employed outside agriculture, leased out its land. This was a cash rental, at around 800-900 Rs/*bigha*, to other Jats. In this village, the local measure *bigha* is equivalent to one-fifth of an acre. In the Jaunpur village, before the introduction of mechanical irrigation and land consolidation (1964), most farmers leased out their distant plots to middle and low caste peasants. It was also common to give a small plot on lease to permanent labourers, as part of their payment. Both these kinds of annual sharecropping have generally ceased. In 1993, 15 per cent of Brahmin and Thakur landowners leased out land throughout the year: seven landowners who were working and staying elsewhere, and three of the local landowners. The sharecroppers were from the low and middle castes. The sharecropping was commonly done on an '*adiya*' (50–50) basis with fertiliser and seed costs shared and sharecroppers providing all other inputs, including labour. Since the late 1980s, leasing out on contract had also taken place. In 1993, three landowners working wholly outside the village had leased all their land out on contract basis. The land was leased for a full year, with a certain amount of the main crops (usually wheat and paddy; the amount depended on the extent to which the landowner paid for seeds and fertiliser) fixed as payment. The balance of these crops, plus the full amount of any other crops grown by tenants in between the two main crops, belong to the tenant.

18. Landowners decided what to grow (paddy), and when the various agricultural tasks, for example, application of fertiliser, irrigation and harvesting, should be undertaken. They also provided all inputs except labour, for example, tractorised ploughing, seeds, fertiliser, and irrigation. The labourers received one-fifth of the harvest as their payment.

19. Similar systems for the minor crops of Urad Dal and Maize also exist but are less widespread.

20. This form of sharecropping was seen as more productive than the *adhiya* system where all inputs as well as the harvest were shared on a 50–50 basis, as it was more likely that proper inputs were provided.

21. Another type of seasonal leasing out in the Jaunpur village was for the cultivation of maize during the *kharif* season, but that had become quite rare by the 1990s.

22. The Chamars of Jaunpur village have a history of labour migration spanning back at least three generations.

23. More men and even some women from the Jaunpur village have left for the Bombay labour market during the 1990s, even though the Chamars find that it is not as easy as it used to be to pick up work there. There do not seem to be any difficulties for the Muzaffarnagar Chamars to find more work in the brick kilns.

24. In the western fieldwork village, migrant labourers return for the wet season when the brick

kilns are shut down, and when work such as paddy growing is available in the village. From 1993, migrant workers have even stopped returning to the village for wheat harvesting, another relatively well paid job. In the eastern fieldwork village the Chamars say that from 1993, the amount of agricultural work they do has halved. However, practically all migrant labourers (still) return for peak season work in this case.

25. Following Marx, the freedom of wage labour is a core element of capitalist relations of production. 'Free' wage labour is free in a double sense: labourers are 'freed' from the ownership of the means of production and hence 'free' (compelled) to sell their labour power. Unfree labourers (a product of pre-capitalist labour relations), on the other hand are tied to specific masters and specific working conditions. While unfree labour relations are maintained through extra-economic compulsion, there is no extra-economic compulsion directly involved in free labour relations. See Tom Brass [1994b: 255–60] as well as Mohan Rao [this volume] for a discussion of the classical Marxist view on unfree labour .

It has been suggested by several writers that a means to ensuring a cheap and docile labour force in India is to curtail the bargaining power of the labourer through establishing unfree labour relations [T. Brass, 1990; Byres, 1981: 436]. While it is debatable whether, as Brass seems to suggest, unfree labour relations can co-exist with free labour relations within developed capitalism in the long term [Brass, 1994b: 271–4], it is unsurprising that such labour relations might play an important role in class struggle within the less than fully developed capitalism in rural India, and, under these conditions, be a means of capitalist accumulation strategies.

The free/unfree distinction has little to do with the duration of the labour contract, i.e. yearly versus daily contracts. Nevertheless, in the Indian context, it is this last distinction, often phrased as 'attached' or 'permanent' versus 'casual' labour, which is most commonly made, both in government publications and, as we shall see later, in other studies [Thorner, 1962b: 175; T. Brass, 1990: 37–8]. In contrast, in a landmark study from 1957, Daniel Thorner used the free-unfree distinction to group labour relations in Indian agriculture into four sub-groups of free labour relations and three sub-groups of unfree labour relations [Thorner, 1962a]. The basic characteristic of unfree agrarian labour relations is that the labourer cannot refuse to work for a particular employer, because of 'traditional attachment to a family or an estate, indebtedness for a sum larger than can ordinarily be repaid, allotment by the employer of a plot of land, and tenancy on the employer's holding' [Thorner, 1962a: 38]. Thorner emphasised that the length of the labour relation was not significant in itself. Yearly, seasonal, daily or task-specific contracts could all form the basis of free labour relations, if labourers were free to terminate the employment. Thus, unfree labour relations could take the form of full-time work on annual (or longer) contracts, of being at the beck-and-call of the landowner, or of having to perform *begar* or unpaid labour service for the landowner on specified occasions, often as part of a tenancy arrangement. Tom Brass [1990] has taken this argument further by pointing to the increase in debt bonding among short-term and casual labourers in Punjab and Haryana. He sees this situation as springing from changes in the agricultural labour process since the Green Revolution, and more generally as part of a capitalist accumulation strategy here.

For Thorner, debt is only one of several possible strands of the dependency on which unfree labour relations can be based. While the form and duration of the specific unfree relation can vary, the dependency relations on which unfree labour relations are based are always of a long-term, for example, life-time or more, character [Thorner, 1962a: 22].

Again, Brass has added to this by arguing that, as part of their inclusion in a capitalist accumulation strategy, unfree labour relations in India today have themselves become monetised, that is, transformed into debt bondage relations [Brass, 1995: 99–100].

26. The specific arrangement and terminology for the permanent labour relations varied, with several different types existing in both villages. Generally, permanent labourers worked for the same employer for a number of years even though they were, formally, engaged annually at onset of the *kharif* (monsoon) cropping season. See Lerche [1995] for a detailed description.

27. The workers had been (re)settled on government land next to a railway line for as long as they remember. Whether the original settlement process described above is a myth or

factually correct is not important in the present context. What matters is that the story legitimised the notion that labourers 'belonged' to specific landowning households.

28. The exact proportion is difficult to estimate as the survey of local agricultural labourers counts households, whereas the migrant labourers are hired and counted as individuals. The number of members of households working as agricultural labourers varies. If, for example, the household takes paddy growing on lease or wheat harvesting on contract, all adults who are not in government jobs and most children would participate, whereas in other cases, only one or two household members may engage in agricultural labour. The proportion of permanent labourers to all agricultural labourers is here based on a conservative estimate of two agricultural labourers per agricultural labour household.

29. The one local permanent labourer is an unmarried Jat in his 40s who is mentally handicapped.

30. Some farmers claimed they paid up to Rs 800 per month for experienced workers but this was denied strongly by the low caste people of the village. It seems that labourers on yearly contracts were paid Rs 600 per month. It was not possible to interview the migrant workers as I was not there during the right season.

31. The Bihari workers are generally picked up by jobbers at Delhi railway station. The more experienced workers make their own way to the villages of west UP and, we were told, may go on to Punjab for wheat harvest and paddy transplanting work there, before returning home. The Nepalese workers were brought to the village by a local Jat who used to go to Nepal and, through a labour contractor there, bring 10–12 workers to the village. He promised them Rs 800 per month but paid them only Rs 400, claiming that the Rs 800 was their wage in Nepali Rupees, not in Indian Rupees. However, when he went this winter (1997) with two friends, they were attacked by local Nepalese, beaten up, their money taken, and they were tied up and abducted. One escaped but the other two were killed.

32. These percentages are based on the number of households with members (male or female) working as agricultural labourers throughout the year, whenever work is available.

33. The Chamar workers who constituted around 30 per cent of households working for landowners throughout the year had been able to stop taking loans from the Jats in the 1970s. Employees from other castes routinely took loans, but often from the big Jat moneylenders rather than employer who did not always have the cash needed.

34. The exception is the tying of the sugarcane paid at 10 kg of wheat per *bigha*. This arduous task is performed during the busy summer months.

35. Around 40 per cent of all households from the Chamar, Jhimar and Jogi castes rear cattle or possess their own milch cows.

36. A labourer from the Muzaffarnagar village would earn Rs 50–70 or even more per day working in a brick kiln in Punjab in 1998, while wages in agriculture are around Rs 25–30 per full working day.

   According to the migrant brick kiln workers of the village, the brick kilns of Punjab and Haryana pay Rs 70–100 per 1000 bricks. Brick kiln workers, working in pairs, would most often do 1500 to 2000 bricks per day - a long working day as it takes around 5 hours for two people to do 1000 bricks, excluding the clay preparation which is done the previous evening. They claim that it is common to return after nine months work with savings of Rs 4–5,000 per pair, and that some manage up to Rs 20,000. The workers claim that labour relations in the kilns are free. No debt bondage exists and they can move on to other kilns if they want. This is a far cry from the bondage in the Muzaffarnagar kilns in the late 1970s described by Suneet Chopra [1985].

   Local brick kilns in Muzaffarnagar pay around Rs 55–60 per 1,000 bricks and employ mainly workers from Bihar.

   In agriculture, on the other hand, when and if work is available, the wage is around five kg of wheat for a full working day, or three kg of wheat for half a day. However, different tasks are paid at different rates, with harvesting and threshing commanding the top pay. Comparisons between wages are further complicated by the fact that the best paid work is performed on piece-rate payments. For example, wheat harvesting is paid by 20–25 kg of wheat per *bigha*, notwithstanding the number of persons participating or the time it takes, and wheat threshing commands one kg of wheat per 40 kg threshed.

37. While they have been successful in keeping wages below the levels of other parts of the region, a full day's wage increased from 1 kg of wheat in the late 1970s to 2 1/2 kg in the late 1980s; and to 3, 4 and 5 kg by 1993, a level at which it has remained. The monetary value of the wage varies with the wheat price which in the early 1990s was Rs 5 per kg. In 1998 it was Rs 6 per kg.

38. In 1998, the Chamars reported that daily wages in Bombay were around Rs. 70 per day, which compared favourably to the Rs 25–30 per full working day paid in the village – when work was available.
    The Rs 25–30 refers to a full day's agricultural work in most tasks. For hard work such as digging soil or levelling fields the wage was Rs 40.

39. These strike actions and the politicisation of the Chamar labourers of the village are discussed in Lerche [1995].

40. For example, for half a day's transplanting work they were paid 1¼ kg of wheat in the early 1980s. Throughout the 1980s, this increased gradually and reached 3 kg in 1993 – on a par with the west UP village. However, while in the west, wages have not increased since then, the transplanting wage was raised to 4 kg through strike action in the east in 1994. Similarly, the payment for half a day's ploughing went up from Rs 10 in 1993 to Rs 15 or 3 kg of wheat in 1994. In 1998, it was still 3 kg or, if paid in cash, between 15 and 20 Rs as the wheat price fluctuates. (In 1994, the price of 1 kg of wheat in the village was Rs 5. Since then, it went above Rs 7 to come down to Rs 6 in 1998).
    As with most half day wages, the ploughing wage also included a light breakfast (most full day wages include breakfast and lunch). Both permanent ploughmen (*halwars*) and ploughmen hired for the day received this pay; permanent ploughmen are only paid when they are actually working. (The one *tatwar* (traditional farm servant) of the village is paid Rs 300 per month or around Rs 10 per day, plus breakfast and lunch.)

41. The 1980 cut off line is chosen to reconcile two conflicting aims. On the one hand, studies of the early phases of the Green Revolution, particularly in parts of central and east UP should be excluded. On the other hand, a fair number of case studies should be included; a more recent cut-off line was therefore found to be too strict.

42. The surveys also showed that in the five villages, between 14 per cent and 26 per cent of landless households' income came from dairy work, that is, from keeping milch cows and selling milk.

43. Dipankar Gupta does not provide any information on when, and for how long, fieldwork was carried out. However, it seems that the book is based on a number of brief visits, each of 2–3 days' or a week's duration.

44. Gupta guess-stimates that in the two other villages which were less remote, 'the tendency for the landless to seek work outside the village is far more pronounced' [*Gupta*, 1997: 29].

45. Up to 1970, it was only rich households which engaged in job migration, while middle-ranking households were mainly occupied locally. Altogether, around 50 per cent of households in the village were involved in migrant work in 1987 [*Saith and Tankha*, 1997: 113].

46. The village is Karimpur which was first studied by the Wisers in the 1920s [*Wiser*, 1988].

47. The study mentions this as part of an argument about how the more lucrative government jobs have more or less passed the Jatabs by [*Drèze*, 1997].

48. In an article from 1996, Srivastava dates the fieldwork to 1985–87 and 1990–91 [*Srivastava*, 1996: 229].

49. Without quantifying her data, she states that while sharecropping was 'still common' in 1984, since 1975 inverse sharecropping had begun as peasants owning less than two acres 'often' leased out their land to bigger landowners as 'modern farming is expensive', while big landowners had withdrawn land from sharecropping between 1975 and 1984 [*Wadley*, 1996: 214].

50. Agricultural labour inquiries from 1950–51 and 1956–57 attempted to distinguish between attached labourers and casual labourers and to list the level of indebtedness of the different groups. However, according to Daniel Thorner, this resulted in the mix-up of various types of labour contracts, and a thoroughly unreliable result. There were other problems as well [*Thorner*, 1962b]. After the official abolition of 'bonded labour' in 1976, several surveys

focused narrowly on debt bondage generated quite diverse results concerning the numbers of debt bonded labourers in UP and in India in general (see, for example, Government of India [1991a: 101; 1991b: annexe A] for an outline).

51. While the Camar tenants, including the ploughmen, were often indebted to their Thakur, most of their borrowing was actually from a small group of Thakur money- and grain lenders [*Cohn*, 1954].

52. Cohn's study is particularly relevant to the study of rural labourers as it is the only one of the 1940s and 50s anthropological village studies which focuses on an (untouchable) agricultural labour community, namely the Chamars.

53. This is the case with, for example, Miriam Sharma's study from Allahabad (east UP) [*Sharma*, 1978: 168], and Shrinath Singh's study from Jaunpur based on fieldwork in 1969–70 [*Singh*, 1976: 171–5].

54. In the villages studied by Saxena 73 per cent of the area was irrigated, mainly by canal (53 per cent of irrigation) or tubewell (27 per cent) [*Saxena*, 1969]. Had other means of irrigation been more common (as they were in the villages I studied) the proportion of permanent labourers might have been even higher. For example, open well irrigation or the Persian wheel (*rehat*) require a higher input of continuos labour power.

55. As reason for this development it only offers the unease of the labourers with working conditions as attached labourers [*Saxena*, 1969: 99].

56. For example, in the Muzaffarnagar village, '72 per cent of debtor tenants are employed by their landlords, and only one-third of these are employed on a strictly contractual basis' [*Srivastava*, 1989b: 500].

57. Regarding credit-labour interlinkages, each village had only seven cases of credit being repaid, at least partially, through labour services [*Srivastava*, 1996: 243].

58. With one exception, a big landowner who made use of both credit–labour interlinkages and interseasonal linkages [*Drèze and Mukherjee*, 1989: 244].

59. In the Aligarh village studied by Saith and Tankha the number of 'permanent and semi-permanent' farm servants fell from 12 to 4 from 1970 to 1987 [*Saith and Tankha*, 1997: 105–6]. Similarly, while the leatherworkers [Chamars] were 'essentially bonded labourers in 1925' in the Mainpuri District of west UP studied by Wiser (in 1925) and Wadley (in 1984), this type of labour relation died out in the 1960s together with many Jajmani relations [*Wadley*, 1996: 212, 222].

60. The fact that such confrontations have not been reported does not mean that they did not take place. However, it seems to me that the fieldwork based studies of labour conflicts from the 1940s and 1950s which placed the earliest conflicts in the 1920s should have been able to pick up earlier conflicts had they occurred. It is my experience that villagers may recall conflicts and events that took place 50 to 60 years ago, that is, for these early studies back to the last decades of the nineteenth century.

61. The Bhakti movement, the Ravidas untouchable religious societies, the Adi Hindu untouchable ideology, and Ambedkar's dalit social and political movement, all emphasised different aspects of the fight against caste-based discrimination, ranging from agitation against untouchables' performance of polluting occupations and tasks, and propagating an emulation of high caste norms, to more direct attempts to undermine and attack higher castes' control. Several groups under the Hindu Mahasabha (a reform society for mainstream caste Hindus) also sought to reform or 'uplift' the untouchables. These movements were mainly active in towns [*Gooptu*, 1993; *Kananaikil*, 1993: 401–3; *Prashad*, 1996: 553]. Nevertheless, their importance for rural untouchables should not be underestimated, as shown by some of the case studies below.

62. It is thus wrong to claim that the left did not take up struggles of rural labourers, as Omvedt does. The communists took up the grievances and struggles of agricultural labourers, albeit as a secondary aim for them in the general struggle against landlordism [*A. Gupta*, 1996; *Omvedt*, 1986].

63. The fact that the Hindu reform society Arya Samaj held a strong position in the area at the time was one reason for this, even though no Chamars from the village were active in the organisation [*Cohn*, 1954: 124, 252–3].

64. From the same village, Opler and Singh report several strike and non-co-operation actions

by labourers for 'higher wages or better treatment from their employers' in the years before Independence [*Opler and Singh*, 1952: 181]. They also point to the uneven politicisation that was taking place by comparing the Jaunpur village to a village in the neighbouring Allahabad district, where no labour actions took place.

65. Similar politicisation from the same period is reported from a study of a village in Delhi state adjacent to west UP by Oscar Lewis. Here, partly as a result of the inspiration from the Arya Samaj movement and the Congress party, the Chamars refused to pay house tax to the Jats in 1926. Even though the Chamars lost that year's case through the courts and local oppression, the Jats did not collect the tax from 1928 to 1938 when they managed to instigate the tax system again until Independence. Between 1928 and 1947, there were four other court cases between Chamars and Jats, involving issues such as Jats having beaten up a Chamar, the Chamars' refusal to collect dead animals, and their refusal to guard the Jat harvest against thieves and animals. Finally, at Independence, the legal bulwark that the Jats had made use of till then – the legally binding status of the recorded traditional village duties of the lower castes (the *wajib-ul'aiz*) – was abolished, and the Jats gave in in disputes about house tax and the carrying of dead animals [*Lewis*, 1958: 72–5].

66. This is not surprising; even debt bondage is possible only if landowners can enforce this outlawed relation, which requires that the state, with its ties to the dominant elite, does not attempt to stop them.

67. The practice of untouchability was outlawed after Independence, government quotas for scheduled castes and scheduled tribes were introduced within the educational system and government employment, and programmes directed towards the 'upliftment' of the scheduled castes were set in motion. However, such programmes were at best partially implemented, and the more direct route to satisfying the needs of the rural poor, namely giving land to untouchable agricultural labourers was never seriously contemplated [*Omvedt*, 1986: 174–76]. It can be argued, therefore, that policy was aimed more at satisfying the scheduled caste elite than the masses [*Shah*, 1990].

In the 1970s, the Congress party and Indira Gandhi did, however, acquire a pro-poor image through policy announcements such as her 'fight against poverty' programme of 1971, and the abolition of bonded labour in 1975–76. In UP, the ruling Congress party followed suit with debt relief for landless agricultural labourers in 1974 as well as other pro-poor, pro-low caste initiatives [*Hasan*, 1989: 147; *Omvedt*, 1995: 155].

68. In the Jaunpur village, the Chamars referred to the fight against poverty campaign, while in the Muzaffarnagar village they referred to debt abolition when explaining why they broke the borrowing relations with their employers.

69. The improvements in living standards among low caste rural workers registered in my and Srivastava's case studies seem to point in a different direction to the general trend in poverty rates in the early 1990s registered by the National Sample Surveys. According to Abhijit Sen's [1997] estimate of the Rural Headcount Poverty from 1973–74 to 1993–94, based on NSS data and on the Planning Commission's Expert Group, rural poverty decreased steadily during the first part of this period, to reach a low in 1989–90 and 1990–91, both in UP and at All India level. However, rural poverty increased dramatically in 1992 following the introduction of structural adjustment policies. In 1993–94, it fell back to a level in-between the 1992 peak and the previous lower levels. In UP, the rural poverty headcount was 35 per cent in 1990–91, 48 per cent in 1992, and 43 per cent in 1993–94 [*Sen*, 1997: 97]. This trend probably means that material conditions have worsened for rural labourers in general in UP, but this is not necessarily the case. Rural labourers, who at any rate are likely to subsist below the poverty line, have not necessarily become poorer just because others have fallen below the poverty line; it depends on what caused the movement. One way of answering this question is the approach chosen here, that of looking at case studies.

70. Omvedt's figures are based on the Rural Labour Inquiry 1974–75, Table 2.3(b).

71. However, the majority of untouchables did not gain access to jobs or education via the reservation schemes. In their discussion of the reservation policy Oliver Mendelsohn and Marika Zicziany point out that the 1.5 million untouchable government employees only constitute 1.25 per cent of all untouchables in India. They also conclude that reservation

regarding education has had virtually no effect [*Mendelsohn and Zicziany*, 1998:133–45]. Their detailed analysis compares favourably with the undocumented pronouncement by Rajendra Sharma that the reservation policies of 1994 had benefited 16 per cent of untouchables in various unspecified ways [*Sharma*, 1994: 153].

72. The development of a radical untouchable petty bourgeoisie in the central UP town of Kanpur had also been documented [*Gooptu*, 1993].

73. In many cases it is the caste-based hamlet that forms the boundary of immediate solidarity bonds and the only unit for action by the agricultural labourers. Labourers may also take action across hamlet and caste boundaries, but even such wider actions are often phrased in caste, rather than class terms: the 'small' castes against the 'big' castes. Similarly, the dominant landowners' answer to strikes, *naka bandi*, hits all lower caste members irrespective of class. *Naka bandi* is the total ban on any trespassing by labouring communities on the landowners' land, in effect stopping the lower castes from collecting fodder and even from having a place to defecate. Collective beatings and collective atrocities such as burning down a whole hamlet or murdering local labour leaders are also part of employers' arsenal [*Byres*, 1981: 440; *Gill*, 1995: 445].

74. For the construction of ethnic, religious and caste identities, see, for example, Paul Brass [1991] and van der Veer [1987] and, for an overview, Dipankar Gupta [1996]. The concept of identity as construct compares favourably with more traditional attempts to see the present importance of caste categories as a result of the survival of primordial religious identities as, for example, Francine Frankel does [*Frankel*, 1990].

75. While RPI's core support came from untouchables, especially the Jatavs, their main alliance partner in the successful 1962 elections was the Muslim group. The electoral success of RPI was short-lived as Muslim voters soon returned to the Congress party [*Hasan*, 1989: 118–20].

76. In the 1989 UP assembly election, the two communist parties received less than two percent of the votes altogether [*Hasan*, 1998: Appendix, Table 2.4]

77. The chronologies of Omvedt and of Mendelsohn and Vicziany do not agree. For example, Omvedt claims that DS-4 was formed in 1982 and not in 1981. She also does not mention that Kanshi Ram established an earlier version of BAMCEF back in 1971. Here, I have chosen to follow the more detailed outline of BSP's history given by Mendelsohn and Vicziany [1998].

78. Opposed to the terms 'untouchable', 'ex-untouchable', 'Harijan' or 'scheduled caste', 'dalit' is an explicitly political term. It refers to the untouchable group but 'implies demands for social justice and empowerment' [*Sharma*, 1994: 14].

79. According to some sources, the percentages used by the BSP are 90 per cent and 10 per cent (see, for example, Mendelsohn and Vicziany [1998: 223]).

80. This political agenda also makes sense electorally, as they can thereby widen their possible support to encompass more than the 22 per cent of the UP population who are untouchables.

81. There is no doubt that the Bahujan alliance between various caste groups takes place according to conditions set by untouchables. Therefore it is difficult to agree with Omvedt that the BSP can be seen as a modern carrier of the South Indian low caste political tradition, which mainly expressed the aspirations of low but not untouchable castes [*Omvedt*, 1996: 345].

82. The sweepers who in some places still remove the night soil, often remain in close patron-client relations with their employers. They often do not feel much affinity with the Chamars who treat them as a low ranking caste. They also have a long history of association with the Congress Party and with Hindu upliftment movements from the Arya Samaj of the 1930s to the present-day BJP [*Prashad*, 1995: 337–8; 1996: 552; *Pai*, 1997: 2313; *Pai and Singh*, 1997: 1358].

83. Omvedt, who seems to agree with the BSP's analysis of social relations in India, argues that instead of challenging the high caste elite, socialism has been useful to it. Her argument deserves to be quoted at some length:

Socialism (in vague Marxist form) was useful to the elite in several ways: 1) It represented a powerful intellectual force claiming world-wide salience that totally rendered irrelevant the question of caste; (2) it provided the ideological basis for a managed economy which gave a long-standing fillip to the brahman bureaucracy, as opposed to rather upstart banias who from time to time had associated themselves with the bahujan movement; (3) it gave the elite an opportunity to claim themselves to represent – as party leaders and activists – the greatest force for equality, seeming to fulfil at least some mass demands; (4) by making land reforms central to this it provided for equality at the bottom and focused struggles among the lowest and low-middle caste sections while leaving as a secondary matter the question of education and intellectual dominance. There is nothing so striking as the degree to which the elite has promoted land reform on the one hand, and dragged its feet on universal comprehensive education, on the other. Socialism was thus, in the Indian context, a brahminical socialism, or what Marx and Engels described as 'feudal socialism' [*Omvedt*, 1997: 1967].

84. Mendelsohn and Vicziany report similar assertions by Kanshi Ram [*Mendelsohn and Vicziany*, 1998: 225].
85. One Kanshi Ram slogan may be translated as 'Brahmins, Banias and Thakurs [all high castes, JL] are thieves, the rest are with us' [*Omvedt*, 1996: 346]. Its UP leader Mayawati, dubbed a 'firebrand of a woman', has allegedly called Mahatma Gandhi (the revered Father of the Nation) the biggest enemy of untouchables, and sees caste and caste-ism as an invention of Brahmins and Brahminical scripts, 'an obscenity thrust upon 85 per cent of the population'. The link back to the Ambedkar movement and the RPI is obvious, even regarding the style of propaganda. Thus, an RPI slogan reported from Aligarh district in 1962 urged voters to 'Blacken the faces of Thakurs, Brahmans and Lalas [Banias]' [*Brass*, 1985: 231]. Untouchables are also encouraged to fight back against their oppressors. For example, a BSP state minister allegedly responded to the murder of a local BSP activist by calling for the crowd to 'take three of their lives for the one of our people they have killed', and high caste government officials are told to support local untouchables or face the consequences [*Frontline*, 11 March 1994: 4–8].
86. During 1997, Mayawati's government even decided that 25 per cent of all posts of Police Station in-Charge should be manned by untouchables [*Government of Uttar Pradesh*, 1997: 9].
87. For example, it was stipulated that all government offices should be open for hearing public grievances and complaints from 9 to 10 am each day. The government also sanctioned new administrative posts in all UP's districts, specifically focusing on the well-being of the untouchables.
88. In 1997, 15,000 Ambedkar villages were provided with extra funds in all government programmes, and within these villages 60 per cent of all beneficiaries had to be from the untouchable castes. This programme was initiated before the BSP came to power, but the BSP extended it considerably, in terms of numbers of villages covered and especially funding. Of the 15,000 Ambedkar villages, 4025 were included by the BSP government during 1997, and 7000 million Rupees were expected to be spent on the programme in 1997 [*Government of Uttar Pradesh*, 1997: 11], including housing schemes giving beneficiaries house construction grants of Rs 20,000 per household, increased scholarships to untouchables in primary and secondary education, and old age pensions, government construction work which, it was stipulated, should employ local low castes, installing of electricity and drinking water supplies in, and building metalled link roads to, untouchable hamlets, etc.
89. Until the early 1990s, police and courts generally acted on behalf of high caste landowners, within certain limits on how blatantly this could be done [*Lerche*, 1995].
90. Nevertheless, the wages were still well below the official minimum wage of the region. The payment for half a day's paddy transplantation increased from 3 kg of wheat to 4 kg in 1994. Since then, this wage has been stable, but pay for some other tasks in agriculture has increased. In 1998, most full day's tasks were paid Rs 30, or sometimes only Rs 25. More arduous jobs such as digging soil were paid Rs 35–40. The government stipulated minimum wage was Rs 47, which is paid to labourers by various government development projects.

91. For example, in 1971, the Thakurs' murder of a Chamar strike leader forced the Thakurs to compromise on wages in order to avoid court action [*Lerche*, 1995].
92. They did, however, still perform the stipulated *begar* for their priority Thakurs.
93. In 1998, she had become the organisational secretary of the BSP district organisation.
94. The full grant is Rs 20,000. The remaining Rs 3,400 should have been given a few months after the Mayawati government fell but never appeared.
95. The old 'core tenants' from the middle ranking castes: the Yadav, the Kormi and the Moria were all now highly efficient small or middle peasants. As elsewhere in east UP, these groups formed the core of the SP party's support base (though at the 1998 election the Morias were split as the BSP fielded a Moria candidate). Pals and Muslims also voted for the SP, while Kathiks, as in many other parts of UP, voted for the BJP. All other low and untouchable castes voted BSP (for example, Chamar, Bhar, Dhobi, Nai, Lohar, Bodhai, Kahar, Teli, Musehar, Mallah).
96. Most of the Chamars from the second biggest hamlet of the village stopped doing any agricultural labour at all after their hamlet was burned down in a labour conflict in 1983.
97. While factional conflicts within the Jat community has always been common, this was the first time that one Jat faction had approached the Chamars for support against the other. Previously, conflicts among the Jats had not been any others' business.
98. Most importantly, a community hall for the Chamars worth Rs 85,000 was under construction during our visit in 1998.
99. The 'Scheduled Castes and Scheduled Tribes (Prevention of Atrocities) Act'.
100. The communists organised strikes and demonstrations in west UP for the rural poor during the 1950s and 1960s, and were active in several 'land grab' movements from the 1970s onwards, especially in east UP, where landless people led by the party took possession of land illegally held by landlords. The Communist parties organised agricultural workers in agricultural labour unions, and initiated struggles against bonded labour arrangements and for allocation to labourers of land held by landlords above permitted land ceilings [e.g., *J. Singh*, 1992: 88, 93–4; *Singh*, 1986; *Chopra*, 1985].
101. At the last election, only one CPI(M) candidate and no CPI candidates were elected from UP to the Lok Sabha, the Indian Parliament. This represents a major downturn in public support. The two communist parties were strongest in the 1960s. In 1967, they had six MPs elected in UP. In 1989, they still got three seats while in 1991, they only got one (*The Hindu*, 6 Feb. 1998). The defections of local level communist cadres to the BSP was an issue that representatives of both CPI and CPI(M) interviewed in 1998 brought up themselves, denying the 'rumours' of such defections which they assumed we were aware of.
102. AIAWU was founded in 1981 and held its first conference in 1982. The UP branch also held its first conference in 1982 [*AIAWU*, 1982b: 1, 43].
103. Thus, in 1989, the AIAWU General Secretary again criticised DS-4 and the BSP, but now it was acknowledged that these organisations had built their strength by 'highlighting the genuine problems of the oppressed and downtrodden'. The problem with the BSP approach was still seen as its caste approach which 'isolate[s] them [the untouchables] from the mainstream of the masses struggling to achieve a better life' [*AIAWU*, 1989: 24–5]. In 1992, the General Secretary noted even more pointedly that DS-4 and BSP had responded better to the oppression of untouchables than the AIAWU. While the criticism from 1989 was maintained, the analysis was now that the emergence of DS-4 and BSP was a response to the 'alarming' increase in atrocities against untouchables [*AIAWU*, 1992: 16] – a response that the AIAWU and CPI(M) had not been able to provide.
104. In Jaunpur district, where CPI and not CPI(M) was the strongest communist party, a member of the CPI district secretariat acknowledged that the fight against 'social oppression' was important for low caste workers, and that the BSP had brought this to the fore. According to him, the CPI had now accepted that an analysis of social as well as economic contradictions was necessary, and analysis of inter-caste contradictions, not least because control or lack of control over economic means was caste based. Moreover, the party now stressed developing a communist leadership from dalit castes in response to the BSP politics, as it realised that high caste communists could not command support from

dalits [Singh, interview, 1998].

The Muzaffarnagar District Secretary of AIAWU was also UP Vice President of AIAWU as well as member of its all India Central Committee, and member of the CPI(M) district secretariat of Muzaffarnagar. He argued, similarly, that it had been a mistake for the CPI(M) not to organise agricultural labourers against caste based non-economic oppression. Instead, the party tried to mobilise the agricultural labourers on farmers' issues, especially better prices, as well as on labour issues. This he saw as grounded in the bias of CPI(M) cadres who were mainly from middle and upper castes. As an example of the problematic mass line of the party, he argued that CPI(M) members would talk about the rights of Chamar labourers in political speeches, but when they went to villages, they would stay with the Jats. 'If we do not stay in their place, why should they come to us?' (Jagmohan, interview, 1998). Moreover, he argued that the BSP was in a much easier position than the CPI(M) as it could attack peasant employers directly and openly while the CPI(M) always had to think of the long-term consequences.

105. For UP examples, see, for example, AIAWU[1996: 25; 1992: 30].

106. CPI(M) criticised itself for not raising the specific demands of the agricultural labourers sufficiently strongly in as early as 1966. Since then, it has undertaken several adjustments in its policy towards agricultural labourers, including the formation of the All India Agricultural Workers Union. This, however, has not led to any overall rethinking of its class analysis nor of its class alliance policy.

REFERENCES

AIWU, 1982a, Statement of Policy and Constitution. Adopted by the First Conference (Midnapore, West Bengal) 11 Nov. 1982.

AIAWU, 1982b, General Secretary's Report to 24th Session of the All Kisan Sabha (Midnapore, West Bengal, 8 to 11 Nov. 1982).

AIAWU, 1985, Proceedings of the Meeting of All India Council of AIAWU held at Munger (Bihar) 3 to 5 July 1985.

AIAWU, 1986, 2nd All India Conference 1986 9, 10, 11 and 12 Dec. 1986 Palghat – Kerala.

AIAWU, 1988, Proceedings, Report and Resolutions of the General Council of the All India Agricultural Workers Union at Allahabad (UP): 26–28 Feb. 1988.

AIAWU, 1989, Proceedings, Report and Resolutions of the General Council of the All India Agricultural Workers Union at Khammam (AP) 1 May 1989.

AIAWU, 1992, Documents of the Third Conference of AIAWU 17–19 April 1992, Samastipur (Bihar).

AIAWU, 1996, Documents IVth All India Conference 2–4 Nov, 1996, Khammam (AP).

Bhalla, G.S. and D.S. Tyagi, 1989, Patterns in Indian Agricultural Development: A District Level Study, New Delhi: Institute for Studies in Industrial Development.

Brass, Paul, 1980a, 'The Politicization of the Peasantry in a North Indian State: I', Journal of Peasant Studies, Vol. 7, No. 4, pp. 395-426.

Brass, Paul, 1980b, 'The Politicization of the Peasantry in a North Indian State: II', The Journal of Peasant Studies, Vol.8, No.1, pp.3–36.

Brass, Paul, 1985, 'Caste, Caste Alliances, and Hierarchy of Values in Aligarh District', in Paul Brass, Caste, Faction and Party in Indian Politics, Vol.II. Delhi: Chanakya Publications, pp.207–79.

Brass, Paul, 1990, The Politics of India since Independence, Cambridge: Cambridge University Press.

Brass, Paul, 1991, Ethnicity and Nationalism: Theory and Comparison, New Delhi: Sage.

Brass, Paul, 1997a, 'General Elections, 1996, in Uttar Pradesh. Divisive Struggles Influence Outcome', Economic and Political Weekly, Vol.32, No.38, pp.2403–21.

Brass, Paul, 1997b, The Theft of an Idol, Princeton: Princeton University Press.

Brass, Tom, 1990, 'Class Struggle and the Deproletarianisation of Agricultural Labour in Haryana (India)', The Journal of Peasant Studies, Vol.18, No.1, pp.36–67.

Brass, Tom, 1994a, 'Post-Script: Populism, Peasants and Intellectuals, or What's Left of the Future?', in *New Farmers' Movements in India, The Journal of Peasant Studies, Special Issue*, Vol.21, Nos.3/4, pp.246–86.

Brass, Tom, 1994b, 'Some Observations on Unfree Labour, Capitalist Restructuring and Deproletarianization', *International Review of Social History*, Vol.39, No.2, pp.255–75.

Brass, Tom, 1995, 'Reply to Utsa Patnaik: If the Cap Fits ...', *International Review of Social History*, Vol.40, No.1, pp.93–117.

Breman, Jan, 1993, *Beyond Patronage and Exploitation. Changing Agrarian Relations in South Gujarat*, Delhi: Oxford University Press.

Breman, Jan, Kloos, Peter and Ashwani Saith (eds.), 1997, *The Village in Asia Revisited*, Delhi: Oxford University Press.

Byres, T.J., 1981, 'The New Technology, Class Formation and Class Action in the Indian Countryside', *The Journal of Peasant Studies*, Vol.8, No.4, pp.405–54.

Chopra, Suneet, 1985, 'Bondage in a Green Revolution Area: A Study of Brick Kiln Workers in Muzaffarnagar District', in Utsa Patnaik and Manjari Dingwaney (eds.), *Chains of Servitude. Bondage and Slavery in India*, Bombay: Orient Langman, pp.162–86.

Cohn, Bernard, 1954, 'The Camars of Senapur: A Study of the Changing Status of a Depressed Caste', unpublished Ph.D. dissertation, Cornell University.

CPI(M), 1993, Review of the Work on Kisan Front and Future Tasks (Adopted by the Central Committee in its meeting, 16–18 April, 1993).

CPI(M), 1995, Political Organisational Reports 15th Congress CPI(M), 3–8 April 1995, Chandigarh.

CPI(M), 1997, Policy Resolutions of the Communist Party of India (Marxist-Leninist).

Desai, A.R. (ed.), 1986, *Agrarian Struggles in India after Independence*, Delhi: Oxford University Press.

Dev, S. Mahendra and Ajit K. Ranade, 'Agricultural Growth, Employment and Poverty in Uttar Pradesh: Some Recent Trends', in G.K. Chadha and Alakh N. Sharma (eds.), *Growth, Employment and Poverty. Change and Continuity in Rural India*, New Delhi: Vikas Publishing House for Indian Society of Labour Economics, pp.346–64.

Drèze, Jean, 1997, 'Palanpur, 1957–93. Occupational Change, Land Ownership and Social Inequality', in Breman, Kloos and Saith [1997: 126–74].

Drèze, Jean and Anindita Mukherjee, 1989, 'Labour Contracts in Rural India: Theories and Evidence', in Sukhamoy Chakravarty (ed.), *The Balance Between Industry and Agriculture in Economic Development. Proceedings of the Eighth World Congress of the International Economic Association, Delhi*, V. Pandit (volume reporter): Vol.3: Manpower and Transfers, IEA Conference Vol.88. London: Macmillan, pp.233–65.

Drèze, Jean, Lanjouw, Peter and Nicolas Stern, *Economic Mobility and Agricultural Labour in Rural India: A Case Study*, DEP No.35. London School of Economics.

Duncan, Ian, 1988, 'Party Politics and the North Indian Peasantry: The Rise of the Bharatiya Kranti Dal in Uttar Pradesh', *The Journal of Peasant Studies*, Vol.16, No.1, pp.40–76.

Duncan, Ian, 1997, 'Agricultural Innovation and Political Change in North India: The Lok Dal in Uttar Pradesh', *The Journal of Peasant Studies*, Vol.24, No.4, pp.246–68.

Election Commission, 1998, 'Votes Polled in States/UTs by Parties', http://www.eci.gov.in

Frankel, Francine, 1990, 'Conclusion. Decline of a Social Order', in Francine Frankel and M.S.A. Rao (eds.), *Dominance and State Power in Modern India: Decline of a Social Order*, Vol.II. Delhi: Oxford University Press, pp.482–517.

Frontline, 1994, by Praveen Swamy, 'Conflicts in UP', 11 March, pp.4–8.

Frontline, 1995, by Venkitesh Ramakrishnan, 'Remains of the Day', 1 Dec., pp.30–31.

Frontline, 1997, by Venkitesh Ramakrishnan, 'Opportunism Inc.', 18 April, pp.13–19.

Frontline, 1997, by Venkitesh Ramakrishnan, 'Violence Unabated', 2 May, pp.34–5

Frontline, 1997, by Venkitesh Ramakrishnan, 'Deepening Social Divisions', 31 Oct., pp.119–21.

Fukanaga, Masaaki, 1993, *Society, Caste and Factional Policies: Conflict and Continuity in Rural India*, New Delhi: Manohar.

Gill, Sucha Singh, 1995, 'Unionising Agricultural Labour: Some Issues', *The Indian Journal of Labour Economics*, Vol.38, No.3, pp.443–53.

Gooptu, Nandini, 1993, 'Caste and Labour: Untouchable Social Movements in Urban Uttar Pradesh in the Early Twentieth Century', in Peter G. Robb (ed.), *Dalit Movements and the Meanings of Labour in India*, SOAS Studies on South Asia, Delhi: Oxford University Press, pp.277–98.

Government of India, Ministry of Labour, 1991a, *Report of the National Commission on Rural Labour*, Vol.I, New Delhi.

Government of India, Ministry of Labour, 1991b, *Report of the National Commission on Rural Labour*, Vol.II, New Delhi.

Government of Uttar Pradesh, Information and Public Relations Department, 1997, *Major Decisions and Achievements of UP Government under the Dynamic Leadership of Ms. Mayawati and Steps Taken to Perpetuate the Memory of Great Heroes of Social Change*, Lucknow.

Gupta, Amit Kumar, 1996, *The Agrarian Drama: The Leftists and the Rural Poor in India. 1934–51*. New Delhi: Manohar.

Gupta, Dipankar, 1996, *Political Sociology in India. Contemporary Trends*, Hyderabad: Orient Longman.

Gupta, Dipankar, 1997, *Rivalry and Brotherhood. Politics in the Life of Farmers in Northern India*, Delhi: Oxford University Press.

Hasan, Zoya, 1989, *Dominance and Mobilisation. Rural Politics in Western Uttar Pradesh 1930–1980*, New Delhi: Sage.

Hasan, Zoya, 1998, *Quest for Power. Oppositional Movements and Post-Congress Politics in Uttar Pradesh*, Delhi: Oxford University Press.

Herring, Ronald J., 1984, 'Economic Consequences of Local Power Configurations in Rural South Asia', in Meghnad Desai, Susanne Rudolph, Ashok Rudra (eds.), *Agrarian Power and Agricultural Productivity in South Asia*, Berkeley, CA: University of California Press, pp.198–249.

The Hindu, 1998, 'Mulayam Makes the Going Tough for CPI, CPI(M)', Special Correspondent, 6 Feb.

Ilaiah, Kancha, 1994, 'BSP and Caste as Ideology', *Economic and Political Weekly*, Vol.29, No.12, pp.668–9.

Indian Express, 1994, 'Mulayam in a Fix Over Meerut Firing', Express News Service, 2 April.

India Today, 1997, 'A Captive Legacy', by S.N. Bhaumik with S. Misra, 1 Sept., pp.46–8.

Jeffey, Craig, 1998, '"He became cheeky, so we punched out his teeth": Rural Violence and an Agrarian Elite in North-West India', paper presented for the Graduate Forum 26 Jan. 1998, Cambridge, mimeo.

Kananaikil, Jose, 1993, 'The Emerging Dalit Identity in India', *Social Action*, Vol.43, No.4, pp.401–11.

Kothari, 1994, 'Rise of the Dalits and the Renewed Debate on Caste', *Economic and Political Weekly*, Vol.29, No.26, pp.1589–94.

Kumar, P.K. Sanal, 1995, 'Changing Political Equations: A View in UP Politics', *Social Action*, Vol.45, No.3, pp.340–8.

Lerche, Jens, 1995, 'Is Bonded Labour a Bound Category? - Reconceptualising Agrarian Conflict in India', *The Journal of Peasant Studies*, Vol.22, No.3, pp.484–515.

Lewis, Oscar, 1958, *Village Life in Northern India. Studies in a Delhi Village*, Urbana, IL: University of Illinois Press.

Lynch, Owen, 1969, *The Politics of Untouchablility. Social Mobility and Social Change in a City of India*, New York: Columbia University Press.

Mahar, J. Michael, 1972, 'Agents of Dharma in a North Indian Village', in J. Michael Mahar (ed.), *The Untouchables in Contemporary India*, Tucson, AR: University of Arizona Press, pp.17–35.

'Mankind' (a report from), 1986, 'Countrywide Civil Disobedience Movement', in Desai [1986: 83–106].

Mendelsohn, Oliver, 1993, 'The Transformation of Authority in Rural India', *Modern Asian Studies*, Vol.27, No.4, pp.805–42.

Mendelsohn, Oliver and Marika Vicziany, 1998, *The Untouchables: Subordination, Poverty and the State in Modern India*, Cambridge: Cambridge University Press.

Misra, Amaresh, 1993, 'Land Struggle in Uttar Pradesh', *Economic and Political Weekly*, Vol.28, No.39, p.2059.

Misra, Amaresh, 1994a, 'Evading the Land Issue', *Economic and Political Weekly*, Vol.29, No.13, pp.723–4.

Misra, Amaresh 1994b, 'Meerut Firing: A Turning Point?', *Economic and Political Weekly*, Vol.29, No.18, pp.1054–5.

Misra, Amaresh, 1995, 'Opportunities for the Left', *Economic and Political Weekly*, Vol. 30, No. 46, pp. 2910-2911.

Misra, Amaresh, 1996, 'Politics in Drift', *Economic and Political Weekly*, Vol.31, No.10, pp.585–6.

Misra, Amaresh, 1997, 'Transfer of Power: Permutations and Combinations', *Economic and Political Weekly*, Vol.32, No.38, pp.2383–4.

Omvedt, Gail, 1985, 'Capitalist Agriculture and Rural Classes in India', in Iqbal Khan (ed.) *Fresh Perspectives on India and Pakistan. Essays on Economics, Politics and Culture*, Oxford: Bougainvillea Books, pp.98–142.

Omvedt, Gail, 1986, 'Caste, Agrarian Relations and Agrarian Conflicts', in Desai [1986: 168–95].

Omvedt, Gail 1994a, *Dalits and the Democratic Revolution: Dr. Ambedkar and the Dalit Movement in Colonial India*, New Delhi: Sage Publications.

Omvedt, Gail, 1994b, 'Kanshi Ram and the Bahujan Samaj Party', in K.L. Sharma (ed.), *Caste and Class in India*, Jaipur: Rawat Publications, pp.153–69.

Omvedt, Gail, 1995, *Dalit Visions: The Anti-Caste Movement and the Construction of an Indian Identity* (Tracts for the Times No.8), London: Sangam Books.

Omvedt, Gail, 1996, 'The Anti-Caste Movement and the Discourse of Power', in T. V. Sathyamurthy (ed.), *Social Change and Political Discourse in India: Structures of Power, Movements and Resistance, Vol.3: Region, Religion, Caste, Gender and Culture in Contemporary India*, New Delhi: Oxford University Press, pp.334–54.

Omvedt, Gail, 1997, 'In Search of the Indian Nation', *Economic and Political Weekly*, Vol.32, No.31, pp.1966–7.

Opler, Morris and Rudra Datt Singh, 1952, 'Two Villages of Eastern Uttar Pradesh (UP), India: An Analysis of Similarities and Differences', *American Anthropologist*, 54, pp.179–90.

Pai, Sudha, 1997, 'Dalit Assertion in UP', *Economic and Political Weekly*, Vol.32, No.37, pp.2313–15.

Pai, Sudha and Jagpal Singh, 1997, 'Politicisation of Dalits and Most Backward Castes', *Economic and Political Weekly*, Vol.32, No.23, pp.1356–61.

Pathak, S.N., 1987, *Land Reforms and Change in Rural Society*, Allahabad: Chugh Publications.

Pinto, Ambrose, 1995, 'The Birth of a Dalit Regime', *Social Action*, Vol.45, No.3, pp.349–55.

Prashad, Vijay, 1995, 'May Days of Mayavati', *Economic and Political Weekly*, Vol.30, No.23, pp.1357–8.

Prashad, Vijay, 1996, 'The Untouchable Question', *Economic and Political Weekly*, Vol.31, No.6, pp.551–9.

Rana, M.S., 1994, *Bharatiya Kisan Union and Ch. Tikait*, Meerut: Paragon Publications.

Ranade, Sudhanshu, 1989, 'A Communist Perspective on Development Strategy for Rural India', *The Journal of Peasant Studies*, Vol.16, No.4, pp.542–74.

Saith, Ashwani and Ajay Tankha, 1997, 'Longitudinal Analysis of Structural Change in a North Indian Village, 1970–87', in Breman, Kloos and Saith [1997: 79–125].

Saxena, R.C., 1969, *Agricultural Labour:. Wages and Living Conditions in Meerut*, Bombay: Bhatkal Books International.

Sen, Abhijit, 1997, 'Structural Adjustment and Rural Poverty: Variables that Really Matter', in G.K. Chadha and Alakh N. Sharma (eds.), *Growth, Employment and Poverty: Change and Continuity in Rural India*, New Delhi: Vikas Publishing House for Indian Society of Labour Economics, pp.110–22.

Sen, Sunil, 1982, *Peasant Movements in India: Mid-nineteenth and Twentieth Centuries*, Calcutta: K.P. Bagchi.

Shah, Ghanshyam, 1990, 'The Bourgeoise Party and Deprived Communities', in Ghanshyam Shah (ed.), *Capitalist Development: Critical Essays*, Bombay: Popular Prakashan, pp.343–69.

Sharma, Miriam, 1978, *The Politics of Inequality. Competition and Control in an Indian Village* (Asian Studies at Hawaii, No.22), Hawai: University Press of Hawai.

Sharma, Rajendra, 1994, 'Constructing 'Dalit' Identity', *Link*, Vol.37, No.1, pp.13–15.

Sharma, Rita and Thomas T. Poleman, 1994, *The New Economics of India's Green Revolution: Income and Employment Diffusion in Uttar Pradesh*, Delhi: Vikas Publishing House.

Singh, Abha Lakshmi, Fazal Shahab and Haroon Sajjad, 1996, 'Employment of Landless Labourers Inside and Outside the Villages in Aligarh District, UP', *Indian Journal of Regional Science*, Vol.28, No.1, pp.13–26.

Singh, Jagpal, 1992, *Capitalism and Dependence: Agrarian Politics in Western Uttar Pradesh 1951–1991*, Delhi: Manohar.

Singh, Rajendra, 1979, 'Peasant Movements in Uttar Pradesh', in M.S.A. Rao (ed.), *Social Movements in India. Volume One: Peasant and Backward Classes Movements*, New Delhi: Manohar, pp.91–148.

Singh, Rajendra, 1986, 'Agrarian Social Structure and Peasant Unrest: A study of Land-Grab Movement in District Basti, East UP', in Desai [1986: 538–65].

Singh, Shrinath, 1976, *Modernisation of Agriculture: A Case Study in Eastern Uttar Pradesh*, New Delhi: Heritage Publishers.

Srinivasulu, K., 1994, 'Centrality of Caste: Understanding UP Elections', *Economic and Political Weekly*, Vol.29, No.4, pp.159–60.

Srivastava, Ravi, 1989a, 'Tenancy Contracts During Transition: A Study Based on Fieldwork in Uttar Pradesh (India)', *The Journal of Peasant Studies*, Vol.16, No.3, pp.339–95.

Srivastava, Ravi, 1989b, 'Interlinked Modes of Exploitation in Indian Agriculture During Transition: A Case Study', *The Journal of Peasant Studies*, Vol.16, No.4, pp.493–522.

Srivastava, Ravi, 1994, 'Planning and Regional Disparities in India', in Terence J. Byres (ed.), *The State and Development Planning in India*, Delhi: Oxford University Press, pp.147–219.

Srivastava, Ravi, 1995, 'India's Uneven Development and Its Implication for Political Processes: An Analysis of some Recent Trends', in T.V. Sathyamurthy (ed.), *Social Change and Political Discourse in India: Structures of Power, Movements and Resistance, Vol.2: Industry and Agriculture in India since Independence*, Delhi: Oxford University Press, pp.219–47.

Srivastava, Ravi, 1996, 'Agrarian Change and the Labour Process', in Peter Robb (ed.), *Meaning of Agriculture: Essays in South Asian History and Economics*, Delhi: Oxford University Press, pp.228–50.

Srivastava, Ravi, 1997, 'Change and Resilience in Producer Strategies in Uttar Pradesh Agriculture', in Breman, Kloos and Saith [1997: 199–236].

Stokes, Eric, 1978, *The Peasant and the Raj: Studies in Agrarian Society and Peasant Rebellion in Colonial India*, Cambridge: Cambridge University Press.

Thorner, Daniel, 1962a, 'Employer–Labourer Relationships in Agriculture', in Thorner and Thorner [1962: 21–38].

Thorner, Daniel, 1962b, 'The Agricultural Labour Enquiry: Reflections on Concepts and Methods', in Thorner and Thorner [1962: 173–88].

Thorner, Daniel and Alice Thorner, 1962, *Land and Labour in India*, London: Asia Publishing House.

Van der Veer, Peter, 1987, 'God Must be Liberated: A Hindu Liberation Movement in Ayodhya', *Modern Asian Studies*, Vol.21, No.2, pp.283–303.

Wadley, Susan S., 1996, *Struggling with Destiny in Karimpur, 1925–1984*, New Delhi: Vistaar Publications.

Whitehead, Judy, 1991, 'The State and Oppositional Discourse in Central Uttar Pradesh', *Social Scientist*, Vol.19, Nos.8–9, pp.3–25.

Wiser, William, 1988, *The Hindu Jajmani System*, Lucknow: Lucknow Publishing House [originally published 1936].

Agrarian Power and Unfree Labour

J. MOHAN RAO

I. INTRODUCTION

In the half-century since independence, the growth performance of Indian agriculture handily outpaced the negative trend of the half-century preceding independence. Quite clearly, something went well or at least better than before. High-yielding varieties appearing like manna from heaven and lifting the economy from precarious external dependence have been the obvious candidate. Regional variations in performance may be then attributed to agro-climatic differences and the relative availability of suitable new varieties. Yet, this characterisation falls well short of a proper understanding of the historical record (in both periods) and, more so, of regional variations. Nor does it even pretend to ask whether Indian agriculture has come close to fulfilling the promise of available technologies. Even in terms of the proximate determinants of performance, it suffices to note that irrigation by itself is a major contributor to growth besides being an inseparable complement of the Green Revolutionary varieties. Hence, historical changes and regional variations in production relations and political processes which structure investments and incentives, in both public and private domains, have deservedly commanded wide attention.[1] The agrarian labour regime, in particular, is central to any understanding of the dynamics of Indian agriculture; both the utilization of resources (including labour) and their development over time, not to mention the distribution of growth gains, hinge on it.

But the agrarian labour regime is not only source but also destination of changes in agricultural resources, technologies, policies and performance. And for the post-independence period, there is ample evidence of change amidst continuity in labour relations. Even without radical changes in the distribution of control over land and other means of production (along the lines, say, of the enclosure movement), employment relations seem to have

J. Mohan Rao, Department of Economics, University of Massachusetts at Amherst. The author would like to thank Tom Brass for the stimulating exchange of views they had on this account at the LSE–SOAS conference and also for his thoughtful written comments. The author alone is responsible for any errors.

evolved qualitatively during this half century. While neither the robust elements of continuity nor the substantial variations over space should be underplayed, the following stylised shifts seem fairly widespread: from caste-based or personally bonded labour sometimes secured by debt frequently extending across generations to long- and short-duration credit contracts apparently with no such tying; from informally defined and open-ended obligations to formal contractual arrangements; from relations based on 'extra-economic' sanctions to ones based on voluntary agreements; from a reliance on intra-village labour exchanges to the conjoint employment of local and migrant workers; and, from permanent farm labour to casual labour. These shifts seem broadly to be correlated also with the growth of non-agricultural employment. At the same time, however, poor peasants' and labourers' livelihoods remain precarious as they continue to carry land leases at very low returns to their labour, often pay high interest rates especially for consumption loans and, face insufficient and uncertain employment in the labour market.[2]

These shifts have prompted the thorny question whether there has been an historic change in rural India from forms of unfree labour to free or proletarianised labour, from custom and coercion to contract, perhaps even from feudal or semi-feudal relations to capitalist relations. The issue is by no means confined to the employment relation proper for it is easily extended to include tenancy and credit relations as well. It is complicated by the substructure of continuities in the labour regime: the puzzling multiplicity of forms of labour, land and credit exchanges and payment systems often coexisting in the same locales; by the fragmentation of rural markets and the inter-local variations in wages or access to employment and credit this generates; by the tangled gender and caste correlates of class. Agrarian power is exercised by individuals and sometimes by tacit or open coalitions; it is expressed in both personalised and institutionalised relationships; its instrumentalities range from the sheer pressure of labourers' survival imperative to the long arm of law and order; it is bound up with ideologies of local patronage but has increasingly resorted to the trans-local politics of caste and class.

In this study, we focus on one aspect of this changing Indian regime: the question of unfree versus free employment (and land and credit) relationships. Section II reconsiders the theoretical basis of the categories freedom/unfreedom employed in both liberal and Marxian thought. We argue that the concepts of unfree and free employment relations, even when they have been consistently defined, do not lie on a continuum because they are based on the incommensurable categories of negative freedom and self-determination. Nor can any clear separation be sustained between labour subject to 'non-economic' coercion versus labour subject exclusively to 'economic' coercion. If there is a case for retaining, nevertheless, the distinction between unfree and not-unfree employment relationships, this must rest on its utility as a tool of historical analysis.

In this light, we reopen (in section III) the Indian debate over agrarian servitude. An important strand of this debate (involving Tom Brass and Surinder Jodhka in the case of Haryana in recent years, and many other scholars and regions in earlier years) concerns the status of attached labourers who work exclusively for a particular employer to whom they are indebted. We concur with Brass who argues that if attached labourers are indeed unfree, this is not related to their being permanent and local workers as opposed to casual and migrant workers. Whether they are unfree must be determined only by reference to any constraints on their freedom to contract and recontract. Brass categorizes them as unfree on the consideration that the production relation in which they find themselves after entering a contract does so constrain them (for example, during the peak season). However, the nature of exchange and production relations associated with attached labour does not clinch the issue of unfreedom, we point out, because heritability of debt plays a potentially critical role. Since field evidence for the late 1980s (see Brass [1990]) shows that the heritability of debt is ubiquitous, it seems plausible that unfreedom is widespread though its actual extent and change over time must be determined from direct evidence on the dynamics of debt and its inheritance.

Even ignoring inheritance, however, there are substantive differences between attached labour relations and the canonical case of industrial proletarians in advanced economies or in the advanced sectors of poor economies. These differences come into focus in section IV where we present an analysis of *production* relations associated with attached labour emphasising the importance of (a) inequality between employers and poor rural labourers, and (b) the absence of certain supportive/protective social institutions regulating property relations, which jointly structure labour-tying credit arrangements in rural India. Section V concludes the study.

II. COERCION AND UNFREE EMPLOYMENT RELATIONS

This sphere that we are deserting, within whose boundaries the sale and purchase of labour-power goes on, is in fact a very Eden of the innate rights of man. There alone rule Freedom, Equality, Property and Bentham. Freedom, because both buyer and seller of a commodity, say of labour-power, are constrained only by their own free will. They contract as free agents, and the agreement they come to is but the form in which they give legal expression to their common will. Equality, because each enters into relation with the other, as with a simple owner of commodities, and they exchange equivalent for equivalent. Property, because each disposes only of what is his own. And Bentham, because each looks only to himself. ... On leaving this sphere ... which furnishes the 'Free-trader Vulgaris' with ... the standard by which he judges a society based on capital and wages, we think we can perceive a change in the physiognomy of our dramatis personae. He, who before was the money-owner, now strides in front as capitalist; the possessor of labour-power follows as his labourer. The one with an air of importance, smirking, intent on business; the other, timid and holding back, like one who is bringing his own hide to market and has nothing to expect but – a hiding' [*Marx*, 1867: 176].

In the Indian debates on the social existence form(s) of labour, employment relations based on politico-juridical or other 'non-economic' coercion have been commonly defined as unfree. Conversely, a free relationship is one entered into voluntarily and without any 'non-economic' duress.[3] The Thorners [1962] categorised a labourer (or borrower or tenant) to be free if he is able to accept or reject the conditions offered by the employer (or lender or landlord). An 'unfree or bond labourer' on the other hand 'does not possess the right or has yielded the right to refuse to work under the terms set by his master. Through custom, compulsion, or specific obligation, the bond labourer is tied to his master's needs. He can neither quit nor take up work for another master without first receiving permission'. Note that this definition of unfreedom deviates from the commonly understood notion by allowing both strictly involuntary and seemingly voluntary origins of unfreedom ('does not possess the right or has yielded the right').

Slaves and serfs are transparently unfree in the Thorners' sense. But are slave owners and feudal lords themselves free, that is, have they no involuntary obligations to their dependants? The answer is by no means self-evident. A slave owner may scale down his slave-holdings through sale or transfer as he sees fit. But in conditions where slaves are economically redundant, this is not necessarily a choice that he and his fellows may be 'free' to exercise not merely because the market for slaves may have collapsed but also because non-market ways of ridding the slaves may be prohibited. Similarly, a lord may choose to keep out strangers who wish to enter his domain but he may not be free to dismiss his incumbent but redundant serfs (which may amount to letting them perish). And this for two reasons. For one, the lord or master may have to discount for the 'malice of the ploughmen' – individual reactions from his dependents which adversely affect production. For another, he may not be able to act with impunity in his own individual interest for fear of provoking collective action by his dependants. On the second count, if we ask what might be the institutional agency imposing restraints on such pre-capitalist masters, one possible answer is 'the state'. For medieval western Europe, the relevant agency was the manorial court or, more plausibly, the village community including the dependent class of serfs.[4] In short, while serf subordination and dependency were institutionalized, so were the means for restraining if not resisting feudal authority. The 'terms set by the master' (a critical clause in the Thorners' definition) are themselves not beyond the purview of laws or customs. It should be clear that the fact that *both* parties have involuntary obligations and are therefore unfree to quit the relationship does not undermine the above conception of unfree relationships.

Arguably, the caste system too contains unfree relations (as defined above) institutionalising an unequal division of labour and hierarchical dominance. Analogously with slavery and serfdom, to the extent that the caste system tied its members in relationships involving obligations not voluntarily chosen, those relationships are unfree notwithstanding their 'reciprocity'. Noting that the caste system was not enforced by any conventional politico-juridical means, Rudra [1994: 89] argued that 'the sanctions of the caste system and the traditions of the village society are surely as much extra-economic as any laws enforced with the help of the police'.[5]

Apart from slaves and serfs, offspring (or other kin) obliged to work off their parents' unpaid debts also do not meet the Thorners' criterion of freedom for, under the force of law or custom that allows debtor and creditor to treat the labour-power of the debtor's offspring as collateral, the offspring are not free to accept or reject the conditions offered by the employer-creditor. That is, the relationship is founded no less on a coercive social rule (one's offspring are one's chattel) than is slavery. While this conclusion holds when viewed from the side of *entry* into the relationship, servitude can presumably be ended, at least in principle, through repayment of the debt so that *exit* out of the relationship is not extra-economically constrained. In this connection, we should note that law or custom concerning bankruptcy is of no avail for if descendants' labour-power can and must be pledged, then obviously, so too can and must one's own labour-power. But indebtedness and associated labour services continue only so long as the debt has not been repaid (in one generation or more).[6] Hence, employment based on inherited debt is a peculiar, *hybrid* relationship: the labourer-debtor is politico-juridically coerced into it but not similarly coerced to remain in it. By the Thorners' definition, such a relationship is not free (because entry is coerced) but it is also not unfree (because exit is not coerced).

Recall that the Thorners' definition of unfreedom allowed the reverse of the above case, that is, it classifies an individual who has voluntarily yielded the right to refuse to work under the terms set by his master as unfree. An example of this is the historical phenomenon of famine slavery, the subjects of which voluntarily entered into what were from the outset known to be unfree relations, and from which they were then not permitted to exit. It has been widely reported in India and elsewhere (for example, Russia).[7] The famine slave relation can take two forms: one is the sale by parents/kinsfolk of their children into slavery and the other is the sale of a person by him/herself (an orphaned child offers him/herself as a slave). By the Thorners' definition, both instances of famine slavery are unfree relationships since exit is precluded. Yet, only the first form of famine slavery arises involuntarily on the part of the person sold into slavery.

Hybrid cases such as servitude to pay off an inherited debt fuse voluntary and involuntary elements. An obvious correction to remove these ambiguities or hybrids is to redefine unfreedom as follows: a relationship is *unfree* if entry into it is politico-juridically coerced *and/or* exit out of it is politico-juridically constrained.[8] Conversely, a relationship is *not unfree* if neither entry nor exit is subject to such external interference. It should be noted that while unfree relationships are typically 'personalized' and life-long, these features may also be present in free relationships.[9] For present purposes, we will retain the Thorners' definition of a 'free' relationship as one in which the parties are able to accept or reject the conditions offered.

Consider now a labour *market* where workers and employers are not politico-juridically unfree in the sense just defined, that is, they enter into employment contracts voluntarily and exit when the conditions of the contract have been met. There is of course no assurance that all workers will be fully employed. Involuntary unemployment may arise from the self-interest of employers (who may choose non-market-clearing wage rates because either the ability or the willingness of workers to work depends on the wage) or because of deficient effective demand or because of minimum wage requirements imposed by law or convention. Can the unemployed be categorized as 'free'? Following the Thorners' definition of a free labourer, there is no sense in which an unemployed worker's condition is the result of a voluntary choice made by him: he simply does not have the opportunity to accept or reject work conditions and wages offered by any employer. Although such a worker is not unfree, he cannot be classified as 'free' either.

Following the same conception, are workers who do find employment to be categorised as 'free'? Several considerations are germane to this issue. One arises from the distinction between labour and labour-power. Labour-power is not only produced for sale but such sale is essentially unproblematic, these being the chief characteristics of a commodity. The sphere of market transactions in labour-power is the 'Free Trade Vulgaris' realm of Freedom (the realm of the 'not unfree' in our definition). Labour, on the other hand, is the chief non-commodity under capitalism. The productive consumption of labour-power, as Marx argued, proceeds in a sphere outside the market.   More than a century later, mainstream economics has recognised this fundamental proposition of Marx *sans* his language. In the mainstream economist's terminology, employment contracts cannot normally be completely specified except at prohibitively high cost. This means that the full conditions of the contract are not known *ex ante*; they are realized only in the actual process of production. But the existence of unemployment makes the employment relationship asymmetric.[10] It enables the employer to enforce worker compliance with greater ease and less cost than otherwise. To that extent, unemployment compels the worker to submit to the employer's authority.[11] To that extent also, employed workers are not free to accept or reject the conditions that unemployment effectively allows employers to 'offer'. In practice of course workers would find it preferable to be employed rather than unemployed so that unemployment enables employers practically to make an offer that workers cannot refuse. Thus, employed workers too do not enjoy 'freedom' in the sense of the Thorners' definition. Although a proletarian, whether employed or unemployed, is not juridically unfree, he is not 'free' either. This dialectical composite of incommensurable categories expresses the fact that there are limits to the commoditisation of labour.

This is not all. If pre-capitalist masters of unfree workers were often themselves unfree, being subject to 'reciprocal' if asymmetric obligations and constraints, it can hardly be otherwise under capitalism. The unemployed cannot be wished away; their presence imposes social costs and/or requires social responses. Mechanisms to enforce property rights in the means of production must be adequate in the face of unemployment and/or the costs of supporting the unemployed must be met by some social device the burden of which will generally if partly rest on profits. Both entail appropriate 'non-economic' coercion of capitalists and of workers. Thus, if the private control of the means of production together with unemployment institutionalises the power of capital over labour in the 'private' sphere of the labour process, this so-called 'economic' coercion is itself simultaneously buttressed and restrained by the necessary politico-juridical coercive mechanisms of the state which sustain the 'public' sphere of the market where Freedom reigns.

Clearly, the concepts of unfree and free employment relations just analysed do not lie on a continuum. Whereas unfreedom pertains to the politico-juridical conditions under which an employment nexus arises or ceases, freedom has to do with the full range of conditions obtaining in and from employment. Steven Lukes has lucidly defined the broader distinction of which this separation between unfree and free labour is a part:

> According to standard liberal views, freedom is the absence of interference or (even more narrowly) coercion. ... Marxism is heir to a wider and richer view ... of *freedom as self-determination*. If, in general, freedom is the absence of restrictions upon options open to agents, one can say that the liberal tradition has tended to offer a very narrow construal of what these restrictions can be (often confining them to deliberate interferences), of what the relevant options are (often confining them to whatever agents in fact conceive or choose), and of agents (seen as separate individuals, pursuing their independently conceived ends, above all in the market-place). Marxism invokes wider notions of the relevant restrictions and options, and of human agency [*Lukes*, 1983: 146; emphasis added].

In applying the liberal standard of Freedom (= not unfreedom), we need to describe, at least implicitly, the choices that face the individuals considered. When we say that an employed proletarian is not politico-juridically forced into a wage employment relation, we seem to be ignoring the politico-juridical coercion that presumably sustains capitalist control of the means of production in the first place. Is this a real omission? If so, what is its warrant? Perhaps, the proletarian in question and all his fellows take the balance of power to be given. But this is not a natural, asocial imperative. Workers who routinely work to earn their rice may, during a famine, successfully confront the authorities and enable themselves to 'earn' their rice by breaking open the rice hoards of the rich. Perhaps, one could then argue that workers in *both* situations are making voluntary choices in the liberal sense.[12] But if even the most basic form of politico-juridical power of the state can, in principle, be rendered ineffective by collective action, then the very notion of politico-juridical coercion breaks down. Put differently, the liberal conception of Freedom fails to specify the variable or variables that enable 'non-economic' coercion to constrict choices in the one situation but not in the other. In other words still, the bifurcation of the totality of a situation facing an individual or a group into elements that are *givens* and others that are the objects of his or their choice is, to say the least, problematic. Such a bifurcation is dependent not only on prevalent 'material' conditions but also on how the agents themselves perceive the situation.[13] Yet, such a bifurcation is necessary for the liberal (Marxian) notion of Freedom (unfreedom) to apply.

The upshot is that no clear separation can be made between labour subject to 'non-economic' coercion versus labour subject exclusively to 'economic' coercion nor between 'unfree' and 'free' labour. On the other hand, we have argued that the distinction between unfree and not-unfree relationships, based on a concept of negative freedom, cannot be sustained either unless the agent's situation is historically (contingently) delimited. It is clear that Marx none the less insisted on employing this latter distinction which was a product of the bourgeois world. An obvious justification is that the distinction captures an important dimension of social-historical experience. More subtly, the distinction may be deployed, particularly when the precise sources of unfreedom are differentiated, as a tool of analysis to provide useful historical insights (or hindsights) relating to the modes of social and production control, the structure of material incentives and the patterns of surplus disposal.

III. EXCHANGES OF CREDIT FOR EMPLOYMENT

Questions concerning freedom versus bondage in rural labour relations in India, notably in relation to 'attached' labour, have aroused much controversy. Consider attached labourers who work exclusively for a particular employer at least as long as the contractually stipulated condition for attachment is met; this condition invariably is a debt. Such labourers are often at their employer-creditor's beck-and-call. Studies from the field report a range of specific characteristics in labour-tying arrangements due no doubt to differences among the regions/locales studied but possibly also because of variations in the questions posed. For example, the caste correlates and bases of class positions are scarcely the same across the various studies. Change over time may also account for some of the differences. In the case of Haryana, for example; the relative status of attached labourers appears to have changed. Whereas Bhalla [1976] found attached labourers in Haryana to be relatively 'privileged' being drawn mostly from marginal land-owning households rather than from the landless or the lowest castes, and to enjoy a higher standard of living than the latter, Brass's [1990] and Jodhka's [1994] studies a dozen years later found that attached labourers not only came from the same low castes as casual workers but also had lower incomes and experienced longer/harder work. Nor are the politico-juridical rules impinging on labour exchanges or production relations that the authors consider to be important identical across the studies.

Nevertheless two broadly different positions are discernible. Some scholars hold contemporary forms of attached labour to be 'free' and distinguishable from traditional forms of unfree tied labour arrangements or at least that contemporary labour-tying is based on the purely 'economic' compulsion of indebtedness.[14] Others see contemporary forms of labour attachment as containing or based on significant elements of unfreedom.[15]

An important strand of this debate, the exchange between Brass and Jodhka on the status of attached labour in Haryana that both scholars studied during the second half of the 1980s, bears scrutiny because it illustrates the main issues of interpretation in this literature.[16] The authors agree on some key features of contemporary forms of attached labour in Haryana: (1) attached labourers *enter* these arrangements voluntarily when they feel 'compelled' by the need for credit; (2) they work longer hours than debt-free unattached workers for the same or lower wage rates; (3) their higher rate of exploitation is due to their dependence on the employer for credit coupled with the restrictions he places on their ability to participate freely in the open labour market. Brass and Jodhka also agree that the traditional form of attachment (that neither author hesitates to call debt bondage) differs from modern forms in that it was (a) attachment to a single employer, long-lived and involved inheritance of the debt by offspring while in modern forms the first two features are frequently absent (on inheritance, Brass believes it applies to modern attached labourers while Jodhka does not); (b) based on the traditional authority of the dominant caste-class of creditor-employers and the ideology of clientelism both of which served to make it conflict-free in comparison with the modern forms which are based on contract and whose proneness to conflict arises precisely from the decline of traditional authority and ideology;[17] (c) a mode of guaranteeing regular subsistence requirements whereas modern attachment is not geared to providing such a guarantee (and often arises from contingent needs such as marriage, house construction or ill-health). Also, contemporary attached labourers resent being attached and essentially tolerate it as a necessary evil whereas traditional bonded workers viewed their bondage more positively as a source of subsistence security.

Their differences are largely interpretive and derive, as Brass recognises, from their divergent understandings about the nature of unfree labour; but even here, on one rather large matter, their interpretations too are concordant. They share the view that permanent (that is, not single-season casual) attached labourers are *unfree* (or unproletarian) although Jodhka is hesitant to go the full distance and equate their ties with debt bondage proper in view of what he calls counter-tendencies to unfreedom arising from the worker's ability to change employer-creditors, to find alternative non-agricultural employment and to 'assert' himself. Their real disagreement is twofold. First, Brass includes all workers – whether permanent or casual, migrants or locals – who have labour obligations arising from debt to their employers, among the *unfree*; Jodhka includes only permanent workers thus excluding casual and migrant workers. Second, whereas Brass sees an ongoing process of deproletarianisation and growing unfreedom (arising from the debt-based attachment of casual and migrant workers),[18] Jodhka finds the contrary to be true (arising from the aforementioned counter-tendencies and indicated by the declining significance of attached permanent labourers).

The fact, relevant to the criterion of unfreedom discussed earlier, appears to be that labourers in Haryana, whether casual or permanent, migrant or local, enter debt-based labour contracts voluntarily and are free, as per contract, to leave the employ of the creditor if and when they repay their debts. Neither entry into nor continuation in these modern-day attached labour relationships is otherwise politico-juridically coerced if debts and associated attached labour obligations are not transferred across generations or among kin. Given the latter *proviso*, then, these relationships must be categorised as not unfree.

Consideration of the heritability of debt, however, complicates somewhat this seemingly transparent picture of 'Freedom' of the attached labourers. The difficulty is both theoretical and empirical. While Jodhka claimed to find 'no case of intergenerational bondage or generational debt transfers' [1994: A-103] in his fieldwork, Brass [1990] found debt inheritance to be the rule. For example, in the not atypical Village B that Brass studied, 'When either an annual servant or a casual labourer died or became incapacitated without first having cleared his debts, these were transferred to his son, even if the latter had formed an economically independent household unit within the village' [*Brass*, 1990: 48]. Elsewhere, other kinsfolk may also be similarly attached.[19] It is significant too that such inheritance applies to permanent and casual workers alike. We are not in a position to adjudicate these contrary findings and so confine our remarks to the authors' interpretations alone.

While claiming that neither casual nor permanent attached workers inherited or transmitted debts, Jodhka nonetheless concludes that the permanent workers but only the permanent workers are unfree. As Brass noted, there is no consistent notion of unfreedom that could support this conclusion. On the other hand, while Brass found rules of heritability to be ubiquitous and concludes that both permanent and casual workers are unfree, heritability *per se* is not the theoretical basis of his conclusion.[20] But empirically too, heritability *per se* cannot support the view that all attached labourers are unfree. Note first that if the debts of an attached labourer are indeed inherited by his son, then, the son's employ with the creditor is involuntary but this does not make the father's relationship with the creditor unfree. Therefore, it is actual *inheritance*, not potential *heritability*, that would make for unfreedom.[21] Since it is no part of Brass's findings that all attached labourers in Haryana had inherited their debts, heritability cannot be the basis of his interpretation. Nevertheless, if inherited debt-based labour services are a marker of unfreedom as we have argued, then, labourers who have such an inherited burden are to be counted as unfree while those who do not should not be so counted. Given the ubiquity of heritability in Brass's sample villages, one may surmise that the actual inheritance of debt is still widespread in Haryana and, therefore, so too is unfreedom. Moreover, his evidence for heritability also supports Brass's general conclusion that bondage among attached labourers does not depend on whether they are casual or permanent.[22] At the same time, however, Brass' finding that many casual and migrant workers entered attached labour relationships on their own rather than through inheritance shows that debt-based attachment *per se* is not an unfree relationship. Finally, while this finding by itself suggests the hypothesis of deproletarianisation over time, the hypothesis can only be tested against direct evidence on the dynamics of debt and its inheritance.

The heritability of debt relations is also central to Rudra's [1987] position regarding their unfree status. But the reasoning by which he makes the connection is different in an instructive way. His argument is that a mere attached labourer secures loans from different creditor-employers and thereby remains independent of each of them. By contrast, inherited debt personalises the relation of credit dependence. This, as Brass points, is a *non sequitar*: inheritance does *not* establish a personalised or 'direct connection between the creditor and a person now engaged in repaying the loan' [1990: 39]. All the same, the issue is not whether inheritance establishes such a personalised relationship but whether it is involuntary. Our view is simply that inheritance of debt is not an act of volition but a consequence of a specific rule that forces the inheritance. This view is in conformity with that of Breman who identified servitude of the hali labourers of Gujarat during the first half of the present century with inherited debt or intergenerational attachment.[23] It is also notable that, contrary to Rudra's argument regarding the 'personalised' nature of inherited servitude, Breman found that hali labourers could move among employers as and when debts were transferred among the latter without ceasing to be unfree.

Recall that our definition of unfreedom requires entry into and/or remaining in a relationship to be involuntary. In the Thorners' definition, unfreedom includes voluntary entry into an unfree relationship so long as any change of status of the worker thereafter depends on the unilateral action of the master and not on anything that the borrower can himself do. As regards inherited debt-based attachment, we are unaware of any historical argument/evidence that repayment could not end such obligations. While indebtedness may be prolonged, it stands to reason that if purely economic circumstances can drive a person into (heritable) attachment, so can they redeem him from it. Hence, by the Thorners' definition, such a relationship is not *unambiguously* unfree.[24] On the other hand, by the same definition, attached labourers in Haryana are not unfree since, both in contract and in practice, they do get out of their relationships if and when they pay off their debts.

IV. PRODUCTION RELATIONS: ATTACHED LABOUR VS. CANONICAL CAPITALISM

We have argued that considering only the nature of *exchange* relations associated with attached labour does not clinch the issue of unfreedom since heritability plays a potentially critical role. Starting with a brief examination of Brass's substantive formulation, we now present a theoretical analysis of the nature of *production* relations associated with attached labour. This highlights the importance of (a) inequality between employers and poor rural labourers and (b) the absence of certain supportive/protective social institutions regulating property relations, which jointly structure labour-tying credit arrangements in rural India. In order to gain this focus, we shall ignore the heritability of debt as a factor.

While taking entry into attached labour relations to be a voluntary act (which implicitly sets aside the issue of heritability), Brass argues that 'it does not follow that the production relation which results will be correspondingly free in terms of the worker's capacity to re-enter the labour market' [*Brass*, 1990: 55]. Thus, it is not so much that the relation cannot be ended through debt repayment but that the worker's options are constrained in various ways *during* his tenure of attachment that makes it unfree. But of course restraints within the production relation are not unique to attached labourers. Classical proletarians too are subject to the employer's authority in the 'hidden abode of production'. The threat by the creditor-employer to recall the debt is different in form but not in substance from the threat by the boss to sack a worker.[25] This is not to say that there are no differences of context between debt-based attached labour and, say, the canonical case of industrial proletarians in advanced economies or in the advanced sectors of poor economies ('canonical capitalism' for short). But the differences do not pertain to Freedom; leaving Bentham aside, they have to do with Equality and with Property instead. To these differences we now turn.

To begin with, although unemployment is a *common* source of worker insecurity and employer power, the virtual absence of social security together with the breakdown of traditional forms of patronage makes for a higher order of insecurity among the rural poor. This insecurity is compounded by the fact that production and earnings have sharp seasonal rhythms. The paucity of assets implies a need for credit to get through the slack season or to meet lumpy expenditures.[26] What meager assets they may have are also generally unacceptable as collateral to formal lenders who ration them out of the queue: they cannot get formal loans because they cannot prove that they do not need them. On the other hand, material assets that may be acceptable to specialized informal lenders are usually severely undervalued as collateral and therefore provide insufficient funds: in this case, the effective interest rate is too high to make for borrower viability. This does not mean that poor borrowers are inherently unviable; only that rural proletarians not only have nothing to sell except their labour-power but also frequently have nothing to pledge except their labour-power.[27] Viability then depends on their finding individuals who value the borrowers' labour-power sufficiently to be willing and able to lend to them. Attached labour – creating a nexus between the income-earning and collateral potentials of the worker-borrower's labour-power – is often the only available resolution of the double bind in which the rural labourer finds himself.

The nature of this resolution must be understood in terms of the production relations it creates. The hypothesis we propose goes as follows. The poor borrower's only worthwhile collateral – his labour-power – may be secured only through its productive consumption, that is, by employing the worker. Ensuring that the labour earnings of the borrower are in fact available to service the debt may not be feasible except by employing him. Stated in less extreme terms, attachment serves to reduce the joint costs of enforcing the labour and credit transactions. In more transparent terms, this just means that the employer-lender's ability to control the labour-power of the worker-borrower is enhanced precisely because the credit and employment transactions are a linked source of profit for him. Given uncertainty in the borrower's earnings, attachment also avoids any conflict of interest over priority of claims of lender versus employer that would otherwise arise. Notwithstanding such 'economies' of control, the effective rate of interest may well be high relative to the rates that the well-to-do must pay.[28]

Both the enhanced control and the enhanced profit must show up in the labourer finding himself obliged in various ways to do the 'bidding' of the creditor-employer. Serving the lender on a beck-and-call basis or, being required to work for the lender alone during the peak season while being left to his own devices in the slack season are the principal manifestations of such control. But these are the contextual forms in which the authority of capital over labour is exercised in the 'hidden abode', not marks of an unfree relationship. The contracts which underpin them are not cemented by politico-juridical coercion. Hence, at least in respect of Freedom, there is nothing to distinguish attached labour from canonical wage-labour.

Beyond our account of labour-tying grounded in production relations, however, further consideration of exchange and property relations allow us to distinguish between rather than assimilate attached labour and classical wage-labour. Rural markets in labour, credit and land tend to be highly fragmented spatially. When this is coupled with the prevalent high levels of property inequality, many poor borrowers find themselves facing localised monopolies in both labour and credit. These are not necessarily literal monopolies with single providers of employment or credit; typically, lose coalitions of lenders or employers (or lender-employers) wield localised power. Under these conditions, borrower or lender does *not* enter 'into relation with the other, as with a simple owner of commodities, and they [do *not*] exchange equivalent for equivalent' [*Marx*, 1867: 176] for such equivalence can only be established by competitive exchange, not under monopoly. Note also that localised monopolies provide the basis for highly personalised and enduring employment-credit relationships although whether these forms will be realized will vary from one situation to another.[29] Whereas Freedom and Equality cohabit the textbook Eden of market exchange, there are good grounds to expect Freedom without Equality to prevail in the typical rural 'markets' where attached labour relations are found. At least in the present argument, Freedom is not contingent upon Equality.

The prevalence of monopolies is not the only or even the most important difference between the two contexts under comparison. The chief difference rather has to do with effective rules of custom or law relating to property rights. Specifically, this consists in the fact that a form of 'limited liability' applies even to individual borrowers in modern or advanced capitalist sectors: in the event of default, their future labour earnings are not required to be used to pay off creditors. In other words, they are free to seek legal protection from attachment. On the other hand, no such rule is effective at least for poor borrowers in rural India. It seems quite plausible that it is this difference that underlies the view common to both Brass and Jodhka that the employment of indebted workers (for a long duration only as Jodhka maintains or irrespective of duration as Brass would insist) amounts to an unfree relationship. Consider the treatment of default or bankruptcy in the two contexts.

Debts are normally secured by some combination of present collateral and future earnings or profits though the distinction between the two may be blurred because of uncertainty concerning future asset values. When expectations are broadly realised, debt servicing proceeds in normal fashion. But in the event of a default, custom, law or the contract itself must establish the priority of claims between debtor and creditor. In effect, this establishes property rights when default occurs. But how is priority to be pre-determined? First consider modern law applicable to defaults. When the debtor's current assets and income fall short of the debt service requirement, a 'default' naturally occurs. Although debtor and creditor may reach an agreement to reschedule payments or otherwise settle the matter, the debtor is nonetheless free to declare bankruptcy under cover of law which would allow him to start afresh. Creditors are then prevented from recovering their contractual dues from the borrower's future earnings. In effect, future earnings are reckoned on a different footing than the rest of the debtor's assets though both elements constitute his property. But this legal interference clearly amounts to an abridgment of the creditor's property right. It enables the borrower figuratively to flee his creditors.[30]

No such legal interference normally occurs in the rural Indian context. For poor labourer-borrowers, as we have seen, pledging future earnings is the normal way to obtain borrowed resources even for subsistence. Given this fact, it should be hardly surprising that future earnings can and routinely are 'attached' to servicing accumulated debt. Implicitly, 'default' occurs when the accumulated debt exceeds the expected earnings-inclusive repayment capacity of the debtor.[31] And default is not an event certain but always probabilistic. But if default is expected (in the probabilistic sense), then, far from extinguishing the attachment, this will typically tighten it (though, of course, the possibility that the debtor will be able in time to repay the debt cannot be ruled out).

Formally, one might say that poor rural debtors could resort to bankruptcy proceedings if they choose to. In practice, however, this will almost never eventuate. There is no dearth of explanations for this. Ignorance of the law or a belief that its workings would be too expensive and biased against the poor borrower probably suffice. The flip side of this coin is that the custom of settling one's debts conflicts with the law. As if these were not sufficient, it seems highly probable that even with effective bankruptcy laws a poor debtor wishing to protect his future 'credit' with his lender(s) would not flee under cover of the law. Localised monopoly power due to the spatial fragmentation of the rural credit market makes this response all but certain. Formally, however, similar considerations may also prompt defaulting borrowers in the canonical context to reach revised arrangements with their creditors rather than resort to bankruptcy.

The formal similarities should not be allowed to mask the substantive differences however. First, explicitly pledging one's labour-power against a loan for subsistence is as common in rural India as it is rare if not non-existent under more advanced capitalism. Over and above this, second, debtors under advanced capitalism are protected by law against the 'catastrophe' of finding one's future earnings in hock to lenders whereas such legal protection of poor rural labourers seems virtually unenforceable, contrary to custom or simply futile from the viewpoint of the would-be-'protected'.

In view of these significant contrasts and the widespread presumption that Freedom of contract is most developed under advanced capitalism, it is perhaps understandable that attached labour in rural India appears to be an instance of unfreedom. Our analysis shows that this appearance is deceptive. So long as politico-juridical constraints coercing one or both of the contracting parties are absent (specifically, this includes the intergenerational transfer of attachment), attached labour is not an unfree relation. While the proviso regarding inheritance is an important historical/empirical issue for our understanding of the past and the present of attached labour, our knowledge in this area remains limited. Apart from the contrasts with advanced capitalism in regard to both Equality and Property, interpretations of debt-based employment in rural India seem to have been strongly influenced also by what scholars have discovered in regard to the actual practice of the inheritance of debts.

V. CONCLUSION

The bases/manifestations of agrarian power and whether these lead to unfree employment (and land and credit) relations has been an important part of the debates on India's rural labour regime. The question remains a thorny one in part because empirically the 'freedom' of contracting is not always easily proved or disproved. In addition, however, unfreedom is liable to manifest itself in such customs as the inheritance of debt even when contractual freedom obtains. In this study, we have reconsidered concepts of unfree and free employment relations and, in that light, reopened a major strand of this debate, namely the status of attached labour in an agriculturally advanced region.

Whereas unfreedom pertains to the politico-juridical conditions under which an employment nexus arises or ceases, positive freedom or self-determination has to do with the full range of conditions obtaining in and from employment. In applying the liberal standard of Freedom (=not unfreedom), the choices that individuals confront must be described. Conventionally, this description implicitly bifurcates the totality of the individual's (or group's) situation into elements that are givens and others that are the objects of his or their choice. Thus, contractual Freedom counts but the politico-juridical constraints that sustain property and property-based power somehow do not. We have therefore maintained that no clear separation can be made between labour subject to 'non-economic' coercion versus labour subject exclusively to 'economic' coercion nor between 'unfree' and 'free' labour. On the other hand, we have argued that, unless the agent's situation is historically (contingently) delimited, the distinction between unfree and not-unfree relationships, based on a concept of negative freedom, cannot be sustained either. But when the basic relations of property and the balance of power are taken to be given, the distinction may be deployed, particularly when the precise sources of unfreedom are differentiated, as a tool of analysis to provide useful historical insights (or hindsights) relating to the modes of social and production control, the structure of material incentives and the patterns of surplus disposal.

With one critical exception, the field descriptions of attached labour in Haryana by Brass and Jodhka do not suggest that the associated contractual relations were reached under politico-juridical duress. Their differences are twofold. First, Brass includes all attached workers – whether permanent or casual, migrants or locals – among the *unfree*; Jodhka includes only permanent workers. Second, Brass finds an ongoing process of deproletarianisation (arising from the debt-based attachment of migrant workers) which Jodhka must deny given the first difference. We find persuasive Brass's argument that if attached labourers are unfree, this is not related to their being permanent and local workers as opposed to casual and migrant workers. Rather, the question must be determined only by reference to any constraints on their freedom to contract and recontract. Brass categorises them as unfree upon the consideration that the production relation in which they find themselves after entering a contract does so constrain them (for example, during the peak season). We argue that considering only the nature of *exchange* relations associated with attached labour does not clinch the issue of unfreedom since heritability plays a potentially critical role (this is the critical exception noted above). Since Brass reports field evidence for the late 1980s showing that the heritability of debt is ubiquitous, it seems plausible that unfreedom is widespread though its actual extent and change over time must be determined from direct evidence on the dynamics of debt and its inheritance.

Setting aside the heritability of debt, a closer examination of the production relations under attached labour shows that the power wielded by the creditor-employer over the debtor-worker is not qualitatively different from the similar power that bosses wields over workers under the 'canonical' forms of capitalism. While consideration of both exchange and production relations thus establishes symmetry between attached labour and capitalism as far as Freedom is concerned, this is not to say that there are no other differences between the two contexts. Indeed, in regard to contractual freedom, the formal symmetry could not be more complete. But the substantive differences remain highly significant.

First, the prevalence of fragmented markets and localized monopolies implies that even exchange relations in rural India tend not to be symmetric, that is, characterised by both Freedom *and* Equality which Marx so eloquently described as the hallmarks of the Eden of competitive market exchange. Second, explicitly pledging one's labour-power against a loan for subsistence is as common in rural India as it is rare if not non-existent under more advanced capitalism. Third, debtors under advanced capitalism are protected by law against the 'catastrophe' of finding one's future earnings in hock to lenders whereas such legal protection of poor rural labourers seems virtually unenforceable or contrary to custom or simply futile (or all of the above) from the viewpoint of the would-be-'protected'. These latter two differences show that the rules of property too are contextually differentiated. Apart from the contrasts with advanced capitalism in regard to both Equality and Property, interpretations of debt-based employment in rural India seem to have been strongly influenced also by what scholars have discovered in regard to the actual practice of the inheritance of debts. It is perhaps understandable, in view of these differences, that attached labour in rural India appears to be politico-juridically fettered.

NOTES

1. For an account of the proximate and ultimate determinants of post-independence agricultural performance, see Rao and Storm [1998].
2. 'Cross-sectionally' also, although the quantitative earnings of labour may be correlated with the qualitative features of labour/land/credit relations, these correlations are contextual rather than ubiquitous and predictable.
3. Among those who take such a position are Breman [1985], Bhalla [1976], Rudra [1987] and Jodhka [1994].
4. See Bloch [1966, 1931] and Postan [1972] on medieval France and Britain respectively.
5. However, an important question that arises from this view is that beliefs and traditions *chosen* voluntarily may not be plainly separable from those *enforced* by social sanctions including socialisation.
6. On the other hand, if the debt is so large that neither the original debtor nor his descendants has any chance of paying it off, then, the relationship will be perpetuated. The probability of the one or the other outcome will, in practice, vary with the context and will be related to the probability of contracting the 'original' debt.
7. I am grateful to Tom Brass for drawing my attention to this case and the issues it raises for alternative conceptions of unfreedom.
8. If abstract consistency alone were at issue, then we could alternatively define the hybrid cases to be *semi-unfree*. We reject this not merely because it may be inelegant but chiefly because it is inconsistent with the widely accepted liberal definition of contractual Freedom which, in the language of liberal economics, is defined as 'free entry and free exit'.
9. Thus, slaves may be sold many times in their lives. On the other hand, most employees of large Japanese corporations remain with them for life.
10. Even if full employment were to prevail in the labour market, the incompleteness of the labour contract still holds. This implies that neither capitalist nor worker is 'free' (since the effective conditions offered under the contract are not known in advance to either side) but there is no implication of asymmetry or symmetry between them.
11. This holds whether or not enforcement is the reason for the existence of unemployment in the first place.
12. When we say 'workers' here, we mean both individual workers and workers as a class. For the purpose of the argument just made, even the decision of individual workers to act concertedly with others may be considered to be a freely available choice.

13. One may of course seek to reduce the latter to the former and thus 'objectively' resolve the problem of bifurcation. But such a resolution elides rather than confront the conundrum between structure and agency.

14. See Breman [1974, 1985], Bhalla [1976] and Rudra [1987].

15. See Brass [1990], Harris [1992], Lerche [1995], Ramachandran [1990], Srivastava [1989], and Thorner and Thorner [1962].

16. Brass [1995, 1996a and 1996b] and Jodhka [1994, 1995 and 1996].

17. This was the primary reason why even though many attached labourers remained in that state for many years (in some cases approaching an entire life time), a typical attached labourer did not remain with a single creditor-employer for any appreciable length of time.

18. 'Deproletarianisation refers to a process of workforce restructuring that involves introducing or reintroducing unfree relations, either by replacing free workers with unfree equivalents or by converting the former into the latter' [Brass, 1995: 697].

19. The term 'heritability' employed in this study is short-hand for both inter-generational transference and transference to other kinsfolk.

20. Brass's rejection of heritability as the test of unfreedom of attached labourers is captured by the following statement: 'the extension of unfreedom from permanent to casual labour, which corresponds to a shift in the immobilising function of debt from a continuous and intergenerational basis to a more period-and-context-specific basis' is an instance of deproletarianisation [Brass, 1995: 697].

21. This is a conclusion of general interest to both historical and contemporary instances of heritability of debt especially since *heritability per se* has been widely taken to be a mark of unfreedom.

22. Brass' empirical findings on the heritability of debts are therefore highly significant for his conclusions. It should be noted that documenting heritability empirically cannot be an easy exercise. No general or uniform picture seems to be available on this issue. Lerche [1995], like Brass in Haryana, reports heritability in eastern Uttar Pradesh. But Breman [1985] concluded that intergenerational transfer of debt bondage has disappeared in south Gujarat.

23. See Breman [1974, 1985]. Breman's central argument is that bondage disappeared along with the custom of inheriting debt-based obligations.

24. Note that the heritability of debt does not imply the perpetuity of debt though this is often taken to be true.

25. Such authority, apart from its utility in production, may also be converted into political influence in both contexts. See Brass (1996a:239) on this point.

26. 'Subsistence' contains 'historical and moral components' no less for the low-caste landless proletarian of rural India than for the urban proletarians of Marx's time. Hence, there is no amoral basis for drawing a distinction between the necessary and discretionary elements in subsistence or consumption loans. Note also that subsistence reproduces the worker and is a necessary cost of production. Hence, another popular distinction – between 'unproductive' consumption loans and direct production loans – has no foundation.

27. See Bhaduri [1977] on the problem of collateral undervaluation and its influence on interest rate determination. The connection between undervaluation, interest rate fixation and borrower viability is developed in Rao [1980].

28. For a formal elaboration of this argument in the context of sharecropping as the mode of organizing and paying for labour, see Rao [1987].

29. See Rao [1988] for an analysis of market fragmentation that helps explain the localization of labour, credit and land relations and the exercise of monopoly power in such relations.

30. The fact that the law also imposes certain restrictions on the ex-bankrupt individual's reentry into the credit market does not detract from the present argument.

31. Under the assumption that debts are not heritable, the period over which such capacity is reckoned is the debtor's own lifetime. Note also that default occurs if there are unpaid debts when an attached labourer dies or is unable to continue working due to illness or age. The lender may be expected to factor this into his decisions.

REFERENCES

Bhaduri, Amit, 1977, 'On the Formation of Usurious Interest Rates in Backward Agriculture', *Cambridge Journal of Economics*, Vol.1, pp.341–52.

Bhalla, Sheila, 1976, 'New Relations of Production in Haryana Agriculture', *Economic and Political Weekly*, 11.

Bloch, Marc, 1966[1931], *French Rural History: An Essay on Its Basic Characteristics*, Berkeley, CA: University of California Press.

Brass, Tom, 1990, 'Class Struggle and Deproletarianisation of Agricultural Labour in Haryana (India)', *The Journal of Peasant Studies*, Vol.18, No.1, pp.36–67.

Brass, Tom, 1995, 'Unfree Labour and Agrarian Change: A Different View', *Economic and Political Weekly*, 30, pp.697–9.

Brass, Tom, 1996a, 'Yet More on Agrarian Change and Unfree Labour', *Economic and Political Weekly*, 31, pp.237–40.

Brass, Tom, 1996b, 'Misinterpreting Unfree Labour in Contemporary Haryana', *Economic and Political Weekly*, 31, pp.2362–4.

Breman, Jan, 1974, *Patronage and Exploitation. Changing Agrarian Relations in South Gujarat, India*, Berkeley, CA: University of California Press.

Breman, Jan, 1985, *Of Peasants, Migrants and Paupers: Rural Labour Circulation and Capitalist Production in West India*, Delhi: Oxford University Press.

Harris, John, 1992, 'Does the 'Depressor' Still Work? Agrarian Structure and Development in India: A Review of Evidence and Argument', *The Journal of Peasant Studies*, Vol.19, No.2, pp.189–227.

Jodhka, Surinder S., 1994, 'Agrarian Changes and Attached Labour: Emerging Patterns in Haryana Agriculture', *Economic and Political Weekly*, Vol.29, pp.A102–6.

Jodhka, Surinder S., 1995, 'Agrarian Changes, Unfreedom and Attached Labour', *Economic and Political Weekly*, Vol.30, No.?, pp.2011–13.

Jodhka, Surinder S., 1996, 'Interpreting Attached Labour in Contemporary Haryana', *Economic and Political Weekly*, Vol.31, No.?, pp.1286–7.

Lerche, Jens, 1995, 'Is Bonded Labour a Bound Category? Reconceptualising Agrarian Conflict in India', *The Journal of Peasant Studies*, Vol.22, No.3, pp.484–515.

Lukes, Steven, 1983, 'Emancipation', entry in Tom Bottomore, Laurence Harris, V. G. Kiernan and Ralph Miliband (eds.), *A Dictionary of Marxist Thought*, Cambridge, MA: Harvard University Press.

Marx, Karl, 1967[1867], *Capital: A Critique of Political Economy*, Vol.1, New York: International Publishers.

Postan, M.M., 1972, *The Medieval Economy and Society*, Harmondsworth: Penguin.

Ramachandran, V.K., 1990, *Wage Labour and Unfreedom in Agriculture: An Indian Case Study*, Oxford: Oxford University Press.

Rao, J. Mohan, 1980, 'Interest Rates in Backward Agriculture', *Cambridge Journal of Economics*, Vol.4, pp.159–67.

Rao, J. Mohan, 1987, 'Productivity and Distribution under Cropsharing Tenancy', *World Development*, Vol.15, pp.1163–78.

Rao, J. Mohan, 1988, 'Fragmented Rural Labour Markets', *The Journal of Peasant Studies*, Vol.15, No.2, pp.238–57.

Rao, J. Mohan and Servaas Storm, 1998, 'Distribution and Growth in Indian Agriculture', in Terence J. Byres (ed.), *The Indian Economy: Major Debates since Independence*, Delhi: Oxford University Press.

Rudra, Ashok, 1987, 'Land Relations in Agriculture: A Study in Contrast', *Economic and Political Weekly*, 32.

Rudra, Ashok, 1994, 'Unfree Labour and Indian Agriculture', in Kaushik Basu (ed.), *Agrarian Questions*, Delhi: Oxford University Press.

Srivastava, Ravi, 1989, 'Interlinked Modes of Exploitation in Indian Agriculture: A Case Study', *The Journal of Peasant Studies*, Vol.16, No.4, pp.493–522.

Thorner, Daniel and Alice, 1962, *Land and Labour in India*, Bombay: Asia Publishing House.

Rural Labour in Uttar Pradesh: Emerging Features of Subsistence, Contradiction and Resistance

RAVI S. SRIVASTAVA

Studies on socio-political and economic changes in the large Northern Indian state of Uttar Pradesh have paid some attention to the changes in the scenario as a result of the growing ascendancy of the 'middle castes' and the vertical cleavages among the dominant elite.[1] Relatively little attention has been paid to the changing conditions of the low castes and the labouring classes who constitute a significant proportion among the poor. Since the rural poor in Uttar Pradesh are not overtly organised to any significant extent, it is not surprising that action on their behalf aiming at changing their condition has gone largely unnoticed.

It would be facile to suggest that such conflict or resistance has either been absent or is a new feature in the rural scene in Uttar Pradesh (UP). A number of careful studies carried out in the state in the 1950s documented the contradictions and struggles between the poor and dominant classes.[2] Recent studies of UP villages have also uncovered an arena of conflict and resistance in several parts of the state.[3] A careful gleaning of the evidence, both from our study as well as others suggests, however, that changes affecting the social, economic and political environment in which the poor are made to operate have added new dimensions and assertiveness to these classes in recent years.

The conflict between the dominant and the (hitherto) dependent classes has acquired different characteristics and intensity at different times and may range from issues relating to traditional rights (such as the *jajmani* system[4]) and issues of *izzat* (honour) to issues relating to land and the labour market, as well as mobilisations aimed at control of institutions at the local or supra-local levels. Even though the elements and structures of dominance

Ravi S. Srivastava, Department of Economics, University of Allahabad, India. This study arises out of a research project funded by the Indo-Dutch Project on Alternatives in Development (IDPAD). Assistance received for the Project is gratefully acknowledged. The author is also grateful to his research colleagues, Dr G.K. Lieten and Dr R.K. Khasnabis, to an anonymous IDPAD referee, and to the editors of *The Journal of Peasant Studies* for their help and comments.

demonstrate considerable resilience, the changes in the nature of dependence, contradictions and ensuing resistance analysed in this study have significant implications for the restructuring of labour relations within villages, and still wider ramifications for the political articulation of the labouring classes. The shifts in local as well as state politics can both be understood in terms of, and have implications for, these changes.

The study specially focuses on an important area of conflict – namely that centring on the agricultural labour market – and aims to delineate the extent to which labour market changes are embedded in a wider socio-economic and political dynamic – a point which is missed in orthodox analyses of the rural labour market.

It is based on a field study of six *gram panchayats*[5] carried out during 1993–95 in Muzaffarnagar, Rae Bareli and Jaunpur districts of Uttar Pradesh, which lie in the Western, Central and Eastern regions of the state respectively.[6] The location of the study areas is shown in the map given at the end.

The study draws on evidence from three sources: (1) a census survey of households which forms the basis of the results on distribution of land holdings and occupational structure and the relationship between caste and class; (2) a sample survey of households which form the basis of the results on tenancy and wage labour; (3) unstructured individual and group interviews with men and women in the *panchayats* (village councils).

ACCESS TO LAND

Land Ownership

The results on distribution of owned land, given in Tables 1 and 2, demonstrate the relationship between caste and land ownership in the study villages. The leading land owning groups in each of the panchayats continue to be members of castes which traditionally held superior (proprietary or sub-proprietary) rights in each of the areas: *Jats* in Muzaffarnagar, upper caste Hindus (*Brahmins* and *Thakurs*) in Jaunpur, and upper caste Hindus and Muslims in Rae Bareli.[7] But there are considerable inter-panchayat variations in the pattern of land ownership, partly induced by changes which have occurred in recent decades.

The Jats own nearly all the cultivable land (97.2 per cent) in *Siswa* and about four-fifths of land in *Newa* (both in Muzaffarnagar district). Brahmin land owners own more than three-quarters of the land in *Belapur* (Jaunpur district) while Brahmin and Thakur landowners together own two-thirds of land in neighbouring *Birpur*. Upper caste share in land ownership is smaller in the two Rae Bareli panchayats. Brahmin and Thakur landowners own

TABLE 1
PERCENTAGE OF LAND OWNED BY SOCIAL GROUPS WITHIN EACH
LAND-OWNERSHIP CATEGORY

Village and Caste Group	Land Ownership Group (in acres)									
	<0.5 acres		0.5–2.5 acres		2.5–7.5 acres		>7.5 acres		Total	
(1)	(2)	(3)	(4)	(5)	(6)	(7)	(8)	(9)	(10)	(11)
	% hh	% land owned	% hh	% land owned	% hh	% land owned	% hh	% land owned	% hh	% land owned
1. SISWA										
Upper	14.3	42.9	85.5	88.2	100.0	100.0	100.0	100.0	66.7	97.2
OBC	57.1	0.0	5.8	7.9	0.0	0.0	0.0	0.0	21.0	1.6
SC	28.6	57.1	8.7	3.9	0.0	0.0	0.0	0.0	12.4	1.2
Total	*100.0*	*100.0*	*100.0*	*100.0*	*100.0*	*100.0*	*100.0*	*100.0*	*100.0*	*100.0*
2. NEWA										
Upper	2.3	17.6	41.5	43.0	80.5	83.5	82.2	84.8	34.3	78.6
Muslim	32.3	23.5	36.2	34.6	14.6	12.3	11.1	9.6	27.1	13.8
OBC	23.7	11.8	14.9	15.9	4.1	3.8	6.7	5.6	16.1	5.9
SC	41.7	47.1	7.4	6.5	0.8	0.4	0.0	0.0	22.5	1.7
Total	*100.0*	*100.0*	*100.0*	*100.0*	*100.0*	*100.0*	*100.0*	*100.0*	*100.0*	*100.0*
3. JASRA										
Upper	0.0		2.6	2.8	14.5	14.5	33.3	31.2	4.3	11.1
Muslim	41.8	13.3	30.4	28.9	23.6	23.1	33.3	41.1	32.6	27.5
OBC	15.3	26.7	31.4	31.6	29.1	34.2	16.7	12.5	26.3	30.6
SC	42.9	60.0	35.6	36.7	32.7	28.1	16.7	15.2	36.9	30.9
Total	*100.0*	*100.0*	*100.0*	*100.0*	*100.0*	*100.0*	*100.0*	*100.0*	*100.0*	*100.0*
4. TEKA										
Upper	4.9	0.0	6.5	9.7	22.1	23.2	60.7	66.9	19.1	42.6
OBC	53.7	80.0	58.1	53.8	58.8	56.4	35.7	27.4	54.3	42.5
SC	41.5	20.0	35.5	36.6	19.1	20.4	3.6	5.7	26.6	14.9
Total	*100.0*	*100.0*	*100.0*	*100.0*	*100.0*	*100.0*	*100.0*	*100.0*	*100.0*	*100.0*
5. BIRPUR										
Upper	6.8	0.0	64.4	70.2	64.0	66.0	57.1	71.0	40.2	67.6
Muslim	6.8	0.0	0.0	0.0	0.0	0.0	0.0	0.0	2.8	0.0
OBC	36.5	52.6	26.0	21.5	12.0	16.1	42.9	29.0	29.1	22.8
SC	50.0	47.4	9.6	8.3	24.0	17.9	0.0	0.0	27.9	9.6
Total	*100.0*	*100.0*	*100.0*	*100.0*	*100.0*	*100.0*	*100.0*	*100.0*	*100.0*	*100.0*
6. BELAPUR										
Upper	5.0	0.0	50.0	52.4	77.4	81.1	94.7	95.9	43.2	77.8
Muslim	10.9	13.3	0.9	0.5	0.0	0.0	0.0	0.0	4.1	0.5
OBC	23.8	30.0	35.5	33.6	22.6	18.9	5.3	4.1	26.7	17.2
SC	60.4	56.7	13.6	13.5	0.0	0.0	0.0	0.0	26.0	4.5
Total	*100.0*	*100.0*	*100.0*	*100.0*	*100.0*	*100.0*	*100.0*	*100.0*	*100.0*	*100.0*

Source: Census survey of households.

TABLE 2
PERCENTAGE HOUSEHOLDS AND LAND OWNED ACCORDING
TO SOCIAL GROUP

Village and Caste Group	Land Ownership Group (in acres)									
	<0.5 acres		0.5–2.5 acres		2.5–7.5 acres		>7.5 acres		Total	
(1)	(2)	(3)	(4)	(5)	(6)	(7)	(8)	(9)	(10)	(11)
	% hh	% land owned	% hh	% land owned	% hh	% land owned	% hh	% land owned	% hh	% land owned
1. SISWA										
Upper	7.1	0.3	42.1	18.4	40.0	51.5	10.7	29.7	*100*	*100*
OBC	90.9	0.0	9.1	100.0	0.0	0.0	0.0	0.0	*100*	*100*
SC	76.9	33.3	23.1	66.7	0.0	0.0	0.0	0.0	*100*	*100*
Total	33.3	0.7	32.9	20.3	26.7	50.1	7.1	28.9	*100*	*100*
2. NEWA										
Upper	3.3	0.4	21.5	5.9	54.7	50.9	20.4	42.7	*100*	*100*
Muslim	60.1	2.9	23.8	26.8	12.6	42.8	3.5	27.6	*100*	*100*
OBC	74.1	3.4	16.5	28.8	5.9	30.5	3.5	37.3	*100*	*100*
SC	93.3	47.1	5.9	41.2	0.8	11.8	0.0	0.0	*100*	*100*
Total	50.4	1.7	17.8	10.7	23.3	48.0	8.5	39.6	*100*	*100*
3. JASRA										
Upper			33.3	10.8	53.3	57.7	13.3	31.5	*100*	*100*
Muslim	36.0	0.7	50.9	45.5	11.4	37.1	1.8	16.7	*100*	*100*
OBC	16.3	1.3	65.2	44.8	17.4	49.3	1.1	4.6	*100*	*100*
SC	32.6	2.9	52.7	51.5	14.0	40.1	0.8	5.5	*100*	*100*
Total	28.0	1.5	54.6	43.3	15.7	44.1	1.7	11.2	*100*	*100*
4. TEKA										
Upper	5.3	0.1	10.5	2.1	39.5	23.2	44.7	74.7	*100*	*100*
OBC	20.4	0.9	33.3	11.8	37.0	56.7	9.3	30.6	*100*	*100*
SC	32.1	0.7	41.5	22.8	24.5	58.4	1.9	18.1	*100*	*100*
Total	20.6	0.5	31.2	9.4	34.2	42.7	14.1	47.4	*100*	*100*
5. BIRPUR										
Upper	6.9	0.0	65.3	30.9	22.2	33.3	5.6	35.8	*100*	*100*
Muslim	100.0	0.0	0.0	0.0	0.0	0.0	0.0	0.0	*100*	*100*
OBC	51.9	4.4	36.5	27.2	5.8	25.0	5.8	43.4	*100*	*100*
SC	74.0	9.4	14.0	25.0	12.0	65.6	0.0	0.0	*100*	*100*
Total	41.3	1.9	40.8	28.7	14.0	35.3	3.9	34.1	*100*	*100*
6. BELAPUR										
Upper	4.0	0.1	43.7	14.0	38.1	43.6	14.3	42.4	*100*	*100*
Muslim	91.7	80.0	8.3	20.0	0.0	0.0	0.0	0.0	*100*	*100*
OBC	30.8	6.0	50.0	44.6	17.9	49.9	1.3	9.0	*100*	*100*
SC	80.3	10.6	19.7	17.6	0.0	0.0	0.0	0.0	*100*	*100*
Total	34.6	3.0	37.7	20.8	21.2	41.8	6.5	34.4	*100*	*100*

Source: Census survey of households.

42.6 per cent land in *Teka-Janwa*, a share matched by *Other Backward Castes* (OBCs), while in *Jasra* they now own only 11.1 per cent land. Some of the upper strata (*Ashraf*) Muslims are important landowners in *Jasra*, and have, indeed, displaced the upper caste Hindus from their erstwhile position of dominance.

Upper caste dominance appears more formidable when one examines their position as large, dominant landowners. Significantly, the share of upper castes in large holdings, given by Column 9 of Table 1, is invariably greater than their share in total land owned *in each of these villages*. This is clearly their key to a dominant position in land and labour markets. However, members of other low caste groups (non-upper caste Hindu or Muslim) also own large landholdings in some of the panchayats and their share in such holdings ranges from one-third to two-fifths in three of the panchayats (*Jasra*, *Teka* and *Birpur*).

Jasra is, indeed, quite an exception as each of the three major caste groups (Muslim, OBC and *Scheduled Castes*) own nearly equal share of land. However, this overstates lower caste control over land, since upper caste (Hindu and Muslim) landholders still own more than 70 per cent of large holdings and since the holdings of the lower castes are often of poorer quality with poorer access to irrigation. But the pattern of distribution of holdings is quite significant and imparts a degree of autonomy to land-owning members of these castes. Almost all groups have gained land at the expense of upper caste Hindus. A number of scheduled caste (SC) households have also received *pattas* (non-transferable land deeds for small plots of government land) of 3 to 5 bighas (1.6 to 3 acres) of government *usar* (alkaline) land, and nearly four-fifths have been able to claim possession of this land.

Upper caste landowners have lost some land to lower caste, mainly OBC cultivators, in all the panchayats surveyed in eastern and central Uttar Pradesh. A *Yadav* cultivator in Belapur told us that in that village the Brahmins have been slowly selling their land and renting out their trees to contractors, and in the process have lost some of their clout. This account was echoed in the other villages we surveyed in these regions. 'There was a time when *Yadavs* had to provide *begar* (unpaid labour). But gradually we have become stronger. Now we can stand up to the Brahmins. Some of them are selling their land. I, myself, have bought land from them at a rather high price.'

The imperfect correspondence between caste and landownership is brought out quite forcefully in Table 2 which shows the intra-caste group distribution of landownership. Even though upper caste households continue to dominate the landholding structure in several of the villages, a significant proportion of them are marginal cultivators owning less than 2.5

acres of land. In *Birpur*, more than 70 per cent upper caste cultivators own
less than 2.5 acres of land. Even in *Siswa*, where Jats monopolise ownership
of large landholdings, nearly half the Jat households own less than 2.5 acres
of land. On the other hand, while the proportion of medium to large
landowners is generally not large among OBCs and SCs, a little less than
half the OBC households and about one-quarter SC households are medium
or large cultivators in *Teka-Janwa*.

The scheduled caste households are at the base of the landowning
structure in most villages. Excluding the small Muslim populations in
Birpur and Belapur, the proportion of landlessness (measured here as
households owning less than 0.5 acres of land) is highest among scheduled
castes in four of the panchayats. But in two others (*Jasra* and *Siswa*),
landlessness is higher among Muslims and OBCs respectively.

Column 2 of Table 1 shows the share of each caste group among landless
households. SC, OBC and Muslim households comprise 85 per cent to 100
per cent of the landless households in these villages. The share of scheduled
castes among landless households ranges from 29 per cent in *Siswa* to 60
per cent in Bela. This share among the landless is higher than that for any
other caste group in five of the six panchayats. However, it is the non-
scheduled caste groups that form the majority of the landless households in
four out of the six panchayats.

The pattern of land ownership in the six panchayats leads to several
main conclusions. First, upper caste (inclusive of intermediate caste)
Hindus own a higher proportion of land compared to other major caste
groupings in five of the panchayats. Only in one panchayat is their share in
total land ownership distinctly lower than that of Muslims, OBCs or even
SCs, while in another, OBCs own nearly as much land as the upper castes.
Second, however, the upper and intermediate castes are still predominant
among the large landowners in all the gram panchayats studied, except one
where Muslims (also belonging to the upper caste) predominante among big
landowners. Together upper caste Hindus and Muslims still own between 67
to 100 per cent of the land in large holdings. Third, despite these results, the
traditional proprietary castes in the eastern and central UP panchayats have
been losing land whereas there is a small accretion of land holdings of the
OBCs, as well as the SCs, the latter mainly through government land
distribution programmes. Fourth, the proportion of landlessness or near-
landlessness is higher among scheduled castes than among any other caste
group in four of the panchayats. Scheduled caste households also constitute
the largest proportion of landless households in five panchayats.
Notwithstanding this, non-scheduled caste households form a majority of
landless households in four panchayats. Together, however, scheduled caste,
OBC and Muslim households comprise an overwhelming proportion of

land-poor households. Fifth, there is a varying degree of differentiation in land ownership among all castes, including the upper and intermediate castes – many of whom are marginal owners of land and some are virtually landless, the OBCs, and, to a lesser degree, even the SCs.

Landlease

The landlease market in the study areas has served to increase access to land of the primarily land-poor households from the lower castes to a limited extent. The traditional pattern of leasing is still common in the UP villages, with large/medium landowners leasing out land and landless/small landowners leasing in land (Figure 1). Moreover, scheduled castes and backward castes (in that order) predominate among the lessees, while upper/intermediate castes and Muslims are predominant among the lessors (Figure 2). However, the land poor have fairly limited access to land through leases in the study areas. Only about 16 per cent of the households lease in land, and the percentage of landless households leasing in some land is also nearly the same. The percentage of land leased to land owned varies from 1.5 per cent in *Siswa* to 23 per cent in *Teka-Janwa* (Table 3).[8] The nature of the lease market, their regional differences, and their implications are quite similar to those described in Srivastava [1989a, 1997].

In *Siswa*, in a few cases, landless tenants (belonging to the OBCs) have taken land on seasonal lease from the *Jat* land owners for paddy cultivation. Landowners provide all material inputs and appropriate four-fifths of the output as rent. The main sources of credit for the poor households are well-to-do cultivators or friends and relatives. Interest rates are generally four per cent per month, but range from two per cent to ten per cent monthly.

FIGURE 1
PERCENTAGE TO TOTAL AREA LEASED IN/OUT

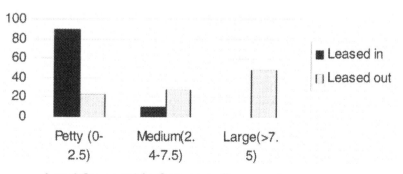

FIGURE 2

PERCENTAGE DISTRIBUTION OF LESSEES AND LESSORS BY SOCIAL GROUP

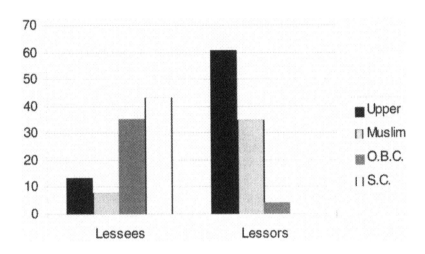

There are also a few cases of annual leases in *Newa* (where generally wheat-sugarcane is grown) on cash rents or crop share. Where annual leases and cash rents are involved, most of the lessors and lessees are middle/rich peasants from the intermediate castes (Jats). In the case of cash rents, the annual rent payable is about Rs 3,000 per acre. Seasonal leases involving paddy cultivation are quite common in *Newa*. Here the lessors (who are from the upper or intermediate castes or are Muslims) bear the entire cost of cultivation while the labour and field supervision is supplied by the tenant who receives one-sixth of the output as rent. The seasonal lessees are generally Muslims or SCs. The poorer households have access to the organised credit markets only through subsidised government credit schemes for asset creation for the rural poor such as the Integrated Rural Development Programme (IRDP). Rates of interest vary between two to four per cent monthly. While Muslim and OBC poor households take recourse to credit from the rich farmers, it is more uncommon to find poor SC households borrowing from rich farmers. Instead, if necessary, they rely on *mehajans* (trader-moneylenders) and 'friends and relatives'.

Many of the poor households in *Teka-Janwa*, mostly from the OBC cultivating castes and the SCs, lease in some land to add to their meagre holdings. Among the study *panchayats*, leasing is quite prominent in this *panchayat* – 23 per cent of the area was reported to be leased in (see Table 3). Leased area was 70 per cent of owned area for households owning less

TABLE 3
PERCENTAGE OF LAND LEASED TO CULTIVABLE LAND OWNED
(BY LAND OWNERSHIP CATEGORY)

Village	Land Ownership Category			
	Petty (0–2.5)	Middle (2.5–7.5)	Large (>7.5)	Total
1. Leased In				
Siswa	6.2	0.0	0.0	0.8
Newa	1.7	0.0	0.0	0.2
Jasra	18.8	1.9	0.0	8.2
Teka Janwa	69.9	4.6	0.0	23.0
Birpur	29.3	2.1	0.0	5.5
Belapur	16.7	4.6	0.0	7.6
Total	*25.6*	*1.6*	*0.0*	*5.7*
2. Leased Out				
Siswa	0.0	2.6	0.0	1.5
Newa	8.1	10.9	5.6	7.1
Jasra	9.2	0.0	30.8	11.0
Teka Janwa	6.3	0.0	0.0	1.9
Birpur	0.0	3.3	0.8	1.4
Belapur	2.8	0.0	0.0	1.0
Total	*5.3*	*3.8*	*4.9*	*4.6*

Source: Sample Survey.

than 2.5 acres of land and 53 per cent of the owned area in the case of the SC households. Upper caste – *Thakur* and *Brahmin* – households are the lessors in all cases. Sharecropping arrangements, mostly on a half-half share, are made in July (*Asadh*) and last till April (*Chait*). The labour cost of harvesting is deducted before the division of the crop and the by-product. Input costs (usually only fertiliser costs, or sometimes fertiliser as well as irrigation costs) are shared between the tenant and landlord. Cropping decisions are either taken jointly or only by the tenants.

Land-leases are also not uncommon in *Jasra* with about nine per cent of the operated area under lease. Land is rented out on a half-half crop-share basis and land owners and tenants share in the paid out costs (of irrigation and fertiliser). Seed loans are obtainable from the landowners at a 50 per cent interest, deductible from the harvest. Lessors belong to the upper castes (both Hindu and Muslim) but there is also a sprinkling of lessors (about one-sixth) from the OBCs. Lessees are mostly from the SCs (more than half) and the lower castes among Muslims (about one-fifth), but OBC and upper caste cultivators (one-fifth and one-tenth of all lessees) also lease in land.

There is not much land available for sharecropping in *Birpur* as resident landholders have increasingly taken to some form of self-cultivation. Only

5.5 per cent of owned land is reported to be under lease. For SCs, however, the area under lease is one-third of their owned area. The prevalent form of tenancy is the half-half share but there are some variations both in the pattern of output sharing (whether net or gross; with or without by-products), as well as the sharing in input costs. The lessors belong to the upper castes, and exceptionally to the OBCs. The lessees belong to the OBCs and SCs.

In *Belapur*, poor lower caste cultivators have also been leasing in land from the upper caste *Brahmin* proprietors. Such leasing, on a half-half share basis with sharing in the cost of fertiliser and irrigation, till recently was quite common. Poorer quality and distant plots of land were leased out or given as payment for labour services to SC households. The amount of land under tenancy has declined since 1993 due to incidents reported below in which landowners unilaterally repudiated tenancy agreements and did not allow sharecroppers to harvest the crop, and presently only about eight per cent of the area is reported to be under tenancy. The lessees belong to the SCs in about three-fifths of the cases, to the OBCs in over a quarter of the cases, and, in some exceptional cases, upper caste small cultivators have also leased in land (generally from non-resident relatives).

OCCUPATIONS AND CLASS STRUCTURE

As with landownership, our results regarding distribution of economically active males according to principal occupation confirm a broad correspondence between occupational structure and social status. This is evident from the results for all the villages taken together which are presented at the beginning of Table 4. The percentage of households reporting 'cultivation' as principal occupation is highest among upper and intermediate castes (61 per cent) and smallest among SCs (29 per cent). 'Regular wage employment' and 'Professional, salaried or large business' are also more significant among higher castes. The latter occupations denote not only higher non-agricultural incomes, but are also a source of political and social prestige and power in the rural areas. The OBCs and Muslim castes have an intermediate position in the occupational structure with a higher percentage of workers self-employed in petty trades or artisanal work compared to other castes. The percentage of males from these groups reporting cultivation as principal occupation is lower than that among upper castes, but higher than among SCs. The position of OBCs is also intermediate with respect to professions and salaried employment, but fewer Muslims are employed in the formal sector than scheduled castes. Scheduled caste males are at the base of the occupational structure. A higher proportion among them work as labourers compared to all other caste

TABLE 4
OCCUPATIONAL DISTRIBUTION OF MALE WORKFORCE
(BY PRINCIPAL OCCUPATION)

Village and Occupation Group	Land Ownership Group (in acres)									
	Upper and Intermediate Castes		Other Backward Castes		Muslims		Scheduled Castes		Total	
	Col.%	Row %	Col.%	Row %	Col.%	Row %	Col.%	Row %	Col.%	Row %
ALL VILLAGES										
Labour	6.0	8.1	29.0	25.3	41.3	16.6	55.9	50.1	28.4	*100.0*
Cultivation	61.2	48.4	49.7	25.4	46.7	11.0	29.0	15.2	48.5	*100.0*
Reg. Wage Empye.	8.5	46.2	8.3	28.9	5.0	8.1	4.7	16.8	7.1	*100.0*
Prof. or Business	20.9	63.0	9.6	18.6	4.1	3.7	7.3	14.7	12.7	*100.0*
Others	3.5	40.2	3.5	26.1	2.8	9.8	3.1	23.9	3.3	*100.0*
Total	100.0	38.4	100.0	24.8	100.0	11.4	100.0	25.4	100.0	*100.0*
1. SISWA										
Labour	3.4	11.9	52.0	46.4	–	–	70.	41.7	20.1	*100.0*
Cultivation	70.2	93.2	16.0	5.5	–	–	6.0	1.4	52.8	*100.0*
Reg. Wage Empye.	6.2	75.0	1.3	4.2	–	–	10.0	20.8	5.8	*100.0*
Prof. or Business	20.2	66.3	30.7	25.8	–	–	14.0	7.9	21.3	*100.0*
Total	100.0	70.0	100.0	18.0	–	–	100.0	12.0	100.0	*100.0*
2. NEWA										
Labour	3.6	4.0	54.5	19./1	43.2	25.4	83.3	51.4	37.5	*100.0*
Cultivation	63.8	58.9	38.2	11.2	48.5	23.8	12.0	6.2	45.1	*100.0*
Reg. Wage Empye.	8.0	66.0	4.9	12.8	4.4	19.1	0.5	2.1	5.0	*100.0*
Prof. or Business	24.4	83.3	1.6	1.8	3.9	7.0	4.2	7.9	12.2	*100.0*
Others	0.3	50.0	0.8	50.0	–	–	–	–	0.2	*100.0*
Total	100.0	41.6	100.0	13.2	100.0	22.1	100.0	23.1	100.0	*100.0*
3. JASRA										
Labour	9.5	1.8	8.3	10.6	37.7	35.4	33.0	52.2	25.1	*100.0*
Cultivation	42.9	3.5	69.4	39.4	45.3	18.9	54.2	38.2	56.4	*100.0*
Reg. Wage Empye.	4.8	3.1	12.5	56.3	4.7	15.6	4.5	25.0	7.1	*100.0*
Prof. or Business	42.9	20.9	9.7	32.6	4.7	11.6	8.4	34.9	9.6	*100.0*
Others					7.5	100.0			1.8	*100.0*
Total	100.0	4.7	100.0	32.0	100.0	23.6	100.0	39.8	100.0	*100.0*
4. TEKA-JANWA										
Labour	7.5	6.8	18.8	44.1	–	–	38.2	49.2	22.1	*100.0*
Cultivation	54.7	18.4	67.4	58.9	–	–	47.4	22.8	59.2	*100.0*
Reg. Wage Empye.	13.2	24.1	8.7	41.4	–	–	13.2	34.5	10.9	*100.0*
Prof. or Business	24.5	61.9	5.1	33.3	–	–	1.3	4.8	7.9	*100.0*
Total	100.0	19.9	100.0	51.7	–	–	100.0	28.5	100.0	*100.0*
5. BIRPUR										
Labour	0.8	3.3	10.4	23.3	–	–	29.3	73.3	11.4	*100.0*
Cultivation	63.6	60.2	49.3	25.8	–	–	24.0	14.1	48.5	*100.0*
Reg. Wage Empye.	0.8	100.0			–	–	–	–	0.4	*100.0*
Prof. or Business	7.4	33.3	7.5	18.5	–	–	17.3	48.1	10.2	*100.0*
Others	27.3	42.3	32.8	28.2	100.0	1.3	29.3	28.2	29.5	*100.0*
Total										
6. BELAPUR										
Labour	17.1	21.3	34.3	31.6	50.0	1.3	63.4	45.8	34.3	*100.0*
Cultivation	44.6	50.9	40.6	34.3			22.3	14.8	37.4	*100.0*
Reg. Wage Empye.	17.1	51.6	14.0	31.3	50.0	3.1	8.0	14.1	14.2	*100.0*
Prof. or Business	19.7	63.3	10.5	25.0	–	–	6.3	11.7	13.3	*100.0*
Others	1.6	75.0	0.7	25.0	–	–	–	–	0.9	*100.0*
Total	100.0	42.7	100.0	31.6	100.0	0.9	100.0	24.8	100.0	*100.0*

Note: Row % columns refer to between-caste distribution of male workforce according to each principal occupation. Col.% columns refer to within caste distribution of male workforce according to principal occupation.

Source: Census field survey.

groups, and they also have the lowest proportion of workers reporting 'cultivation' as main occupation.

Despite the broad correspondence noted above, each caste group shows considerable occupational diversification. It is quite important that a small percentage of lower castes have found a niche in salaried occupations, professions and businesses. On the other hand, half the workers reporting labour as principal occupation are not from the scheduled castes, and a small percentage of these (eight per cent) are from the upper castes.

Besides, there are also significant inter-regional and inter-village variations. The share of the upper and intermediate caste groups in professions, salaried jobs and businesses is between three-fifths and fourth-fifths in four of the panchayats (*Siswa, Newa, Teka* and *Belapur*). But in *Birpur*, their share is only about one-third, and in *Jasra* it is only one-fifth (the combined share of upper caste Hindus and Muslims is also about one-third). The share of OBCs in this occupational group is negligible in *Newa* but it varies from about one-fifth in *Birpur* to about one-third in *Teka*. The share of SCs in salaried employment is very significant in *Birpur* (48 per cent). A few SCs have acquired wealth and prosperity, mainly through a foothold in the salaried professions. These include a *Dhobi* (washerman caste) who has now retired as a *Kotwal* (police officer in charge of a district police station) and who plays an important role in village politics. Others include school teachers and a doctor. *Jasra panchayat* also has a high proportion of SCs (35 per cent) among salaried earners and professionals but the share is fairly low in other panchayats (generally below ten per cent).

Cultivation is the most significant occupation among upper castes in all panchayats and OBCs in the four *panchayats* in Eastern and Central regions. But in the two other *panchayats* in Western region, labour is the predominant occupation among OBCs. For scheduled castes, the predominant occupation is 'labour' in five panchayats, but cultivation is more important in the *Jasra panchayat*. The proportion of scheduled males reporting labour as their main occupation ranges from about two-fifths in *Teka, Birpur* and *Jasra* to over two-thirds in *Siswa*, three-quarters in *Belapur* and over four-fifths in *Newa*. Except in *Jasra*, a fairly small percentage report cultivation as their main occupation.

Despite some changes in the occupational structure, an overwhelming proportion of labourers (wage labour, *jajmani* labour, etc.) are from the SCs, OBCs and Muslims. Scheduled castes constitute over one-third to two-thirds of all labourers, while OBCs comprise over ten per cent to one-half of the labourers in each of the villages. In panchayats with a sizeable Muslim population, the Muslims also constitute a large chunk of labourers.

However, the limited process of economic modernisation has had some impact on the traditional locations of power. The evidence that we have is mixed but it does suggest that new vocations and jobs may have contributed to some dispersal of economic (and also as we shall see, political) concentration in the rural areas under study with important implications for rural dynamics.

Class and Caste

Since the evidence on landholdings and occupations provides confirmation both of a considerable degree of convergence and disjuncture between caste and economic status, we have examined the issue directly by constructing a synthetic index of 'class' extending Bharadwaj's fourfold classification [*Bharadwaj*, 1979: 280–81] to include diversification and non-agricultural sources.[9]

Figure 3 which presents the caste-wise distribution of households belonging to the 'dominant' class'shows a very high degree of overlap between high and intermediate castes and the dominant class in several of the panchayats. In two of the panchayats (*Siswa* and *Belapur*), nearly all the dominant class households belong to the higher castes. In another two panchayats (*Newa* and *Teka*) more than three-quarters of the dominant class households belong to these castes, the remaining being Ashraf (upper caste), Muslim and OBC households in *Newa*, and OBC and SC households in *Teka*. Higher caste Hindus constitute less than a third of the dominant class in *Jasra*, but together with Ashraf Muslims they comprise two-thirds of the class. Most of the remaining dominant families are OBCs. A clearer disjuncture between higher castes and the dominant class exists in *Birpur* where upper castes form half of the dominant class, while the remaining are (nearly equally) from OBC and SC families.

Figure 4 gives us the caste-wise dispersion of the 'dependent' class. The main feature here is the minuscule presence of the upper castes in this class. Nearly all are low caste-groups (SC, OBCs and lower caste Muslims). SCs comprise anywhere between one-third (*Siswa*) to three-fifths (*Birpur*) of this class. OBCs constitute between 16 per cent (*Jasra*) and 57 per cent (*Siswa*) of the dependent class. Muslims also comprise a quarter to one-third of this class in *Newa* and *Jasra*.

The caste–class picture in the panchayats shows that, at the upper end, there is a great deal of overlap between the higher castes and the dominant class in four of the *panchayats*. In the fifth *panchayat*, the upper caste group has two distinct entities (Muslim and Hindu). Only in one *panchayat* has a clearer disjuncture occurred despite the large weight of the upper castes in land ownership and hence also as agricultural employers. But caste and class coincide much less as far as the dependent class is concerned. All the low and middle castes are well represented among the dependent class, though the SCs form a slightly larger proportion of this class.

FIGURE 3
CASTE GROUP-WISE DISTRIBUTION OF 'DOMINANT' HOUSEHOLDS

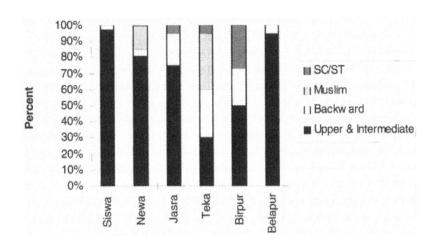

FIGURE 4
CASTE GROUP-WISE DISTRIBUTION OF 'DEPENDENT' HOUSEHOLDS

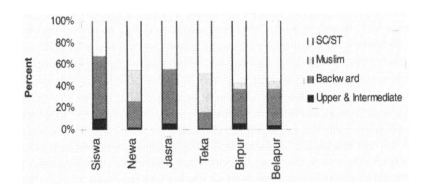

These results imply that high caste groups can be identified in the main with the dominant class and with the exploiting classes (even in *Birpur* where they form only half of the dominant class, they are dominant as landowners and agricultural employers); the dependent class is more multi-caste, although with a high SC proportion. It remains to be seen whether this opens the possibility of class action on common issues or whether the social composition of the dependent class places severe limits on collective action by this class.

FEATURES OF WAGE EMPLOYMENT

This section highlights the main features of the wage employment situation in the study areas. The basic features of wage employment are shown in Figure 5 which shows the distribution of casual labour days in agriculture, non-agriculture (local) and non-agriculture (migrant) employment. A significant result which emerges from these data is that agriculture provides a major share of casual wage employment (in terms of person days) only in two of the *panchayats* in Jaunpur and Rae Bareli. In all other *panchayats*, a major chunk of employment days originates in the non-agricultural sector, and, except in *Siswa*, most of this is through seasonal migration. Table 5 gives average days of employment in each activity. Opportunities of employment in agriculture are low and have declined. Agricultural employment is available for two to three months in a year. On the other hand, for those who work in the non-agricultural sector, the period of employment is longer, about four months. For seasonal migrants, the period is longer still – six to seven months.

Despite the developed agricultural base, and a labour intensive cropping pattern (wheat-paddy-sugar cane), wage employment in the agricultural sector is quite low in the two Muzaffarnagar panchayats and there is not enough year-round work for labourers in agriculture. The *Jat* cultivators in these villages are mainly self-cultivating and this also affects the demand for labour in agriculture. Employers, however, report a shortage of labour in the peak season when labour requirements for wheat harvesting and threshing are high, and when many labourers have migrated or are employed in small cane crushing and indigenous sugar manufacturing units called *kolhus*. Between the two villages, as shown earlier, *Newa* has a higher concentration of landholdings but also a larger proportion of landless labourers. Work on the fields is done both on casual and contract basis. Wage labourers reporting agricultural employment get 76 days of employment in *Siswa* and only 55 days in *Newa*. Moreover, the existing agricultural practices and cropping pattern also provide little scope for female employment. Female participation in agriculture has also declined

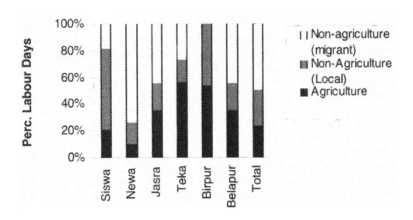

and noticeably, Jat women no longer work on the fields but have the major responsibility for looking after the livestock. Female wage employment in agriculture is only for 55 days on average in *Siswa* and 48 days in *Newa*.

The study areas in Rae Bareli district have witnessed an increase in cropping intensity since the last two decades. The advent of canal irrigation in the 1970s gave a fillip to agriculture in Salon *tehsil*, which is now an important potato growing area, but the canals have run dry since 1990. Even though land has been distributed to the rural poor in all three villages, their effective control over the distributed land varies from about nil in *Teka* to nearly 80 per cent in *Jasra*. This has resulted in some decline in landlessness, but, even so, a large proportion of households are land poor and dependent on wage labour. The average days of employment in agriculture in *Teka-Janwa* are low – only about one-and-a-half months a year. In *Jasra*, agriculture provides employment for a little under two months in the year which amounts to about 35 per cent of total casual wage employment. The period of employment is roughly the same for males and females, but Table 6 shows that only two-fifths of the agricultural labour force is female.

The land–man ratio in Jaunpur district is one of the poorest in the state, making for a large potential labour supply. Despite recent agricultural change in the region as a result of increased irrigation and multiple cropping, agricultural employment is again low and the structure of wage labour employment has shifted away from agriculture. The relative share of agricultural (local), non-agricultural and migrant employment days shows

TABLE 5

AVERAGE DAYS PER LABOURER IN DIFFERENT KINDS OF LABOUR

| Village | Gender | For All Labourers | | | For Labourers Reporting Wage-work | | | |
		Ag. Labour	Non-ag. Labour	Migrant Labour	Ag. Labour	Non-ag. Labour	Migrant Labour	Total Labour
Siswa	M	40	137	29	76	163	180	206
	F	55	–	90	55	–	180	145
	T	42	118	37	71	163	180	197
Newa	M	21	36	119	55	180	198	176
	F	11	6	183	48	100	206	200
	T	18	28	135	54	173	201	181
Jasra	M	32	31	67	52	85	186	130
	F	56	–	–	56	–	–	56
	T	38	22	48	53	85	186	108
Teka Janwa	M	34	14	21	43	54	128	69
	F	43	–	–	43	–	–	43
	T	36	11	17	43	54	128	64
Birpur	M	74	81	–	96	104	–	155
	F	34	–	–	34	–	–	34
	T	60	52		70	104	–	112
Belapur	M	33	31	69	62	68	180	134
	F	39	–	–	39	–	–	39
	T	35	20	45	50	68	180	100
Total	M	32	49	57				138
	F	36	2	66				104
	T	33	37	68	55	124	192	138

Source: Sample Survey.

the increasing importance of the latter two categories in total employment. Despite two or three agricultural crops a year, the demand for agricultural labour has not kept pace with supply. Mechanisation of certain operations, such as ploughing and threshing, the use of weed killers, etc. has reduced the demand for labour in several agricultural operations. With the subdivision of holdings among dominant landholders, many are finding it increasingly difficult to employ labourers on an annual basis and have begun to participate in certain forms of labour themselves. Efforts to side-step wage costs include proliferation of half-day employment assignments. Agricultural employment is available for a very few months only – just over two months a year on average for males, and even less than one-and-a-half months for females. As Table 6 demonstrates, the existing structure of employment implies that agriculture labour is no longer the mainstay for a number of labourers, with just over half the male labourers reporting taking up agricultural employment, even though female labourers are still largely employed in the agricultural sector.

TABLE 6
PERCENTAGE OF WAGE LABOURERS PARTICIPATING IN AGRICULTURAL
LABOUR, NON-AGRICULTURAL LABOUR AND MIGRANT LABOUR TO ALL
WAGE LABOURERS (BY GENDER)

Village	Ag. Labour		Non-Ag. Labour		Migrant Labour		All Labour	
	M	F	M	F	M	F	M	F
Siswa	45	14	72	–	14	69	86	14
Newa	29	6	15	1	45	22	75	25
Jasra	55	34	32	–	32	–	89	11
Teka Janwa	63	20	20	–	13	–	80	20
Birpur	39	36	20	–	–	–	64	36
Belapur	35	35	30	–	25	–	65	35

Note: Activity-wise percentages do not add up to 100 since labourers may participate in more
than one kind of labour. Figures have been rounded off to whole numbers.
Source: Sample Survey.

The agricultural labour force is mainly casual in each of the three areas. Attached labourers are more common in Muzaffarnagar, but the need for farm and domestic servants now is mainly fulfilled through in-migration of labourers from Bihar or Nepal. These labourers often receive very rough treatment at the hands of their *Jat* employers. They reside with their employers and are generally given an initial advance which is treated as a debt with interest should they decide to leave. In several cases, we found that the farm servants were asked to quit with unpaid wages over long periods of time.

There are very few attached labourers in Rae Bareli. Their incidence is higher in Jaunpur but their magnitude has clearly declined. They are employed by dominant *Brahmin* and *Thakur* landholders and work as ploughmen (*halwah*) in what Thorner and Thorner [1962: 22] have described as a beck and call relationship. While the labouring classes themselves look upon such relationships with disfavour, upper caste proprietary groups still try to enforce traditional labour relations and labour compliance with threats and sanctions.

Moti Lal Chamar (of Birpur) says that labourers are unwilling to attach themselves now. Earlier, employers used to give 2 *bigha* (1.25 acre) land and 1 seer of grain per day. But now they only give 5 *biswa* (0.25 *bigha*) land and some have stopped even this. Those cultivators who keep *halwah* (ploughmen) give them 5 *biswa* land to cultivate and 2 kg grain per day. Only those who cannot go out take up this work. The younger people go to the cities or work in the kilns. Some employers still give threats to either work for them or not use their pathways.

The diversification of employment opportunities no doubt gives the labourers some greater leeway. But it also suits the upper caste landowners who can cut back on their traditional obligations, which in any case they find it difficult to meet. At the same time, they can extract labour through modified traditional arrangements and through the threat of violence as the example given below shows:

> Rajji, wife of Ram Sunder Chamar, says that only if we work for them (the upper caste employers) they are happy, if we don't they say that they will cut off our feet. Earlier her husband used to work as a *halwah* at the former *Pradhan*'s (village council chairman) farm who did not give them any land, only wages. Now he is a *halwah* to Matru Brahmin who has given them a *bigha* on crop-share. They produce something from it for subsistence. Her son works in the kiln. 'If we work regularly for them then they say nothing but if we don't, then it will become impossible for us to move or sit around', she ways.

Non-agricultural Employment

While local non-agricultural wage work has undoubtedly gained importance in the study areas, and overall it is nearly equal in importance to agricultural employment, Figure 5 shows that it is sizeable only in *Siswa* where it provides 66 per cent of total employment days. Moreover, even though the number of labourers taking up employment in the non-agricultural sector is quite large, on average while about 70 per cent of labourers participate in the agricultural labour market, only about 30 per cent participate in the non-agricultural labour market and seasonal migration. The main difference, however, is in the small participation by females in non-agricultural wage work.

The sources of local non-agricultural employment are shown in Table 7. The principal source of non-agricultural employment is the construction sector (nearly half the labourers; predominantly in the Eastern and Central districts); followed by agricultural processing (more than one-third of the labourers, concentrated in sugar making in the two Muzaffarnagar *panchayats*). These are followed by the service and transport sector and 'other manufacturing'.

TABLE 7
SECTORAL DISTRIBUTION OF NON-AGRICULTURAL LABOURERS
(PERCENT TO TOTAL)

Village	Agricultural Processing	Other Manufacturing	Construction	Service, Transport	Total
1. Resident Labourers					
Siswa	64	–	36	–	100
Newa	79	–	14	7	100
Jasra	–	–	79	21	100
Teka Janwa	–	–	67	33	100
Birpur	–	29	43	28	100
Belapur	–	–	83	17	100
Total	36	3	48	13	100
2. Migrant Labourers					
Siswa	–	100	–	–	100
Newa	2	98	–	–	100
Jasra	–	7	21	72	100
Teka Janwa	–		25	75	100
Belapur	–		60	40	100
Total	1	71	9	19	100

Source: Sample Survey.

In *Siswa*, where non-agricultural employment is most significant, the two main avenues for such employment are *kolhus* and sugar mills which employ about two-thirds of local non-agricultural workers who are both skilled and unskilled. Labourers belonging to the *Jheenvar* caste specialise in sugar making and often work as skilled labourers. The remaining labourers find employment in the construction sector. Most of this employment is in the village or in rural areas in proximity to it. Non-agricultural employment yields about three-and-a-half months of employment to labourers compared to less than one-and-a-half months from agricultural work.

In *Newa* as well, most local non-agricultural employment is in *kolhus* or sugar mills which together employ about four-fifths of the labourers, while the remaining employment is in construction, transport or service industries. But the opening of the Titawi sugar complex nearby has adversely affected the *kolhu* industry which was the main source of employment. The sugar factory has not absorbed the labour force in adequate numbers and currently only about 15 per cent of *Newa's* male labourers find non-agricultural employment, less than half of those who are employed in agriculture.

Our study areas in Rae Bareli district experienced rapid growth in medium and large industries as a result of deliberate state intervention for about a decade and a half. But the growth of local industry has provided a negligible boost to non-agricultural employment in the sub-district (*tehsil*) headquarters at Salon and expectations of significant increases in non-agricultural employment have been entirely belied. In *Teka*, only one-fifth of the labourers reported having taken work in the non-agricultural sector, mainly in construction and in services or transport. Non-agricultural employment provided less than one-third the quantum of employment provided by agriculture.

The other *panchayat*, *Jasra*, is divided into several hamlets and is now sandwiched between a factory, which started in 1984, and a large agricultural facility which was established in 1989. The factory employs one person from *Jasra*, whereas the agricultural facility gives employment to a few persons on daily minimum wages. But some employment is available to labourers in public work programmes such as the *Jawahar Rozgar Yojana* (JRY), where, by all accounts, the minimum wages of Rs 23 are generally paid. Some opportunity of non-agricultural employment, mainly in the construction sector, is also available in Salon *tehsil* which is only a short distance away from *Jasra*. With all such possibilities added together, non-agricultural employment in the vicinity of the village provides employment to just over half as many labourers as those employed in agriculture. The major source of employment is in the construction sector. The average period of non-agricultural employment per labourer (about three months) is longer than in agriculture.

There is also very limited possibility of non-agricultural employment in the study region in Jaunpur, confined principally to the construction and transport sectors. Non-agricultural employment, principally in the construction sector, is equally meagre and affords over two months of employment to the labourers who take up such employment. With the construction of village approach roads, however, the labour market is now more integrated. Labourers now also travel to neighbouring villages for work in agriculture and in the government sponsored employment schemes.

Migration

One of the significant features of the rural labour market in the study areas is the significant mobility of the workforce to both nearby and distant destinations. Workers without any assets migrate to work as seasonal labourers, those with meagre means take up petty self-employment, while the more fortunate ones move to lucrative vocations or jobs. Many of the seasonal migrants are employed in the brick kilns, in services and transport, in the construction industry, or in processing industries.

Some of the basic features of wage labour migration, based on the sample household survey, are summarised in Figures 6, 7 and 8. More than two-thirds of the labour migrants are below 35 years of age and nearly three-fifths have been migrating for less than ten years. Typically also the

FIGURE 6
PERCENTAGE OF SEASONAL LABOUR MIGRANTS BY AGE

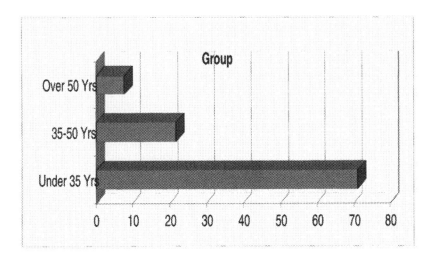

FIGURE 7
PERCENTAGE OF LABOUR MIGRANTS BY DESTINATION

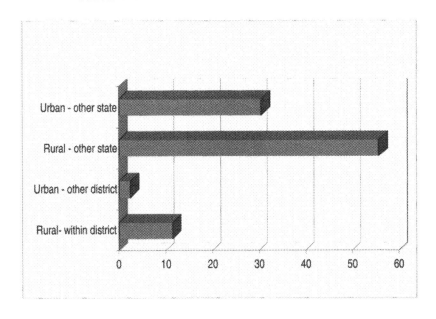

FIGURE 8
YEARS SINCE FIRST OUTMIGRATION OF SEASONAL LABOUR MIGRANTS

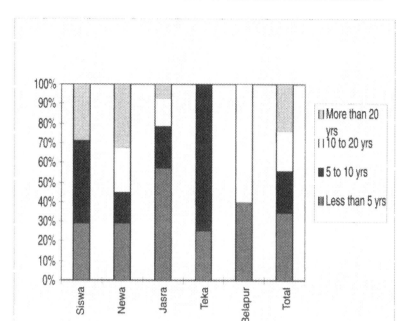

labour migration experienced in these villages is a long distance phenomenon. More than half of the migrants migrate to rural areas in other states; fewer than one-third go to urban areas in other states; about 10 per cent migrate to rural areas in neighbouring districts; and a very small number to urban areas in other districts.

Among the Muzaffarnagar villages, fewer labourers take recourse to migration in *Siswa*. About one-fifth of scheduled caste labourers do migrate, mostly to brick kilns in Haryana, and a few to work in *kolhus* in neighbouring districts. By comparison, a large number of labourers, particularly from the SCs, migrate from *Newa* to seek work in other areas in UP, Haryana or Punjab, mainly in brick kilns and to a lesser extent in *kolhus*. An estimated two-thirds of SC households migrate seasonally to work in brick kilns for six to nine months a year. About two-thirds of wage labourers in *Newa* report seasonal migration for six to seven months a year. Nearly all

TABLE 8
COMPOSITION OF WAGE LABOURERS BY SOCIAL GROUP AND GENDER

Village	Upper & Intermediate		OBC		Muslim		SC		Total	
	M	F	M	F	M	F	M	F	M	F
(1)	(2)	(3)	(4)	(5)	(6)	(7)	(8)	(9)	(2+4+ 6+8)	(3+5+ 7+9)
Siswa			41.5	3.4			44.8	10.3	86.3	13.7
Newa			16.4	2.7	17.8	1.4	41.2	20.5	75.4	24.6
Jasra			13.0	3.7	18.5	3.7	41.7	20.4	73.2	27.8
Semri	6.5		31.2	9.4			42.3	10.6	80.0	20.0
Belapur			25.0		10.0		40.0	20.0	80.0	20.0
Birpur			20.0	5.0			50.0	25.0	70.0	30.0
Total	0.8		21.2	4.7	9.7	1.7	42.4	19.5	74.1	25.9

Source: Sample Survey.

TABLE 9
PERCENTAGE OF WAGE LABOURERS PARTICIPATING IN AGRICULTURAL
LABOUR, NON-AGRICULTURAL LABOUR AND MIGRANT LABOUR TO ALL
WAGE LABOURERS (BY SOCIAL GROUP)

Village	Agricultural Labour			Non-agricultural Labour				Migrant Labour			
	OBC	SC	Muslim	Upper	OBC	SC	Muslim	Upper	OBC	SC	Muslim
Siswa	20.7	37.9	–	–	41.4	31.0	–	–	–	20.7	–
Newa	13.7	16.4	4.1	–	5.5	4.1	6.8	–	5.5	52.0	9.6
Jasra	5.5	60.0	5.5	–	3.6	21.8	0.0	–	3.6	10.9	10.9
Semri	20.0	63.3	–	6.3	10.0	6.7	–	3.3	6.7	3.3	–
Birpur	20.0	75.0	–	–	8.0	12.0	–	–	–	–	–
Belapur	15.0	50.0	5.0	–	5.0	25.0	–	–	20.0	5.0	–

Note: Percentages in columns add up to more than 100 since labourers may participate in more than one kind of labour.

Source: Sample Survey.

migrant employment was reported in the brick kilns. In terms of days of employment, 75 per cent of employment days came from seasonal migration. Migrant labourers in the village cite both economic and non-economic reasons – low agricultural employment, underpayment or delay in payment of wages, harassment, coercion and insecurity of women-folk in the source villages, as well as easy availability of credit and non-discriminatory wage payments in the destinations – as reasons for migration. Usually, the recruiters of the contractors collect them at the beginning of the brick-making season and pay them an advance (Rs 3,000 to 5,000) and provide transport to labourers who migrate to the kilns with their families during the winter and summer months. The practice of giving advances has stopped in the last two to three years but the outflow due to migration has not ebbed. The labourers migrating to these destinations work eight to 12 hours a day and receive piece rate wages which may bring the migrating household daily returns Rs 80 to 90.

In Rae Bareli, a large number of poor households have recourse to seasonal migration. About 13 per cent labourers in *Teka* reported having migrated to other areas for work. These labourers migrate to Salon, Rae Bareli and Lucknow, as well as to distant destinations like Ludhiana where they work as casual labourers, masons, rickshaw pullers, fruit vendors, etc. Some labourers migrate during the lean season (July–October), or for a longer spell which could last till March, the average period of migration being four months. About half the migrants are recent migrants (within five years).

In *Jasra*, members belonging to a number of poorer households from the lower castes and Muslim social groups migrate seasonally. Many of the seasonal migrants are itinerant or petty traders selling cloth, bangles, utensils or other merchandise or are wage-employed in the informal sector. Labour migrants are as significant in *Jasra* as those employed locally in the non-agricultural sector. Added to this is the fact that period of employment is longer for the seasonal migrant (six to seven months). As a result, migrant labour accounts for about two-fifths of total employment days in the village.

In the Jaunpur region, with the extremely limited possibilities of local non-agricultural employment and with the subdivision of land holdings, households have been increasingly having recourse to migration. The migration streams consist of educated villagers who find jobs in the urban formal sector; poor members belonging to all castes who have some assets are self-employed in the informal sector – many among them are itinerant traders, selling their wares in the urban or rural areas; the asset-less who migrate to seek wage employment in near-by villages, in proximate urban areas or even distant places – Jaunpur, Ahmedabad, Surat, Dhanbad – to be absorbed in the burgeoning informal sector. While the sample household survey did not include any labour migrants in *Birpur*, 25 per cent of labourers were seasonal migrants in *Belapur*, and labour migration contributed to over half the total employment days in the village.

Social Composition

We have seen in the preceding section that, using principal occupation as a criterion, rural labourers come mainly from the lower castes (SCs, other backward castes and low caste Muslims). Among these castes, SCs form about half the total number of labourers. Below we use the results of the sample survey on the social and gender characteristics of casual labourers, and also briefly describe the main subsistence strategies of the poorer groups.

As noted earlier, female employment in agriculture appears to have declined throughout and the participation of females from certain castes such as *Jats* (in Muzaffarnagar) and *Yadavs* (in eastern UP) in agricultural on-field work has declined quite significantly. Most women labourers are confined to agriculture where they constitute about two-fifths of the casual labourers. Outside the Western district, there are very few women labourers in non-agricultural employment. There are also a few female migrant labourers in the Western district where migration to the brickfields is a household phenomenon. The contribution of female labour in the upkeep of livestock is also very significant in all the study areas.

While Table 8 summarises the social composition of all wage labourers, Table 9 above gives the percentage of labourers participating in agricultural/non-agricultural work according to social groups. In all sample households, for all the study areas taken together, about 62 per cent of casual labourers come from the scheduled castes and about 26 per cent come from the other backward castes. Muslims contribute the remaining 12 per cent.

Compared to *Siswa*, where casual labourers are equally divided between scheduled castes and OBCs, in *Newa*, 62 per cent of labourers are from scheduled castes and nearly 19 per cent are from backward castes and Muslims each. However, an overwhelming proportion of scheduled caste households work as seasonal migrants rather than being employed in agriculture or local non-agricultural activities. While SC households in *Newa* rely principally on wage labour or to some extent on agricultural sideline activities such as dairying about (86 per cent report labour as the principal occupation), Muslim households in *Newa* are more differentiated. Some own land and rely on agricultural incomes, others are engaged in dairying, milk processing, cloth peddling, handloom weaving and petty trading. The poorer sections among them work as domestic servants or as agricultural labourers. Like the Muslims, the OBC households are also somewhat differentiated. While some among them pursue their traditional vocations, others own and run *kolhus*, often jointly. The poorer households eke out an existence by working in *kolhus* as skilled (*halwai*) or unskilled labour. Livestock rearing and the sale of milk are important sources of subsistence for several poor households. Even though livestock rearing adds to incomes, it does generate a significant structure of dependency. Since there are virtually no open-access grazing grounds, and purchased fodder is expensive, land-poor rearers depend on the collection of fodder from the fields of the farmers. This could be in the form of grass, as by-product in harvesting operations, or (in the important case of sugar cane) the harvesting wage.

In *Teka*, in the sample households, wage labourers in the village belonged either to the SCs (about 45 per cent were male SC and ten per cent female SC) or to the Other Backward Castes (42 male and three per cent female OBC). The location of a milk collection centre for the apex co-operative federation at *Teka* has boosted dairying and a number of poor households combine meagre cultivation with the sale of milk. The labour force in *Jasra* is widely dispersed among all the *purwas* (hamlets) and the lower/middle castes. Again, it is the two scheduled castes of *chamar* and *pasi* who form the core of the labour force. More than half the wage labourers originate from these castes. Members of these castes take up both agricultural and non-agricultural wage work, and also engage in cultivation. The lower Muslim castes (*Shah*) in *Jasra* hamlet are engaged in itinerant trade (fruit vendors, salt vendors, trade in waste products) and singers in bands. The *Nuts* of Dhoomanganj still follow their traditional occupation (acrobatics) but take up sundry employment as and when possible. The *Lohars* (ironsmiths) follow their traditional work but have stopped doing *jajmani* work Their implements are sold in the weekly market near Jasra or in other markets. The *Telis* of the hamlet *Telian ka purwa* are engaged in grain trading. They act as middlemen between farmers and merchants. The *Yadavs* are small and medium cultivators. The *Gaderias* have stopped tending sheep and work at the dairy or other urban centres. As in *Teka*, the *Nais* have stopped *jajmani* and prefer to open a shop or migrate to urban centres. The social composition of the female labour force is narrower than its male counterpart. Women belonging to the *Chamar*, *Pasi*, *Shah*, *Nut* and *Bhunjwa* castes work as labourers. But the *Yadavs* tend to emulate the practice of the higher castes and except in a few cases their womenfolk do not take up work on others' fields.

The poor SC households in *Birpur* form the main component of its casual labour force, as other sections increasingly have taken to petty self-employment or migrate to the urban informal sector. Three-quarters of wage labourers are from these castes. In neighbouring *Belapur*, the structure of local employment is similar to *Birpur*. Here, too, SCs (*Chamar* and *Pasi*) form the mainstay of the agricultural labour force (more than 75 per cent among agricultural labourers). The cultivating backward castes such as *Yadav*, *Pal* and *Kurmi* in the main have withdrawn from agricultural wage labour and rely on cultivation, remnants of their traditional occupation, some wage labour, or petty self-employment in the informal sector. Again, women from the OBCs have a very small presence in the casual labour force.

Essentially, the picture which emerges is that labourers may combine wage labour with a number of other subsistence strategies such as the rearing of livestock, marginal cultivation, and traditional services. Each of these differs in their implications for dependency on, and independence from, the dominant classes.

CONTRADICTIONS, RESISTANCE AND THE AGRARIAN LABOUR MARKET

There are still large disparities in the agricultural wages between the study regions. Wages in *Siswa* are nearly three times as high as the wages in *Teka*. Moreover, except for operations common to both genders, female wages in the eastern and central UP panchayats are about half that for females while there is no apparent disparity between male and female wages in Muzaffarnagar. However, wages in both Jaunpur and Rae Bareli have tended to rise in recent years, while wages in Muzaffarnagar remain high despite assertive agricultural employers.

The dominance of the Jats in the two western UP panchayats has been reinforced by their hold on the social and political institutions – both traditional as well as modern – their influence over state power, and the rise of the Bhartiya Kisan Union (BKU). The traditional panchayats are used both to buttress the authority of the dominant class, as well as a means of conflict resolution. Despite the adverse balance of power, the rural poor have attempted to resist their onslaught through their own caste panchayats, wider forms of organisation, and mobilisations, which have also resulted in strikes. Such action is rare in *Siswa* where both the balance of forces is extremely adverse to the labouring classes and where, on the other hand, the relations between the classes are less openly oppressive. But in *Newa*, a number of collective actions have been reported in recent years. In 1992, the labourers in *Newa* went on a strike demanding a higher wage. The Jats retaliated by threatening the SCs and their women folk with physical and sexual violence, and by banning their movement through the fields. The ban on the cutting of grass was enforced through a *panchayat* edict which imposed a fine of Rs 500 on those who defied the ban. This continued for a few days, at the end of which the labourers had to withdraw the strike. Negotiations on behalf of the principally *Chamar* and Muslim labourers were led by a backward caste (*Jogi*) petty cultivator and labourer after an informal meeting in which he was elected as their spokesperson. Even though the action did not immediately succeed, wages did eventually go up.

One of the underlying sources of tension between the *Jats* and the poorer classes is the treatment of the latter's women folk by the former. In one such incident during our field survey, two drunken *Jat* youths tried to molest an SC girl at pistol point. The SCs held a *panchayat* and raised the issue in the general *panchayat*, held at the Pradhan's house. After some discussion, the Pradhan agreed to conciliate and the SCs were mollified.

Several small cultivators, mainly from the *Jheenvar* OBC, hire and run small *kolhus* in Newa. In 1994, the *Jat* cultivators demanded that the *kolhu* owners be responsible for unloading and weighing the cane. A ban was imposed on supplying cane to the *kolhus* through the *panchayat* unless the farmers' demand was conceded. But since *kolhu* labourers were unwilling to do this work without extra payment, the owners would not concede to the *Jats'* demands. Eventually, the ban was lifted by the *Jat* cultivators who agreed to supply cane to the *kolhus* on pre-existing terms.

The labour market in *Newa* is severally segmented. The important segmentation is between (i) male and female labourers, with a very low participation rate of the latter; (ii) permanent farm servants and casual labour, the former being increasingly imported from other regions and states; (iii) between landless (and assetless) labourers who migrate out with their households and other labour households who still form part of the agricultural labour force. The latter may own some assets, and depend on dominant landholders not only for employment, but also for fodder and grass.

Out-migration from the village has added to the pressure on the agricultural labour market in several ways. The access to urban centres also has widened the political horizons of the labourers. They have become more united on all fronts – social, economic and political. They demand higher wages and smaller working hours, and want to do only specialised kinds of jobs. They will sit idle, refusing to work on the fields of *Jats*, in the certainty that when the season begins, the kiln contractor will arrive on the scene. The near-certainty of employment for six to eight months a year has increased their confidence in facing the *Jats'* challenge. It is not that these labourers are completely satisfied with the arduous working conditions at their destinations. They would be willing to stay and work in the village if there was greater certainty of employment along with a change in attitude of their *Jat* employers.

The higher wages and employment in the non-agricultural sector have led to demands and even strikes for higher wages by labourers in agriculture. Jat landholders, by virtue of their dominance as large landowners and their social cohesiveness, exercise monopsony power in the agrarian labour market. In the face of a wage demand by the labourers, they also retaliate through boycotts, threats, violence, harassment of women-folk, sanctions against labour households on the collection of grass or other agricultural by-products vital for the livestock economy, and sanction against the use of their fields or pathways for movement, for passage of bullocks, and for easing themselves. The actions are often sanctioned by village panchayats. Besides, dominant employers employ a variety of individual stratagems – advances, individual threats and inducements, 'half-day' work, seasonal crop-sharing arrangements – to side-step high wage costs and the higher wages which come to prevail. Even though labourers' strikes rarely succeed, the shortage of labourers at peak times (generally when the cutting of sugar cane and harvesting of wheat coincide) eventually necessitates higher wage offers by employers.

Muzaffarnagar

Daily wages in *Siswa* are 10 kg of grain – generally wheat – in kind or Rs 30 (lean season) to Rs 35 (peak season). Wheat harvesting is paid at the rate of 10 kg per day (both for males and females). *Jat* cultivators in *Siswa*, who own nearly all the cultivable land and take collective decisions regarding the conditions of employment of labourers, clearly enjoy monopsony power in the agricultural labour market. Hence, it is somewhat surprising that wages have risen to their present levels. The main reason for this is the competition for labour during the peak season (October to March) between the non-agricultural enterprises (*crushers*) and the farms. The non-agricultural demand for labour leads the determination of wages in this area. Wages for various types of unskilled labour in the crusher industry approximate around Rs 35 to Rs 40 per day, which are also prevailing wages in other non-agricultural and the agricultural sectors. Skilled work outside agriculture is remunerated at Rs 75–80 per day. Once the prevailing wages are determined, farmers face some degree of resistance towards lowering them during the lean season. However, even here, labourers do report attempts by some farmers to browbeat them into accepting low wages as well as attempts to side-step wage payments by using half-day wage rates.

Agricultural wages in *Newa* are somewhat lower than in *Siswa*, and are also slightly lower in relation to non-agricultural wages. Wage rates in agriculture vary between operations but general wage rates are Rs 30–35 per day, and employment is often by the half day.[10] Added to this is the *Jat* dominance and their frequent non-payment of wages. Labourers complain that employers sometimes take several days work and then delay payment for months. Over the years, the relations between employers and labourers have steadily deteriorated and complaints have increased. Employers complain that, despite rising wages, labourers have become lazy, preferring to work for fewer and more convenient hours. Relations between *Jat* employers and SC labourers in *Newa* are particularly at a low ebb. The latter, who are also significant out-migrants, are extremely reluctant to put up with the ways of their *Jat* employers. As a result, there is diminished contact between the two in the agricultural labour market. Whatever little land is leased out annually is only to poorer *Jats* or members of other communities; while SCs are seasonal lessees in only a small number of cases. The fact that the *Chamars* neither carry out their traditional work, nor prefer to work on the fields of the *Jats*, is a source of friction and harassment.

Rae Bareli

Overall, among the *panchayats* studied, *Teka-Janwa* exhibits the lowest agricultural wages. Agricultural wages in *Janwa* are Rs 8 for females and Rs 10 to 12 for males. In *Teka*, which is geographically isolated and dominated by Thakur landowners, wages are lower still – Rs 5 for women and Rs 8–10 for men. Half-day wages are also in vogue as in *Newa* and are an important means to help employers side-step prevalent daily wages. The spread of wages received by males reflects the different wages paid by large and small cultivators respectively. There are also operation-wise variations, but these are relatively unimportant to the overall picture. Dominant employers often pay a lower wage, as explained to us by a group of labourers:

> Casual labourers in the village have been getting Rs 10 per day. But farm labourers generally get only Rs 5 (for a half-day). The dominant cultivators won't even pay that. They pay anything they please – Rs 3–4. Women get Rs 5 for weeding or transplanting after a full day's work. For potato digging males get 8 kg and females get 4–5 kg, but dominant cultivators again pay less.

Several reasons might be suggested for the persistence of low wages in *Teka-Janwa*. Irrigation, particularly public irrigation has been quite unstable – in fact there has hardly been any water in the canals in recent years; agricultural productivity is low in *Janwa* and still lower in *Teka*; demand for labour has not kept pace with the increasing supply of labourers; the impact of public works on employment has been marginal – most labourers only report 15 to 20 days of employment in them.

Despite the low levels, wages have been under upward pressure notably in the last few years. Male and female labourers recall wage rates of Rs 2 and Rs 0.50 respectively only about 12 years ago. As stated above, these have now risen to Rs 10–12 for males and Rs 8 for females. This is suggestive of some increase in real wage rates over the period.

There are several real forces behind these changes which have resulted in the improved bargaining capacity of the labourers. The various government anti-poverty and land distribution programmes have reduced landlessness and assetlessness and put upward pressure on the supply price of labour. The village and the region also saw a surge in developmental activities during the period that the constituency was represented by former Prime Minister, Rajiv Gandhi. The Soochi minor canal; the electrification of the village, installation of a public tube-well and digging of several wells took place during this period. The contractors offered a wage of Rs 10 in 1989 when the prevailing wage rate was Rs 6. The subsequent reluctance of the labourers to work at the prevailing wage rate compelled the farmers to raise wages in the subsequent year to Rs 8. Contract work is also said to have affected the working hours. Employers report that earlier labourers started work at dawn, now they rarely report for work before 8 a.m. and their working hours have shrunk to merely six hours. They complain that labourers have become more assertive, vocal and demanding. They will not take up work under pressure and have to be requested to come to the fields to take up work. Whether they accept or not is entirely up to their discretion. Further, even though government programmes such as JRY have themselves created a minuscule amount of jobs in the rural areas, the wage offered under the schemes was higher than the prevailing wage rate, which, both employers and labourers concede, fuelled labourer expectations regarding wages.

Moreover, employment generating public works programmes such as the JRY implemented though the village councils (*panchayats*) have given a small boost to rural infrastructure such as village approach roads which has tended to make labour more mobile. The increased mobility of labourers to nearby as well as distant destinations has created more alternative opportunities for employment. The agricultural labourers of *Janwa* now take up work in *Jasra*, while labourers in *Teka* seek work in *Sayar*, where wages are higher. As reported earlier, a number of labourers migrate to urban destinations both within and outside the state, where wages are higher and there is smaller risk of remaining unemployed. Finally, there is also much greater political awareness amongst the labourers due to a number of separate factors (greater media exposure, improved communication and better political articulation, etc.).

According to employers in *Janwa*, demands for wage increases have been more persistent since 1988. Wages have risen from Rs 6 in 1988 to Rs 10–12 in 1994 in *Janwa*. The labourers in *Janwa* are not unionised and demands have not been raised in a very organised manner. Demands for higher wages are generally preceded by informal consultations among labourers and negotiations with employers have been carried out on an individual basis through implicit bargaining:

> A group of labourers from Janwa tell us that agricultural wages have risen to Rs 10–12 or Rs 10 with *Chabaina* (roasted grain and snacks) in the last two years, and this rise has been largely due to greater amount of public works both in and near the village. Wages for female labourers in rice transplanting have also risen. They explain that labourers had made a demand for higher wages, but individual employers initially resisted an increase saying that they would raise wages only if others also raised wages. But later on, when problems of securing labourers at the existing wages arose, wages were raised.

But at least on one occasion (when wages rose from Rs 8 to Rs 10), labourers report that they had gone on an open strike. Local SC labourers had been in the forefront of the strike and had enforced the strike by resisting the import of labour from other villages. *Pasi* women had been vocal and active in the strike.

Most people say that it is generally the small employers in *Janwa* who first concede labourers' demand and raise wages but this is not universal. Ram Lal Gupta, a small cultivator in *Janwa*, says that some years ago he took the first step in increasing wages. Another backward caste small cultivator from *Janwa* feels that small employers tend to raise wages first because they cannot get labourers easily. Large employers are able to resist because labourers are available to them more easily.

As stated earlier, wages in *Teka* are lower than in *Janwa*. While agricultural productivity is also lower in *Teka*, the primary reason depressing wages is a collusive exercise of extra-economic power by the large landed proprietors in the area, which the unorganised labourers are unable to resist. Labourers cite the example of a commercial farmer who had leased in land in *Teka* and paid a higher than prevailing wage. Because of this, he was forced to abandon farming by the *Thakur* landowners. A more glaring instance was reported by a group of SC labourers:

> We had worked in the JRY programme digging a well for about 20 days last year. Because of the insistence of *Thakurs* we were paid wages only at Rs 10 per day. The *Thakurs* said that they did not care what wages were paid to other labourers but *Teka* labourers would not be given anything higher than the prevailing wage. Ultimately the work had to stop halfway (because the contractors were obliged to pay legally stipulated wages), but they (the *Thakurs*) would not relent.

Wage increases are held back through threats and increase very slowly only after wage increases in other villages cause some shortage of labourers here. According to a backward caste labourer in *Teka*:

> Normally wages are Rs 12, but the dominant farmers such as the *Brahmins* and *Thakurs* pay only Rs 10. They say if you do not want to work on Rs 10, then leave the village and go away or if you come for grass or fodder to our fields we will thrash you. Where will you go to ease yourself. In *Janwa*, most people give Rs 12, but in *Teka* the *Thakurs* and *Brahmins* do not allow wages higher than Rs 10 to be paid.

In *Jasra*, agricultural wages have risen from Rs 6 in 1988–89 to Rs 12–15 in 1994 for male labourers and from Rs 4 to Rs 8 for female labourers. Even though the setting up of industries around *Jasra* has belied labourer expectations in terms of jobs, it has affected work attitudes and expectations. There is a consensus that recent demands for wage increases have to do with higher wages paid initially to casual labourers in the factory and the dairy, and since 1989, to wages paid in public works under the JRY, even though these account for a small proportion of labour days for the local labour force. In addition, the allotment of land holdings has also affected labour supply and may have pushed up reservation wages. The development of irrigated agriculture and potato cultivation may have had a favourable impact on demand for labour.

Wage demands were also raised in a more organised manner in *Jasra* and even resulted in a strike in 1992. Initially, the dominant Muslim landholders responded with a counter-boycott, but finally acceded to labourers' demands. Labourers point out that absentee farmers, commercial farmers or small farmers are the first to give in to labourer demand for higher wages. Since smaller cultivators often pay higher wages, while dominant cultivators pay lower (than prevailing) wages, capacity to pay is not a major deterrent. According to the *Pasi uppradhan* of *Jasra*: 'Some Muslims who are non-residents come home for short periods. They are then prepared to pay a higher wage to get work done quickly … On the other hand, there are cultivators who are more dominant ("*dabang*") like the *Pradhan* and they pay a wage which is lower than the going rate.'

The *Pradhan* of *Jasra* singles out the higher wages paid in the construction of the factory as the primary stimulus to rising wages:

> When the factory came up in 1984, its contractors paid a wage of Rs 6 to the labourers when the prevailing wage was Rs 3. Gradually the factory increased the wages and this caused the wages in the village to also rise. The Dairy came up in 1988–89. At that time the wages paid by it was Rs 13 while the wages in the village were Rs 8. When they started giving Rs 13, the village wages rose to Rs 10. Now the wages range from Rs 10 to Rs 15, the agricultural wages range from Rs 10 to Rs 12, while for non-agricultural work it is Rs 15.

Other respondents feel that, as in *Teka-Janwa*, the JRY and temporary shortage of labour has led to wage increases

> According to Shivkumari Pasi, among labourers working on the fields, women get Rs 8, men get Rs 12–15. If they seek work they get Rs 12 but if they are sought out because the employers comes and says, *Bhaiya* (brother), please come, it is important then they get Rs 15. Wages, she says, have increased due to JRY. Labourers have started demanding more after JRY started. Because of the dairy, people now know about the working hours. Labourers who went out

at 6 a.m. now go to work at 9 a.m. because they know that the farmers' need for them is greater.

Labourers cite a number of instances to show how the persistence of low wages comes from a collusive exercise of extra-economic power by the large landed proprietors in the area, which they are unable to resist. Certain large landed proprietors make lower than prevailing wage payments to which the labourers say they acquiesce because of the extra-economic power wielded by these landowners. Again, in a recent case similar to the one in Teka, an outside gentleman farmer near *Jasra* raised the wages of potato digging to Rs 15. This had repercussion for the general level of wages which tended to rise during the operation. But he was compelled to abandon farming after two years.

With greater alternative sources of livelihood, why do the poor still succumb to such coercion? One of the reasons, which was repeated in every gram panchayat, is that they need to use the fields of the dominant landowners – for movement, for easing themselves and for their cattle. The greater this need, the greater is the handle which the large landowners can exercise.

A *Pasi* labourer in *Jasra* put this in the following way:

> I live hemmed in by the fields of the *Thakur-Brahmins* and the Muslims. If I oppose them or ask them for a raise, they say don't you use our fields as well? If I tell them I use the public road, they say well make sure that you don't stray on to our fields. It is better not to run foul of them. These big landowners are able to use their better links to harass us if we dare oppose them.

The feudal clout of the dominant landholders is still very much in evidence in the region and there is some reason to believe that it has an impact on the general level of wages in the area. Even though Salon is a reserved legislative constituency, labourers who come mainly from the SCs have very limited bargaining power.[11] As discussed earlier, the clout of the dominant groups is the most in *Teka*, and in the main as well as adjoining hamlets of *Jasra*. Labourers in the dispersed hamlets of *Jasra* and those of *Janwa* have greater autonomy.

In *Jasra*, the clout of the *Pathans* is greatly felt and workers who are locationally disadvantaged are less prone to raise any demands. If they do raise demands, they may have to contend not only with their employers, but also with other elements of state power. According to a *Pasi* in *Sheetal purwa*:

> We (the SCs in this hamlet) cannot raise demands for wage increases because we live between the upper castes and the *Pathans*. Of course,

we no longer agree to perform *halwahi* and *begar*. But they still tell us 'Look I can't pay you more than this. You should make an exception for me'. Than this exception becomes the rule. Of course, their cajoling is backed by implicit threats. 'Don't you also use our paths and our fields?' If we remonstrate saying that we use the public pathways, they say, 'well then you shouldn't step off it'. Sometimes, we are abused. If we persist in being vocal, we could be implicated in framed up charges. The two of us worked on digging a well at a *Pathan*'s place. We were not paid a *paise*. When I remonstrated he told the police to give me a sound beating. I had to pay a heavy bribe to escape with my honour intact. This is the price we have to pay if we are vocal!

Wages are not low because they (the employers) cannot pay. It is because we are submissive (*Dabbu*). When JRY started, we asked for higher wages. Gradually wages have increased and are now Rs 15. For harvesting we get *Baraukha* (1/13 share) and some left-over grain (*Tari*). It is nothing for the work that we put in. For today's labour in harvesting and threshing *arhar* (pigeon-pea), my wife and I have barely got one kg *arhar*.

Even though economic demands are raised, the immediate cause of the conflict is often non-economic. These changes are also slowly propelling the former landed classes to undertake manual labour themselves. According to a lower caste Muslim woman in *Jasra*:

There is a lot of change now. Five years ago the *harijans*[12] made unity and said that they would not come for work. The *Khans* had misbehaved with a *harijan* that is why the labourers stopped work for nearly two years. The *Khans* did their own work but they were experiencing difficulty. Then the *Pradhan* went to them and asked the *Harijans* to restart work and assured them that the misbehaviour would not recur. It was only then that the *Harijan* labourers started to work again.

The low wages and the oppressive conditions should not obscure the fact that the socio-economic status and working conditions of the lower castes have undergone some improvement. As Basant *Chamar* of the hamlet *Senan ka Purwa* observed:

Fifty years ago we were not allowed to wear new clothes and we could not move freely. But now we can wear new clothes like you. We can sit on the cot along with you. Our working conditions, too, are better.

Ever since the factory has opened we wait for the factory whistle to start our work. Then we work up to 12 noon. After that the work starts at 3 or 4 p.m.

Certain other deep-rooted changes are also occurring in the former *jajmani* castes – *Nai* (barber), *Lohar* (ironsmith), *Bhangi* (scavenger), *Chamar* (skinner of animals/midwife). The *biradari* (caste) movements evident in Jaunpur and described below are also noticeable here. Members of these castes are exhorted by the biradari leaders to stop providing personalised or demeaning services and labour. While change continues to occur, its pace is slow and uneven.

Jaunpur

Agricultural wages in the region around *Birpur* were at their traditional level (*panch pao* or nearly 1.75 kg) till about five years ago. Since then, labourers have demanded higher wages and have also gone on strike on these demands. In the last two years, wage demands and strikes have led to wage increases in kind from 2 to 4 kg of grain. Labourers went on strike in two phases. First, demandig a wage increase from 2 to 3 kg, and then two years later, from 3 to 4 kg. Even though the dominant landholders have resisted these demands, they have not succeeded in holding back the tide. In the first phase employers retaliated using violence and threats of sanctions against labourers on using their fields for gathering, movement or for easing themselves. When the strike continued, employers agreed to raise wages. According to a *harijan* women labourer: 'The labourers went on strike for higher wages. They were beaten up by *Thakurs* and *Brahmins*, harassed and prevented from using their fields. But when their work started suffering, they had to increase wages. Wages were earlier 2 kg, but in 4 years time they have increased to 4 kg.'

A similar sequence of events followed in the second phase but this time without any actual physical violence being inflicted on the labourers. Last *Asadh* (July) labourers took a decision not to work for less than 4 kg per day. Finally, employers and labourers came to a common agreement.

Both labourers and employers cite two explicit reasons for such demands being raised: the payment of higher wages, fixed at the government minimum, in the public work programmes executed under JRY; and the spread, albeit limited, of garden cultivation, in which trader-farmers have made higher wage offers in order to attract labourers from neighbouring villages at the peak period. The existence of alternative livelihood sources through migration which has provided greater staying power during strikes is also cited as a reason.

Upper caste landholders say that there is a marked change in the labourers' attitude and even though their own labour participation is increasing, they depend on hired labour and cannot hold out for long against a strike. Prabhavati Singh, a *Thakur* woman, echoed the sentiments of several of the upper caste respondents whom we interviewed:

> Just as the salaried people go on strike and stop going to offices, the labourers also strike work and stop coming to us. They decided among themselves that they will not come for work till wages are increased. When people started experiencing difficulty in completing work, wages were raised. Some *Thakurs* and *Brahmins* cannot do without labourers. So wages had to be raised. This change in the labourers' attitude has taken place in 4 years.

General agricultural wages in *Belapur* are Rs 20 per day or 3–4 kg in kind. Ploughmen (halwah) are paid 2 kg on land allotment, and 3 kg without such allotment. The *Brahmins* are traditionally non-cultivating and their control over traditional forms of labour allowed them to minimise both supervision and labour costs. Labourers, however, can now, in principle, seek alternative employment in other villages, with higher prevailing wage rates, and through migration, and tend to resist forms of employment which curtail personal freedom. A backward caste labourer highlights this last factor as the principal reason putting upward pressure on agricultural wages in *Belapur*:

> In the neighbouring villages of Pratapgarh, wages were raised first. In these villages, labourers do not demand higher wages but on the contrary farmers call them to work on higher wages. There are only a few cultivators in these villages who start giving higher wages but then the other farmers are compelled to pay the same wages because labourers are no longer available at the lower wages. The farmers who raise wages first also do not do it purely for altruistic reasons. They also have problems. They grow pan leaves, vegetables, etc. These crops demand sowing, weeding, irrigation on time: then only does a good crop come. To get many labourers at the prevailing wage all at the same time is difficult so they resort to offering a higher wage. Then, of course, they even get labourers from neighbouring villages. Because prices are increasing, these trade farmers (*Maurya, Kushwaha,* and *Bari*) do not find it difficult to raise wages. Labourers are also happy. After hearing all this the labourers in *Birpur* and Belapur had started demanding higher wages. The farmers in *Birpur* had started paying the higher wages but the farmers in *Belapur* had initially resisted a wage increase.

There has thus been some simmering tension between *Brahmins* and SC for some years over labour issues. The locational segmentation of the labourers divides them into two groups: those whose home sites are hemmed in on all sides by the employers or their fields, and those who have independent access to their homes/fields. It is the second group of labourers which has been in the forefront of the labourers' struggle and which has also borne the brunt of the retaliation. The employers initially retaliated with the herding of their cattle on the labourers' fields, cutting of the latter's access to their fields, and threat of other sanctions. When the labourers persisted with their demand, a separate issue provided the (*Brahmin*) employers with grounds for a violent retaliation against the (SC) labourers belonging to the most recalcitrant basti (hamlet).

The trouble erupted on 2 March 1993, the day after the festival of *Holi*, when the *Brahmins* of *Belapur* attacked the *Harijan basti* with cries of *Jai Shri Ram* (Victory to Lord Rama).[13] Nearly all the *Brahmin* males in *Belapur* collected and destroyed the tiles of the houses, beat up the *harijans*, and wounded their animals with spears. Their domestic assets and rickshaws (means of livelihood) were smashed and thrown into wells. In the dispute, the *harijans* received most of the injuries, but some *Brahmins* were also injured as *harijans* threw brickbats in self-defence. One of the *harijans* died of his injuries after six weeks. Apart from three families, all other *Brahmin* families participated in the incident.

The immediate cause of the dispute was that on the day of the *Holi* festival, the *harijan* youths were playing with colours and playing their band near Babuganj bazaar. A *Brahmin* elder who was passing asked them to play away from the road. The *harijan* youths, who were possibly drunk, are said to have spoken rudely to him and to have abused him. *Panditji* went back to the village and told others about the incident. The Brahmins felt very upset about the fact that the *harijans* had become so uppish that they had now started abusing the *Brahmins*: 'Till now they had stopped working for us and were having a good time share-cropping our land, now they will abuse us as well! They must be taught a lesson.' Some *Brahmins* went to the place where the *harijan* youths were playing *holi* and there was a heated exchange between them. As this news spread in the village, the *Brahmins* started preparing for an attack on the *basti*. There were discussions through the night and some people were called from neighbouring villages. Some others went to the police station and bribed the officer-in-charge so that he would not intervene in the plans. The *harijans* had got wind of the plans and prepared for the assault in a limited way by collecting brick pieces in their homes. The next day, about 250 *Brahmins* collected in the *mahua* orchard. People say that this was the first time that the *Brahmins* showed such unprecedented unity. Earlier they were always fighting among themselves.

Nearly 40 *Chamar* and *Pasi* males, females and children saw the crowd but could not decide to run away as the women-folk and children would have been exposed to greater danger. The *Brahmins* claim that they did not attack outright and that first about 15 of them went with the aim of making the *harijans* apologise for their behaviour, but seeing them come the *harijans* thought that the attack had begun and started throwing bricks and stones. At this, the entire crowd attacked the *harijan* locality. On being asked why such a petty incident provoked such a huge response, a *Brahmin* youth replied:

> The labourers were demanding higher wages from a year ago. But wages in the village did not increase. Then these *harijans* stopped doing work in the village and started taking up work in other villages and in the cities. They were rearing their cows, buffaloes and goats on our share-cropped land. Their cattle used to graze on our farms. If we asked them to come for work they would say that they don't have the time. Also, they were demanding wages equal to other villages. Some *harijans* had taken loan from the government and were driving rickshaws, tonga, etc. for a living. But they would not work for us. They had become fat on income from outside. They did not have any regard for anyone. Government had given them some land on *patta* (a non-transferable deed). Some farm this land, others have not yet got possession. Some of our land was lying fallow, this was purchased by the *Pals* and *Yadavs* who started tilling it. In Belapur there are now three tube-wells belonging to *Chamars* and one belonging to a *Pasi*. In Birpur one tube-well belongs to a *Chamar* and another to a *Dhobi*. So they have started equating themselves with us. We could not say anything to them because of government laws. When they crossed all limits and abused us on the road, all of us thought we should teach them a lesson so that they do not dare to misbehave again.
>
> Now the *Brahmins* don't call them for work at all. We have also tried to persuade employers in other villages not to give them work but did not succeed in this because those people said that we need to get our work done on time and we will employ anyone if work is to be done. A year has since passed. There are three families of *harijans* who work for us even now. Other labourers are mostly Muslims from the neighbouring village but we give them wage equal to other villages and also give them one meal. The village *harijans* whom we employ are also getting paid at the same rate. We don't call the *harijan* families who were involved in the dispute. We stopped them from working in the JRY project as well. We called labourers from other villages to get that done.

Labourers to whom we spoke confirmed that the root cause of the friction was that they had demanded higher wages, equal to a level already prevailing in other villages. The friction was already high when the *Brahmins* had retaliated and scheduled caste labourers had been forbidden to collect grass and fodder from the landlords' fields. The landowners had also let loose their cattle on the labourers' homestead land. While one group of labourers had invited retaliation, the other group, living in a hamlet closer to the *Brahmin's* locality, had not joined in the demands. In the aftermath of the incident, until recently, employers paid a higher wage of 4 kg to the outside labourers, while the local non-striking labourers were paid a lower wage of 3 kg. However, since small employers had to bear higher transactions costs in importing labour, they had started paying the local labour also at the same rate (4 kg). They also held a meeting of the *gram panchayat* with only the *Brahmin* members, and passed a resolution handing over all village waste land to the forest department. The recalcitrant scheduled castes were also turned away from a JRY road construction site. On their part, the labourers reacted by trying unsuccessfully to organise a counter-boycott, by filing police complaints and using their newly acquired political clout to obtain justice.

For many the incident meant the rupture of a long-standing relationship. Bholanath Chamar told us:

> After the incident, the *Brahmins* stopped us from going even near their fields and cutting grass etc. Anyone who goes near the fields is beaten up by them. I have been working for them since the age of 8, and have worked as a *halwah* for many years. I used to get 1 *bigha* land and about 2 kg wages then. I left *halwahi* 10–15 years ago but used to take land on share. Since 5 years I have been taking 5 *bigha* (3 acres) land on share, but last year, after we did all the work, they did not allow us to harvest the crop. All of them did the same. We made a complaint in *Patti* (the sub-district headquarters) but nothing has come of it so far.

Another old scheduled caste labourer, who had worked as a ploughman for more than 55 years at the same low wages, described to us why he felt the labourers had been able to go on strike for higher wages:

> We stopped going to work because we had some (staying) power. Our work situation is better than before. Earlier no *harijan* had any land. Now we have some land. Some people work here. Others go to other places and earn their living. They have to do this because they can get work for very few days in agriculture. It is now a little better than before because of stricter implementation of government laws but

these people (the dominant *Brahmin* landholders) still want to grab everything.

Another important change is sweeping the *jajmani* occupations in both *Belapur* and *Birpur*. Caste-based associations have been urging their members not to take up demeaning work and threaten them with social excommunication if they do. Virtually all *jajmani* castes – *Nai* (barber), *Dai* (midwives), *Dom* (lifter of dead animals), *Kahar* (washers of vessels), *Kumhar* (potters), *Dhobi* (washermen) – both here and in *Belapur*, have been influenced by this movement. Changes have been occurring in the *jajmani* castes over a long period of time. An old *Chamar* from *Belapur* described the process leading to changes in his traditional work in the following way:

> Earlier we had to lift carcasses and our women undertook delivery of children. Then the *harijans* held a *panchayat* and decided to stop this work. The entire village collected to beat them up for this and they had to run away from their houses. They ran all the way to the police-station where they recited their woes. One police officer came twice to the village. He was bribed Rs 1,000 by a *Brahmin* leader and lodged cases for breach of peace against us. Now this work has entirely stopped. The government midwife comes to the village. Some people (called *hadbiwa*) have come and settled from outside and now lift the carcasses.

The artisan castes in the village deplored the rigid caste based divisions and interactions in the village and pointed out how various castes were giving up work which they considered socially degrading. Earlier the *Nais* used to throw away the used *pattals* (used leafplates). After that this work was done by *Musehras*. Now for some years even they have stopped. However, vestiges of the system remain because of economic compulsions. The change is uneven and is circumscribed by the economic necessity and the social circumstances of the *jajmani* households as the two case studies cited below show:

> Kusum *Nai* has been married for three years. Her in-laws are not alive. Her husband works in a shop in Patti and shares that income with her brother-in-law who looks after 30 houses and gets 4 kg grain per house annually and a sheaf of grain. A change has come about so that *nais* have stopped cleaning after ceremonies (throwing away used leafplates (*pattals*), etc.) six years ago. Earlier they also used to get 1–1.5 *bigha* land, but ever since reservations were implemented, the *Thakur-Brahmins* have taken back their land. Kusum herself had never done traditional work but her in-laws now compelled her to

attend to a few *Thakur* households. This year she went to 4–5 houses around the *Sankrant* festival. She doesn't want to do this work but she has no choice.

Badri Prasad, a *Nai* in *Birpur*, is landless and does *jajmani* work. Every six months he gets 4 kg grain per family. He also gets 1 kg grain in addition to that. He is a widower and has no children. Before consolidation of landholdings (*chakbandi*) took place people also gave land in lieu of *jajmani*. 'Now instead of land they give one sheaf of grain. We had to throw used pattals in any village function.' He is the only *Nai* in the *Thakur basti*. That is why he has to work under their pressure and do what they say. He cannot oppose them in any way.

The *biradari* movements do not appear to have a formal or well-knit structure. They are also more supra-local and regional rather than local. The movement among barbers in Jaunpur, for instance has a spread over at least three adjoining districts (Jaunpur, Pratapgarh and Allahabad) and has caused reverberations in others. The informal leadership of these movements bases itself more on community disapproval rather than sanctions to wean away caste members from demeaning traditional work. But progress is slow, impelled as much by economic forces as by social ones.

SOME IMPLICATIONS FOR AGRICULTURAL WAGE DETERMINATION

This section examines the implications of the emerging characteristics of the rural labour markets in Uttar Pradesh for wage determination in the light of the fieldwork evidence from the study panchayats presented in the preceding sections. It abstracts from several important features of the agrarian labour market such as heterogeneity of wage payment systems and labour contracts, gender characteristics, and interlinkage with land-lease and other transactions, except in passing and focuses on the factors influencing the daily wage rate for casual male agricultural labourers.[14] The 'daily wage rate' is a concept which has a clear meaning in the study areas despite the complexity in the prevailing wage payment systems.[15]

A number of macro studies of the Indian rural labour market have highlighted separate aspects such as the growth of non-farm employment and rise in agricultural wages in hitherto agriculturally backward regions during the 1980s. The rise in agricultural wages is seen as mainly demand determined. Micro-theories of the rural labour market still draw on the equilibrium demand-supply model, the adequacy of which has been seriously questioned; variants of the efficiency-wage hypothesis or on linked labour contracts, both of which have limited empirical validity. In a cross-sectional study of wage rate variations, Bardhan [1984: 47–61] has confirmed the importance of demand and supply factors but wages do not come anywhere near market clearing levels. Bardhan adduced several alternative explanations which stress peak season labour demand and forward contracts to show why rural wages are always positive [*Bardhan*, 1984: Chs.5 and 6]. Equilibirium demand and supply models are shown as satisfactory by some authors [e.g., *Bliss and Stern*, 1982] since labour markets clear, despite considerable evidence to the contrary. Variants of the efficiency wage hypothesis which attempt to explain positive and downwardly-rigid wages have also been found wanting since labour contracts are mainly casual and of short duration [cf. *Ray*, 1987; *K. Bardhan*, 1989].

Agricultural changes are evident in the study areas of the Eastern and Central regions, but, as we have shown, there is no spurt in the demand for labour; the increase necessitated by changes in the cropping pattern has been counteracted by mechanisation of key operations, such as ploughing, irrigation and threshing, as well as by a change in employer attitudes towards participation in farm labour. The latter changes are uneven across regions but are partly evident even across Eastern Uttar Pradesh. Thus, in all likelihood, demand for agricultural labour has lagged behind increasing supply and this can thus not by itself explain the prevailing wage situation, namely an upward pressure.

We have focused on a number of factors due to which wages have been under upward pressure. In contrast to our earlier study [*Srivastava*, 1996] as well as to Rudra [1982, 1992: 402–24] and Bardhan and Rudra [1986], this study has highlighted the considerable mobility of labourers in the rural areas in Uttar Pradesh. The increase in village approach roads in the last few years under the JRY has also helped to create a more generalised agricultural labour market and to break down isolation. Various factors – higher wage earnings in non-agricultural employment and in public works, inter- or even intra-village differentials in agricultural wages; improvement in the asset position of labourers and an increase in alternative means of livelihood – have put upward pressure on the prevailing wages in agriculture and have also implied higher reservation wages, in the sense that workers will not easily accept a lower wage even in lean seasons.

Demands for higher wages have been put across in a number of ways by the labourers, including in a few cases collective actions which have taken the form of strikes. By and large employers in all the study areas have resisted collective demands for wage increases by organising counter-boycotts. The important aspects of employer strategy in all three study areas have been sanctions against workers on the use of fields for grass and fodder, for movement and for easing themselves, and the use or threat of violence (their own violence or that of the state machinery) against workers. Some of these arenas constitute areas of 'one-sided dependence' in which labourers have no direct bargaining power. The sanctions succeed or fail depending on the extent that they affect the workers, which in turn depends on such factors as the location of their habitations and their dependence on fodder and grass, and the extent to which the employers can collectively implement them. The predominance of such 'extra-economic' factors in determining the outcome of labour demands could be seen as an element of market failure (see Singh [1992] for a similar description).

However, even where there is no overt collective action by workers or if the collective action of labourers fails, the implicit 'go-slow' by the labourers at lower-than-reservation-wages may still lead to (sections of) employers having to raise wages. Such wage increases may occur during the peak periods. This is because the peak period is characterised by acute competition among employers to secure a large volume of labourers in a relatively short period. As a result, employer solidarity is most difficult to achieve and sustain during this period, and individual employer strategies to secure labour – such as the use of advances or threats – may yield only partial results. However, large employers, or a section of such employers, do use a variety of economic and extra-economic devices to side-step the prevailing wages, and often pay a lower wage. At the same time, peak-period tightening of the labour market is only part of the story since wage payment practices during the peak period are generally quite distinct.[16] The prevailing wage which is often the subject of negotiation is the 'daily wage' which prevails at other times of the year, including the lean season, when involuntary unemployment exists in all our study villages.[17] It would thus appear that employer requirements, though seasonally variable, are themselves quite inflexible during any given season. Thus wage revisions are not explicable in terms of peak period demand and supply. This evidence again points towards the inadequacy of equilibrium demand-supply models in wage rate determination in the agricultural labour market [cf. *Rajaraman*, 1985]. Even though large employers often do employ various strategies, such as loans and advances or land-lease to secure labour supply at lower than market price as depicted by Bardhan [1984: Chs.4 to 6] or Bardhan and Rudra [1978, 1981], these specific strategies, including the fragmentation of the labour market that they entail, appear not to have had more than a marginal impact on the general labour market dynamics in these areas.

In the light of the evidence described in the preceding sections, labourers can be said to form expectations regarding the wage rate, which is then determined through implicit or explicit bargaining. This process is not very unlike the one described by Rudra [1982] even though the evidence refutes his characterisation of the rural labour market as essentially isolated and splintered.[18]

While the impact of the Employment Guarantee Scheme in Maharashtra in the labour market has been analysed by several researchers [cf. *Acharya*, 1990; *Ravallion, Dutt and Chaudhuri*, 1993], the impact of country-wide employment generation schemes such as the Jawahar Rozgar Yojana on employment and wage rates has not still been adequately researched. As shown above, while the impact of Jawahar Rozgar Yojana on employment has been small in Eastern Uttar Pradesh, it appears to have played an important role in shaping the wage expectations of agricultural labourers. Even though macro-social factors have not been analysed here, they also have played a crucial role in determining worker expectations and demands. In recent years, labourers in Uttar Pradesh have moved towards more explicit collective action in favour of their demands. An important change has also taken place in the *jajmani* occupations which involved some of the most socially degrading work. Caste panchayats have prohibited such work, under threat of ostracism.

The labour market in Uttar Pradesh is thus witnessing a twofold change. First, there is a decline in the pervasiveness of customary relationships. Second, the enlarged set of livelihood opportunities, the growth of a more generalised labour market, and the increase in social consciousness have put the customary institutional wage under upward pressure. The downwardly-rigid reservation wage which replaces the customary wage is the product of a gamut of economic and extra-economic factors. Employer strategies to beat back wage increases rely not only on economic devices but also directly on extra-economic coercion and on areas (outside of the labour market) where labourers have little or no bargaining power [*Srivastava*, 1989b].

DEPENDENCE AND RESISTANCE: SOME CONCLUSIONS

This study has provided evidence of the strategies pursued by the poorer households and of changes in the economic and social relations between the labouring classes and the dominant groups/classes in the study *panchayats*.

The labouring classes pursue a mix of strategies based on traditional services, hiring out of labour and petty self-employment, both within and outside agriculture. A very large proportion of those who hire out labour in the study villages are drawn from the SCs, OBCs and lower Muslim castes. The core of the labour force – about half in all the villages taken together – is formed by the SCs. Many of the poorer households combine wage labour and cultivation with traditional *jajmani* services. The extent and nature of tenancy varies from village to village, but on the whole, about one in six households lease in land. The tenants are from the poor or middle peasant groups, and belong largely to the backward or SCs. Poor households have little access to institutional credit (other than the credit guaranteed by the government in the anti-poverty programmes) and have to depend on large cultivators, professional money lenders and friends and relatives to meet their credit requirements.

Many other modes of subsistence which could supplement the incomes oɪ the poor are not unmixed blessings as they reinforce elements of dependence. Livestock rearing, for example, increases the dependence of the poor on the fields and fodder of the rich. This dependence is greater in the Muzaffarnagar *panchayats* where open access fields and common property resources have shrunk at a more rapid rate.

The evidence presented in this study shows that there has been a decline in the pervasiveness of traditional relationships, whether labour or *jajmani*. The pace of this change (already at an advanced stage in Muzaffarnagar) has been quite marked in the eastern and central UP *panchayats*. Both dominant landholders and labourers concede that extant relationships are no longer sustainable. But the pace of change is uneven.

There has been, alongside, a diversification in the employment structure of the labourers from agriculture to non-agriculture. An important component of the non-agricultural employment opportunities is non-local, linked to migration, both on an individual and household basis. Even though more labourers still seek employment in agriculture than in any other activity, in many of the areas studied non-agriculture has emerged as a more major source of employment.

The growth of non-agricultural employment opportunities, the more limited public works employment, as well as other factors – such as some increase in land and asset ownership among the rural poor – have increased reservation wages in agriculture. Again these changes have been more marked in the eastern and central UP *panchayats*. In the western UP *panchayats*, the small, indeed negative, difference between local wages and government stipulated minimum wages and the lesser importance of land distribution to the poor, reduces the roles of these two factors.

Disputes between the poor and dominant classes have centred on both economic and non-economic issues and span a range, from individual to well-articulated collective demands, which have both local as well as supra-local origins. While caste no doubt is an important factor (and one of several) in both facilitating and impeding class solidarity, the struggles that we have cited from all three areas have rarely been confined to one caste or caste-group and labourers' mobilisations have spanned caste differences.

MAP SHOWING LOCATION OF STUDY DISTRICTS AND PANCHAYATS

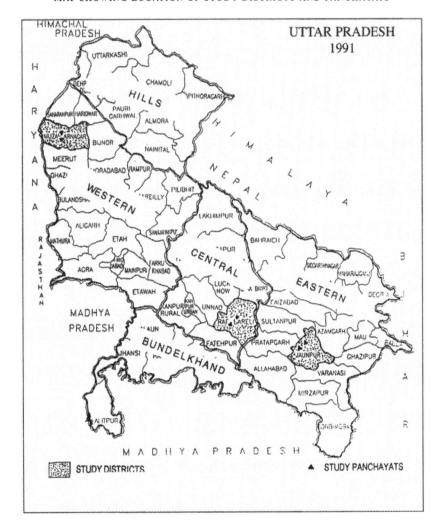

Also, significantly, the struggles have not focused on caste issues but, clearly, on class issues. At the same time, the evidence that we have presented also demonstrates the limited nature of organisation, and absence of sustained mobilisation, among the poorer classes in the study areas. The reactions of the dominant groups have also varied – from bargaining to threats and actual violence. With a decline in both social legitimacy and economic patronage, the threats are mostly extra-economic, centring on violence and the exclusion of the poor from common property resources and traditionally sanctioned uses of private fields. Domination may have been facilitated by *jati* or *biradari* solidarity, but it clearly is organised around class interests and class issues.

The changes discussed in this study have implications for, and inter-relate with, macro-social and political dynamics. Since the late 1980s, a significant feature in Uttar Pradesh has been the growing independent political assertion of the *dalits*.[19] State level politics in the state has been in a flux, and there has been a rise of new political parties and coalitions. A major factor in state politics has been the rise of the Bahujan Samaj Party (BSP) which has a significant support base among the scheduled castes and OBCs. During the period in which the fieldwork was initially carried out, the BSP had a political coalition with the Samajwadi Party (SP) which has a strong political base among the minorities and the peasantry belonging to the backward castes in the eastern and central parts of the state. The political conjuncture arising out of this coalition appears to have accelerated struggles against the hegemony of the well-entrenched landed proprietors belonging to the upper castes. But after 1995, the BSP–SP coalition broke down and the BSP formed coalitions with the Hindu communalist BJP on two different occasions. The shifting alliances are also bound to have some implications for village level dynamics but these have not been analysed by us here.

NOTES

1. See Yogendra Singh [1961]; Brass [1965, 1985 (especially Chs.4 and 8)]; Gould [1984]; Duncan [1988]; Kohli [1987]; Hasan [1989a, 1989b]; Fukunaga [1993].
2. Interestingly, the locality of many of the studies is quite close to the areas of the present study. Lewis [1958] documents changes in *Chamar–Jat* relations, under the impact of the reform movement, greater education and increased employment in the organised sector, in a village near Delhi. Cohn [1955] has described emerging contradictions between *Chamars* and *Rajputs* in a village of Jaunpur district since the first local elections in 1938. In a restudy after *zamindari* abolition, Cohn observed a deterioration in their condition due to land alienation [*Cohn*, 1959, reprinted in *Cohn*, 1987]. For a village near Lucknow where *zamindari* abolition had taken place, Majumdar, Pradhan, Sen and Misra [1955: 191–2] report the refusal of *Chamars* to perform *begar*, while the barbers refused to draw water for the Thakurs, wash their utensils, remove their leaf plates.
3. See, for instance, Miriam Sharma [1979: 160–83] for Varanasi district; Jagpal Singh [1992: 64–83] for Meerut district; Lerche [1994, 1995] for Muzaffarnagar and Jaunpur; and Rajendra Singh [1978, 1988] for *Basti*.
4. In the traditional *jajmani* system, diverse providers of services, ranging from barbers, washermen, ironsmiths to priests provide personalised services to a household or a group of upper-caste and land-owning households called the *jajmans*, for which they may be typically provided with a share of the agricultural produce and a number of other prerequisites. There are a complex set of traditional rights and obligations between the providers of services and the *jajmans*, which are increasingly a source of contention.

5. *Gram panchayats* or village councils are the lowest unit of self-government in India. In UP each village council now consists of one or more villages with a total voter strength of about 1,000. In our case, except in one *panchayat* (*Teka-Janwa*) which consisted of two villages, villages and *panchayats* coincided.

6. The State of Uttar Pradesh in Northern India is often divided into five relatively homogeneous agro-climatic regions. Apart from the three selected for this study, the other two are the UP Hills and Bundelkhand (Southern Uttar Pradesh). The differences between these regions extend to agro-ecological, social and demographic characteristics and agrarian relations which have resulted in different development outcomes [cf. *Lieten and Srivastava*, forthcoming: Ch.2]. The disparities between the agriculturally backward Eastern region and developed Western region of UP have been the subject of intense debate. Until 1968–70, the disparity between them was not only large but increasing [*Singh*, 1985]. However, by the early 1990s, the differences between the regions have marginally narrowed owing to growth impulses in the hitherto backward regions and the share of the Eastern region in total foodgrain production increased [*Lieten and Srivastava*, forthcoming]. Between 1968–71 and 1988–91, the growth rate of foodgrain production in the Eastern region was higher at 4.05 per cent, compared to 3.6 per cent in the Central region and 3.4 per cent in the Western region [*Singh*, 1997]. During this period, agricultural wage disparities between the regions have also declined [*Lieten and Srivastava*, forthcoming].

   The selection of districts within the regions was done purposively to cover contrasting situations at the local and regional levels. Muzaffarnagar has been at the centre of a peasant movement led by the Bhartiya Kisan Union (BKU); whereas the area of Raebareli studied was at the centre of development initiatives from above as many members of the Nehru-Gandhi family were elected from here to the parliament. Jaunpur, with a high man-land ratio and petty landlordism is quite typical of many Eastern UP districts (for details of the study areas, see Lieten and Srivastava [forthcoming: Ch.3].

7. The following terms are used to denote the caste groups/strata in the study areas: *Upper Caste Hindus* refers to high castes such as *Thakurs, Brahmins* and *Kayasthas*. The terms *Other Backward Castes* (OBC) or *Backward Castes* denote a heterogeneous group of middle castes, which are considered *socially and economically backward* on the whole and are entitled to positive discrimination under the Constitutional provisions of Article 16(4). The *Intermediate Castes* are also middle castes like the Jats but are not considered backward and hence are not eligible for positive discrimination. *Scheduled Castes* (SC) are at the bottom of the caste hierarchy and are notified in the Constitution (Scheduled Caste) Order of 1950, in accordance with the provisions of Article 340 of the Constitution. They are also entitled to various measures of reservation and positive discrimination. The Muslims have also been stratified into two groups of which the upper strata (*Ashraf*) consists of Sheikh, Saiyad, Moghul and Pathan (Khan). Upper castes Hindus and Muslims along with Jats are the traditional proprietary groups in the rural areas of UP [cf. *Saxena*, 1984].

8. We have taken the higher of the two figures (leased in/leased out to land owned) because of likely underreporting.

9. Households have been classified into four classes based on the following criteria:

   (1) *Dominant*: Households with agricultural surpluses based on systematic hiring in of labour or leasing out of land, or with superior sources of non-agricultural incomes (large business or contractors, superior professions).

   (2) *Upper Middle*: Households with net hiring in of labour supplementing family labour, small lessors, inferior but regular sources of non-agricultural income.

   (3) *Lower Middle*: Households who are small (net) hirers out of labour, or are skilled casual labourers, are in the main self-employed in agriculture or non-agriculture with petty and generally irregular incomes.

   (4) *Poor (Dependent)*: Households who are principally hirers out of casual labour or traditional services in agriculture or non-agriculture.

10. Cane tying is paid per bigha rates which vary from round to round at time rates which are Rs 15–20 for adults and Rs 10 for minors. Cane digging is paid a wage of 5 kg wheat per half day. Wheat harvesting is paid a wage of 25 kg per bigha or 1 in 25 bundles. Labour in wheat threshing is paid a wage of 1.5 kg per quintal. Outside agriculture, prevailing wages were

Rs 80 for skilled and Rs 40 for unskilled workers. Wage rates for brick-making vary between destinations – from Rs 62 per thousand in UP to Rs 90 per thousand in Punjab and Chandigarh. Farm servants are paid Rs 400–600 monthly, with food and clothes. Local farm servants are additionally given 5 kg gur and 1 quintal wheat annually.

11. We have elsewhere noted the role of extra- economic coercion in shaping the characteristics of the labour market in UP [*Srivastava*, 1989b, 1996]. This study also notes how different wage rates may come to prevail in relation to different categories of employers purely as a result of extra-economic coercion.

12. Literally meaning 'God's people', a term popularised by Gandhi for the untouchable (SC) castes.

13. While 'Jai Siya-Ram' is a normal form of greeting in Uttar Pradesh, 'Jai Shri Ram' has been converted into a militant incantation and greeting by the communalist Hindu forces such as the *Vishwa Hindu Parishad*.

14. The prevailing agricultural wage rate for males is twice that of females in two of the study areas, while both wage rates are equal in the third. However, as stated above, the gender characteristics of the agricultural labour market is a theme not pursued here.

15. Even though there is an unambiguous notion of the 'prevailing wage', our evidence here and elsewhere does not corroborate the notion of an uniform prevailing wage, suggested in several other studies, notably that of Rudra [1982]. Instead, we find that the prevailing wage generally lies within a small band due to any of the following reasons: (i) small inter-seasonal fluctuations; (ii) differences in wages paid by small and large (dominant) cultivators; (iii) transition from a lower to a higher wage.

16. Harvesting wages, for instance, are generally paid as a share of the crop. In some areas in Uttar Pradesh, labourers have demanded an upward revision of this share. In other cases, employers allege, and I have often found to be true, that labourers take more than the stipulated share, simply because of their improved bargaining power at that time. With rising productivity, where employers have the upper hand, fixed kind wages have been substituted for the share, as in our two west Uttar Pradesh villages. However, here too, these wages are higher than those prevailing at other times.

17. As far as the peak periods are concerned, there was evidence of labour shortage in the West Uttar Pradesh villages, and to a much lesser extent in the two East Uttar Pradesh villages. The study found no evidence of such shortage in the Central Uttar Pradesh villages.

18. The isolation of the labour market also figured in our own earlier study of the agrarian labour market in Uttar Pradesh. One of the principal conclusions here is that this isolation is breaking down in our present study villages.

19. Literally meaning the 'downtrodden', *dalit* is part of the political lexicon referring to the low castes, particularly the scheduled castes and tribes.

REFERENCES

Acharya, Sarthy, 1990, 'The Maharashtra Employment Guarantee Scheme: A Study of Labour Market Intervention', *ARTEP Working Paper*, May, Delhi: ARTEP.

Bardhan, K., 1983, 'Economic Growth, Poverty, and Rural Labour Markets in India: A Survey of Research', *World Employment Research Working Papers*, ILO, Geneva.

Bardhan, K., 1989, 'Poverty, Growth and Rural Labour Markets', *Economic and Political Weekly*, Review of Agriculture, 25 March.

Bardhan, P.K., 1982, 'Agrarian Class Formation in India', *The Journal of Peasant Studies*, Vol.10, No.1, pp.73–93.

Bardhan, P.K., 1984, *Land, Labour and Rural Poverty: Essays in Development Economics*, Delhi: Oxford University Press.

Bardhan, P.K. and A. Rudra, 1978, 'Interlinkage of Land, Labour and Credit Relations: An Analysis of Village Survey Data in East India', *Economic and Political Weekly*, Annual Number, Feb., pp.367–84.

Bardhan, P.K. and A. Rudra, 1981, 'Terms and Conditions of Labour Contracts in Agriculture:

Results of a Survey in West Bengal 1979', *Oxford Bulletin of Economics and Statistics*, Feb., pp.89–111.

Bardhan, P.K. and A. Rudra, 1985, 'The Domain of Rural Markets: Results of a Survey in West Bengal, 1981–1982', Economic and Political Weekly, *Review of Agriculture*, 21–28 Dec., pp.A153–4.

Bardhan, P.K. and A. Rudra, 1986, 'Labour Mobility and the Boundaries of the Village Moral Economy', *The Journal of Peasant Studies*, Vol.13, No.3, pp.96–115.

Bharadwaj, K., 1979, 'Towards a Macro-economic Framework for a Developing Economy: The Indian Case', *The Manchester School*, Sept. pp.270–302.

Binswanger, H.P. and M.R. Rosenzweig (eds.), 1984, *Contractual Arrangements, Employment and Wages in Rural Labour Markets in Asia*, New Haven, CT and London: Yale University Press.

Bliss C. and N. Stern, 1982, *Palanpur: A Study of an Indian Village*, Oxford: Oxford University Press.

Brass, Paul, 1965, *Factional Politics in an Indian State: The Congress Party in Uttar Pradesh*, Berkeley, CA: University of California Press.

Brass, Paul, 1985, *Caste, Faction and Party in Indian Politics, Volume One: Faction and Party*, Delhi: Chanakya.

Cohn, Bernard S., 1955, 'The Changing Status of a Depressed Caste', reprinted in A.R. Desai (ed.), 1961, *Rural Sociology in India*, Bombay: Popular Prakashan, pp.668–85.

Cohn, B.S., 1959, 'Some Notes on Law and Change in Village India', *Economic Development and Cultural Change*, 8, pp.79–93; reprinted in Cohn, Bernard S., 1987, *An Anthropologist among the Historians and Other Essays*, Delhi: Oxford University Press.

Drèze, Jean and Mukherjee, Anindita, 1989, 'Labour Contracts in Rural India: Theories and Evidence', in S. Chakravarty (ed.), *The Balance Between Agriculture and Industry in Economic Development*, Vol.III, London: Macmillan.

Duncan, Ian, 1988, 'Party Politics and the North Indian Peasantry: The Rise of the Bhartiya Kranti Dal in Uttar Pradesh, *The Journal of Peasant Studies*, Vol.16, No.1, pp.40–75.

Frankel, Francine R. and M.S.A. Rao, 1989, *Dominance and State Power in Modern India*, Delhi: Oxford University Press.

Fukunaga, Masaaki, 1993, *Society, Caste and Factional Politics: Conflict and Continuity in Rural India*, New Delhi: Manohar.

Gould, Harold A., 1984, 'Politics of Agrarian Unrest in U.P.: Who Co-opted Whom?', *Economic and Political Weekly*, Vol.1, No.49, pp.2084–8.

Hasan, Zoya, 1989a, 'Power and Mobilization: Patterns of Resilience and Change in Uttar Pradesh Politics', in Frankel and Rao [1989].

Hasan, Zoya, 1989b, *Dominance and Mobilisation: Rural Politics in Western Uttar Pradesh 1930–1980*, New Delhi: Sage Publications.

Kohli, Atul, 1987, *The State and Poverty in India: The Politics of Reform*, Bombay: Orient Longman.

Lerche, Jens, 1994, 'New Wine in Old Bottles: Caste, Local Action, Social Movements and General Elections. Scheduled Caste Agricultural Workers in Uttar Pradesh, India', paper presented at the XIII World Congress of Sociology, Bielfeldt, Germany, July.

Lerche, Jens, 1995, 'Is Bonded Labour a Bound Category? Reconceptualising Agrarian Conflict in India', *The Journal of Peasant Studies*, Vol.22, No.3, pp.484–515.

Lewis, Oscar, 1958, *Village Life in Northern India*, Urbana, IL: University of Illinois Press.

Lieten, G.K. and Ravi Srivastava, forthcoming, *Unequal Partners: Power Relations, Devolution and Development in Uttar Pradesh*, New Delhi: Sage.

Majumdar, D.N., Pradhan, M.C., Sen, C. and S. Misra, 1955, 'Intercaste Relations in Cohanakallan, a Village Near Lucknow', *Eastern Anthropologist*, 8, March–Aug., pp.191–214.

Rajaraman, Indira, 1985, 'Returns to Labour in Developing Country: India, *World Employment Programme Research Working Paper*, ILO, Nov.

Ravallion, Martin, Dutt, Gaurav and Shubnum Chaudhuri, 1993, 'Does Maharashtra Guarantee Scheme Guarantee Employment? Effects of the 1988 Wage Increase', *Economic Development and Cultural Change*, Vol.41, No.2, pp.251–76.

Ray, Shovan, 1987, 'Returns to Rural Labour in Asia', *World Employment Programme Research Working Paper*, ILO, Sept.

Rudra, A., 1978, 'Class Relations in Indian Agriculure', *Economic and Political Weekly*, 3, 10 and 17 June.

Rudra, A., 1982, 'Extraeconomic Constraints on Agricultural Labour: Results of an Intensive Survey in Some Villages near Santiniketan, West Bengal', *Asian Employment Programme Working Papers*, ILO, Geneva.

Saxena, N.C., 1984, 'Caste, Land and Political Power in Rura Uttar Pradesh', paper presented at the Conference on 'Caste, Class and Dominance', University of Pennsylvania, May.

Sharma, Miriam, 1979, *The Politics of Inequality: Competition and Control in an Indian Village*, Hawaii: University Press of Hawaii.

Singh, Ajit Kumar, 1985, *Agricultural Development and Rural Poverty*, New Delhi, Ashis Publishing.

Singh, Ajit Kumar, 1997, 'Agricultural Growth, Employment and Poverty in Uttar Pradesh: Some Recent Trends', in G.K. Chaddha and A.N. Sharma (eds.), *Growth, Employment and Poverty: Change and Continuity in Rural India*, New Delhi: Vikas Publishing House, pp.346–64.

Singh, Jagpal, 1992, *Capitalism and Dependence: Agrarian Politics in Western Uttar Pradesh 1951–1991*, Delhi: Manohar.

Singh, Rajendra, 1978, 'Peasant Movements in Uttar Pradesh: A Study in the Politics of Land and Land Control in Basti District, 1801–1907', in M.S.A. Rao (ed.), *Social Movements in India, Volume 1, Peasant and Backward Classes Movement*, New Delhi: Manohar.

Singh, Rajendra, 1988, *Land, Power and People: Rural Elite in Transition, 1801–1970*, New Delhi: Sage.

Singh, Yogendra, 1961, 'The Changing Power Structure of Village Community: A Case Study of Six Villages in Eastern U.P.', in A.R. Desai (ed.), *Rural Sociology in India*, Bombay: Popular Prakashan, pp.668–85.

Srivastava, Ravi, 1989a, 'Tenancy Contracts During Transition: A Study Based on Fieldwork in Uttar Pradesh', *The Journal of Peasant Studies*, Vol.16, No.3, pp.339–95.

Srivastava, Ravi, 1989b, 'Interlinked Modes of Exploitation in Indian Agriculture: A Case Study', *The Journal of Peasant Studies*, Vol.16, No.4, pp.493–522.

Srivastava, Ravi, 1996, 'Agrarian Change and the Labour Process', in Peter Robb (ed.), *Meanings of Agriculture*, New Delhi: Oxford University Press, pp.132–5.

Srivastava, Ravi, 1997, 'Change and Resilience in Producer Strategies in Indian Agriculture', in Jan Breman, Peter Kloos and Ashwani Saith (eds.), *The Village in Asia Revisited*, Delhi: Oxford University Press.

Thorner, D. and A. Thorner, 1962, *Land and Labour in India*, New Delhi: Allied Publishers.

Patterns of Accumulation and Struggles of Rural Labour: Some Aspects of Agrarian Change in Central Bihar

KALPANA WILSON

INTRODUCTION

The unprecedented scale of the massacre of 61 women, children and men belonging to low caste labouring families at Lakshmanpur Bathe in Jehanabad district on the night of 1 December 1997, the latest in a concerted campaign of terror by the landlord-sponsored Ranvir Sena, brought tensions in Central Bihar sharply into national focus in India. The mainstream media attempted to explain the massacre as resulting from either 'caste conflict' or 'land disputes'. Clearly however, the forces underlying such atrocities cannot be understood simply in these terms: while the inextricably interrelated questions of land and caste are indeed at the root of the battle being waged in the plains of Bihar, what is at issue is the very nature of power in the region.

Today, ownership of land and other assets, caste dominance, political position, and control over the state apparatuses and their resources all intersect in a way which is by no means unique to Bihar, but which takes a particularly potent form here. This system is by no means a static one – for instance, as we will see, technological developments have had a significant impact, particularly on larger cultivators of the intermediate castes – but it has proved able to incorporate such change.

By contrast, the movements of agricultural labourers and poor peasants in the region have challenged the very basis of the existing social formation. First, they are attempting to transform the relations of production in agriculture, which still underpin the power of the dominant landowners, even when agriculture is no longer their main source of income. Second,

Kalpana Wilson, Research student in the Department of Economics, School of Oriental and African Studies, Thornhaugh Street, Russell Square, London WC1H 0XG. This contribution could not have been written without the help, support and inspiration of friends and comrades in Hilsa block and beyond. The author would also like to thank in particular Professor Terry Byres for his valuable comments and suggestions, and continuing encouragement.

they are confronting oppressive caste relations, and at a level – that of dalit agricultural labourers and their employers – where these are almost inseparable from class relations. Thirdly, in waging these struggles, these movements, particularly those led by the Communist Party of India (Marxist-Leninist) are coming into direct conflict with sections of landowners with a variety of wider connections both political and criminal; such confrontations are widening the base of the movement to smaller cultivators and others who face harassment by these networks. This has intensified the perceived threat to the hitherto unchallenged political power of dominant landowners.

It is in the context of such developments that this study attempts to identify the underlying shifts in patterns of surplus accumulation during the period from the 1970s to the 1990s and to outline the specific changes in production relations which have emerged from these shifts on the one hand, and the movement of agricultural labourers on the other.

CHANGING PATTERNS OF ACCUMULATION: THE EXPERIENCE OF NALANDA DISTRICT, 1970s–90s

Naresh Ram, a dalit agricultural labourer who lives in a village dominated by large landowners of the Kurmi caste in Hilsa, a block of Bihar's Nalanda District, uses the following example to explain how things have and haven't changed in his village during the last 15 years: 'Before if I remained sitting on the khatia outside my house when a landowner walked through this tola, he would abuse me or even beat me up. Now after we have got organised, I can carry on sitting here and invite him to sit down. But if I were to go to his house and sit down next to him on the khatia outside, it would be a different matter …'.

As this suggests, the change in the relationship between agricultural labourers and the landowners who employ them has been a complex one. It is one which has resulted not from a thoroughgoing transformation of production relations or the collapse of the dominant caste-based ideology, but from a perceived shift in the balance of forces generated by developments both within and beyond the agrarian economy.

However, the experience of Nalanda district is very different from the picture of stagnation which is often painted as a backdrop to accounts of 'agrarian conflict' in Central Bihar. On the contrary, changes here in the 1970s led observers to hail the potential emergence of 'peasant capitalism' among the cultivating landowners of intermediate, 'backward' castes who dominate the area. But subsequent developments raise questions as to whether it is possible for such a trajectory to be followed within the framework of the existing state and social formation, and suggests that a more resilient force for change may lie elsewhere.

Based primarily on fieldwork carried out in 1995–96 in Chandkura, a village which was surveyed as part of an earlier study in the early 1980s, and 11 other villages in Hilsa, this study suggests that while the conditions for the development of capitalism were generated in the 1970s, the period from the mid-1980s onwards has seen a virtual 'stalling' of this process. This is reflected particularly in the absence of land concentration on any significant scale and the use of productive assets by large landowners primarily to extract surpluses from the growing numbers of small and marginal cultivators.

The study argues that a section of the rich peasantry which emerged in the 1970s began in the 1980s to follow the path taken earlier by higher caste, non-cultivating landowners. Surpluses accumulated in agriculture were diverted into unproductive avenues and used to enter networks of politicians, bureaucrats and criminals which allowed them to appropriate development resources on a large scale. This was one of the factors leading to a crisis in the availability of key inputs – notably the 'de-electrification' of large areas – making agricultural investment even less profitable.

The 1990s saw two further developments which intensified these patterns. First, the New Economic Policies adopted from 1991 onwards led to the cutting of subsidies on agricultural inputs and sharp rises in fertiliser and diesel costs in particular. Secondly, the economic and political consolidation of a section of the backward caste peasants which had been underway since Independence, and which had been accelerated by the developments in the 1970s, was reflected in the political arena, culminating in the coming to power of Laloo Prasad Yadav's Janata Dal government in 1990. This direct access to state power further reinforced the tendency for surpluses to be diverted away from agriculture in the areas of incipient peasant capitalism and into what has been called 'primitive accumulation' through corruption and crime [Das, 1992: 74], a phenomenon which is symptomatic of the nature of state power in Bihar; not surprisingly, therefore, the Janata Dal / Rashtriya Janata Dal era has also witnessed the further collapse of the region's infrastructure.

The study goes on to look at the specific impact upon production relations of sustained struggles waged by agricultural labourers. It discusses the significance for such struggles of caste and gender-based expressions of social power, and suggests that a number of changes in production relations during the last 15 years, relating in particular to wages, the nature and extent of attached and casual labour, and changes in patterns of tenancy and of credit, represent either acceptance by employers of demands put forward by agricultural labourers, or essentially defensive attempts to maintain the *status quo*. At the same time the wider connections of one section of large landowners is changing the very nature of class confrontations.

I. THE RISE AND FALL OF 'PEASANT CAPITALISM'?

Bihar's post-independence experience until the early 1970s did little to change the overall picture of a state with a stagnant and unproductive agricultural sector. And despite relatively favourable conditions in the Central Bihar districts, growth rates remained low even in these areas. Thus during the period 1962–65 to 1975–78 triennia, all Bihar districts recorded low (two per cent or less) growth in overall yields. In Central Bihar, the old districts of Shahabad and Patna were included in those recording between one and two per cent growth, while Gaya recorded between zero and one per cent. In terms of foodgrains output, the overall compound growth rate in Bihar between 1962 and 1965 and 1970–73 was only 1.74 per cent, with no district showing high growth rates. Figures suggest that during the period between the triennia ended 1970–71 and 1983–84 this meagre growth rate actually declined further to only one per cent per annum [*Mahendra Dev*, 1988: A-111; *Bhalla and Alagh*, 1979: 29–30; *CMIE*, 1995).

However, a wide-ranging study conducted in 1981/2 and 1982/3 by the A.N Sinha Institute of Social Studies (ANSISS) in conjunction with the ILO [*Prasad et al.*, 1988], while confirming much of this picture, did identify certain trends which suggested that potentially transformative changes might be occurring among a specific group and in specific regions of the state.

This group were 'backward' caste – predominantly Kurmi – peasants employing a combination of wage and family (including female) labour, cultivating anything between 0.5 and 10 acres and using tubewell irrigation. Villages where this group is dominant are concentrated in the Central Bihar districts, particularly Patna and Nalanda (where two of the 12 villages in the study were located). The irrigation ratio is high in these areas, while the incidence of sharecropping tenancy is low in relation to other parts of the state, and a notably high proportion of workers are agricultural labourers (see Table 1).

In summary, the study found that this group of households were at the forefront in the installation of tubewells which were the major source of assured irrigation, and in the adoption of High Yield Varieties and the use of fertilisers. While overall it was found that 'the extent of innovation which was witnessed in the area of biological technology has yet to unfold in the realm of mechanisation' [1988: 549], the larger landholders among this group also had the highest value of machinery, productive assets, and capital investment in agriculture, and obtained more and larger 'modern' (institutional) loans than others. Kurmi peasants were characterised by relatively high values of marketed output per acre, and these values were substantially higher for larger landholdings.

TABLE 1
NALANDA DISTRICT: SELECTED INDICATORS

		Nalanda			Bihar			All India		
1	Average operational holding (hectares)	0.61			0.87			1.69		
2	Net sown area as % of reporting area	76.21			44.43			46.3		
3	Gross irrigated area as % of gross cropped area	76.16			36.31			30.72		
4	% of cultivating households leasing in land	16.5			19.73			15.85		
5	% of tenancies sharecropped	45.7			61.94			38.74		
6	As % of main workers:	Male	Female	Total	Male	Female	Total	Male	Female	Total
	Cultivators	43.42	27.54	39.61	45.81	31.54	43.41	40.01	34.55	38.75
	Agricultural labourers	37.22	64.27	43.71	33.02	57.92	37.21	20.90	43.56	26.15
	Household industry	3.73	2.72	3.49	2.66	2.86	2.69	3.33	4.63	3.63
	Other workers	15.63	5.47	13.19	18.51	7.68	16.69	35.76	17.26	31.47

Sources:
Rows 1–3: Centre for Monitoring Indian Economy (CMIE) Profiles of Districts, November 1993
Rows 4 and 5: Column 1 – Census of India 1981, Columns 2 and 3 – National Sample Survey 37th Round, 1981–82.
Note: NSS figures refer to operational holdings, Census figures refer to cultivating households.
      Row 6: Census of India 1991.

This group was identified as having the potential to 'lead' a transformation of the agrarian sector, and specifically contrasted with the predominantly upper caste landlord class which dominated large parts of the state.

Chandkura, one of the villages surveyed in the study, is in Hilsa block of Nalanda district. The study described it as 'a good example of the prosperity of the middle peasant village, which is typical in this part of Bihar'. The Kurmi 'big and middle' peasants who dominated the village were found to have 'a high degree of aptitude for adopting new technology: the village had a high use of chemical fertiliser, HYV seeds and fairly extensive mechanisation in agriculture' [*Prasad et al.*, 1988: 88].

Today, a number of observations suggest that in Chandkura at least, this trend has not continued in the direction predicted in the early 1980s. Whereas the spread of irrigation to cover about half of total cultivated land by the time of the earlier survey was associated with the advent of electricity (however sporadic the supply) and was mainly through private tubewells and pumpsets, during the 1980s electricity disappeared completely from the village, making cultivators dependent on diesel operated pumpsets which were far costlier. The costs of fertiliser were also perceived by even the largest cultivators to be inhibiting the accumulation of surpluses, although both these inputs continued to be used extensively. But there had been little further mechanisation or other technological change. Land concentration still did not appear to be occurring on any significant scale while fragmentation of holdings through inheritance was widespread. Meanwhile there had been a decline in the system of attached labour in favour of casual labour and a relative increase in the wages of the latter.

Class and Caste in Chandkura

Chandkura is a village of 236 households, of whom almost half belong to the 'scheduled' Chamar and Dusadh castes. More than 90 per cent of this group of households are primarily dependent on earnings from agricultural wage labour in the same village. None own more than two acres or operate more than 2.7 acres of land.

Kurmi Mahatos, classified as an 'Other Backward Caste' (OBC) in Bihar, constitute the most numerous single caste in the village, accounting for 65 households. These are predominantly landowning households with cultivation as their main source of income, and both men and women working in the fields. However there is considerable variation both in the size of owned and operated holdings, and in the combination of wage and family labour employed. Much smaller numbers of 'OBC' Yadav and Koeri households are similarly distributed among the poor, middle and rich peasants of the village. Those belonging to traditional service castes such as

Beldar (potters), Barhi (carpenter) and Nai (barber) accounted for another 42 households relying on a combination of jajmani occupations, agricultural and other manual labour and the cultivation of very small landholdings. Although not all classified as 'scheduled castes', these groups have a very low caste status in the region. Among upper castes, there are three Rajput households, all primarily dependent on urban white-collar employment, and one Brahman household, which combined performing ceremonies with auto-rickshaw driving and cultivating a marginal landholding.

Fifty per cent of households in Chandkura are completely landless, and a further 21 per cent own less than one acre. At the other end of the spectrum, nine households own and operate more than ten acres. Despite the absence of any landholdings greater than 25 acres in the village, this leads to a very skewed distribution of both land owned and land operated. 70 per cent of households own only 7.5 per cent of the total land cultivated, compared to 64 per cent owned by the top 10 per cent of households. For land operated, the figures are 13 per cent and 53 per cent.

Only 19 per cent of households lease in land, with the vast majority of tenants owning less than one acre, and leasing in small amounts of land averaging 1.2 acres from the biggest landowners in their own and neighbouring villages. Nearly all these landowners retain most of their land for self-cultivation. There are no instances of leasing in by rich peasants, or by those owning more than five acres. Except for one household sharecropping one acre belonging to a Brahman family living in another village, all leases are today on a fixed rent basis.

The major dividing line according to which the majority of inhabitants of Chandkura and other villages in Hilsa define themselves is that between 'kisans' (literally peasants) and 'mazdoors' (workers). This is partly an expression of the fact that the area is dominated by landowners of the Kurmi Mahato caste, traditionally a peasant caste. It also reflects contemporary reality in which the central class contradiction is between landless or near-landless agricultural labourers, and employers who themselves engage in cultivation, with very few non-cultivating landlords.

However, it also underlines the complex relationship between caste and class in the area. While the vast majority of scheduled caste households hire out agricultural labour, and include virtually no 'middle' or 'rich' peasants, Kurmis and other 'middle' castes are widely distributed among different peasant classes and there are even a handful of households among them who hire out agricultural labour. In this situation the 'kisan' identity plays a vital role in unifying the middle-caste peasantry under the hegemony of the small number of rich peasants who are the major employers, sources of credit and leasers of land in each village. This becomes particularly significant in periods when class conflict between rich peasants and labourers intensifies:

the 'kisan' identity combines elements of caste and class, but is primarily defined by its distinction from the 'mazdoors', those who depend on selling their labour power, and who by definition belong to lower castes.

Irrigation and Cropping Patterns

When explaining how agriculture has changed, older inhabitants of Chandkura and other villages in Hilsa still frequently cite the drought of 1965–66 as the most significant turning point. Until then, agriculture was essentially rainfed. As crops failed repeatedly, cultivators in Hilsa began to adopt the new varieties of wheat being promoted as part of the Green Revolution package. This set up immediate pressures towards the mechanisation of irrigation and private tubewells spread rapidly among larger landowners in the first half of the 1970s.

By 1977, Nalanda district as a whole was proving a 'notable exception' to the comparatively low levels of private tubewell irrigation in the eastern Gangetic plains [Dhawan, 1977: A103]. By the early 1980s the ANSISS/ILO study confirmed that 'tubewells have been adopted in a big way by the Kurmis, most of them situated in … Nalanda District. There is no canal in Nalanda District. In fact Nalanda is one of the few districts where the so-called `Green Revolution' has succeeded significantly' [Prasad et al., 1988: 537). In Chandkura itself, more than 50 per cent of net sown area was irrigated at least once, and 99 per cent of irrigation was from private tubewells.

Chandkura's experience illustrates the key role of irrigation which has been characterised as the 'leading input in Asian agriculture'. Ishikawa [1967] identified three successive roles for irrigation in the transition from a less to a more productive 'stage' of this agriculture. First, it stabilises harvest fluctuations arising from variable rainfall. It then allows a second crop to be introduced. Finally it makes possible increased applications of fertiliser and the use of improved varieties and techniques. A more recent study observes that for West Bengal and Bangladesh, these have been simultaneous, rather than successive, effects; a 'modified' version of the second effect is identified, in which irrigation contributes not to the introduction of a second crop, but to a change in the crop composition [Boyce, 1987: 199].

In Chandkura, the rabi crop changed significantly, both in composition and area sown, with the area under wheat increasing from negligible levels in the mid-1960s to 18 per cent of net sown area by 1981–82, partially at the expense of unirrigated crops like khesari, gram and masoor. High Yielding Varieties of rice requiring substantial applications of fertilisers were also introduced. Another significant development was the increased cultivation of onions from 1975 onwards. These require intensive application of irrigation and other capital inputs as well as labour, and by 1981 'continual power failures' were already affecting yields. The main crops cultivated in the village were 'bhadai and aghani paddy, wheat, maize (rabi, garma and bhadai) khesari, potato, onion, gram and masoor' [*Prasad et al.*, 1988: 87]. Yields of paddy had also increased substantially: average yields in the village in 1981–82 were 800kg per acre, almost double the district average in 1970–71.

In terms of cropping patterns, there have been a number of further changes during the last 15 years. Wheat cultivation has expanded further at the expense of other rabi crops, notably khesari, and is now the major rabi crop, although almost all landholders continue to cultivate a small amount of khesari, chana(gram) and masoor. Onion cultivation has also increased significantly across landholding sizes: most cultivators only devote a small proportion of their land to onion growing, but these take up a large proportion of total capital investment, with irrigation, fertiliser and labour costs per acre highest.

However, there is now only one paddy crop in the village – the aghani(kharif) crop. The cultivation of bhadai paddy and maize, which were mainly rainfed, stopped in the early 1980s as a result of a climatic shift: whereas previously the pre-monsoon rains came in June, they now do not begin until the second week of July. And the cumulative effect of the use of tubewells and pumpsets has been that in the weeks preceding the rains, the water table goes down far lower than it used to.

Yields of wheat have increased steadily and in 1995–96 average yields were 894 kg per acre, almost double their 1981–82 levels of 480 kg per acre. Rice yields also increased, but less dramatically, to an average of 1102 kg per acre.

Landholding Patterns

Observers of agrarian change have identified a number of phenomena which may be associated with a process of expanded reproduction among a particular section of cultivators. One of these is the gradual concentration of land in the hands of this group. This process is clearly not taking place in Chandkura: referring to land losses and gains during the five years preceding the survey in 1981–82, the ANSISS/ILO report noted that, for the study villages as a whole,

> Not much can be inferred from the data as to which of the land size groups is gaining or losing relative to the others. If anything, the smallest landsize category, up to one acre seems to be faring relatively better. But the understatement of gain is probably disproportionately concentrated in the larger landholding size groups. Therefore, it

would not be reasonable to infer that land transactions are greatly changing the pattern of land distribution' [*Prasad et al.*, 1988: 464–5].

This absence of 'land transactions' on any significant scale seems to have persisted during the 1980s and early 1990s: only 20 per cent of households reported any change in the amount of land they owned during the last 15 years. Significantly, 50 per cent of these referred to the division of land through the process of inheritance or the separation of joint families into more than one household. Of those who had purchased land, more than 70 per cent had done so using earnings from government service outside the village. The amounts of land involved were also very small, averaging 0.58 acres.

And while the lease market as well as the land market has been an important avenue for land concentration elsewhere, there are no cases of leasing in by rich peasants, which appears to be a non-existent phenomenon in the area.[1]

While reliable data on land distribution is not available for the earlier period, a comparison of the distribution of households by class in 1981–82 and 1995–96 confirms the impression that the tendency in Chandkura has been towards dispersion rather than concentration of both owned and operated land. On the one hand, it shows a substantial increase in the number of small and marginal cultivators: using the ANSISS/ILO study's (admittedly somewhat problematic) classification, those classified as 'poor middle peasant' households – neither hiring in nor hiring out agricultural labour – have increased from only 3.7 per cent of total households in 1981–82 to 19.3 per cent in 1995–96, when average land cultivated by them was 1.7 acres. (50 per cent of these households are primarily dependent on non-agricultural income) 'Middle peasant' households, who do hire in labour, have also increased from 11.2 per cent to 15 per cent of households, similarly cultivating an average of only 1.8 acres. This seems to be at least partially accounted for by a decline in the percentage of 'big peasant' households (defined by a combination of resource endowment and the exclusion of female household members from cultivation) from 20.3 per cent to only 7.7 per cent. However, the point to be noted is that this has not led to a greater concentration of land in the hands of big peasants. In fact the average area cultivated per household has either declined or remained constant for all classes between 1981–82 and 1995–96. While the top 20 per cent of households in terms of size of area cultivated now cultivate a slightly higher percentage of total land under cultivation, the average area cultivated by these households has also declined slightly from six acres to 5.4 acres.

Another striking aspect of the landholding pattern in Chandkura is the extent of fragmentation of holdings. The average number of plots per operated holding in 1995–96 was extremely high at 6.6, compared to an all-

Bihar figure of 2.8 in 1991–92 [*Government of India*, 1996a: A19]. The average size of plots was highest among those operating five acres and above, but even this group operate plots of an average size of only 1.3 acres. In addition plots are frequently irregular in shape. There may be a number of reasons for this phenomenon. In particular, population density – and the dependence of the population on agriculture – is high, while the quality of the land is variable. This means that inheritance usually involves not only division of holdings but fragmentation into smaller and smaller plots to ensure that each heir receives a comparable share of lands of different quality and type. At the same time, as we have seen, tenancy in this area involves the leasing out by the larger landowners of small plots to tenants of whom the majority are small landowners themselves, and also involves leasing out tiny plots as partial payment to attached labourers, leading to further fragmentation of operated holdings.

This too has significant implications for the process of agrarian transformation: as Byres [1988: 184] notes,

> For rich peasants, who may be proto-capitalists, fragmentation is likely to constitute a significant barrier to accumulation. Development of the productive forces faces a powerful constraint: whether that development takes a purely bio-chemical or a mechanised form (that is, on the one hand, for example, new seeds, the application of non-organic fertilisers, new forms of non-mechanised irrigation; on the other, tractors, tube-wells, etc.). Fragmentation poses especially difficult problems for mechanisation.

But despite the fact that land consolidation has been a stated goal of agricultural policy at both the all-India and the state-level since before Independence, there have been no state-sponsored attempts at land consolidation in Hilsa development block.[2] In fact, Bihar's Land Consolidation Department has now been formally abolished [*Jha*, 1997: 108]. Jannuzi argues that such policies were in any case modelled on conditions in Punjab and inappropriate to Eastern India where 'to have diverse holdings was favoured by many, in circumstances where the quality of land was not homogeneous, as a way of ensuring, for example, that it would be possible to plant different crops in different seasons … This was a rational means by which cultivators could seek to maximise their economic security' [*Jannuzi*, 1996: 12]. But under the conditions prevailing today, cultivators of different sizes in Chandkura and elsewhere in Hilsa consider having one's land in one place a definite advantage – for example, Rajaram Mahto, a Kurmi rich peasant of Chandkura who was particularly proud of his skills as a farmer told me that while he was not the largest landowner in Chandkura, he was the only one to have so much land in one place – all his 12 acres were in one plot – and that this was something he had achieved in his lifetime through judicious buying and selling of land. Other cultivators in the village also commented on this as something both remarkable and desirable.

In fact, there are a few instances of groups of landowners elsewhere in Hilsa – big and middle peasants – attempting consolidation themselves – but these were reported to have failed because of the uneven quality of land and the economic inequalities between those exchanging land. Overall it seems that without state intervention, awareness among landholders of the disadvantages associated with fragmentation has not in itself been a powerful enough force to overcome the barriers to consolidation and the impulses to further subdivision of holdings. But if the state itself to a large extent reflects the nature and interests of the dominant classes within the region, this lack of intervention by the state also reflects the fact that a strong rich peasantry with capitalist tendencies, capable of acting as a 'class-for-itself' and pushing through policies which would facilitate its own development, has failed to emerge in Bihar, despite the initial indicators noted in the early 1980s.[3]

Mechanisation

The ANSISS/ILO study found significantly higher levels of investment in 'modern agricultural capital goods' among the dominant landowners in Chandkura when compared to other groups across Central and North Bihar. Excluding irrigation, this referred to threshers, power tillers and tractors. In 1995–96, there were 18 threshers, three power tillers and five tractors owned in the village. Nearly all of these had been bought in the late 1970s or early 1980s. However, two points should be noted in this context. First, in comparison to areas which have already witnessed agrarian transformation on the lines predicted for Chandkura in 1981–82, the incidence of use of these machines was and has remained low. For example, Agarwal [1983: 36] cites Cost of Cultivation Studies carried out in Punjab in 1971–72, which found that 41.24 per cent of cultivators of HYV wheat used tractors or a combination of bullock ploughs and tractors for ploughing. For threshing, 71.71 per cent used mechanical threshers. In Chandkura in 1995–96, only 16 per cent of cultivators of HYV wheat used tractors or a combination of bullock ploughs and tractors for ploughing, while 29.27 per cent used mechanical threshers. Both sets of data refer to both owned and hired implements.[4]

Secondly, while tractors are by far the most expensive of the items categorised as 'modern agricultural capital goods', their presence should not necessarily be seen as indicative of changes in the process of agricultural production. Significantly, the only tractor bought in the last ten years had been purchased (along with a trailer) by one of the biggest landowners in the village exclusively for the purpose of hiring out for construction and transport work in the surrounding villages. The use of tractors primarily for non-agricultural purposes by landowners owning ten acres and above is now a common phenomenon in Hilsa, and in fact throughout Central Bihar. During the decade from the early 1970s to the early 1980s, it was these landowners who had access to a large proportion of the institutional credit available for the purchase of agricultural machinery, and they frequently took loans for one or more tractors. In the same period, construction of houses in villages, district towns and in Patna emerged as a major avenue for investment of the surpluses being generated by the spurt in productivity in agriculture. Thus it was possible to realise substantial returns to an investment in a tractor by hiring it out for transporting building materials. In addition, the poor condition of most roads and the inadequacy of public transport in the region means that tractors can also be profitably hired out for transporting produce from villages to local markets, as well as for carrying passengers. Drivers are employed by the owners – in Hilsa, they are usually from other villages, and belong to the same Kurmi caste as the owners, a feature which is discussed in more detail below.

On the other hand, tractors are not completely absent from agriculture in Chandkura. They are hired out by their owners to other cultivators in this and neighbouring villages for ploughing. The use of tractors – by 17 per cent of cultivating households in 1995–96 – was spread across landholding sizes and surprisingly, if the biggest size group cultivating 10 acres or more (and including all the tractor owners) is excluded, the use of tractors is highest in the size group 0.51–1 acre. The reason for this is that it is those cultivators who cannot afford to keep bullocks and do not own ploughs who resort to hiring in tractors for ploughing, at a rate of Rs 300 per acre, despite the fact that the size and shape of their fields makes them difficult to plough effectively using a tractor. With the increased use of HYVs, the period within which ploughing must take place has become shorter. As a result ploughs and bullocks are not available for hire in this period. In some cases larger landowners continued to use ploughs even when owning tractors.

Power tillers, being smaller, are actually more suited to conditions in Chandkura. But relatively few were available for hire – at higher rates of Rs 400 per acre. All this suggests that given the pattern of small landholdings and the extent of fragmentation, the role which tractors can play in the transformation of Chandkura's agriculture is limited. They are clearly not displacing wage labour on any significant scale (small cultivators do their own ploughing). Rather their owners – the large landowners who were given loans to buy them in the 1970s and early 1980s – are now using them to extract a rental surplus from marginal and small cultivators, a phenomenon which also has significant implications for an analysis of the process of peasant class differentiation.[5]

Inputs, Infrastructure and the Administration

Perhaps the biggest change which has taken place in the process of agricultural production in Chandkura since the early 1980s relates to irrigation. By 1981–82, the extension of irrigation through tubewells in Chandkura had more or less come to a standstill. According to the ANSISS/ILO study, the total area improved by private tubewell irrigation in the five years preceding the study period had been only three per cent of the total cultivated area. In fact the spread of tubewell irrigation coincided with the advent of electricity in the early 1970s and as the study noted, by the early 1980s, the electricity supply was already sporadic. By 1983/84 it was cut off completely. And from the late 1970s onwards, there was a switch to diesel powered pumpsets as a result of the absence of electricity. In 1995–96, excluding a very marginal amount of river irrigated land, diesel pumpsets used with open borings were the sole method of irrigation in use in the village.This pattern of a shift from electric to diesel powered irrigation in the late 1970s or early 1980s is replicated throughout Hilsa. Only in one village in my survey was electricity still sporadically supplied, and in this case it was not usually available at the time of year it was needed for irrigation.

The National Commission on Agriculture noted as early as 1976 that

> nearly a third of private tubewells are diesel operated notwithstanding the fact that electric pumps are cheaper both in capital and operating cost. This situation has arisen because of inadequate and unsatisfactory supply of power. The persisting shortage of power in most parts of the country, particularly in North India where groundwater resources are abundant, has hampered the rapid growth of electrically operated tubewells and farmers keen on having their own source of irrigation have turned to the more expensive diesel pumpsets ... [*Government of India*, 1976a: 21].

While it was hoped that 'The present tendency ... will disappear before long with the improvement in the power position', in Bihar at least the power crisis has deepened during the last two decades.

Mozoomdar [1990: 28] points out that inadequate investment in power in Bihar (excluding the industrial and coalfield regions) has led to slow growth in electricity consumption. Thus in Central Bihar, 30.73 kwh per capita were consumed in 1965–66, rising to 41.23 in 1977–78 and 44.09 in 1984–85, as compared to all-India figures of 61.33, 120.73 and 154.00. According to Sharma [1996: 16] on a conservative basis, the State was deficient in power in relation to total requirement to the extent of at least 40% in 1993-94. Most parts of the rural area of the State go without power for days together. Overwhelming majority of State and private tubewells are idle for lack of electricity. The farmers have largely changed over to diesel pumps which are costly in terms of maintenance and operating charges. The acute power crisis has affected not only the level of agricultural production but also a whole range of rural activities – processing of grains, storage, production in small rural industries etc.

Different classes of cultivators in Chandkura are unanimous in identifying the increased costs of irrigation as one of the principal factors currently preventing them from accumulating agricultural surpluses on any significant scale. In the mid-1970s it was observed that the per unit cost of irrigation with a diesel tubewell was approximately twice that of irrigation with an electric tubewell, while the figures for mobile diesel pumpsets were even higher [*Dhawan*, 1977: A98]. Today this differential has increased further, with operating costs of diesel pumpsets now almost four times as high as that of electric tubewells. Frequent shortages of diesel also force pumpset users to buy diesel on the black market, pushing costs up even further.[6]

This has exacerbated the problem of economies of scale associated with mechanised irrigation on small fragmented holdings.[7] However the fact that in Chandkura, as elsewhere in Hilsa, diesel pumpsets are used not with tubewells but with fairly densely scattered open borings partially counteracts this effect, by allowing diesel pumpset owners to move them from plot to plot, and even more importantly, to hire out their pumpsets to other cultivators. Thus in 1995–95, 83.3 per cent of those households cultivating any land in the village used diesel pumpsets. Of these, 48 per cent owned their own pumpsets, a further 48 per cent hired them in from others in the village, and the remainder borrowed them.

Diesel pumpsets are the most widely distributed of mechanical inputs, with four of the 64 sets in Chandkura being owned by households who hire out casual labour and also own small amounts of land. However, those hiring in pumpsets are overwhelmingly small and marginal cultivators. This extension of irrigation to small and marginal holdings is the major factor accounting for the further increase in cultivated area irrigated at least once to approximately 73 per cent in 1995–96.

The changes which have occurred in the production patterns of small and marginal cultivators in Hilsa, the reasons for their adoption of new technology, and the nature of their integration into the market will be explored elsewhere. But it is evident that with owners charging Rs 10–20 per hour plus the costs of diesel, rental costs for irrigation along with other input costs are too high for these marginal cultivators to be able to accumulate any significant surpluses as a result of increases in yields.

Fertiliser costs have also increased significantly since 1991. Wholesale fertiliser prices went up by nearly 50 per cent between 1990 and 1992 alone after remaining virtually unchanged throughout the 1980s [*Government of India*, 1992].

In terms of actual costs to the cultivator, cost of cultivation studies for Bihar show that fertiliser costs adjusted against the farm harvest price index remained almost constant between 1972–72 and 1983–84 [*Government of India*, 1991, 1996b; *Jha*, 1997]. By 1995–96, however, cultivators in Hilsa were paying approximately Rs 10 per kg nutrients, as compared to the cost of cultivation studies figures of approximately Rs 5 per kg nutrients for the entire period from 1980–81 to 1987–88 [*Government of India*, 1991, 1996b]. The post-1991 fertiliser price increase means that in Hilsa, a maund of rice is today the equivalent of only one 50 kg sack of urea where previously it was worth two. Prices of fertiliser on the black market, on which small and marginal cultivators without connections with the administration were the most dependent, are substantially higher.

If 'de-electrification' has had a profound impact on agricultural production in Hilsa, other factors symptomatic of a crisis of the state infrastructure in Bihar as a whole have also had a detrimental effect. The absence of roads and the high cost of transport forces surplus-producing cultivators in many villages to sell their produce at lower rates to traders who come to the villages. However, the most widely cited problem in all the villages surveyed – including Chandkura – is the chronic lack of availability of inputs such as fertilisers, pesticides, and seeds as well as diesel, and the consequent escalation of black-market prices for these inputs. These are usually appropriated by the Block level administration and a section of rich peasants who have links with the bureaucracy and local politicians, to be resold on the black market.

This process, while inevitably difficult to assess quantitatively, is also inextricably linked to the nature of the state in Bihar. The appropriation of development resources by unproductive upper caste landlords through the manipulation of state apparatuses is not a new phenomenon in Bihar. But current developments in Hilsa suggests that a section of Kurmi and other 'OBC' rich peasants who were able to accumulate significant agricultural surpluses in the 1970s are now following a similar route, diverting resources into the 'unproductive' but far more lucrative avenues of tertiary activities inextricably linked to political careerism, corruption and crime. As Das [1992: 25] observes: '... the proliferation of the bureaucracy, the enormous accretion of power with the government and the rise of corruption and crime as the fastest modes of accumulation changed occupational patterns and and social urges. The plateauing off of agricultural growth was contrasted with the immense opportunities availed by those who had access to governmental position and patronage.'

These structures can only reinforce the 'stalling' of agricultural development which we believe to have occurred in this part of Central Bihar, both by denying key resources to the more production-orientated section of cultivators, and by providing more lucrative avenues for the diversion of whatever surpluses are accumulated in agriculture away from productive reinvestment. It also gives an indication of the kind of constraints – inherent within the nature of state power in Bihar – which would need to be overcome if this stalling is not to be a permanent one.

II. AGRICULTURAL LABOUR – CHANGING RELATIONS

The social distinction between those who perform wage labour on other's land and those who limit themselves to the cultivation of their own holdings is an extremely sharp one throughout Central Bihar. For agricultural labourers in Hilsa furthermore, the correlation between class position and caste status is as we have seen very strong. The term 'mazdoor' or labourer connotes a position in both hierarchies – a 'mazdoor' is by definition low caste. The fact that labourers are defined, both by others and by themselves, as a cohesive community in this sense has important implications for their ability to organise.

It is also significant that while paid labour by any household member on another's land denotes a 'mazdoor' household, it is the participation of women in such labour which is at the heart of the definition. As far as agriculture is concerned, only women of a low caste work 'outside'. (For women of the upper 'backward' castes – Kurmis, Koeris and Yadavs – there is no stigma attached to cultivating family holdings, but upper-caste women are prohibited from doing any work in the fields). The pervasive – albeit contested – influence of feudal high caste norms in this respect is partly responsible for the withdrawal of women – particularly younger daughters-in-law – from paid agricultural labour by dalit labour households who acquire alternative sources of income and/or land. However an equally important factor which makes women's wage labour undesirable both to dalit women themselves and their families is the other side of upper caste morality – the sexual harassment and even rape of women labourers working in the fields which higher caste employers long considered their birthright. Altogether, it is clear that the complex notion of family 'izzat' or honour is crucially affected by women participating in wage labour far more in Central Bihar than appears to be the case in most of South India and even some other parts of the North.[8]

At the same time, with rice the major crop, it is women's paid labour which assures the employer of realising his surplus – women are solely responsible for the labour-intensive and time-bound task of transplanting, and play a major role in harvesting the crop. Given the overall scarcity of employment, few labour households can afford to prevent women from working in these periods of peak labour demand. But this also means that women are at the forefront of agitations demanding higher wages, refusing to work en masse during the transplanting and harvesting seasons. These aspects of agrarian class relations are explored further below.

Agricultural wage labour in Chandkura and other villages in Hilsa takes two forms. Casual labourers are paid daily wages in kind, fixed in advance, except during harvesting when they are paid a predetermined fraction of what they harvest. Attached labourers are employed on one year oral contracts, but are also paid on a daily basis in kind. They receive a small plot (usually 10–12 katthas, approximately one third of an acre) to cultivate.

Male attached labourers are generally employed for non-mechanised ploughing, and in addition carry out maintenance work in the fields including looking after the drainage system. They also take part in harvesting and in uprooting the paddy seedlings (a task carried out by men during the transplanting season, while women are replanting). Unpaid labour, in tasks such as cutting grass and bringing in animals, existed previously but is no longer widespread. Those who employ attached labourers in Chandkura do not give work to the women family members of male attached labourers for most of the year. However during transplanting and harvesting, these women have to carry out the work on the employer's land before accepting employment anywhere else, even though wage rates are often lower. In fact this guaranteed supply of female labour during peak periods is a key advantage of attachment from the employer's point of view.

It is important to note that the position of attached labourers in Chandkura is somewhat different from that of those in upper-caste dominated areas who are often referred to as 'farm servants'. Under the latter system, both men and women carry out a variety of tasks both in the fields and in the compound. Employers in Chandkura are almost all of the Kurmi caste and almost universally the men engage in cultivation themselves: labourers, whether attached or casual, are employed only for specific tasks in the fields. This also means that even male attached labourers only receive a maximum total of six months work per year. And while attached labourers can (and in fact are usually compelled to) seek other employment when there is no work at all provided by their employer, unlike casual labourers they are not 'free' to do so in periods when there is some work to be done, but not enough to earn a daily wage. As we will see, this has been one of several reasons for labourers preferring casual labour in the context of changing patterns of non-agricultural employment.

While the employer generally provides the seeds and sometimes also the plough and bullocks for the cultivation of the attached labourer's plot, the labourers provide all other inputs, including fertilisers and diesel pumpsets which they hire from the employer at standard rates. This is in contrast to the situation observed in 1981–82 when it was found that electric powered tubewell irrigation was provided free by employers to attached labourers, and was seen as one of the mechanisms through which attachment was reinforced [*Prasad et al.*, 1988: 538].

People who had been attached labourers in the past described the classic interlocking of loan and labour markets in which on entering a contract they were given a sum of money and made to put a thumb print on an 'agreement' according to which the 'loan' along with unspecified amounts of interest had to be paid back before they could leave the employer. In 1995–96 however attached labourers were not automatically given loans by their employers. (Approximately 31 per cent of attached labourers as compared to 15 per cent of casual labourers took loans from 'kisans' currently employing them.) Several attached labourers stated that they took loans (usually between Rs 100 and Rs 300) only if they needed them for an emergency such as illness or a funeral. These loans were subject to the same interest rates (6 per cent per month) as other loans given by 'kisans' to 'mazdoors', but did not require collateral. However until these loans were paid back (with interest) the labourers could not leave the employer. In some villages crops from the allotted land were seized by the landowner if the labourer defaulted on the loan at the end of the year. In Chandkura, however, the most significant factor preventing labourers from defaulting on loans was the fact that if they did so they would not be able to get further credit in emergencies from any of the 'kisans' in the village.

In fact there appears to have been a shift from interlocked relationships between individuals to those between classes in the village. Thus the agricultural labourers of the village, whether casual or attached, are primarily dependent on the group of large landowners of the village for credit. Credit available to them from other sources, generally moneylenders and gold merchants in Hilsa town, was on substantially less favourable terms. Interest is always charged in such 'kisan-mazdoor' transactions (in contrast, smaller cultivators of the Kurmi caste can often get loans interest-free from larger ones). As we will see, this becomes particularly significant in periods when class contradictions intensify.

While we do not have information on the precise extent of attached labour in Chandkura in the late 1960s, it is evident that the 1970s saw a substantial decline in the proportion of labourers who were attached throughout Hilsa. A large proportion of agricultural labourers describe being 'bonded' in the 1960s or can recall their parents working under these conditions. Thus by 1981–82, 59 per cent of agricultural labourer households had no members working as attached labourers. Similar shifts in the structure of labour demand have been observed elsewhere in India in the context of the introduction of tubewell irrigation, which has been estimated to reduce the labour time required for irrigation by up to 75 per cent [*Rudra*, 1971; *Byres*, 1972]. The changes in cropping intensity and the spread of HYVs which accompanied tubewell irrigation increased demand for labour, but intensified seasonal peaks in this demand, reinforcing the shift away from permanent labour. But the limited introduction of tractors in the area in the latter half of the 1970s, did not, as elsewhere, mean the employment of permanent labourers whose work included driving them: tractor drivers in Hilsa are generally, like their owners, from cultivating Kurmi families, they receive a monthly salary of Rs 500–700, and do not identify themselves in any way as agricultural labourers. In any case, as we have seen, tractor driving is not exclusively, or even primarily an agricultural occupation in Hilsa.

However, the major impact of these processes had already been felt by the time the first study of Chandkura took place in 1981–82. Although there has been a further extension of irrigation during the last 15 years, this has been largely a result of the adoption of diesel pumpset irrigation by small and marginal cultivators of the dalit castes. These households have never employed attached labourers; in fact, they hire out both male and female labour. During peak seasons, many of them meet additional needs by exchanging labour, particularly women's labour, with other similar households. Thus the impact of the second, post-electricity phase of extension of irrigation has had far less impact on the structure and extent of demand for wage labour in Chandkura.

Further changes in the cropping pattern in this period have also been limited so far in their effects on demand for labour. As we have noted, onion growing has increased even in the smallest landholding size categories. Cultivation of onions requires intensive labour, and operations are extremely time-bound. This means that even the smallest cultivators, who do not employ labour at any other time, have to employ wage labour for weeding and harvesting the onions. Further increases could have important effects on the structure of demand for labour within the village: weeding is performed entirely by women, and is paid at the same rate as paddy transplantation. However onions are also a very capital intensive crop – requiring larger applications of fertilisers, pesticides and in particular irrigation than any other crop (onions need 12 to 13 waterings as compared to two waterings for wheat). Given the constraints described earlier, it seems unlikely that in this area there will be a rapid expansion beyond current levels in the immediate future.

The other crop which has seen considerable expansion during the last 15 years, wheat, by contrast, mainly provides male employment in ploughing and sowing during the rabi season when it is grown, particularly as threshing is largely mechanised. However this too has not been sufficient to change the basic pattern of demand for labour which provides a maximum of six months regular employment, peaking in July/August when kharif paddy is transplanted by women labourers, and November/December when it is harvested.

Yet from the point of view of agricultural labourers in Chandkura, it is the 1980s and 1990s which have seen the most significant changes in both the nature of agricultural labour and relationships between employers and labourers in the village. This can only be understood by looking at changes which are occurring beyond the confines of the village. One of these is the pattern of change in the non-agricultural employment available to labouring households in Hilsa during the 1980s and 1990s.

Alternative Sources of Employment for Rural Labour Households

Nalanda district has not been an area of high outmigration in comparison to other parts of Bihar. The ANSISS/ILO survey found that for the villages surveyed in Nalanda, only eight per cent of all households had outmigrant members, compared to 17 per cent at an all-Bihar level [*Prasad et al.*, 1988: 136]. (The incidence of migration did not however vary widely across classes although the type of work carried out by migrants from different classes was very different [1988: 125].)

However, from the point of view of labour households in this area, in the 1970s and 1980s migration represented the main possibility for non-agricultural employment. In Hilsa there were three main types of migration open to these households. First, there was migration to Calcutta and the surrounding area for work in jute mills. Although the Magadh region of Central Bihar which includes Nalanda has historically been a less important source of Bihari workers for the jute mills of Bengal than the Bhojpur region [*de Haan*, 1997], it still provided considerable numbers. However, with the decline of the jute industry in the 1980s and 1990s, this is no longer a significant source of employment in Hilsa. In 1995-96, only two households in Chandkura had members who were currently jute mill workers, although there were a number of men in the village who had retired from this work.

Secondly, and this was a much more recent phenomenon which emerged in the 1980s, men migrated to work in small factories in Punjab, Haryana, UP and the Delhi area. These were small scale units such as metal processing or furniture making, based in small urban centres rather than big cities. Men doing these jobs stayed away for periods ranging from five months to one year. Earnings could vary between Rs 300 to Rs 1,000 per month, out of which all living expenses had to be met. It was generally felt that the harsh working conditions together with isolation made it difficult to continue with such work for long periods. We do not have data on the extent of such migration in different periods. But in the light of the sharp decline in employment growth in the secondary sector particularly since the late1980s [*Bhalla*, 1997: 222] I would hypothesise that this source of employment is a declining one.

The third type of migration involved both men and women going to work as construction labour or loaders or in brick kilns elsewhere in Central Bihar. This is the only type of migration which has not declined. In fact there appears to be a growing trend of groups of women or whole families migrating further afield to Haryana, Punjab and Kanpur (UP) to work in brick kilns. Where entire families migrate, they sometimes leave in September or October, and only return in July, when there is work available – mainly for women – in paddy transplanting. This type of migration was prevalent in several villages surveyed in 1995–96. Labourers said that one of the reasons was that in the wake of struggles over wages, local landowners were refusing to give them consumption loans, which had enabled them to survive the lean season in the village in the past (see below).

Today the most important source of employment outside the village for both men and women is daily wage labour on construction sites in neighbouring villages or in Hilsa town. This is now an important source of income during the lean season for the majority of agricultural labour households. In addition, several men from agricultural labour families in the village have become 'rajmistris' or masons during the last fifteen years and this is now a significant source of income for their families, although household members still participate in agricultural labour during peak seasons. My survey also found that in 1995–96, about one quarter of 'jajmani' caste households were no longer participating in agriculture at all. But this again was the result of an increase in construction and loading work rather than a revival of 'traditional' occupations.

The boom in construction has been mainly the result of the investment of the agrarian surpluses generated in the 1970s and early 1980s in 'conspicuous consumption'. Large new two and three storey houses both in the villages and in Hilsa town, are, along with extravagant weddings, enormous dowries and in some cases a formidable array of licensed and unlicensed weapons, potent symbols of the upward mobility of a section of the rich peasants of the area. These are the major sources of expenditure for that group which has been able to consolidate the improvement in their class status afforded by technological change and increased yields by integrating themselves into the political and bureaucratic structures and networks which allow them to divert and appropriate a large portion of the Block's development resources. This is clearly not a stable situation and construction work is liable to dry up as quickly as it proliferated.

It should also be borne in mind that employment in the construction sector does not indicate the kind of development which would create an expansion in opportunities for non-agricultural employment in general in rural Central Bihar. As Bhalla points out, construction is a 'residual sector' to which 'underemployed workers gravitate ... as a last resort' (Bhalla, this volume). Jha [1997: 45] refers to the use of the term 'distress diversification' to describe the movement of agricultural labour household members into low productivity/low earning non-agricultural work of this type.[9]

The labour market in Chandkura has never of course been completely isolated, and it has long been common practice for casual agricultural labourers to occasionally work for employers in adjacent villages. In fact, this mobility, as well as the physical proximity of villages which are often less than a kilometre apart, has been a key factor in determining the impact of class conflicts. But a more recent development for agricultural labourers in Hilsa has been the increased demand for labourers for large-scale potato and onion cultivation in the Jalla area of neighbouring Patna district. In Chandkura, agents come to the village and recruit men in groups of ten or twenty for the potato harvest in March and the onion harvest in April. In a number of other villages, however, whole families go to Patna district for a period of two to four months between January and April. They construct their own shelters on the land of the rich peasant employers. During this period each adult can earn between Rs 25 and Rs 40 daily.

Thus both of the major types of employment which were available to rural labour households outside their own villages in 1995–96, construction work and contract agricultural work, take place in nearby areas, are relatively short term, and are generally engaged in by both women and men. The change in the nature of employment available has several implications.

First, whereas earlier forms of non-agricultural employment involved long-distance migration, and essentially removed a small number of people from the socio-economic arena of the village for long periods, today non-agricultural employment is engaged in by a far greater proportion of labouring households, but can only offer a secondary source of income. Whereas previously it was seen an escape route, as we will see today the availability of local construction work in particular has helped labourers to demand higher wages for agricultural labour from employers in the village, by allowing them to sustain long disputes.

Secondly, the emergence of contract work in a neighbouring district has had a direct impact on the expectations of agricultural labourers by providing an opportunity (albeit for a limited period of the year) of earning more within the agricultural sector itself.

Thirdly, both these types of employment involve labourers being exploited by employers from the same class and caste as the village landowners. Thus it has intensified rather than defusing contradictions between labourers and employers in the village. For example dalit labourers in Bhokila (one of the villages in my survey) described how one of them had been taken to another village to work on the construction of a new house for a local rich peasant landowner. A wall collapsed killing the young man. The landowner brought back the body and told his father that he had died of dysentry. But they found out what had really happened and this led to a campaign to have the landowner prosecuted (this ultimately failed due to the witnesses' fear of retaliation).

Fourthly, the participation of women and/or entire families rather than lone men in these activities means that the additional income has a greater impact on household consumption levels: as a number of studies have shown, women invariably spend a greater proportion of their earnings on family necessities [e.g., *Kelkar and Gala*, 1990: 101; *Agarwal*, 1994: 28–9]. Women's participation also reinforces all the effects described above, making alternative sources of earning more directly comparable with those in the village. And the availability of alternative sources of employment for women workers has a particularly important effect on disputes during periods of peak labour demand for agricultural operations in the village, since it is women's labour which is most in demand at these times.

Apart from increasing the bargaining power and confidence of labourers, strengthening their resistance to unequal relations based on caste, and intensifying class contradictions, the increased availability of work outside the village in 1995–96 meant that agricultural labourers in Chandkura felt that their earning capacity was now substantially greater if they were unattached and free to take up both non-agricultural casual daily labour and agricultural contract work. This is despite the fact that permanent labourer households carried out an average of 94 more persondays local agricultural wage labour per household in a year.

However, it is important to note that even in the case of unattached workers, local agricultural wage labour remained their primary source of income, and improving the conditions of this labour was a major concern. In fact one of the most significant effects of the growth in construction work in Hilsa was that it helped labourers to sustain long disputes with agricultural employers. These struggles are discussed in more detail in the following section.

Agricultural Labourers' Struggles

While there are a number of earlier instances of agricultural labourers in Hilsa organising to demand basic improvements in the conditions of their lives, during the 1980s these struggles entered a new and more concerted phase with the emergence of the movement led by the CPI(ML) (Liberation).

Agitations led by the CPI(ML) began in Hilsa in 1979. As elsewhere in Bihar, the base and local leadership of the party was drawn from among the mainly dalit landless agricultural labourers and poor peasants. The main focus of the movement in its intial phase was wages, forced attachment of labour through debt, and caste-based or 'social' oppression. In several villages, mobilisation began around women's resistance to rapists of the higher caste landed classes. While this movement had direct links with earlier struggles which had taken place elsewhere in central Bihar in the early 1970s, the catalyst for its emergence in this area at this juncture was the visibly growing profits of a section of the rich peasantry, which had not been paralleled by an increase in the wages of labourers. As a local activist of the movement explained, 'here we don't have landlords owning hundreds of acres as in some other parts of Bihar, but the rich peasants, the new economic class, are exploiting people brutally, and they are a target of our struggle. They are attacking women, attacking labourers. They have supported the big landowners – like the Mahants – against our movement.'

Nor had there been a decline in the everyday experiences of humiliation and brutality faced by the dalit rural poor – and particularly dalit women – at the hands of the economically powerful higher castes. In fact this type of coercion had intensified as opportunities for rapid accumulation by the richer landowners grew and contradictions with labourers sharpened, and was increasingly occurring even in villages which, dominated by 'backward caste' cultivating landowners, had been relatively free of the extremes of feudal oppression.

By 1980 a wave of strikes had begun, demanding an increase in wages. In a survey of 12 villages in the block where wage-related struggles had occurred, I found that in all these villages, strikes often lasting from the period of rice transplanting in July/August until the harvest in November/December, had taken place between 1980 and 1988. In all except one case, it was these struggles which had established the wage rate for casual labour which still predominates in the area, 2 kg rice and 0.5 kg sattu, with or without a 250 gm 'nasta' (breakfast), and one out of every 12–15 bundles harvested. Often strikes had taken place in tens of villages simultaneously, and this was a key factor in preventing the employers from bringing in labour from other villages. Meanwhile in some villages, the labourers were able to negotiate a wage rise with the employers without going on strike after wages had increased in neighbouring villages. This was the case in Chandkura, where wages increased in 1988.

During these struggles, demands were also raised relating to the attachment of labour by employers. It was then still common for employers to give loans to permanent labourers in order to compel them to remain working indefinitely for lower wages, ostensibly to pay off an ever-growing debt. The movement advised labourers not to take such loans if they could avoid it, and demanded that all such debts should be cancelled. This was one of the major factors which led to the virtual disappearance of long-term attached labour, which had previously lasted entire lifetimes. However as we will see, one of the responses of employers in many villages to labourers organising in general, and to the resulting decline in debt bondage in particular, has been to withdraw from the credit market, refusing to give loans to labourers altogether.

Struggles for land redistribution were launched in this block a few years later, focussing on two main types of land seizure – that of 'gair mazarua' (government and public commons) land illegally occupied – and often left uncultivated – by the larger landowners of the village, and that of sections of the huge tracts of land controlled by religious Maths. These campaigns generated a response which had as much to do with the threat posed to the authority of the dominant classes as with the actual land at stake.

For example, in Baradih, one of the villages in my survey, 19 acres illegally occupied by large landowners were seized in 1982. One night the dalit 'tola' of the village was invaded by armed members of the Kurmi landowners' army, the Bhoomi Sena (see note 13). The hut of a family belonging to the Bhuniya scheduled caste who had been active supporters of the movement was set alight with the occupants inside. The family only just managed to escape with their lives. But the police refused to take any action against the culprits.[10] As well as organising armed attacks (supported by the police) on the labourers and poor peasants, the landowners used the mechanism of concertedly denying them access to key resources. Thus, for example, in Bairiganj, where the landowners are Awadhia Kurmis who do not engage in cultivation, at the height of a struggle to capture vested land, landowners tried to physically prevent the labourers from leaving the village, even setting up barricades on the roads out of the village and manning them with arms. At the same time they imposed a 'social boycott' by denying them their established right to graze their cattle and cut grass on the landowners' fields.

Women played a central role in all these struggles. Strikes took place during the periods of peak labour demand – paddy transplanting which only women are considered capable of doing, and paddy harvesting in which women participate heavily. It was therefore women who initially placed wage demands before employers, and subsequently collectively refused to work. (Women labourers in one village dominated by upper caste Bhumihar landowners related how, faced with losing the entire paddy crop during a strike, the employers frantically summoned home all the available males of their families from the towns – but still would not break the taboo on Bhumihar women working in the fields. However, as everyone knows, the women said, men can never do a good job of transplanting, and they still lost a lot of the crop.)

Women have also led marches of thousands to physically occupy land for redistribution, and have been at the forefront of resistance and protest against the repression unleashed by the landowners and the police. It is women who, armed with bricks, small scythes or houshold utensils, have driven the police out of their villages when they have arrived heavily armed in midnight or dawn raids, or who have surrounded police jeeps and snatched back those arrested, even forcing the police to apologise in some instances.[11]

Women who had participated in such struggles often referred to women's courage and determination, that they were 'prepared to fire a gun' if necessary. Because of the movement's focus on rape and sexual harassment by upper castes, they perceived these struggles as primarily struggles for their own dignity. At the same time, these women's involvement has led to their challenging oppressive domestic relations – particularly domestic violence, cases of abandonment of women by husbands, and the increasing incidence of dowry among dalit families. This remains a contested area for the movement at a local level, with many village-level male activists continuing to believe that such issues should not be within the scope of the movement, even while the All-India Progressive Women's Association, (AIPWA), which is linked to the CPI(ML), is trying to strengthen its network at the village level to take up questions of women's oppression.

The practice of paying women labourers less than their male counterparts prevails throughout Central Bihar. In Hilsa, there were a small number of cases where men received three kgs of rice and women only two; what was universal was for women to receive a smaller 'nasta' (breakfast) despite the fact that they often have to feed young children who accompany them to work out of this amount. Despite women's participation in wage struggles, the question of unequal wages has not been addressed. In several cases women themselves as well as men have given the explanation that men's work – such as uprooting paddy seedlings for transplanting and carrying harvested bundles – is 'heavier', despite the fact that tasks performed by women are equally if not more arduous. Again, the existence of women's organisations with some degree of autonomy appears to be a crucial factor in getting such questions onto the agenda of the movement. According to a recent survey carried out in four Central Bihar districts by the Bihar unit of AIPWA,

> our study shows that men and women receive equal wages only in areas where wage levels are very low. And where agricultural labourers have succeeded through struggles in pushing up wages, the increases agreed have not been equal. This is defended on the basis of the social understanding that women have less physical strength. Even some women labourers offered this argument. This shows the power of received patriarchal notions. The struggle for equal wages is thus not just for economic equality, but has to also be directed against patriarchal prejudices [*Chaubey*, 1996].

Changing Relationships

The most striking aspect of the movement is that it enabled the dalit poor and landless to challenge the practices which underpin the social and economic authority of both the older and the more recently emerged dominant classes throughout central Bihar. These are forms of oppression based on caste and gender as much as class. Thus dalit women frequently explain that the men from higher caste landowning families used to sexually harrass and abuse them, physically assault them if they missed a day's work, or refuse to allow them to take breaks to drink water telling them to drink the water in the drainage canals, but now they no longer 'dare' do these things. As the comment cited at the beginning of this study illustrates, this primarily reflects a perception among all classes and castes that there has been a shift in the balance of forces in those villages where the CPI(ML) has a presence, rather than a change in the mentality of the landowners.

In Hilsa a very small number of dalit households – two or three in most villages – have experienced a significant improvement in their economic situation during the last 15 years as a result of having a family member in an urban white collar job, usually in government service. This has enabled them to build pucca houses and in some cases to buy tiny plots of land and to withdraw partially or completely from agricultural labour. It is noticeable that the members of such families are usually enthusiastic supporters of the CPI(ML). This is firstly because the change in their economic status originates outside the village and has had little impact on their relative position within the agrarian hierarchy – at most such households have shifted from total reliance on agricultural wage labour to marginal self-cultivation, usually supplemented by hiring out of family labour. Secondly they continue to be subject to the daily expressions of the social power of the dominant castes within the village. But it appears from discussions with them that it is the CPI(ML)'s ability to project itself as a progressive force in wider terms – challenging feudal and caste-based practices, corruption and crime – as much as its commitment to village-level struggles that attracts this section of dalit communities.[12]

Although still below the minimum rate set by the Bihar government, wage rates have increased in response to the demands made by labourers in Hilsa. The standard wage rate for casual labour, both male and female, is now 2 kgs rice and 0.5 kg sattu, with labourers in some villages being also given 'nasta' (breakfast). Significant inter-village disparities in wages persist however, with casual labourers in some villages still getting the old rate of one kachchi seer (approximately 800 g).

In the case of attached labour, there is much more variation: in villages where the majority of labourers are still attached, they too receive this rate, as well as a small plot of land for self-cultivation. But in villages where the majority of labourers are casual, attached labourers are paid substantially less. Thus in Chandkura, whereas all casual labourers now receive 2 kg rice and 0.5 kg sattu, there is no fixed rate for attached labourers, who are paid on average 1.59kg of rice, with some receiving as little as 1 kg.

The question of harvest wages is more complex. For casual labourers in Chandkura, the wage had almost universally risen in 1988 to one out of every 14 bundles harvested, from a previous rate of one out of every 21 bundles harvested. Similarly in the other villages surveyed, harvest wages increased in the 1980s from one out of 21 to one out of 12–15 bundles.

In the wake of struggles over wages and an increase in the agreed rates, there have been a number of changes in employers' daily practices which reflect direct or indirect attempts to reduce the labourers' share in the produce. In Chandkura during harvesting there are frequent arguments in which the employers try to reduce the size of the bundles taken by the labourers. In other villages too employers are now for the first time insisting on choosing or making up the bundles themselves. In Murarpur, a Bhumihar-dominated village, labourers now have to carry the harvested crops to the landowners' homes before they are paid. In Baradih, conflict has developed over the number of hours worked by the labourers, with the employers demanding that they start earlier.

More significantly, perhaps, employers have responded to successful agitations over wages by withdrawing from credit and tenancy relations with the labourers. In Chandkura and several other villages surveyed, the surplus-producing landowners, who were previously the main source of credit for all types of agricultural labourers, have begun refusing to give loans without collateral to casual labourers and simultaneously increased interest rates substantially. In Murarpur, the landowners stopped leasing out land on a crop-sharing basis to the labourers after the most recent wage struggle in 1995. Elsewhere too, landowners became unwilling to lease out on a sharecropping basis, the only form of lease accessible to most landless labourers, after wage struggles had occurred, leading to a substantial decline in the incidence of sharecropping in Hilsa. The reasons given by the landowners were that they could no longer ensure that they got their share of the produce, and also that if the labourers could lease in land, they would no longer be available to work on the landowners' self-cultivated land.

This underlines the 'collectively interlocked' nature of the relationship between 'kisans' and 'mazdoors' in Hilsa noted above. While labourers were relatively rarely dependent solely on their employers for leases or credit, their dependence on the large landowners of the village as a whole, which they consciously articulated as the dependence of one class upon another, meant that 'class for itself' action by the labourers in the labour market could lead to similarly conscious and co-ordinated action by the dominant class in the lease and credit markets.

Observers of the trajectory of capitalist development in Haryana have pointed out that in the context of an increased and more time-specific demand for labour, the interlocking of labour and credit markets can be used to undermine attempts to organise by labourers and create 'new' forms of attachment suited to the needs of capitalist employers [*Bhalla*, 1976; *Brass*, 1995].

However, the withdrawal of credit and land from casual labourers which has occurred in Hilsa does not appear to be primarily a systematic attempt to create new relations of dependence, but rather a long term extension of the 'social boycott' strategy of withdrawing key resources in a bid to maintain the *status quo* – particularly as far as wages are concerned – in the context of an agricultural economy where the process of accumulation has essentially come to a standstill. Thus in several villages, credit had been withdrawn across the board from attached as well casual labourers, while there were also instances of landowners refusing to provide plots of land to attached labourers in the aftermath of struggles over vested land.

In Chandkura, however, several labourers who had entered into contracts as attached labourers in 1995–96 had done so (as in the earlier period) in order to get a loan without collateral in an emergency, along with a small plot which would help them pay off the loan. But these labourers too expressed an aversion to this form of employment, and were determined not to remain attached for long, not only because daily wages were lower, but because of the element of feudal coercion which remained in the relationship – for example, if the labourer could not come to work on a particular day, his wages might be witheld the next day. The labourers use of the term 'bandhua' (bonded) as opposed to 'chhuta' (free) reflects their continuing perception of a strong element of coercion in the relationship.

And most importantly, the period when these changes occurred has witnessed a further reduction in the incidence of attached labour in both relative and absolute terms: the proportion of agricultural labourer households with at least one member employed as an attached labourer has declined from 41 per cent of agricultural labour households in 1981–83 to only 26 per cent in 1995–96. My survey indicates that a similar decline has occurred in at least 50 per cent of the villages in Hilsa. In villages where struggles had occurred but where attached labour was still prevalent, labourers regarded this as an indication of their current lack of organisation and relative weakness within the overall balance of class forces in the village.

Landowners employing labour throughout Hilsa complained of a decline in the availability of labour, the increase in labour costs, and the labourers' 'unwillingness to work', which they attributed to new sources of employment 'in the towns' as well as the 'misleading' of the labourers by the CPI(ML). But the evidence suggests that in general they have been unable to effectively resist the changes initiated by the agricultural labourers' movement in the area through the introduction of new forms of attachment or dependence.

At the same time, the involvement of one section of the dominant classes in Hilsa in networks of criminals, bureaucrats and politicians stretching across central Bihar and beyond has changed the very nature of class confrontations since the early 1980s. On the one hand, landowners are now more on the defensive, and less likely to respond to agitations by labourers as in the past, by personally orchestrating violence against them. And for the moment, perhaps because of the heterogeneity, in both caste and economic terms, of the dominant classes, there is no consolidated landowners' army active in Hilsa.[13] On the other hand, that section which has links with criminal gangs and their ubiquitous patrons in political parties and the administration are able to use them to unleash brutal attacks on anyone who challenges their dominance. (Nalanda has the distinction of having the highest number of licenced arms of any district in Bihar [*Gupta*, 1997] – many more are unlicensed). Today it is those with such connections, the major source of capital accumulation in the area, who, regardless of caste background, are adopting the coercive practices previously associated with the extremes of feudalism. Thus in a case in Hilsa in early 1997, supporters of a medium-sized landowner who was also a Janata Dal MLA killed an agricultural labourer who wanted to work elsewhere. The man was treated as a bonded labourer although he had no debts. Although the killers had the support of the Block Development Officer and several other MLAs, mass protests by the people of the village succeeded in having them arrested.

This 'criminalisation' of the landowners' response, which has intensified during the 1990s, has also affected the nature of the agricultural labourers' movement in Hilsa, as elsewhere in central Bihar. Precisely by continuing to wage struggles on issues affecting the lives of landless agricultural labourers and poor peasants, the CPI(ML)-led movement has found itself posing a challenge to forces whose terror tactics extend beyond the dalit poor and landless to other sections of rural society, particularly small cultivators from the backward castes. Significantly whereas CPI(ML)'s direct attempts to win over 'middle peasants' in the late 1980s had relatively little impact,[14] this tenacity, expressed in a new wave of wage and land-related struggles since 1992, seems to be effectively widening the support base of the movement to include new sections of the working people.

CONCLUSION – FORCES FOR CHANGE IN THE CONTEXT OF A STALLED TRANSITION

In summary, this study suggests that the process of transition to a more dynamic agriculture based on 'peasant' capitalism which appeared to have begun in parts of Central Bihar in the 1970s has encountered constraints which are rooted in both the agrarian structure itself and the nature of State power in Bihar. The agrarian economy of Central Bihar is, first, characterised by acute inequalities and an extremely high incidence of landlessness. Secondly, small and marginal landholdings predominate in the region. Thirdly, even the small number of dominant 'big' landowners rarely cultivate large tracts of land. And in the absence of land consolidation, their holdings generally consist of a large number of small plots, while the persistence of chronic fragmentation continually increases the numbers of small holdings.

This study argues that the impetus towards 'peasant capitalist' development which emerged in certain parts of Central Bihar under uniquely favourable conditions in the 1970s has not been powerful enough to effect a transformation of these structures along the lines observed elsewhere in the country (notably Punjab, Haryana and western UP). Instead surpluses accumulated in this phase were used in such a way as to exacerbate the 'stalling' of capitalist development. Whatever substantial surpluses have been accumulated in agriculture have been diverted into more lucrative avenues such as contracting and organised crime, which are inextricably linked to political parties and the state.

This is also one of the factors behind the virtual collapse of the infrastructure since the early 1980s, leading to spiralling costs of production, which in turn has served to reinforce a situation where it is more profitable for rich peasants to use their assets to extract a rental surplus from poor peasants – whether through moneylending, hiring out equipment, or using their control over the local bureaucracy to appropriate and re-sell subsidised inputs – than to invest in agricultural production.

Further, these activities, and the very nature of the state in Bihar which facilitates them, are underpinned by the continuing stranglehold of the dominant classes over rural society. The left-led movements of dalit agricultural labourers, who are the most exploited section of this society, pose a direct threat to this power. And the experiences of the land and particularly wage struggles which are currently forming the central thrust of these movements suggest that they represent the most resilient and potent force for change in the region today.

First, evidence suggests that it is the movements of agricultural labourers which have been responsible for the most significant changes in production relations which have occurred during the last 15 years. Again in contrast to regions where production-oriented capitalist development has taken root, employers have not been able incorporate new forms of control of labour into processes of production.

Secondly, these struggles are today bringing the movement into direct conflict with a network of criminal gangs, politicians, administrators and landowners, and as a result the CPI(ML), which has led this movement, is being identified by increasing sections of society as providing the only resistance to the endemic corruption and criminalisation rooted in the agrarian economy.

Finally, in the current context demands for higher wages ultimately face limits set by the stalling of capitalist development in agriculture. But it is precisely when these limits are exposed through struggles that wider goals of political and economic transformation take on the character of mass demands. Similarly the limited scope for redistribution of ceiling surplus and vested land in much of Central Bihar, which is currently seeing fragmentation and subdivision rather than capitalist concentration of holdings, is serving only to reinforce and widen a growing popular conviction of the neccessity of a fundamental reorganisation of the distribution and use of land and resources, which will require a radical change in the character of the state in Bihar and beyond.

NOTES

1. At an all-India level, National Sample Survey data indicates that 'during the last two decades, while the concentration ratio of ownership of land remained by and large unchanged, that of operational holdings rose sharply ... a fact that is entirely consistent with the phenomenon ... of an increasing tendency of large and semi-medium holdings to lease in land from the marginal and small ones' [Government of India, 1996a: 24].

2. The National Commission on Agriculture noted in 1976 that while an Act for compulsory land consolidation had been passed in Bihar in 1956, 20 years later only three per cent of the total cultivable area of the State was reported to have been consolidated [Government of India, 1976b].

3. The existence of such a class was vital to the effective implementation of consolidation in Punjab, Haryana and western UP. For example, Byres [1988] has analysed the role of Charan Singh as an 'organic' intellectual of the rich and middle peasantry who as such was instrumental in bringing about a number of key reforms, including land consolidation, in Uttar Pradesh.

4. Landholding size and distribution is clearly a key issue here – while Chandkura has a relatively high ratio of tractors to operated area, the actual incidence of access to tractors for cultivators can only be assessed by taking into account the relatively small average size of holdings and the uneven distribution of resource endowments among cultivators.

5. Particularly relevant in this context is the work of the so-called Agrarian Marxists carried out in the Soviet Union during the 'NEP' period of the 1920s, under conditions where land had been redistributed and could no longer be bought or sold. L.N. Kritsman argued that, despite this, 'a process of expropriation of the agricultural surplus was taking place between peasant farms in a systematic way' [Cox, 1984: 57] based on ownership of scarce working animals and farm stock which could be hired out by those with 'excess' capacity to 'exploit weaker farms and ... accumulate capital' [1984: 12–13]. However, the question of how such capital is subsequently deployed is, as we have suggested, of equal importance for an assessment of the potential for capitalist development in Central Bihar.

6. It should be noted that the disappearance of electricity itself cannot account for the slowing down of any process of capitalist development which may have been occurring. Rich peasants in other regions which have experienced similar problems have not responded in the same way. For example, in a study of the farmers' movement in UP, Patnaik and Hasan note that western UP, the centre of 'growth of capitalist production', 'lagged surprisingly in the number of electrified villages ... with only 30 per cent of villages having access to electricity, close to the state average. Evidently, machinery is to a large extent powered by other fuel sources' [Patnaik and Hasan, 1995: 285]. In fact, along with remunerative prices, a reliable power supply and the waiving of electricity bills were key demands of the 'farmers' movement in UP [1995: 290–2]. This political expression, primarily by rich peasants, of their demands as capitalist farmers, which can be observed in different forms in Punjab, UP and Haryana can be contrasted with the absence of any such movement in Bihar and underlines the difference in the extent to which capitalist farmers have developed as a class. The fact that rich peasants in central Bihar have now reverted to non-productive forms of accumulation suggests that the relatively more favourable price and infrastructural conditions of the 1970s may have played a key role in generating short-term development, which, however, the underlying structure of the agrarian economy and society could not sustain.

7. It has been calculated that, in the mid-1970s, the 'minimum economic size' of landholding for a diesel-operated tubewell, taking into account a number of factors including the extent of fragmentation and the availability of credit, varied from 1.5 acres in Punjab and Haryana to 14.4 acres in Bihar and 20.5 acres in West Bengal [Dhawan, 1977: A102].

8. For example, see Kapadia's work on Tamil Nadu [1992, 1996] and da Corta and Venkateshwarlu (this volume) who suggest that among labourers in Andhra Pradesh, 'men's own withdrawal from paid work is much more important to their status than their wives' withdrawal'. Chowdhry [1993] observes that in Haryana, fragmentation of holdings among non-scheduled caste cultivators has meant that 'status considerations' have been

'superseded' and 'it is the male, by and large, who continues to operate his own holding, sending out the female for wage work, while he himself might explore the possibility of outside employment, particularly in the urban centres' [1993: A-144]. Key determinants of variations in the attitude to women's work seem to be twofold. First, the extent – and durability – of pre-capitalist patriarchal relationships and the hegemony of upper caste ideology (for a discussion of this see Chakravarti [1995]). For example, in Central Bihar, the joint family, in which women are considered possessions of the family and repositories of its honour, prevails even among poor dalit households, in contrast to the situation described by Kapadia for Tamil Nadu where 'among the impoverished Pallars there were no joint families, only nuclear households' [Kapadia, 1992: 231]. Secondly, the degree and nature of capitalist penetration and capitalist development. The latter may have a number of direct and indirect regionally specific effects which shape attitudes to women's paid labour in agriculture including classic polarisation and proletarianisation of poor peasants, the emergence of sources of non-agricultural employment for men, the collapse of the joint family or even the collapse of the nuclear family with men withdrawing completely from family subsistence.

9. Bihar as a whole has a particularly high proportion of agricultural labourers among women, second only to Andhra Pradesh among major states in 1991, as does Nalanda district itself (see Table 1). This is partially explicable in terms of the fact that Bihar among the major states also has the second highest proportion of agricultural labourers among main workers of both sexes, and the highest proportion among male main workers; enumeration of women cultivators may also be particularly ineffectual in Bihar. Yet the sharp disparities between male and female main workers' participation in wage labour are undeniably significant.

At the same time, Bihar and Uttar Pradesh have been the only states where the increase in the proportion of agricultural labourers among women main workers has not been higher than that for men during the period 1961–91 (da Corta and Venkateshwarlu – this volume). It is thus worth briefly examining some of the explanations put forward for this perceived 'feminisation' of agricultural wage labour, and considering their current relevance to the Central Bihar scenario and whether they may be potentially relevant in the future.

A number of observers have linked 'feminisation' to technological changes which have brought about higher participation of women in agricultural tasks as a whole, particularly in the 1980s (see da Corta and Venkateshwarlu – this volume, for a summary of this 'neo-liberal' literature) In response to this 'feminisation of agriculture' hypothesis, Banerjee argues that the increase in women's employment was confined to five states – Andhra Pradesh, Madhya Pradesh, Maharashtra, Tamil Nadu and UP, where 'women have been the traditional mainstay of three crops – paddy, sugar cane and cotton. A further intensification of their cultivation over this period was probably the main factor behind the additional work days for women. So far, there are no signs of any change in the technologies of cultivating these crops, so, when cultivation is intensified, women get more work' [Banerjee, 1997: 435].

However, other writers have argued that the significant change is the increase in rural women's dependence on wage labour, and agricultural labour in particular. Unni suggests that a fall in the percentage of days in wage employment for rural households as a whole reflects a diversification of earning opportunities for these households, which is however not shared by women: 'among men, the percentage of wage employed days declined even in labour households without land, but among women, it increased in such households until 1983. Thus, while men in labour households were able to find other kinds of work, women remained mainly casual workers' [Unni, 1997: 460]. In fact in areas where women had been employed in the rural secondary sector, they were pushed out on a massive scale by the New Economic Policies associated with liberalisation from 1991 onwards [Bhalla, 1997; Unni, 1997]. Da Corta and Venkateshwarlu (this volume) cite new non-agricultural employment opportunities for men as well as the acquisition of small plots of land by previously landless households resulting from state policies specific to Andhra Pradesh – in this context men withdraw from agricultural wage labour to cultivate their own plots while women continue to work on others' land. Chowdhry [1993] refers to downward rather than upward mobility in the context of rural Haryana, with poor peasant households increasingly sending women out for agricultural labour while men continue to cultivate their own holdings or seek alternative employment.

However, my observations suggest that none of these situations are likely to emerge in Central Bihar in the immediate future. Firstly, as we have seen, non-agricultural employment has to date remained concentrated in construction and related areas such as brick-kilns, where women are generally employed alongside men. My survey found similar levels of participation by both men and women in this activity. The emergence of employment opportunities which are heavily biased towards men is itself an indicator of a specific pattern of development (see for example Sharma and Poleman [1994], for a description of the emergence of permanent employment in small-scale industrial units in small towns in western Uttar Pradesh). Such development, as I argue elsewhere in this study, is in Bihar seriously constrained by the very nature of the state's institutional structures. Secondly, in Central Bihar land redistribution by the state has been negligible; in the few cases where previously landless labourer households have been able to acquire small plots through savings or in some cases participation in collective struggles for land redistribution, both male and female members of such households have been compelled to continue to work as agricultural labourers – the only cases of withdrawal I came across were in fact of women. Thirdly as suggested above, the continuing dominance of essentially feudal notions about women and status in Central Bihar acts as more of a constraint on women performing agricultural labour than men. This is the case even for dalit households and is all the more applicable to poor peasants of non-dalit castes.

Da Corta and Venkateshwarlu (this volume), Kapadia [1992] and Chowdhry [1993] have argued that in a context of different relationships to the means of production, women labourers should be regarded as belonging to a different class from their male relatives. However, such arguments cannot be generalised without a careful examination of domestic relations and the nature of the family as an institution in the area under discussion. Questions raised by Marxist feminist writers include: do domestic relations (such as the type of work done by the woman in the household) continue to be shaped by the class position of the men in the family – which may, as in Chowdhry's study, be that of a poor peasant? Does the dominant ideology – reproduced within the family – lead the woman to identify with the class position of her husband? Have changes in production relations led to the weakening or collapse of the family as a patriarchal institution? In the Bihar context at least, Kelkar and Gala's concept of the 'mediated class position of women' appears to be a more fruitful one: discussing the question of women's equal access to land and property and parity of agricultural wages, they argue that 'while it is true that marriage does give women access to material resources, this is not the same as having a direct relationship to the means of production. For women, class is mediated through their sexual ties and related services to men. If such sexual ties are broken and sexual services withdrawn, women no longer enjoy access to material resources. Class analysis in India has not included the mediated class position of women' [Kelkar and Gala, 1990: 85].

10. Chaudhry gives the following illustration of the relationship between dominant landowners and the state apparatuses: 'on October 22, 1981, the Bhoomi Sena held an armed demonstration of about 3,000 people in defiance of prohibitory orders ... The police was not only escorting this illegal procession but was even distributing pamphlets and raising slogans. This armed procession of landlords ... included Diwaker Sharma and Jaiprakash Singh of Congress(I), Subhas Chandra Singh, vice-president of the Patna district BJP and Siddeshwar Singh of the CPI. Lok Dal activists were also reported to have been present in the procession' [Chaudhry, 1988: 55]. Even more explicit was police collaboration in the massacre at Ekwari, Bhojpur carried out by the Ranvir Sena on 10 April 1997. The police accompanied the Ranvir Sena men around the village, knocked at the doors of poor dalit households in the village and got them opened on the pretext of making enquiries, thus allowing the Ranvir Sena men to enter the houses and kill those inside.

11. A recent instance of this occurred in Bargaon village in Bhojpur district in the wake of the Lakshmanpur Bathe massacre perpetrated by the Ranvir Sena. Police entered the village in the early morning with the intention of arresting some local CPI(ML) activists. They were observed by three women in the fields on the outskirts of the village. They alerted others and within minutes 70 or 80 women had surrounded the police and prevented them from taking anyone away for several hours (in this case the police finally succeeded in making the arrests

but only after radioing for reinforcements from several police camps which were nearby).

12. This section of dalit communities form an important part of the Bahujan Samaj Party (BSP)'s base in neighbouring UP. Bihar's history of left activism, and specifically the emergence and development of the Marxist-Leninist stream, in recent decades may be one reason why the BSP has failed to make inroads in the state.

13. Large landowners of Nalanda district were active in one of the earliest of these armies or 'senas', the Bhoomi Sena, a Kurmi organisation formed in 1982 which operated in Patna, Gaya, Jehanabad and Nalanda districts. The Bhoomi Sena continued until the late 1980s, when it collapsed after some of its key leaders were targeted by armed squads of the CPI(ML) and several others were given life sentences as the main accused in the 1980 Pipra massacre in Patna district (carried out by an earlier incarnation, the Kisan Suraksha Samiti) in which fourteen labourers and poor peasants of both dalit and Kurmi castes were killed [*Chaudhry*, 1988; *Patnaik*, 1990; *Bhatia*, 1997a]. Both these 'senas' however were dominated by the minority of traditionally non-cultivating Awadhia Kurmi landlords.

The period from 1994 to the present has seen the rise of the Ranvir Sena, an armed gang representing upper caste (Bhumihar and increasingly also Rajput) landed interests. The Ranvir Sena, which was formed in Bhojpur, is now also active in upper caste-dominated areas of several adjoining districts of Central Bihar, and has carried out a series of massacres of dalit labourers, which have been characterised by their scale and barbarity and in particular by their extreme violence against women [*Bhatia*, 1997a and 1997b; *Chaubey*, 1998]. The Ranvir Sena can also be distinguished from earlier 'landlord armies' which have been active in the region by the extent of its resource mobilisation with funds flowing in from upper caste-controlled coal and steel mafias in Bokaro and Dhanbad; and by its organic links with the Hindu fascist Bharatiya Janata Party (BJP) which provides it with direct and systematic support. One reason for this is that the assertion of the rural poor in the electoral arena, where CPI(ML) candidates won several seats in the last Assembly elections in 1995, has been perceived as a threat to the hitherto unchallenged political power of upper caste landowners in these areas: the last few years have seen these landowners who previously aligned with the Congress Party, increasingly putting their faith in the BJP as an effective representative of their interests. This also partly accounts for the peculiarly political character of the Ranvir Sena, with the scale, timing and other features of recent massacres in Bhojpur, Patna and Jehanabad seemingly determined by clear electoral calculations.

Currently the rich peasants of the Kurmi caste who are dominant in Nalanda district are represented politically by the Samata Party, which was formed in 1995 in response to perceived Yadav dominance within the Janata Dal. The Samata Party fought the last two elections in alliance with the BJP; at the time of writing, Samata Party leaders George Fernandes (MP for Nalanda constituency) and Nitish Kumar (MP for Barh) have just been inducted into the BJP-led national government. The impact of the much increased strength of this alliance in Bihar after the 1998 elections on ground realities remains to be seen.

14. A full discussion of the changing strategies of the CPI(ML) in Central Bihar in the 1980s and 1990s is beyond the scope of the present study, but will form part of a more detailed analysis of the subject.

REFERENCES

Agarwal, Bina, 1983, *Mechanization in India Agriculture: An Analytical Study Based on the Punjab*, New Delhi: Allied Publishers

Agarwal, Bina, 1994, *A Field of One's Own: Gender and Land Rights in South Asia*, Cambridge: Cambridge University Press

Banerjee, Nirmala, 1997, 'How Real is the Bogey of Feminization?', *Indian Journal of Labour Economics*, Vol.40, No.3, pp.427–38.

Bhalla, Sheila, 1976, 'New Relations of Production in Haryana Agriculture', *Economic and Political Weekly*, Vol.11, No.13, 27 March, pp. A23–A30

Bhalla, Sheila 1997, 'Trends in Poverty, Wages and Employment in India', *Indian Journal of Labour Economics*, Vol.40, No.2, pp.213–22.

Bhalla, G.S. and Y.K.Alagh, 1979, *Performance of Indian Agriculture: A District-wise Study*, New Delhi: Sterling.

Bhatia, Bela, 1997a, 'Reasserting Dominance in the Face of Resistance: Caste Senas and the Naxalite Movement in Central Bihar', paper presented at a workshop on 'Rural Labour Relations in India', London School of Economics, 19 and 20 June.

Bhatia, Bela, 1997b, 'Massacre on the Banks of the Sone', *Economic and Political Weekly*, Vol.32, No.51, 20–26 Dec., pp.3242–5.

Boyce, James K., 1987, *Agrarian Impasse in Bengal – Institutional Constraints to Technological Change*, Oxford: Oxford University Press.

Brass, Tom, 1995, 'Unfree Labour and Agrarian Change – A Different View', *Economic and Political Weekly*, Vol.30, No.13, 1 April, pp.697–8.

Byres, T.J., 1972, 'The Dialectic of India's Green Revolution', *South Asian Review*, Vol.5, No.2, pp.99–115.

Byres, Terence J., 1988, 'Charan Singh (1902-87): An Assessment', *The Journal of Peasant Studies*, Vol.15, No.2, pp.139–89.

Centre for Monitoring Indian Economy (CMIE), 1993, *Profiles of Districts*, Nov., Bombay: Economic Intelligence Service.

Centre for Monitoring Indian Economy, 1995, *India's Agricultural Sector – A Compendium of Statistics*, Sept., Bombay: Economic Intelligence Service.

Chakravarti, Uma, 1995, 'Gender, Caste and Labour – Ideological and Material Structure of Widowhood', *Economic and Political Weekly*, Vol.30, No.36, 9 Sept., pp.2248–56.

Chaubey, Saroj, 1996, 'Saman Kam, Saman Mazdoori', *Samkalin Lokyudh*, 15 Sept., p.4.

Chaubey, Saroj, 1998, 'Women Resist Feudal-Fascist Terror', *Women's Voice*, No.1, pp.5–6.

Chaudhry, Praveen K., 1988, 'Agrarian Unrest in Bihar – A Case Study of Patna District 1960–1984', *Economic and Political Weekly*, Vol.23, Nos.1 and 2, 2–9 Jan., pp.51–6.

Chowdhry, Prem, 1993, 'High Participation, Low Evaluation – Women and Work in Rural Haryana', *Economic and Political Weekly*, Vol.28, No.52, 25 Dec., pp.A135–48.

Cox, Terry, 1984, 'Class Analysis of the Russian Peasantry: The Research of Kritsman and his School', *The Journal of Peasant Studies*, Vol.11, No.2, Jan., pp.11–60.

Das, Arvind N., 1992, *The Republic of Bihar*, New Delhi: Penguin.

Dhawan, B.D., 1977, 'Tubewell Irrigation in the Gangetic Plains', *Economic and Political Weekly*, Vol.12, No.39, pp.A91–104.

Government of India, Ministry of Agriculture and Irrigation, 1976a, *Report of the National Commission on Agriculture*, Part 5, 'Resource Development', New Delhi: Government of India.

Government of India, Ministry of Agriculture and Irrigation, 1976b, *Report of the National Commission on Agriculture*, Part 15, 'Agrarian Reforms', New Delhi: Government of India.

Government of India, Ministry of Agriculture, (Directorate of Economics and Statistics, Department of Agriculture and Co-operation), 1991, *Cost of Cultivation of Principal Crops in India*, New Delhi: Government of India.

Government of India, Ministry of Agriculture (Directorate of Economics and Statistics, Department of Agriculture and Co-operation), 1992, *Agricultural Prices in India*, New Delhi: Government of India.

Government of India, Ministry of Planning and Programme Implementation, (National Sample Survey Organisation, Department of Statistics), 1996a, *Some Aspects of Operational Holdings, N.S.S. 48th Round, 1991–92*, New Delhi: Government of India.

Government of India, Ministry of Agriculture, (Directorate of Economics and Statistics, Department of Agriculture and Co-operation), 1996b, *Cost of Cultivation of Principal Crops in India*, New Delhi: Government of India.

Gupta, Shaibal, 1997, 'Local Entrepreneurship in Bihar – Social Context and Economic Constraint', paper presented at 'Bihar in the World and the World in Bihar', a conference organised by the Asian Development Research Institute and the European Science Foundation, 16–19 Dec., Patna.

Ishikawa, Shigeru, 1967, *Economic Development in Asian Perspective*, Tokyo: Kinokuniya Bookstore.

Jannuzi, F. Tomasson, 1996, *India's Persistent Dilemma: The Political Economy of Agrarian*

Reform, New Delhi: Orient Longman.

Jha, Praveen K., 1997, *Agricultural Labour in India*, New Delhi: Vikas Publishing House.

Kapadia, Karin, 1992, 'Every Blade of Green: Landless Women Labourers, Production and Reproduction in South India', in Sharma and Singh (eds.), [1992].

Kapadia, Karin, 1996, *Siva and her Sisters – Gender, Caste and Class in Rural South India*, Delhi: Oxford University Press.

Kelkar, Govind and Chetna Gala, 1990, 'The Bodhgaya Land Struggle', in Sen [1990].

Mahendra Dev, S., 1988, 'Prospects of Enhancing Labour Productivity in Indian Agriculture', *Economic and Political Weekly*, 24 Sept., pp.A106–13.

Mozoomdar, Ajit, 1990, *Bihar – Problems of Development*, New Delhi: Centre for Policy Research.

Patnaik, B.N., 1990, 'Harijans' Franchise: An Alibi of Class Conflict (a Case Study of Danwar-Bihta Massacre)', Patna, Harijan Study Centre, A.N. Sinha Institute of Social Studies (mimeo).

Patnaik, Utsa and Zoya Hasan, 1995, 'Aspects of the Farmers' Movement in Uttar Pradesh in the Context of Uneven Capitalist Development in Indian Agriculture', in Sathyamurthy [1995].

Prasad, Pradhan H., Rodgers, Gerry B., Gupta, Shaibal, Sharma, Alakh N. and B. Sharma, 1988, 'The Dynamics of Employment and Poverty in Bihar', Patna, A.N.Sinha Institute of Social Studies (mimeo).

Rudra, Ashok, 1971, 'Employment Patterns in Large Farms of Punjab', *Economic and Political Weekly*, Vol.6, No.26, pp.A89–94.

Sathyamurthy, T.V (ed.), 1995, *Social Change and Political Discourse in India – Structures of Power, Movements of Resistance, Vol.2, 'Industry and Agriculture'*, Delhi: Oxford University Press.

Sen, Ilina (ed.), 1990, *A Space Within the Struggle – Women's Participation in People's Movements*, New Delhi: Kali for Women.

Sharma, Alakh N. and Seema Singh (eds.), 1992, *Women and Work*, Patna, Indian Sociey of Labour Economics.

Sharma, Alakh N., 1996, 'Development, Economic Reforms and the Poor: The Case of Bihar', paper prepared for the IDPAD Seminar on 'Liberalisation and the Poor: Impact, Opportunities and Barriers', Hyderabad, 7–9 Feb.

Sharma, Rita and Thomas T. Poleman, 1994, *The New Economics of India's Green Revolution: Income and Employment Diffusion in Uttar Pradesh*, New Delhi: Vikas Publishing House.

Unni, Jeemol, 1997, 'Women Workers in Agriculture: Some Recent Trends', *Indian Journal of Labour Economics*, Vol.40, No.3 pp.453–70.

Abstracts

Introduction
KARIN KAPADIA and JENS LERCHE

This volume is the outcome of the Workshop on 'Rural Labour Relations In India Today' held in London in 1997. The aim was to analyse the emerging development trajectories of rural labour relations and labour struggles in India, based on studies from its different states. The organisers wished to see examined, *inter alia*, how accumulation patterns and the balance of power between classes facilitated and shaped labour relations. Important was the extent to which agricultural employment was being substituted by non-agricultural employment, and whether, consequently, rural labourers were being de-linked from their old masters in ways which broke previous exploitative relations; or whether such relations were being maintained, or even extended to new groups. Discussion of the role of the state in rural labour relations was also called for. It is argued that the papers show that politicisation among rural labourers is taking place. However, the papers also point to a range of elements that qualify the politicisation process when it is evaluated from a class perspective, not the least being that rural labour politicisation may strengthen or even depend on intraclass divisions such as gender and caste.

Rural Labour Relations in India: Persistent Themes, Common Processes and Differential Outcomes
T.J. BYRES

The paper has three aims: (1) to identify and consider those major persistent themes which inform this volume; (2) to distinguish, within those themes, whatever common processes, with respect to labour relations in the Indian countryside, can be observed in the contributions published; and (3) to suggest what the studies reveal about differential outcomes within the Indian social formation. The overarching theme of class conflict is singled out and that of the nature and impact of state intervention noted. A series of 'stylised shifts', or clear general tendencies, are seen to be in evidence in the analyses, which suggest the operation of vigorous emancipatory processes. The limitations and contradictions inherent in these emancipatory processes are discussed, the influences which condition class struggle are highlighted, and the crucial role of the state (and, in particular, the significance of poverty alleviation programmes) stressed. It is argued, finally, that a primary analytical task is to pursue a far more systematic interpretation of regional variations in the Indian social formation than is currently available.

Liberalisation, Rural Labour Markets and the Mobilisation of Farm Workers: The Haryana Story in an All India Context
SHEILA BHALLA

In India, the new economic policy, especially after 1991, has been associated with a contraction of public spending on economic and social infrastructure, with technological and structural changes which have caused a decline in the employment generating capacity of economic growth, a widening of the gap between farm labour productivity and labour productivity in all other sectors and a substantial rise in the number of rural people living in absolute poverty. In Haryana, a Green Revolution state, which enjoyed exceptionally high agricultural and industrial output growth rates during the 1990s, employment contracted or stagnated in both agriculture and manufacturing, and poverty soared. Simultaneously, during the 1990s, there was a significant awakening of rural Haryana wage workers as a class, but it is not clear how much this development had to do with worsening labour market conditions. Much of it may be attributable to the way in which the Haryana agricultural workers' union was organised during this period. Some of their most successful mobilisations involved joint action, either with the All India Kisan Sabha and other left-led peasant and agricultural workers' organisations, or with a union representing industrial and other non-farm workers. It is noteworthy that whatever victories were won, were won largely through the intermediation of governments – central, state or local. No major agricultural workers' union victories were recorded in Haryana which emerged from direct confrontations of agricultural labourers with their employers.

Unfree Relations and the Feminisation of Agricultural Labour in Andhra Pradesh, 1970–95
LUCIA DA CORTA and DAVULURI VENKATESHWARLU

Neo-liberal writers have argued that 'green revolution' induced agricultural growth in south India is largely responsible for rising wages, increased land ownership among landless labourers and even some equalisation in land owned between rich and poor. Such growth is now also seen to be responsible for a faster rise in women's employment relative to men (known as the 'feminisation' of agricultural wage labour), for declining wage differentials, and for a rise in women's 'empowerment'. These views are examined afresh in light of evidence gathered from villages in Andhra Pradesh. It is argued that male agricultural labourers were the chief beneficiaries of state policies that helped men escape from traditional permanent bonded relations and to engage in petty commodity production and non-agricultural employment. Agrarian capitalists responded to the resulting rise in labour costs by commission trading, based on tied harvest arrangements, in order to secure the labour of smallholders indirectly, and intensifying non-permanent forms of attached labour. The latter were designed to secure male labour for exclusively male work and in order to replace male workers seeking emancipation and higher wages with cheaper, unfree female labour for the remaining agricultural tasks. Female labour was cheaper and less free than male labour because men shifted more of the responsibility for family provisioning on to women by spending more outside the home and by refusing wage work as a protest against low, tied wages. As a consequence, the cost of men's struggle for emancipation was women's unfreedom. Under these circumstances, feminisation of labour was largely disempowering for women.

Rural Labour Relations and Development Dilemmas in Kerala: Reflections on the Development Dilemmas of a Socially Transforming Labour Force in a Slowly Growing Economy
K.P. KANNAN

Kerala is well known for its achievements in the sphere of social development; and these include a rapid and high-level mobilisation and organisation of workers, regardless of location and sectoral occupation. Such a process of social development without a commensurate transformation of the productive forces has, however, presented Kerala with some major dilemmas. In this study the political economy of labour and development is considered, via treatment of the respective roles of labour unions, state and capital in the rural context. Three major dilemmas are examined: (1) technological choice in the face of trade union resistance and rising labour costs; (2) the mismatch between labour supply and labour demand, as a result of the changing job expectations of the younger generation; and (3) the failure of the state to attract new investment in the context of liberalisation of the Indian economy. There is a close relationship between the dynamics of labour relations and the emergence of these dilemmas. The study presents an analysis of how this works out in concrete terms: in relation to rural labour relations in the rice cultivation sector, where these dilemmas have pushed the trade unions, state and farmers to reconsider their earlier strategies.

Politics of the Poor: Agricultural labourers and Political Transformations in North India
JENS LERCHE

This contribution addresses the question of how local agrarian labour relations and labour struggles, and class- and caste- based emancipatory processes, relate to the wider political development of the north Indian state of Uttar Pradesh (UP). It argues that in UP rural labourers have experienced a number of important positive changes since Independence, and are increasingly able to assert what they now perceive to be their rights. Rural labour struggles have intensified and, in spite of counter actions by middle and big peasants, the position of labourers has improved. The 1990s have seen an extraordinary development in UP, whereby low caste BSP (Bahujan Samaj Party) governments have actually been voted in. This has been both a result of a catalyst for some of these developments. Part I of this study examines the development of rural class relations in UP since Independence, through an analysis of sharecropping and labour relations, local labour struggles and the overall position of rural labourers until the early 1990s. Part II concentrates on the issue of caste- and class-based policies and mobilisation among rural labourers in the 1990s, including a discussion of why the BSP has been more successful than the communist parties in mobilising rural labourers.

Agrarian Power and Unfree Labour
J. MOHAN RAO

This study contributes a theoretical analysis of unfree and free employment relations and reopens the Indian debate on the unfree status of attached labour. It is argued that the concepts of unfree and free employment relations are based on the incommensurable categories of negative freedom and self-determination. Nor can any clear separation be sustained between labour subject to 'non-economic' coercion versus labour subject exclusively to 'economic' coercion. In this light, the study specifies the production relations through which agrarian power is exercised and thereby identifies the substantive differences between attached labour in rural India and wage labour under canonical forms of capitalism.

Rural Labour in Uttar Pradesh, India: Emerging Features of Subsistence, Contradiction and Resistance
RAVI S. SRIVASTAVA

While conflict and struggle between the poor and dominant classes has never been absent from the rural scene in Uttar Pradesh, evidence examined in this study suggests that recent changes may have added new dimensions and assertiveness to the poor. The changes in the nature of dependence, contradictions and ensuing resistance analysed in this study have significant implications for the restructuring of labour relations within villages, and still wider ramifications for the political articulation of the labouring classes. The study aims to delineate the extent to which labour market changes are embedded in a wider socio-economic and political dynamic – a point which is missed in orthodox analyses of the rural labour market.

Patterns of Accumulation and Struggles of Rural Labour: Some Aspects of Agrarian Change in Central Bihar
KALPANA WILSON

Agrarian conflict in Central Bihar has frequently been ascribed to the 'stagnant' and unchanging nature of the rural economy. It is suggested here that in reality, this region has witnessed major changes in patterns of surplus appropriation and investment during the last 25 years. An initial spurt of capital accumulation among a section of larger landowners employing wage labour provided the catalyst for the emergence in the late 1970s of an organised movement of mainly dalit agricultural labourers. This movement has continued to develop despite a subsequent slowing down of the process of accumulation in agriculture in the face of constraints rooted in the agrarian structure itself and the nature of State power in Bihar. The interrelated questions of class, caste and gender which have shaped this movement are discussed, and it is suggested that a number of changes in production relations during the last 15 years represent either acceptance by employers of demands put forward by agricultural labourers, or essentially defensive reactions to such demands. At the same time, employers are constantly developing new strategies to attempt to neutralise or reverse gains made by labourers.

Name Index

Subject Index

and unpaid work *(begar)* 77–8, 91–3, 110, 116, 147, 189, 191, 197, 199, 236
see also Feminisation of attached labour relations in agriculture

Bonded labour
see under Attached labour relations in agriculture

Capitalist farmers 53, 57, 60, 62, 82, 85, 86, 87, 91, 103, 109, 116, 223, 296, 297, 317, 327, 349
Capitalist penetration of agrarian society 1, 2, 3, 15, 53–4, 57, 62–3, 144–5, 149, 198–9, 223, 317–19, 326, 347–8, 350
widening of wage employment 144–5
Castes
Badhai/Barhi 322, 236
Bania 227, 235
Beldar 321
Bhangi 299
Bhar 236
Bhumihar 342, 352
Bhuniya 341
Brahmin 83, 93, 115, 187, 206, 228, 234, 264, 267, 271, 295, 297, 299, 300–305, 312, 322
Chamar 187, 189–94, 196, 200–3, 206, 208, 212–17, 227–34, 236–7, 281, 289, 290, 293, 298, 299, 302–4, 311, 321
Dalit, *see under* Scheduled Castes
Dhobi 236, 274, 302, 304
Dusadh 321
Halpati 4, 183
Harijan, *see under* Scheduled Castes
Jat 14, 67, 187, 192, 202, 203, 216–18, 224, 227, 230, 233, 236, 264, 268, 290, 277–8, 280, 288, 290, 291, 292–3, 311, 312
Jheenvar 282, 291
Jhimar 187, 189, 228, 230
Jogi 187, 228, 230, 290
Kahar 236, 304
Kamma 83
Kathik, 236
Kayastha 312
Khan 298
Koeri 332
Kumhar 304
Kurmi 236, 289, 317, 319, 321–2, 323, 326, 331, 332–5, 341, 352
Lohar 236, 289, 290
low castes 227, 228, 234, 235, 263, 287, 316, 322, 332. *see also* Scheduled Castes
Mallah 236

middle caste 228, 237, 263, 273, 275, 312, 316, 317, 321 *see also* Other Backward Castes
Moria 236
Mughal 312
Musehar 236, 304
Muslim 85, 206, 234, 236, 264–9, 270–72, 273–4, 175–6, 286, 287, 288, 290, 296–8, 302, 309, 311
Nai 236, 289, 299, 304, 305, 322
Nut 289
Other Backward Castes (OBC) 83, 217, 265–76, 286, 288–91, 309, 311, 312, 317–19, 321–2, 331, 332, 340, 347
see also middle caste
Pal 236, 289, 302
Pallar 350
Pasi 289, 295, 296, 297, 302
Pathan 297–8
Rajput, *see under* Thakur
Reddy 83, 85, 93
Saiyad 312
Scheduled Castes (SC) 4, 5, 7, 15, 50, 54, 58, 60, 61, 83–4, 118, 200–202, 206–12, 215, 216, 218, 219, 221, 225–6, 233–6, 265–9, 270–72, 273–4, 275–6, 285–6, 287, 288, 289, 295, 297–8, 301–4, 309, 311, 312, 313, 317, 321–2, 332, 335, 339, 340, 342, 343–4, 348, 350–52 *see also* low caste
Scheduled Tribes (ST) 83
Shah 289
Sheikh 312
Thakur 187, 196, 201, 203, 212–5, 218, 232, 235, 236, 264, 271, 280, 293, 295, 297, 299, 300, 305, 311, 312, 322, 352
Vaisya 88–91
Yadav 187, 193, 228, 288, 289, 302, 321, 332, 352
untouchable *see under* Scheduled Castes
upper caste 187, 193, 203, 206, 208–10, 221, 234–5, 237.263, 264–9, 271–2, 273–4, 275–6, 286, 300, 311, 312, 318, 322, 331–3, 350, 352
Class analysis, methodology 80–81, 119, 275, 312.
Class formation
class–for–itself 12, 14, 17, 20, 65, 144–5, 327, 345
emancipatory processes 2–8, 13, 14–16, 17–19, 20–22, 62, 84, 146, 162, 166, 182–4, 193, 200, 201–2, 203, 207, 210, 211, 212–15, 216, 218, 219, 221, 225–6, 227, 232, 233, 291, 294, 296, 300, 317, 339, 343, 344
pauperisation 72

Books of Related Interest

Agrarian Movements in India: Studies on 20th Century Bihar
Edited by **Arvind N Das**

The papers in this volume trace peasant movements from the early twentieth century through to the Naxalite activity of the recent past. They both give an overview of such struggles and detail the forces which gave rise to them. The response of the state – both the colonial state and the post-colonial state – is also identified.

152 pages 1982
0 7146 3216 3 cloth
Library of Peasant Studies No. 5

Sharecropping and Sharecroppers
Edited by **T J Byres**

This is an original and important collection of essays, in which sharecropping and sharecroppers are examined both in general terms, and in a rich variety of regional contexts. Sharecropping raises difficult theoretical issues which in this volume are given, for the first time, extensive rigorous treatment.

288 pages 1983
0 7146 3223 6 cloth
Library of Peasant Studies No. 6

FRANK CASS PUBLISHERS
Newbury House, 900 Eastern Avenue, Newbury Park, Ilford, Essex IG2 7HH
Tel: +44 (0)181 599 8866 Fax: +44 (0)181 599 0984 E-mail: info@frankcass.com
NORTH AMERICA
5804 NE Hassalo Street, Portland, OR 97213, USA
Tel: 800 944 6190 Fax: 503 280 8832 E-mail: cass@isbs.com
Website: www.frankcass.com

Plantations, Proletarians and Peasants in Colonial Asia

Edited by **E Valentine Daniel, Henry Bernstein** and **Tom Brass**

This is a unique volume on labour in the major plantation areas of colonial Asia, combining detailed historical studies with comparative and theoretical reflection, and written by an international group of scholars. It will be of considerable interest to economic and social historians of Asia, and of colonial plantations elsewhere, and to all those concerned with the political economy of agrarian change in the modern world.

320 pages 1992
0 7146 3467 0 cloth
Library of Peasant Studies No. 11

New Farmers' Movements in India

Edited by **Tom Brass**
Preface by **T J Byres**

The essays in this collection focus on the reasons for and background to the emergence during the 1980s of the new farmers' movements in India. In addition to a more general consideration of the economic, political and theoretical dimensions of this development, there are case studies which cover the farmers' movements in Maharashtra, Uttar Pradesh, Punjab and Karnataka.

290 pages 1995
0 7146 4609 1 cloth   0 7146 4134 0 paper
Library of Peasant Studies No. 12

FRANK CASS PUBLISHERS
Newbury House, 900 Eastern Avenue, Newbury Park, Ilford, Essex IG2 7HH
Tel: +44 (0)181 599 8866 Fax: +44 (0)181 599 0984 E-mail: info@frankcass.com
NORTH AMERICA
5804 NE Hassalo Street, Portland, OR 97213, USA
Tel: 800 944 6190 Fax: 503 280 8832 E-mail: cass@isbs.com
Website: www.frankcass.com

Agrarian Questions

Essays in Appreciation of T J Byres

Edited by **Henry Bernstein** and **Tom Brass**

This collection celebrates T J Byres' seminal contributions to the political economy of the agrarian question.

Four essays in the volume build directly on his work and four complementary essays address peasant politics and communist strategy in North China in the 1920s; globalisation and restructuring in the Indian food industry; foreign trade as a mechanism of economic retrogression in 'agriculture-constrained' economies; and the reasons for China's success and Russia's failure at the end of the twentieth century. Uniting the various themes of the essays is the demonstration of the continuing vitality and relevance of a critical, historical and comparative materialist analysis of agrarian questions exemplified by the intellectual project of T J Byres and its achievements.

Contributors: *Henry Bernstein, Tom Brass, Massoud Karshenas, Graham Dyer, R G Tiedemann, Jairus Banaji, Prabhat Patnaik and Peter Nolan.*

256 pages   1996
0 7146 4774 8   cloth   0 7146 4332 7   paper
Library of Peasant Studies No. 14

FRANK CASS PUBLISHERS
Newbury House, 900 Eastern Avenue, Newbury Park, Ilford, Essex IG2 7HH
Tel: +44 (0)181 599 8866 Fax: +44 (0)181 599 0984 E-mail: info@frankcass.com
NORTH AMERICA
5804 NE Hassalo Street, Portland, OR 97213, USA
Tel: 800 944 6190 Fax: 503 280 8832 E-mail: cass@isbs.com
Website: www.frankcass.com